S0-DQR-450

2020

California Environmental Quality Act

CEQA Guidelines

Appendices & Index to the Guidelines

Notice

While every effort has been made to assure the accuracy of this publication, this book is not an official document. Should any difference or error occur in this book, the actual law will take precedence.

ACEC
AMERICAN COUNCIL OF ENGINEERING COMPANIES
California

2020 Publications Order Form

Order No.	Publication Name	Member	Public Agency	Non-Member	# Copies	Total Cost
FS	Full set of eight California Statute Books (Items 1-8 Discounted)	$99.00	$189.00	$270.00		
1.	✷2020 Professional Engineers Act, Professional Land Surveyor's Act, Geologist and Geophysicist Act, State Board Rules	$14.00	$26.60	$38.00		
2.	2020 Subdivision Map Act & Index	$14.00	$26.60	$38.00		
3.	✷2020 California Environmental Quality Act & CEQA Guidelines	$14.00	$26.60	$38.00		
4.	2020 Planning and Zoning Laws	$14.00	$26.60	$38.00		
5.	2020 Land Use Laws—Environmental Permit Reform Act, Endangered Species Act (CA) and Coastal Act	$14.00	$26.60	$38.00		
6.	✷2020 Water and Environmental Laws- Water Quality, Supply, and Infrastructure Improvement Act of 2014, Water Quality, Underground Storage, and Urban Water Mgmt. Planning Laws, and Rules of the Dept. of Water Resources	$17.00	$34.30	$49.00		
7.	2020 Procurement & Liability Laws-Laws Impacting Engineering and Surveying—Public-Private Partnerships, Professional Liability, Design Build, High Speed Rail Authority and Additional Laws	$14.00	$26.60	$38.00		
8.	✷2020 Prevailing Wage Laws	$14.00	$26.60	$38.00		
CS	Complete Agreement Form Set (electronic) Items 9, 10, 11, 12, 13, & 14	$300.00	$1,500	$2,250		
9.	Form A.E—Client/Consultant (electronic)	COMP	$400.00	$600.00		
10.	Form A.1.E—Client/Consultant (electronic)	COMP	$400.00	$600.00		
11.	Form C.E—Consultant/Subconsultant (electronic)	COMP	$400.00	$600.00		
12.	Written Contract Waiver Form (electronic)	$11.00	$22.00	$33.00		
13.	Mechanics' Preliminary Lien Notice (electronic)	$200.00	$400.00	$600.00		
14.	California Design Professional Lien (electronic)	$200.00	$400.00	$600.00		
15.	2019 ACEC CA Salary, Benefits & Business Practices Survey	$300.00	*not available*	$500.00		
16.	2008 Drainage Law Syllabus	$75.00	$150.00	$225.00		
17.	2007 Subdivision Map Act Syllabus	$75.00	$150.00	$225.00		

ACEC
AMERICAN COUNCIL OF ENGINEERING COMPANIES
California

2020 Publications Order Form

Placing an Order:

To order online visit our website:

www.acec-ca.org

or

Email or mail this form to:

ACEC California
1303 J Street, Suite 450
Sacramento, CA 95814
Phone: 916-441-7991
Email: bliu@acec-ca.org

Please allow 2 to 3 weeks for delivery during the months of Jan.-March.

✱Updater Notification Service
Four of ACEC California's statute books are subject to revision during the course of the year due to changes in CA Regulations. To be notified of changes as they occur throughout the year, we offer the Updater Notification Service. The service is a flat fee that covers all 4 books and costs $25 for Members, $70 for Public Agencies and $100 for Non-Members. Notifications are sent via email to the email associated with your order. Notifications are good through 12/1/20.

Method of Payment

Subtotal: _____

Outside City of Sacramento/State rate sales tax (add 7.25%) _____

City of Sacramento sales tax (add 8.25%) _____

Shipping By Quantity:

EACH FULL SET COUNTS AS EIGHT ITEMS

1 item = $3
2-6 items = $8
7-15 items = $10
16+ items = $15

Total Standard Shipping: _____

Rush Shipment Option:

Federal Express account number required (for Rush Shipments only) Cost of standard overnight shipping is billed to your FedEx account. In addition, please include a rush fee of $15 for members and $25 for nonmembers in your total payment.

FedEx Account #:_____ Rush Fee: _____

✱Updater Notification Service _____

TOTAL DUE: _____

Ship to:
Name: _____

Firm/Agency:_____

Address: _____

City/State/Zip:_____

Phone: _____

✱Email: _____
Required for order to be processed.

☐ VISA ☐ Mastercard ☐ AMEX ☐ Check Payable to ACEC CA PO# _____

Card Number:_____ Expiration Date:_____ CVC#_____

Signature:_____ Billing Address:_____

To avoid order duplication, if you have previously emailed **this** order, please mark this box. ☐

ACEC
AMERICAN COUNCIL OF ENGINEERING COMPANIES
California

ACEC California Offers Updater Notification Service

Four of ACEC California's statue publications are subject to revision during the course of the year due to changes in CA Regulations. As a service to help readers stay up-to-date, ACEC California offers an Updater Notification Service. Purchasers of the service receive notice of changes to all the following publication if and when they take affect.

- Professional Engineers Act, Professional Land Surveyors Act, Geologist and Geophysicist Act, State Board Rules

- California Environmental Quality Act and CEQA Guidelines

- Water and Environmental Laws

- Prevailing Wage Laws

For one flat fee, readers receive updates for all four publications as the changes take affect. The Updater Notification Service costs $25 for members, $70 for public agencies and $100 for non-members. Add the service to your 2020 publications order to stay on top of any changes to CA regulations throughout the year.

Notifications are sent via email to the email provided with your order and are good through December 1, 2020.

ACEC California Chapters

Bay Bridge Chapter
Central California Chapter
Channel Coast Chapter
East Bay Chapter
Kern County Chapter
Los Angeles County Chapter
Marin Chapter
Monterey Bay Area Chapter
Mother Lode Chapter
Napa-Solano Chapter
North Coast Chapter
Northern Chapter
Orange County Chapter
Peninsula Chapter
Redwood Region Chapter
Riverside-San Bernardino Chapter
San Diego Chapter
San Joaquin Valley Chapter
San Luis Chapter
Santa Clara County Chapter
Sequoia Chapter
Sierra Chapter

ACEC
AMERICAN COUNCIL OF ENGINEERING COMPANIES
California

What is ACEC California?

The American Council of Engineering Companies of California (ACEC California) and its predecessor organizations have represented the business and professional interests of engineers, land surveyors and providers of construction related services since the early 1950's. ACEC California is dedicated to enhancing the design and related professions, protecting the general public, and promoting the private enterprise system.

How is ACEC California organized?

ACEC California is the California affiliate of the American Council of Engineering Companies (ACEC), that represents the interests of design firms nationwide. ACEC California is comprised of 22 local chapters with approximately 1,000 member firms. Member firms range in size from sole proprietorships to multi-national corporations and provide the following professional services: civil, structural, geotechnical, electrical, and mechanical engineering; land surveying; environmental; consulting; and construction services, the last of which includes inspection, project management, and program management.

What does ACEC California do?

ACEC California promotes cooperation among member firms for the public interest and the general advancement of the professions. ACEC California's goals are accomplished primarily through the work of its statewide committees and chapters. The functions of its component units during the year include tasks that vary from administrative and liaison assignments, to professional objectives, to responsibility for improving business practices.

How does ACEC California benefit its members?

ACEC California sponsors and supports legislation that further the public interest and the professional practice of its members. Through ACEC California, members have a strong voice at all levels of government: locally through the chapter organizations, at the state level through ACEC California and at the national level through ACEC. Additionally, ACEC California offers a variety of group insurance programs, sponsors webinars on business management, legal and regulatory issues, and publishes various professional and business manuals and forms.

How can I learn more about ACEC California?

To find out more about ACEC California, including information about membership, visit our website at www.acec-ca.org or contact our membership director, Christian Anger, at the ACEC California office. The staff can also put you in touch with members in your area who can tell you about the activities of their local chapter. Firms that are located out of state may join ACEC California as a non-resident member firm.

ACEC California
1303 J Street, Ste. 450
Sacramento, CA 95814
p: 916-441-7991
f: 916-441-6312
e-mail: staff@acec-ca.org
www.acec-ca.org

Table of Contents

California Environmental Quality Act

California Environmental Quality Act

as amended January 1, 2020

§§21000−21189.57

Public Resources Code

State of California

Changes made to CEQA during 2019 are as follows:

Section	Effect	Bill #	Chapter	Effective
21060.2	Add	AB 1560	631	1/1/20
21064.3	Amend	AB 1560	631	1/1/20
21080.14	Add & Repeal	AB 1824	466	1/1/20
21080.21	Amend	AB 1824	466	1/1/20
21080.25	Repeal by Sunset Date			1/1/20
21080.27	Add & Repeal	AB 1197	340	9/26/19
21080.28	Add	AB 782	181	1/1/20
21080.37	Repeal by Sunset Date			1/1/20
21080.50	Add & Repeal	SB 450	344	1/1/20
21098	Amend	SB 242	142	1/1/20
21099	Amend	AB 1824	466	1/1/20
21108	Amend	AB 1824	466	1/1/20
21152	Amend	AB 1824	466	1/1/20
21152.1	Amend	AB 1824	466	1/1/20
21159.25	Amend	AB 991	497	1/1/20
21161	Amend	AB 1824	466	1/1/20
21163	Add & Repeal	SB 744	346	1/1/20
21163.1	Add & Repeal	SB 744	346	1/1/20
21163.2	Add & Repeal	SB 744	346	1/1/20
21163.3	Add & Repeal	SB 744	346	1/1/20
21163.4	Add & Repeal	SB 744	346	1/1/20
21177	Amend	AB 1824	466	1/1/20

Notes

For the reader's convenience, all new language adopted in 2019 is printed in **bold italics**.

The titles to each statute section printed in bold have been added by ACEC California for the reader's convenience. The titles are not part of the law.

Public Resources Code

Division 13. Environmental Quality

Chapter 1. Policy

21000. **State agencies shall regulate to prevent environmental damage**

The Legislature finds and declares as follows:

(a) The maintenance of a quality environment for the people of this state now and in the future is a matter of statewide concern.

(b) It is necessary to provide a high-quality environment that at all times is healthful and pleasing to the senses and intellect of man.

(c) There is a need to understand the relationship between the maintenance of high-quality ecological systems and the general welfare of the people of the state, including their enjoyment of the natural resources of the state.

(d) The capacity of the environment is limited, and it is the intent of the Legislature that the government of the state take immediate steps to identify any critical thresholds for the health and safety of the people of the state and take all coordinated actions necessary to prevent such thresholds being reached.

(e) Every citizen has a responsibility to contribute to the preservation and enhancement of the environment.

(f) The interrelationship of policies and practices in the management of natural resources and waste disposal requires systematic and concerted efforts by public and private interests to enhance environmental quality and to control environmental pollution.

(g) It is the intent of the Legislature that all agencies of the state government which regulate activities of private individuals, corporations, and public agencies which are found to affect the quality of the environment, shall regulate such activities so that major consideration is given to preventing environmental damage, while providing a decent home and satisfying living environment for every Californian.

[Amended, Chapter 947, Statutes of 1979]

21001. **Requires governmental agencies to develop standards and procedures and to consider alternatives**

The Legislature further finds and declares that it is the policy of the state to:

(a) Develop and maintain a high-quality environment now and in the future, and take all action necessary to protect, rehabilitate, and enhance the environmental quality of the state.

(b) Take all action necessary to provide the people of this state with clean air and water, enjoyment of aesthetic, natural, scenic, and historic environmental qualities, and freedom from excessive noise.

(c) Prevent the elimination of fish or wildlife species due to man's activities, insure that fish and wildlife populations do not drop below self-perpetuating levels, and preserve for future generations representations of all plant and animal communities and examples of the major periods of California history.

(d) Ensure that the long-term protection of the environment, consistent with the provision of a decent home and suitable living environment for every Californian, shall be the guiding criterion in public decisions.

(e) Create and maintain conditions under which man and nature can exist in productive harmony to fulfill the social and economic requirements of present and future generations.

(f) Require governmental agencies at all levels to develop standards and procedures necessary to protect environmental quality.

(g) Require governmental agencies at all levels to consider qualitative factors as well as economic and technical factors and long-term benefits and costs, in addition to short-term benefits and costs and to consider alternatives to proposed actions affecting the environment.

[Amended, Chapter 947, Statutes of 1979]

21001.1. Public agency projects not exempt

The Legislature further finds and declares that it is the policy of the state that projects to be carried out by public agencies be subject to the same level of review and consideration under this division as that of private projects required to be approved by public agencies.

[Added, Chapter 1514, Statutes of 1984]

21002. No project approval if feasible alternative or mitigation measures; project may be approved if conditions make project infeasible

The Legislature finds and declares that it is the policy of the state that public agencies should not approve projects as proposed if there are feasible alternatives or feasible mitigation measures available which would substantially lessen the significant environmental effects of such projects, and that the procedures required by this division are intended to assist public agencies in systematically identifying both the significant effects of proposed projects and the feasible alternatives or feasible mitigation measures which will avoid or substantially lessen such significant effects. The Legislature further finds and declares that in the event specific economic, social, or other conditions make infeasible such project alternatives or such mitigation measures, individual projects may be approved in spite of one or more significant effects thereof.

[Amended, Chapter 676, Statutes of 1980]

21002.1. Purpose, use, and application of EIRs; lead agency functions

In order to achieve the objectives set forth in Section 21002, the Legislature finds and declares that the following policy shall apply to the use of environmental impact reports prepared pursuant to this division:

(a) The purpose of an environmental impact report is to identify the significant effects on the environment of a project, to identify alternatives to the project, and to indicate the manner in which those significant effects can be mitigated or avoided.

(b) Each public agency shall mitigate or avoid the significant effects on the environment of projects that it carries out or approves whenever it is feasible to do so.

(c) If economic, social, or other conditions make it infeasible to mitigate one or more significant effects on the environment of a project, the project may nonetheless be carried out or approved at the discretion of a public agency if the project is otherwise permissible under applicable laws and regulations.

(d) In applying the policies of subdivisions (b) and (c) to individual projects, the responsibility of the lead agency shall differ from that of a responsible agency. The lead agency shall be responsible for considering the effects, both individual and collective, of all activities involved in a project. A responsible agency shall be responsible for considering only the effects of those activities involved in a project which it is required by law to carry out or approve. This subdivision applies only to decisions by a public agency to carry out or approve a project and does not otherwise affect the scope of the comments that the public agency may wish to make pursuant to Section 21104 or 21153.

(e) To provide more meaningful public disclosure, reduce the time and cost required to prepare an environmental impact report, and focus on potentially significant effects on the environment of a proposed project, lead agencies shall, in accordance with Section 21100, focus the discussion in the environmental impact report on those potential effects on the environment of a proposed project which the lead agency has determined are or may be significant. Lead agencies may limit discussion on other effects to a brief explanation as to why those effects are not potentially significant.

[Amended, Chapter 1230, Statutes of 1994]

21003.   Legislative intent; concurrent; integration with other review procedures; information data base; efficiency

The Legislature further finds and declares that it is the policy of the state that:

(a) Local agencies integrate the requirements of this division with planning and environmental review procedures otherwise required by law or by local practice so that all those procedures, to the maximum feasible extent, run concurrently, rather than consecutively.

(b) Documents prepared pursuant to this division be organized and written in a manner that will be meaningful and useful to decisionmakers and to the public.

(c) Environmental impact reports omit unnecessary descriptions of projects and emphasize feasible mitigation measures and feasible alternatives to projects.

(d) Information developed in individual environmental impact reports be incorporated into a data base which can be used to reduce delay and duplication in preparation of subsequent environmental impact reports.

(e) Information developed in environmental impact reports and negative declarations be incorporated into a data base which may be used to make subsequent or supplemental environmental determinations.

(f) All persons and public agencies involved in the environmental review process be responsible for carrying out the process in the most efficient, expeditious manner in order to conserve the available financial, governmental, physical, and social resources with the objective that those resources may be better applied toward the mitigation of actual significant effects on the environment.

[Amended, Chapter 1130, Statutes of 1993]

21003.1. Early identification of significant effects, alternatives and mitigation

The Legislature further finds and declares it is the policy of the state that:

(a) Comments from the public and public agencies on the environmental effects of a project shall be made to lead agencies as soon as possible in the review of environmental documents, including, but not limited to, draft environmental impact reports and negative declarations, in order to allow the lead agencies to identify, at the earliest possible time in the environmental review process, potential significant effects of a project, alternatives, and mitigation measures which would substantially reduce the effects.

(b) Information relevant to the significant effects of a project, alternatives, and mitigation measures which substantially reduce the effects shall be made available as soon as possible by lead agencies, other public agencies, and interested persons and organizations.

(c) Nothing in subdivisions (a) or (b) reduces or otherwise limits public review or comment periods currently prescribed either by statute or in guidelines prepared and adopted pursuant to Section 21083 for environmental documents, including, but not limited to, draft environmental impact reports and negative declarations.

[Added, Chapter 85, Statutes of 1985]

21004. Legislative intent; public agency authority

In mitigating or avoiding a significant effect of a project on the environment, a public agency may exercise only those express or implied powers provided by law other than this division. However, a public agency may use discretionary powers provided by such other law for the purpose of mitigating or avoiding a significant effect on the environment subject to the express or implied constraints or limitations that may be provided by law.

21005. Disclosure and abuse of discretion

(a) The Legislature finds and declares that it is the policy of the state that noncompliance with the information disclosure provisions of this division which precludes relevant information from being presented to the public agency, or noncompliance with substantive requirements of this division may constitute a prejudicial abuse of discretion within the meaning of Sections 21168 and 21168.5, regardless of whether a different outcome would have resulted if the public agency had complied with those provisions.

(b) It is the intent of the Legislature that, in undertaking judicial review pursuant to Sections 21168 and 21168.5, courts shall continue to follow the established principle that there is no presumption that error is prejudicial.

(c) It is further the intent of the Legislature that any court, which finds, or, in the process of reviewing a previous court finding, finds, that a public agency has taken an action without compliance with this division, shall specifically address each of the alleged grounds for noncompliance.

[Amended, Chapter 1230, Statutes of 1994]

21006. CEQA is integral to agency decision making

The legislature finds and declares that this division is an integral part of any public agency's decisionmaking process, including, but not limited to, the issuance of permits, licenses, certificates, or other entitlements required for activities undertaken pursuant to federal statutes containing specific waivers of sovereign immunity.

[Added, Chapter 272, Statutes of 1998]

Chapter 2. Short Title

21050. California Environmental Quality Act cited

This division shall be known and may be cited as the California Environmental Quality Act.

[Amended, Chapter 1312, Statutes of 1976]

Chapter 2.5. Definitions

21060. Definitions applicable to Act only

Unless the context otherwise requires, the definitions in this chapter govern the construction of this division.

21060.1. "Agricultural land"

(a) "Agricultural land" means prime farmland, farmland of statewide importance, or unique farmland, as defined by the United States Department of Agriculture land inventory and monitoring criteria, as modified for California.

(b) In those areas of the state where lands have not been surveyed for the classifications specified in subdivision (a), "agricultural land" means land that meets the requirements of "prime agricultural land" as defined in paragraph (1), (2), (3), or (4) of subdivision (c) of Section 51201 of the Government Code.

[Added, Chapter 812, Statutes of 1993]

21060.2. "Bus rapid transit"; "Bus rapid transit station"

(a) *"Bus rapid transit" means a public mass transit service provided by a public agency or by a public-private partnership that includes all of the following features:*

(1) *Full-time dedicated bus lanes or operation in a separate right-of-way dedicated for public transportation with a frequency of service interval of 15 minutes or less during the morning and afternoon peak commute periods.*

(2) *Transit signal priority.*

(3) *All-door boarding.*

(4) *Fare collection system that promotes efficiency.*

(5) *Defined stations.*

(b) *"Bus rapid transit station" means a clearly defined bus station served by a bus rapid transit.*

[Added, Chapter 631, Statutes of 2019]

21060.3.   "Emergency"

"Emergency" means a sudden, unexpected occurrence, involving a clear and imminent danger, demanding immediate action to prevent or mitigate loss of, or damage to, life, health, property, or essential public services. "Emergency" includes such occurrences as fire, flood, earthquake, or other soil or geologic movements, as well as such occurrences as riot, accident, or sabotage.

[Added, Chapter 1312, Statutes of 1976]

21060.5.   "Environment"

"Environment" means the physical conditions which exist within the area which will be affected by a proposed project, including land, air, water, minerals, flora, fauna, noise, objects of historic or aesthetic significance.

[Added, Chapter 1154, Statutes of 1972]

21061.   "EIR"

"Environmental impact report" means a detailed statement setting forth the matters specified in Sections 21100 and 21100.1; provided that information or data which is relevant to such a statement and is a matter of public record or is generally available to the public need not be repeated in its entirety in such statement, but may be specifically cited as the source for conclusions stated therein; and provided further that such information or data shall be briefly described, that its relationship to the environmental impact report shall be indicated, and that the source thereof shall be reasonably available for inspection at a public place or public building. An environmental impact report also includes any comments which are obtained pursuant to Section 21104 or 21153, or which are required to be obtained pursuant to this division.

An environmental impact report is an informational document which, when its preparation is required by this division, shall be considered by every public agency prior to its approval or disapproval of a project. The purpose of an environmental impact report is to provide public agencies and the public in general with detailed information about the effect which a proposed project is likely to have on the environment; to list ways in which the significant effects of such a project might be minimized; and to indicate alternatives to such a project.

In order to facilitate the use of environmental impact reports, public agencies shall require that such reports contain an index or table of contents and a summary. Failure to include such index, table of contents, or summary shall not constitute a cause of action pursuant to Section 21167.

[Amended, Chapter 1312, Statutes of 1976]

21061.1. "Feasible"

"Feasible" means capable of being accomplished in a successful manner within a reasonable period of time, taking into account economic, environmental, social, and technological factors.

[Added, Chapter 1312, Statutes of 1976]

21061.2. "Land evaluation and site assessment"

"Land evaluation and site assessment" means a decision making methodology for assessing the potential environmental impact of state and local projects on agricultural land.

[Added, Chapter 812, Statutes of 1993]

21061.3 "Infill site"

"Infill site" means a site in an urbanized area that meets either of the following criteria:

(a) The site has not been previously developed for urban uses and both of the following apply:

    (1) The site is immediately adjacent to parcels that are developed with qualified urban uses, or at least 75 percent of the perimeter of the site adjoins parcels that are developed with qualified urban uses, and the remaining 25 percent of the site adjoins parcels that have previously been developed for qualified urban uses.

    (2) No parcel within the site has been created within the past 10 years unless the parcel was created as a result of the plan of a redevelopment agency.

(b) The site has been previously developed for qualified urban uses.

[Amended, Chapter 728, Statutes of 2008]

21062. "Local agency"

"Local agency" means any public agency other than a state agency, board, or commission. For purposes of this division, a redevelopment agency and a local agency formation commission are local agencies, and neither is a state agency, board, or commission.

[Amended, Chapter 222, Statutes of 1975]

21063. "Public agency"

"Public agency" includes any state agency, board, or commission, any county, city and county, city, regional agency, public district, redevelopment agency, or other political subdivision.

[Added, Chapter 1154, Statutes of 1972]

21064. "Negative declaration"

"Negative declaration" means a written statement briefly describing the reasons that a proposed project will not have a significant effect on the environment and does not require the preparation of an environmental impact report.

[Added, Chapter 1312, Statutes of 1976]

21064.3. "Major transit stop"

"Major transit stop" means a site containing *any of the following:*

(a) *A*n existing rail *or bus rapid* transit station.

(b) *A* ferry terminal served by either a bus or rail transit service.

(c) *T*he intersection of two or more major bus routes with a frequency of service interval of 15 minutes or less during the morning and afternoon peak commute periods.

[Amended, Chapter 631, Statutes of 2019]

21064.5. "Mitigated negative declaration"

"Mitigated negative declaration" means a negative declaration prepared for a project when the initial study has identified potentially significant effects on the environment, but (1) revisions in the project plans or proposals made by, or agreed to by, the applicant before the proposed negative declaration and initial study are released for public review would avoid the effects or mitigate the effects to a point where clearly no significant effect on the environment would occur, and (2) there is no substantial evidence in light of the whole record before the public agency that the project, as revised, may have a significant effect on the environment.

[Amended, Chapter 1230, Statutes of 1994]

21065. "Project"

"Project" means an activity which may cause either a direct physical change in the environment, or a reasonably foreseeable indirect physical change in the environment, and which is any of the following:

(a) An activity directly undertaken by any public agency.

(b) An activity undertaken by a person which is supported, in whole or in part, through contracts, grants, subsidies, loans, or other forms of assistance from one or more public agencies.

(c) An activity that involves the issuance to a person of a lease, permit, license, certificate, or other entitlement for use by one or more public agencies.

[Amended, Chapter 1230, Statutes of 1994]

21065.3. "Project-specific effect"

"Project-specific effect" means all the direct or indirect environmental effects of a project other than cumulative effects and growth-inducing effects.

[Added, Chapter 1039, Statutes of 2002]

21065.5. "Geothermal exploratory project"

"Geothermal exploratory project" means a project as defined in Section 21065 composed of not more than six wells and associated drilling and testing equipment, whose chief and original purpose is to evaluate the presence and characteristics of geothermal resources prior to commencement of a geothermal field development project as defined in Section 65928.5 of the Government Code. Wells included within a geothermal exploratory project must be located at least one-half mile from geothermal development wells which are capable of producing geothermal resources in commercial quantities.

[Added, Chapter 1271, Statutes of 1978]

21066. "Person"

"Person" includes any person, firm, association, organization, partnership, business, trust, corporation, limited liability company, company, district, county, city and county, city, town, the state, and any of the agencies and political subdivisions of those entities, and, to the extent permitted by federal law, the United Sates, or any of its agencies or political subdivisions.

[Amended, Chapter 272, Statutes of 1998]

21067. "Lead agency"

"Lead agency" means the public agency which has the principal responsibility for carrying out or approving a project which may have a significant effect upon the environment.

[Added, Chapter 1154, Statutes of 1972]

21068. "Significant effect on the environment"

"Significant effect on the environment" means a substantial, or potentially substantial, adverse change in the environment.

[Added, Chapter 1312, Statutes of 1976]

21068.5. "Tiering" or "tier"

"Tiering" or "tier" means the coverage of general matters and environmental effects in an environmental impact report prepared for a policy, plan, program or ordinance followed by narrower or site-specific environmental impact reports which incorporate by reference the discussion in any prior environmental impact report and which concentrate on the environmental effects which (a) are capable of being mitigated, or (b) were not analyzed as significant effects on the environment in the prior environmental impact report.

[Added, Chapter 967, Statutes of 1983]

21069. "Responsible agency"

"Responsible agency" means a public agency, other than the lead agency which has responsibility for carrying out or approving a project.

[Added, Chapter 1312, Statutes of 1976]

21070. "Trustee Agency"

"Trustee agency" means a state agency that has jurisdiction by law over natural resources affected by a project, that are held in trust for the people of the State of California.

[Added, Chapter 744, Statutes of 2004]

21071.   "Urbanized area"

"Urbanized area" means either of the following:

(a) An incorporated city that meets either of the following criteria:

(1) Has a population of at least 100,000 persons.

(2) Has a population of less than 100,000 persons if the population of that city and not more than two contiguous incorporated cities combined equals at least 100,000 persons.

(b) An unincorporated area that satisfies the criteria in both paragraph (1) and (2) of the following criteria:

(1) Is either of the following:

(A) Completely surrounded by one or more incorporated cities, and both of the following criteria are met:

(i)   The population of the unincorporated area and the population of the surrounding incorporated city or cities equals not less than 100,000 persons.

(ii) The population density of the unincorporated area at least equals the population density of the surrounding city or cities.

(B) Located within an urban growth boundary and has an existing residential population of at least 5,000 persons per square mile. For purposes of this subparagraph, an "urban growth boundary" means a provision of a locally adopted general plan that allows urban uses on one side of the boundary and prohibits urban uses on the other side.

(2) The board of supervisors with jurisdiction over the unincorporated area has previously taken both of the following actions:

(A) Issued a finding that the general plan, zoning ordinance, and related policies and programs applicable to the unincorporated area are consistent with principles that encourage compact development in a manner that does both of the following:

(i)   Promotes efficient transportation systems, economic growth, affordable housing, energy efficiency, and an appropriate balance of jobs and housing.

(ii) Protects the environment, open space, and agricultural areas.

(B) Submitted a draft finding to the Office of Planning and Research at least 30 days prior to issuing a final finding, and allowed the office 30 days to submit comments on the draft findings to the board of supervisors.

[Added, Chapter 1039, Statutes of 2002]

21072.   "Qualified urban use"

"Qualified urban use" means any residential, commercial, public institutional, transit or transportation passenger facility, or retail use, or any combination of those uses.

[Added, Chapter 1039, Statutes of 2002]

21073.   California Native American tribe

"California Native American tribe" means a Native American tribe located in California that is on the contact list maintained by the Native American Heritage Commission for the purposes of Chapter 905 of the Statutes of 2004.

[Added, Chapter 532, Statutes of 2014]

21074.   Tribal cultural resources

(a) "Tribal cultural resources" are either of the following:

    (1) Sites, features, places, cultural landscapes, sacred places, and objects with cultural value to a California Native American tribe that are either of the following:

        (A) Included or determined to be eligible for inclusion in the California Register of Historical Resources.

        (B) Included in a local register of historical resources as defined in subdivision (k) of Section 5020.1.

    (2) A resource determined by the lead agency, in its discretion and supported by substantial evidence, to be significant pursuant to criteria set forth in subdivision (c) of Section 5024.1. In applying the criteria set forth in subdivision (c) of Section 5024.1 for the purposes of this paragraph, the lead agency shall consider the significance of the resource to a California Native American tribe.

(b) A cultural landscape that meets the criteria of subdivision (a) is a tribal cultural resource to the extent that the landscape is geographically defined in terms of the size and scope of the landscape.

(c) A historical resource described in Section 21084.1, a unique archaeological resource as defined in subdivision (g) of Section 21083.2, or a "nonunique archaeological resource" as defined in subdivision (h) of Section 21083.2 may also be a tribal cultural resource if it conforms with the criteria of subdivision (a).

[Added, Chapter 532, Statutes of 2014]

Chapter 2.6. General

21080.   Names, types of projects requiring EIRs; exclusions; substantial evidence standard; mitigation substitution

(a) Except as otherwise provided in this division, this division shall apply to discretionary projects proposed to be carried out or approved by public agencies, including, but not limited to, the enactment and amendment of zoning ordinances, the issuance of zoning variances, the issuance of conditional use permits, and the approval of tentative subdivision maps unless the project is exempt from this division.

(b) This division does not apply to any of the following activities:

    (1) Ministerial projects proposed to be carried out or approved by public agencies.

(2) Emergency repairs to public service facilities necessary to maintain service.

(3) Projects undertaken, carried out, or approved by a public agency to maintain, repair, restore, demolish, or replace property or facilities damaged or destroyed as a result of a disaster in a disaster-stricken area in which a state of emergency has been proclaimed by the Governor pursuant to Chapter 7 (commencing with Section 8550) of Division 1 of Title 2 of the Government Code.

(4) Specific actions necessary to prevent or mitigate an emergency.

(5) Projects which a public agency rejects or disapproves.

(6) Actions undertaken by a public agency relating to any thermal powerplant site or facility, including the expenditure, obligation, or encumbrance of funds by a public agency for planning, engineering, or design purposes, or for the conditional sale or purchase of equipment, fuel, water (except groundwater), steam, or power for a thermal powerplant, if the powerplant site and related facility will be the subject of an environmental impact report, negative declaration, or other document, prepared pursuant to a regulatory program certified pursuant to Section 21080.5, which will be prepared by the State Energy Resources Conservation and Development Commission, by the Public Utilities Commission, or by the city or county in which the powerplant and related facility would be located if the environmental impact report, negative declaration, or document includes the environmental impact, if any, of the action described in this paragraph.

(7) Activities or approvals necessary to the bidding for, hosting or staging of, and funding or carrying out of, an Olympic games under the authority of the International Olympic Committee, except for the construction of facilities necessary for the Olympic games.

(8) The establishment, modification, structuring, restructuring, or approval of rates, tolls, fares, or other charges by public agencies which the public agency finds are for the purpose of (A) meeting operating expenses, including employee wage rates and fringe benefits, (B) purchasing or leasing supplies, equipment, or materials, (C) meeting financial reserve needs and requirements, (D) obtaining funds for capital projects necessary to maintain service within existing service areas, or (E) obtaining funds necessary to maintain those intracity transfers as are authorized by city charter. The public agency shall incorporate written findings in the record of any proceeding in which an exemption under this paragraph is claimed setting forth with specificity the basis for the claim of exemption.

(9) All classes of projects designated pursuant to Section 21084.

(10) A project for the institution or increase of passenger or commuter services on rail or highway rights-of-way already in use, including modernization of existing stations and parking facilities. For purposes of this paragraph, "highway" shall have the same meaning as defined in Section 360 of the Vehicle Code.

(11) A project for the institution or increase of passenger or commuter service on high-occupancy vehicle lanes already in use, including the modernization of existing stations and parking facilities.

(12) Facility extensions not to exceed four miles in length which are required for the transfer of passengers from or to exclusive public mass transit guideway or busway public transit services.

(13) A project for the development of a regional transportation improvement program, the state transportation improvement program, or a congestion management program prepared pursuant to Section 65089 of the Government Code.

(14) Any project or portion thereof located in another state which will be subject to environmental impact review pursuant to the National Environmental Policy Act of 1969 (42 U.S.C. Sec. 4321 et seq.) or similar state laws of that state. Any emissions or discharges that would have a significant effect on the environment in this state are subject to this division.

(15) Projects undertaken by a local agency to implement a rule or regulation imposed by a state agency, board, or commission under a certified regulatory program pursuant to Section 21080.5. Any site-specific effect of the project which was not analyzed as a significant effect on the environment in the plan or other written documentation required by Section 21080.5 is subject to this division.

(c) If a lead agency determines that a proposed project, not otherwise exempt from this division, would not have a significant effect on the environment, the lead agency shall adopt a negative declaration to that effect. The negative declaration shall be prepared for the proposed project in either of the following circumstances:

(1) There is no substantial evidence, in light of the whole record before the lead agency, that the project may have a significant effect on the environment.

(2) An initial study identifies potentially significant effects on the environment, but (A) revisions in the project plans or proposals made by, or agreed to by, the applicant before the proposed negative declaration and initial study are released for public review would avoid the effects or mitigate the effects to a point where clearly no significant effect on the environment would occur, and (B) there is no substantial evidence, in light of the whole record before the lead agency, that the project, as revised, may have a significant effect on the environment.

(d) If there is substantial evidence, in light of the whole record before the lead agency, that the project may have a significant effect on the environment, an environmental impact report shall be prepared.

(e) (1) For the purposes of this section and this division, substantial evidence includes fact, a reasonable assumption predicated upon fact, or expert opinion supported by fact.

(2) Substantial evidence is not argument, speculation, unsubstantiated opinion or narrative, evidence that is clearly inaccurate or erroneous, or evidence

of social or economic impacts that do not contribute to, or are not caused by, physical impacts on the environment.

(f) As a result of the public review process for a mitigated negative declaration, including administrative decisions and public hearings, the lead agency may conclude that certain mitigation measures identified pursuant to paragraph (2) of subdivision (c) are infeasible or otherwise undesirable. In those circumstances, the lead agency, prior to approving the project, may delete those mitigation measures and substitute for them other mitigation measures that the lead agency finds, after holding a public hearing on the matter, are equivalent or more effective in mitigating significant effects on the environment to a less than significant level and that do not cause any potentially significant effect on the environment. If those new mitigation measures are made conditions of project approval or are otherwise made part of the project approval, the deletion of the former measures and the substitution of the new mitigation measures shall not constitute an action or circumstance requiring recirculation of the mitigated negative declaration.

(g) Nothing in this section shall preclude a project applicant or any other person from challenging, in an administrative or judicial proceeding, the legality of a condition of project approval imposed by the lead agency. If, however, any condition of project approval set aside by either an administrative body or court was necessary to avoid or lessen the likelihood of the occurrence of a significant effect on the environment, the lead agency's approval of the negative declaration and project shall be invalid and a new environmental review process shall be conducted before the project can be reapproved, unless the lead agency substitutes a new condition that the lead agency finds, after holding a public hearing on the matter, is equivalent to, or more effective in, lessening or avoiding significant effects on the environment and that does not cause any potentially significant effect on the environment.

[Amended, Chapter 523, Statutes of 2013]

21080.01.   Facility in San Luis Obispo County excluded

This division shall not apply to any activity or approval necessary for the reopening and operation of the California Men's Colony West Facility in San Luis Obispo County.

[Added, Chapter 958, Statutes of 1983]

21080.02.   Facility in Kings County excluded

This division shall not apply to any activity or approval necessary for or incidental to planning, design, site acquisition, construction, operation, or maintenance of the new prison facility at or in the vicinity of Corcoran in Kings County as authorized by the act that enacted this section.

[Added, Chapter 931, Statutes of 1985]

21080.03.   Prisons in County of Kings and County of Amador (Ione) are excluded

This division shall not apply to any activity or approval necessary for or incidental to the location, development, construction, operation, or maintenance of the prison in the County of Kings, authorized by Section 9 of Chapter 958 of the Statutes of 1983, as amended, and of the prison in the County of Amador (Ione), authorized by Chapter 957 of the Statutes of 1983, as amended.

[Added, Chapter 931, Statutes of 1985]

21080.04. Napa Valley train included

(a) Notwithstanding paragraph (10) of subdivision (b) of Section 21080, this division applies to a project for the institution of passenger rail service on a line paralleling State Highway 29 and running from Rocktram to Krug in the Napa Valley. With respect to that project, and for the purposes of this division, the Public Utilities Commission is the lead agency.

(b) It is the intent of the Legislature in enacting this section to abrogate the decision of the California Supreme Court "that Section 21080, subdivision (b) (11), exempts Wine Train's institution of passenger service on the Rocktram-Krug line from the requirements of CEQA" in Napa Valley Wine Train, Inc. v. Public Utilities Com., 50 Cal. 3d 370.

(c) Nothing in this section is intended to affect or apply to, or to confer jurisdiction upon the Public Utilities Commission with respect to, any other project involving rail service.

[Amended, Chapter 91, Statutes of 1995]

21080.05. Railroad right-of-way on the Peninsula

This division does not apply to a project by a public agency to lease or purchase the rail right-of-way used for the San Francisco Peninsula commute service between San Francisco and San Jose, together with all branch and spur lines, including the Dumbarton and Vasona lines.

[Added, Chapter 1283, Statutes of 1989]

21080.07. Prisons in County of Riverside and County of Del Norte are excluded

This division shall not apply to any activity or approval necessary for or incidental to planning, design, site acquisition, construction, operation, or maintenance of the new prison facilities located in any of the following places:

(a) The County of Riverside.

(b) The County of Del Norte.

[Added, Chapter 933, Statutes of 1985]

21080.09. Higher education projects

(a) For purposes of this section, the following definitions apply:

(1) "Public higher education" has the same meaning as specified in Section 66010 of the Education Code.

(2) "Long range development plan" means a physical development and land use plan to meet the academic and institutional objectives for a particular campus or medical center of public higher education.

(b) The selection of a location for a particular campus and the approval of a long range development plan are subject to this division and require the preparation of an environmental impact report. Environmental effects relating to changes in enrollment levels shall be considered for each campus or medical center of public higher education in the environmental impact report prepared for the long range development plan for the campus or medical center.

(c) The approval of a project on a particular campus or medical center of public higher education is subject to this division and may be addressed, subject to the other provisions of this division, in a tiered environmental analysis based upon a long range development plan environmental impact report.

(d) Compliance with this section satisfies the obligations of public higher education pursuant to this division to consider the environmental impact of academic and enrollment plans as they affect campuses or medical centers, provided that any such plans shall become effective for a campus or medical center only after the environmental effects of those plans have been analyzed as required by this division in a long range development plan environmental impact report or tiered analysis based upon that environmental impact report for that campus or medical center, and addressed as required by this division.

[Added, Chapter 659, Statutes of 1989]

21080.1. EIR, negative declaration, or mitigated negative declaration determination by lead agency; consultation

(a) The lead agency shall be responsible for determining whether an environmental impact report, a negative declaration, or a mitigated negative declaration shall be required for any project which is subject to this division. That determination shall be final and conclusive on all persons, including responsible agencies, unless challenged as provided in Section 21167.

(b) In the case of a project described in subdivision (c) of Section 21065, the lead agency shall, upon the request of a potential applicant, provide for consultation prior to the filing of the application regarding the range of actions, potential alternatives, mitigation measures, and any potential and significant effects on the environment of the project.

[Amended, Chapter 1230, Statutes of 1994]

21080.2. Time limit for determination; extensions

In the case of a project described in subdivision (c) of Section 21065, the determination required by Section 21080.1 shall be made within 30 days from the date on which an application for a project has been received and accepted as complete by the lead agency. This period may be extended 15 days upon the consent of the lead agency and the project applicant.

[Amended, Chapter 586, Statutes of 1984]

21080.3. Lead agency shall consult with all responsible agencies prior to determination, assistance by the Office of Planning and Research

(a) Prior to determining whether a negative declaration or environmental impact report is required for a project, the lead agency shall consult with all responsible agencies and trustee agencies. Prior to that required consultation, the lead agency may informally contact any of those agencies.

(b) In order to expedite the requirements of subdivision (a), the Office of Planning and Research, upon request of a lead agency, shall assist the lead agency in determining the various responsible agencies and trustee agencies, for a proposed project. In the case of a project described in subdivision (c) of Section 21065, the request may also be made by the project applicant.

[Amended, Chapter 744, Statutes of 2004]

21080.3.1. Consultation with California Native American tribes

(a) The Legislature finds and declares that California Native American tribes traditionally and culturally affiliated with a geographic area may have expertise concerning their tribal cultural resources.

(b) Prior to the release of a negative declaration, mitigated negative declaration, or environmental impact report for a project, the lead agency shall begin consultation with a California Native American tribe that is traditionally and culturally affiliated with the geographic area of the proposed project if: (1) the California Native American tribe requested to the lead agency, in writing, to be informed by the lead agency through formal notification of proposed projects in the geographic area that is traditionally and culturally affiliated with the tribe, and (2) the California Native American tribe responds, in writing, within 30 days of receipt of the formal notification, and requests the consultation. When responding to the lead agency, the California Native American tribe shall designate a lead contact person. If the California Native American tribe does not designate a lead contact person, or designates multiple lead contact people, the lead agency shall defer to the individual listed on the contact list maintained by the Native American Heritage Commission for the purposes of Chapter 905 of the Statutes of 2004. For purposes of this section and Section 21080.3.2, "consultation" shall have the same meaning as provided in Section 65352.4 of the Government Code.

(c) To expedite the requirements of this section, the Native American Heritage Commission shall assist the lead agency in identifying the California Native American tribes that are traditionally and culturally affiliated with the project area.

(d) Within 14 days of determining that an application for a project is complete or a decision by a public agency to undertake a project, the lead agency shall provide formal notification to the designated contact of, or a tribal representative of, traditionally and culturally affiliated California Native American tribes that have requested notice, which shall be accomplished by means of at least one written notification that includes a brief description of the proposed project and its location, the lead agency contact information, and a notification that the California Native American tribe has 30 days to request consultation pursuant to this section.

(e) The lead agency shall begin the consultation process within 30 days of receiving a California Native American tribe's request for consultation.

[Added, Chapter 532, Statutes of 2014]

21080.3.2. California Native American tribes: mitigation measures; consultation; conclusion

(a) As a part of the consultation pursuant to Section 21080.3.1, the parties may propose mitigation measures, including, but not limited to, those recommended in Section 21084.3, capable of avoiding or substantially lessening potential significant impacts to a tribal cultural resource or alternatives that would avoid significant impacts to a tribal cultural resource. If the California Native American tribe requests consultation regarding alternatives to the project, recommended mitigation measures, or significant effects, the consultation shall include those topics. The consultation may include discussion concerning the type of environmental review necessary, the significance of tribal cultural resources, the significance of the project's impacts on the tribal cultural resources, and, if necessary, project alternatives or the appropriate measures for preservation or mitigation that the California Native American tribe may recommended to the lead agency.

(b) The consultation shall be considered concluded when either of the following occurs:

(1) The parties agree to measures to mitigate or avoid a significant effect, if a significant effect exists, on a tribal cultural resource.

(2) A party, acting in good faith and after reasonable effort, concludes that mutual agreement cannot be reached.

(c) (1) This section does not limit the ability of a California Native American tribe or the public to submit information to the lead agency regarding the significance of the tribal cultural resources, the significance of the project's impact on tribal cultural resources, or any appropriate measures to mitigate the impact.

(2) This section does not limit the ability of the lead agency or project proponent to incorporate changes and additions to the project as a result of the consultation, even if not legally required.

(d) If the project proponent or its consultants participate in the consultation, those parties shall respect the principles set forth in this section.

[Added, Chapter 532, Statutes of 2014]

21080.4. Notice of determination; time requirements for reply

(a) If a lead agency determines that an environmental impact report is required for a project, the lead agency shall immediately send notice of that determination by certified mail or an equivalent procedure to each responsible agency, the Office of Planning and Research, and those public agencies having jurisdiction by law over natural resources affected by the project that are held in trust for the people of the State of California. Upon receipt of the notice, each responsible agency, the office, and each public agency having jurisdiction by law over natural resources affected by the project that are held in trust for the people of the State of California shall specify to the lead agency the scope and content of the environmental information that is germane to the statutory responsibilities of that responsible agency, the office, or the public agency in connection with the proposed project and which, pursuant to the requirements of this division, shall be included in the environmental impact report. The

20

information shall be specified in writing and shall be communicated to the lead agency by certified mail or equivalent procedure not later than 30 days after the date of receipt of the notice of the lead agency's determination. The lead agency shall request similar guidance from appropriate federal agencies.

(b) To expedite the requirements of subdivision (a), the lead agency, any responsible agency, the Office of Planning and Research, or a public agency having jurisdiction by law over natural resources affected by the project that are held in trust for the people of the State of California, may request one or more meetings between representatives of those agencies and the office for the purpose of assisting the lead agency to determine the scope and content of the environmental information that any of those responsible agencies, the office, or the public agencies may require. In the case of a project described in subdivision (c) of Section 21065, the request may also be made by the project applicant. The meetings shall be convened by the lead agency as soon as possible, but not later than 30 days after the date that the meeting was requested.

(c) To expedite the requirements of subdivision (a), the Office of Planning and Research, upon request of a lead agency, shall assist the lead agency in determining the various responsible agencies, public agencies having jurisdiction by law over natural resources affected by the project that are held in trust for the people of the State of California, and any federal agencies that have responsibility for carrying out or approving a proposed project. In the case of a project described in subdivision (c) of Section 21065, that request may also be made by the project applicant.

(d) With respect to the Department of Transportation, and with respect to any state agency that is a responsible agency or a public agency having jurisdiction by law over natural resources affected by the project that are held in trust for the people of the State of California, subject to the requirements of subdivision (a), the Office of Planning and Research shall ensure that the information required by subdivision (a) is transmitted to the lead agency, and that affected agencies are notified regarding meetings to be held upon request pursuant to subdivision (b), within the required time period.

[Amended, Chapter 738, Statutes of 2000]

21080.5. Regulatory plan in lieu of EIR; limits programs; interdisciplinary approach

(a) Except as provided in Section 21158.1, when the regulatory program of a state agency requires a plan or other written documentation containing environmental information and complying with paragraph (3) of subdivision (d) to be submitted in support of an activity listed in subdivision (b), the plan or other written documentation may be submitted in lieu of the environmental impact report required by this division if the Secretary of the Resources Agency has certified the regulatory program pursuant to this section.

(b) This section applies only to regulatory programs or portions thereof that involve either of the following:

(1) The issuance to a person of a lease, permit, license, certificate, or other entitlement for use.

21

(2) The adoption or approval of standards, rules, regulations, or plans for use in the regulatory program.

(c) A regulatory program certified pursuant to this section is exempt from Chapter 3 (commencing with Section 21100), Chapter 4 (commencing with Section 21150), and Section 21167, except as provided in Article 2 (commencing with Section 21157) of Chapter 4.5.

(d) To qualify for certification pursuant to this section, a regulatory program shall require the utilization of an interdisciplinary approach that will ensure the integrated use of the natural and social sciences in decisionmaking and that shall meet all of the following criteria:

(1) The enabling legislation of the regulatory program does both of the following:

(A) Includes protection of the environment among its principal purposes.

(B) Contains authority for the administering agency to adopt rules and regulations for the protection of the environment, guided by standards set forth in the enabling legislation.

(2) The rules and regulations adopted by the administering agency for the regulatory program do all of the following:

(A) Require that an activity will not be approved or adopted as proposed if there are feasible alternatives or feasible mitigation measures available that would substantially lessen a significant adverse effect that the activity may have on the environment.

(B) Include guidelines for the orderly evaluation of proposed activities and the preparation of the plan or other written documentation in a manner consistent with the environmental protection purposes of the regulatory program.

(C) Require the administering agency to consult with all public agencies that have jurisdiction, by law, with respect to the proposed activity.

(D) Require that final action on the proposed activity include the written responses of the issuing authority to significant environmental points raised during the evaluation process.

(E) Require the filing of a notice of the decision by the administering agency on the proposed activity with the Secretary of the Resources Agency. Those notices shall be available for public inspection, and a list of the notices shall be posted on a weekly basis in the Office of the Resources Agency. Each list shall remain posted for a period of 30 days.

(F) Require notice of the filing of the plan or other written documentation to be made to the public and to a person who requests, in writing, notification. The notification shall be made in a manner that will provide the public or a person requesting notification with sufficient time to review and comment on the filing.

(3) The plan or other written documentation required by the regulatory program does both of the following:

(A) Includes a description of the proposed activity with alternatives to the activity, and mitigation measures to minimize any significant adverse effect on the environment of the activity.

(B) Is available for a reasonable time for review and comment by other public agencies and the general public.

(e) (1) The Secretary of the Resources Agency shall certify a regulatory program that the secretary determines meets all the qualifications for certification set forth in this section, and withdraw certification on determination that the regulatory program has been altered so that it no longer meets those qualifications. Certification and withdrawal of certification shall occur only after compliance with Chapter 3.5 (commencing with Section 11340) of Part 1 of Division 3 of Title 2 of the Government Code.

(2) In determining whether or not a regulatory program meets the qualifications for certification set forth in this section, the inquiry of the secretary shall extend only to the question of whether the regulatory program meets the generic requirements of subdivision (d). The inquiry may not extend to individual decisions to be reached under the regulatory program, including the nature of specific alternatives or mitigation measures that might be proposed to lessen any significant adverse effect on the environment of the activity.

(3) If the secretary determines that the regulatory program submitted for certification does not meet the qualifications for certification set forth in this section, the secretary shall adopt findings setting forth the reasons for the determination.

(f) After a regulatory program has been certified pursuant to this section, a proposed change in the program that could affect compliance with the qualifications for certification specified in subdivision (d) may be submitted to the Secretary of the Resources Agency for review and comment. The scope of the secretary's review shall extend only to the question of whether the regulatory program meets the generic requirements of subdivision (d). The review may not extend to individual decisions to be reached under the regulatory program, including specific alternatives or mitigation measures that might be proposed to lessen any significant adverse effect on the environment of the activity. The secretary shall have 30 days from the date of receipt of the proposed change to notify the state agency whether the proposed change will alter the regulatory program so that it no longer meets the qualification for certification established in this section and will result in a withdrawal of certification as provided in this section.

(g) An action or proceeding to attack, review, set aside, void, or annul a determination or decision of a state agency approving or adopting a proposed activity under a regulatory program that has been certified pursuant to this section on the basis that the plan or other written documentation prepared pursuant to paragraph (3) of subdivision (d) does not comply with this section shall be commenced not later than 30 days from the date of the filing of notice of the approval or adoption of the activity.

(h) (1) An action or proceeding to attack, review, set aside, void, or annul a determination of the Secretary of the Resources Agency to certify a regulatory program pursuant to this section on the basis that the regulatory program does not comply with this section shall be commenced within 30 days from the date of certification by the secretary.

(2) In an action brought pursuant to paragraph (1), the inquiry shall extend only to whether there was a prejudicial abuse of discretion by the secretary. Abuse of discretion is established if the secretary has not proceeded in a manner required by law or if the determination is not supported by substantial evidence.

(i) For purposes of this section, a county agricultural commissioner is a state agency.

(j) For purposes of this section, an air quality management district or air pollution control district is a state agency, except that the approval, if any, by a district of a nonattainment area plan is subject to this section only if, and to the extent that, the approval adopts or amends rules or regulations.

(k) (1) The secretary, by July 1, 2004, shall develop a protocol for reviewing the prospective application of certified regulatory programs to evaluate the consistency of those programs with the requirements of this division. Following the completion of the development of the protocol, the secretary shall provide a report to the Senate Committee on Environmental Quality and the Assembly Committee on Natural Resources regarding the need for a grant of additional statutory authority authorizing the secretary to undertake a review of the certified regulatory programs.

(2) The secretary may update the protocol, and may update the report provided to the legislative committees pursuant to paragraph (1) and provide, in compliance with Section 9795 of the Government Code, the updated report to those committees if additional statutory authority is needed.

(3) The secretary shall provide a significant opportunity for public participation in developing or updating the protocol described in paragraph (1) or (2), including, but not limited to, at least two public meetings with interested parties. A notice of each meeting shall be provided at least 10 days prior to the meeting to a person who files a written request for a notice with the agency and to the Senate Committee on Environmental Quality and the Assembly Committee on Natural Resources.

[Amended, Chapter 76, Statutes of 2013]

21080.8. Exclusion for conversions

This division does not apply to the conversion of an existing rental mobilehome park to a resident initiated subdivision, cooperative, or condominium for mobilehomes if the conversion will not result in an expansion of or change in existing use of the property.

[Added, Chapter 272, Statutes of 1990]

21080.9. **Local government and state universities or colleges exempt in preparation and adoption of local coastal plan or long-range land use development plan; certification by California Coastal Commission not exempt**

This division shall not apply to activities and approvals by any local government, as defined in Section 30109, or any state university or college, as defined in Section 30119, as necessary for the preparation and adoption of a local coastal program or long-range land use development plan pursuant to Division 20 (commencing with Section 30000); provided, however, that certification of a local coastal program or long-range land use development plan by the California Coastal Commission pursuant to Chapter 6 (commencing with Section 30500) of Division 20 shall be subject to the requirements of this division. For the purposes of Section 21080.5, a certified local coastal program or long-range land use development plan constitutes a plan for use in the California Coastal Commission's regulatory program.

[Amended, Chapter 961, Statutes of 1979]

21080.10. **Act not applicable to: extensions of time for general plan; residential housing for low or moderate income families, agricultural employees**

This division does not apply to any of the following:

(a) An extension of time, granted pursuant to Section 65361 of the Government Code, for the preparation and adoption of one or more elements of a city or county general plan.

(b) Actions taken by the Department of Housing and Community Development or the California Housing Finance Agency to provide financial assistance or insurance for the development and construction of residential housing for persons and families of low or moderate income, as defined in Section 50093 of the Health and Safety Code, if the project that is the subject of the application for financial assistance or insurance will be reviewed pursuant to this division by another public agency.

[Amended, Chapter 1039, Statutes of 2002]

21080.11. **Act not applicable to State Lands Commission settlements**

This division shall not apply to settlements of title and boundary problems by the State Lands Commission and to exchanges or leases in connection with those settlements.

[Added, Chapter 1463, Statutes of 1982]

21080.13. **Act not applicable to railroad grade separation projects**

(a) This division shall not apply to any railroad grade separation project that eliminates an existing grade crossing or that reconstructs an existing grade separation.

(b) (1) Whenever a state agency determines that a project is not subject to this division pursuant to this section, and it approves or determines to carry out the project, the state agency shall file a notice with the Office of Planning

25

and Research in the manner specified in subdivisions (b) and (c) of Section 21108.

(2) Whenever a local agency determines that a project is not subject to this division pursuant to this section, and it approves or determines to carry out the project, the local agency shall file a notice with the Office of Planning and Research and with the county clerk in each county in which the project will be located in the manner specified in subdivisions (b) and (c) of Section 21152.

[Amended, Chapter 143, Statutes of 2015]

21080.14. Act not applicable to closure of a railroad grade crossing; crossing for high-speed rail

(a) *This division does not apply to the closure of a railroad grade crossing by order of the Public Utilities Commission pursuant to Chapter 6 (commencing with Section 1201) of Part 1 of Division 1 of the Public Utilities Code, if the Public Utilities Commission finds the crossing to present a threat to public safety.*

(b) *This section does not apply to any crossing for high-speed rail, as defined in Section 185012 of the Public Utilities Code, or any crossing for a project carried out by the High-Speed Rail Authority, as described in Section 185020 of the Public Utilities Code, or a successor agency.*

(c) (1) *Whenever a state agency determines that a project is not subject to this division pursuant to this section, and it approves or determines to carry out the project, the state agency shall file a notice with the Office of Planning and Research in the manner specified in subdivisions (b) and (c) of Section 21108.*

(2) *Whenever a local agency determines that a project is not subject to this division pursuant to this section, and it approves or determines to carry out the project, the local agency shall file a notice with the Office of Planning and Research and with the county clerk in each county in which the project will be located in the manner specified in subdivisions (b) and (c) of Section 21152.*

(d) *This section shall remain in effect only until January 1, 2025, and as of that date is repealed.*

[Added & Repealed, Chapter 466, Statutes of 2019]

21080.17. Act not applicable to local ordinances regulating construction of dwelling units and second units

This division does not apply to the adoption of an ordinance by a city or county to implement the provisions of Section 65852.1 or Section 65852.2 of the Government Code.

[Added, Chapter 1013, Statutes of 1983]

21080.18. Act not applicable to closing of school or transfer of students

This division does not apply to the closing of any public school in which kindergarten or any of grades 1 through 12 is maintained or the transfer of students from that public school to another school if the only physical changes involved are categorically exempt under Chapter 3 (commencing with Section 15000) of Division 6 of Title 14 of the California Administrative Code.

[Amended, Chapter 1316, Statutes of 1986]

21080.19. Exclude restriping of streets

This division does not apply to a project for restriping of streets or highways to relieve traffic congestion.

[Added, Chapter 750, Statutes of 1984]

21080.20. Exemption for the approval of a bicycle transportation plan, as defined

(a) This division does not apply to a bicycle transportation plan prepared pursuant to Section 891.2 of the Streets and Highways Code for an urbanized area for restriping of streets and highways, bicycle parking and storage, signal timing to improve street and highway intersection operations, and related signage for bicycles, pedestrians, and vehicles.

(b) Prior to determining that a project is exempt pursuant to this section, the lead agency shall do both of the following:

   (1) Hold noticed public hearings in areas affected by the bicycle transportation plan to hear and respond to public comments. Publication of the notice shall be no fewer times than required by Section 6061 of the Government Code, by the public agency in a newspaper of general circulation in the area affected by the proposed project. If more than one area will be affected, the notice shall be published in the newspaper of largest circulation from among the newspapers of general circulation in those areas.

   (2) Prepare an assessment of any traffic and safety impacts of the project and include measures in the bicycle transportation plan to mitigate potential vehicular traffic impacts and bicycle and pedestrian safety impacts.

(c) If a local agency determines that a project is not subject to this division pursuant to this section, and it determines to approve or carry out that project, the notice shall be filed with the Office of Planning and Research and the county clerk in the county in which the project is located in the manner specified in subdivisions (b) and (c) of Section 21152.

(d) This section shall remain in effect only until January 1, 2021, and as of that date is repealed.

[Amended, Chapter 149, Statutes of 2017]

21080.20.5. Exclusions, notifications and requirements

(a) This division does not apply to a project that consists of the restriping of streets and highways for bicycle lanes in an urbanized area that is consistent with a bicycle transportation plan prepared pursuant to Section 891.2 of the Streets and Highways Code.

(b) Prior to determining that a project is exempt pursuant to this section, the lead agency shall do both of the following:

(1) (A) Prepare an assessment of any traffic and safety impacts of the project and include measures in the project to mitigate potential vehicular traffic impacts and bicycle and pedestrian safety impacts.

(B) The requirement to prepare an assessment pursuant to subparagraph (A) shall not apply if either of the following conditions is met:

(i) Measures to mitigate these impacts are identified in an environmental impact report, negative declaration, or mitigated negative declaration prepared pursuant to this division for the bicycle transportation plan, certified or approved no more than five years prior to making the determination, the measures are included in the plan, and those measures are incorporated into the project.

(ii) An assessment was prepared pursuant to paragraph (2) of subdivision (b) of Section 21080.20 no more than five years prior to making the determination, the measures to mitigate these impacts are included in the plan, and those measures are incorporated into the project.

(2) Hold noticed public hearings in areas affected by the project to hear and respond to public comments. Publication of the notice shall be no fewer times than required by Section 6061 of the Government Code, by the public agency in a newspaper of general circulation in the area affected by the proposed project. If more than one area will be affected, the notice shall be published in the newspaper of largest circulation from among the newspapers of general circulation in those areas.

(c) (1) If a state agency determines that a project is not subject to this division pursuant to this section, and it determines to approve or carry out that project, the notice shall be filed with the Office of Planning and Research in the manner specified in subdivisions (b) and (c) of Section 21108.

(2) If a local agency determines that a project is not subject to this division pursuant to this section, and it determines to approve or carry out that project, the notice shall be filed with the Office of Planning and Research, and filed with the county clerk in the county in which the project is located in the manner specified in subdivisions (b) and (c) of Section 21152.

(d) This section shall remain in effect only until January 1, 2021, and as of that date is repealed.

[Amended, Chapter 149, Statutes of 2017]

21080.21. Exclude pipelines of less than one mile

This division does not apply to any project of less than one mile in length within a public street or highway or any other public right-of-way for the installation of a new pipeline or the maintenance, repair, restoration, reconditioning, relocation, replacement, removal, or demolition of an existing pipeline. For purposes of this section, "pipeline" includes subsurface facilities but does not include any surface facility related to the operation of the underground facility.

[Amended, Chapter 466, Statutes of 2019]

21080.22.   Exclude preparation of general plan amendments; exception

(a)   This division does not apply to activities and approvals by a local government necessary for the preparation of general plan amendments pursuant to Section 29763, except that the approval of general plan amendments by the Delta Protection Commission is subject to the requirements of this division.

(b)   For purposes of Section 21080.5, a general plan amendment is a plan required by the regulatory program of the Delta Protection Commission.

[Added, Chapter 898, Statutes of 1992]

21080.23.   Exclude work on existing pipelines

(a)   This division does not apply to any project which consists of the inspection, maintenance, repair, restoration, reconditioning, relocation, replacement, or removal of an existing pipeline, as defined in subdivision (a) of Section 51010.5 of the Government Code, or any valve, flange, meter, or other piece of equipment that is directly attached to the pipeline, if the project meets all of the following conditions:

(1)   (A)   The project is less than eight miles in length.

　　　(B)   Notwithstanding subparagraph (A), actual construction and excavation activities undertaken to achieve the maintenance, repair, restoration, reconditioning, relocation, replacement, or removal of an existing pipeline are not undertaken over a length of more than one-half mile at any one time.

(2)   The project consists of a section of pipeline that is not less than eight miles from any section of pipeline that has been subject to an exemption pursuant to this section in the past 12 months.

(3)   The project is not solely for the purpose of excavating soil that is contaminated by hazardous materials, and, to the extent not otherwise expressly required by law, the party undertaking the project immediately informs the lead agency of the discovery of contaminated soil.

(4)   To the extent not otherwise expressly required by law, the person undertaking the project has, in advance of undertaking the project, prepared a plan that will result in notification of the appropriate agencies so that they may take action, if determined to be necessary, to provide for the emergency evacuation of members of the public who may be located in close proximity to the project.

(5)   Project activities are undertaken within an existing right-of-way and the right-of-way is restored to its condition prior to the project.

(6)   The project applicant agrees to comply with all conditions otherwise authorized by law, imposed by the city or county planning department as part of any local agency permit process, that are required to mitigate potential impacts of the proposed project, and to otherwise comply with the Keene-Nejedly California Wetlands Preservation Act (Chapter 7 (commencing with Section 5810) of Division 5), the California Endangered Species Act (Chapter 1.5 (commencing with Section 2050) of Division 3

of the Fish and Game Code), and other applicable state laws, and with all applicable federal laws.

(b) If a project meets all of the requirements of subdivision (a), the person undertaking the project shall do all of the following:

(1) Notify, in writing, any affected public agency, including, but not limited to, any public agency having permit, land use, environmental, public health protection, or emergency response authority of the exemption of the project from this division by subdivision (a).

(2) Provide notice to the public in the affected area in a manner consistent with paragraph (3) of subdivision (b) of Section 21092.

(3) In the case of private rights-of-way over private property, receive from the underlying property owner permission for access to the property.

(4) Comply with all conditions otherwise authorized by law, imposed by the city or county planning department as part of any local agency permit process, that are required to mitigate potential impacts of the proposed project, and otherwise comply with the Keene-Nejedly California Wetlands Preservation Act (Chapter 7 (commencing with Section 5810) of Division 5), the California Endangered Species Act (Chapter 1.5 (commencing with Section 2050) of Division 3 of the Fish and Game Code), and other applicable state laws, and with all applicable federal laws.

(c) This section does not apply to either of the following:

(1) A project in which the diameter of the pipeline is increased.

(2) A project undertaken within the boundaries of an oil refinery.

[Amended, Chapter 548, Statutes of 2012]

21080.24. Act not applicable to issuance or modification of air quality permits

This division does not apply to the issuance, modification, amendment, or renewal of a permit by an air pollution control district or air quality management district pursuant to Title V, as defined in Section 39053.3 of the Health and Safety Code, or pursuant to a district Title V program established pursuant to Sections 42301.10, 42301.11, and 42301.12 of the Health and Safety Code, unless the issuance, modification, amendment, or renewal authorizes a physical or operational change to a source or facility.

[Amended, Chapter 548, Statutes of 2012]

21080.25. Definitions

[Repealed, by Sunset Date, effective 1/1/20]

21080.26. Minor alterations to utilities

This division does not apply to minor alterations to utilities made for the purposes of complying with Sections 116410 and 116415 of the Health and Safety Code or regulations adopted thereunder.

[Amended, Chapter 327, Statutes of 2017]

21080.27. Definitions

(a) For purposes of this section, the following definitions apply:

    (1) "Eligible public agency" means any of the following:

        (A) The County of Los Angeles.

        (B) The Los Angeles Unified School District.

        (C) The Los Angeles County Metropolitan Transportation Authority.

        (D) The Housing Authority of the City of Los Angeles.

        (E) The Los Angeles Homeless Services Authority.

        (F) The Los Angeles Community College District.

        (G) The successor agency for the former Community Redevelopment Agency of the City of Los Angeles.

        (H) The Department of Transportation.

        (I) The Department of Parks and Recreation.

    (2) "Emergency shelters" mean shelters, during a declaration of a shelter crisis described in Section 8698.2 of the Government Code, that meet the definition of low barrier navigation center set forth in Section 65660 of the Government Code and meet the requirements of Section 65662 of the Government Code, that is located in either a mixed-use or nonresidential zone permitting multifamily uses or infill site, and that is funded, in whole or in part, by any of the following:

        (A) The Homeless Emergency Aid program established pursuant to Section 50211 of the Health and Safety Code.

        (B) The Homeless Housing, Assistance, and Prevention program established pursuant to Section 50217 of the Health and Safety Code.

        (C) Measure H sales tax proceeds approved by the voters on the March 7, 2017, special election in the County of Los Angeles.

        (D) General bond obligations issued pursuant to Proposition HHH, approved by the voters of the City of Los Angeles at the November 8, 2016, statewide general election.

    (3) "Supportive housing" means supportive housing, as defined in Section 50675.14 of the Health and Safety Code, that meets the eligibility requirements of Article 11 (commencing with Section 65650) of Chapter 3 of Division 1 of Title 7 of the Government Code or the eligibility requirements for qualified supportive housing or qualified permanent supportive housing set forth in Ordinance No. 185,489 or 185,492, and is funded, in whole or in part, by any of the following:

        (A) The No Place Like Home Program (Part 3.9 (commencing with Section 5849.1) of Division 5 of the Welfare and Institutions Code).

        (B) The Building Homes and Jobs Trust Fund established pursuant to Section 50470 of the Health and Safety Code.

        (C) Measure H sales tax proceeds approved by the voters on the March 7, 2017, special election in the County of Los Angeles.

(D) General bond obligations issued pursuant to Proposition HHH, approved by the voters of the City of Los Angeles at the November 8, 2016, statewide general election.

(E) The City of Los Angeles Housing Impact Trust Fund.

(b) (1) This division does not apply to any activity approved by or carried out by the City of Los Angeles in furtherance of providing emergency shelters or supportive housing in the City of Los Angeles.

(2) This division does not apply to any action taken by an eligible public agency to lease, convey, or encumber land owned by that agency, or to any action taken by an eligible public agency to facilitate the lease, conveyance, or encumbrance of land owned by that agency, or to any action taken by an eligible public agency in providing financial assistance, in furtherance of providing emergency shelters or supportive housing in the City of Los Angeles.

(3) This division does not apply to the adoption of Ordinance Nos. 185,489 and 185,492 by the City of Los Angeles in 2018.

(c) If a lead agency determines that an activity is not subject to this division pursuant to paragraph (1) or (2) of subdivision (b) and determines to approve or carry out the activity, the lead agency shall file a notice of exemption with the Office of Planning and Research and the county clerk in the manner specified in subdivisions (b) and (c) of Section 21108 or subdivisions (b) and (c) of Section 21152.

(d) This section shall remain in effect only until January 1, 2025, and as of that date is repealed.

[Added & Repealed, Chapter 340, Statutes of 2019]

21080.28. Act not applicable to specified land transfers

(a) This division does not apply to either of the following:

(1) The acquisition, sale, or other transfer of interest in land by a public agency for any of the following purposes:

(A) Preservation of natural conditions existing at the time of transfer, including plant and animal habitats.

(B) Restoration of natural conditions, including plant and animal habitats.

(C) Continuing agricultural use of the land.

(D) Prevention of encroachment of development into flood plains.

(E) Preservation of historical resources.

(F) Preservation of open space or lands for park purposes.

(2) The granting or acceptance of funding by a public agency for purposes of paragraph (1).

(b) Subdivision (a) applies even if physical changes to the environment or changes in the use of the land are a reasonably foreseeable consequence of the acquisition, sale, or other transfer of the interests in land, or of the granting or acceptance of funding, provided that environmental review *otherwise required by this division occurs before any project approval that would authorize physical changes being made to that land.*

(c) If the lead agency determines that an activity is not subject to this division pursuant to this section and the lead agency determines to approve or carry out the activity, the lead agency shall file a notice with the Office of Planning and Research and with the county clerk in the county in which the land is located in the manner specified in subdivisions (b) and (c) of Section 21152.

[Added, Chapter 181, Statutes of 2019]

21080.29.   Procedures for Los Angeles County; Ballona Channel

(a) A project located in Los Angeles County that is approved by a public agency before the effective date of the act adding this section is not in violation of any requirement of this division by reason of the failure to construct a roadway across the property transferred to the state pursuant to subdivision (c) and to construct a bridge over the adjacent Ballona Channel in Los Angeles County, otherwise required as a mitigation measure pursuant to this division, if all of the following conditions apply:

   (1) The improvements specified in this subdivision are not constructed, due in whole or in part, to the project owner's or developer's relinquishment of easement rights to construct those improvements.

   (2) The easement rights in paragraph (1) are relinquished in connection with the State of California, acting by and through the Wildlife Conservation Board of the Department of Fish and Game, acquiring a wetlands project that is a minimum of 400 acres in size and located within the coastal zone.

(b) Where those easement rights have been relinquished, any municipal ordinance or regulation adopted by a charter city or a general law city shall be inapplicable to the extent that the ordinance or regulation requires construction of the transportation improvements specified in subdivision (a), or would otherwise require reprocessing or resubmittal of a permit or approval, including, but not limited to, a final recorded map, a vesting tentative map, or a tentative map, as a result of the transportation improvements specified in subdivision (a) not being constructed.

(c) (1) If the Wildlife Conservation Board of the Department of Fish and Game acquires property within the coastal zone that is a minimum of 400 acres in size pursuant to a purchase and sale agreement with Playa Capital Company, LLC, the Controller shall direct the trustee under the Amendment to Declaration of Trust entered into on or about December 11, 1984, by First Nationwide Savings, as trustee, Summa Corporation, as trustor, and the Controller, as beneficiary, known as the HRH Inheritance Tax Security Trust, to convey title to the trust estate of the trust, including real property commonly known as Playa Vista Area C, to the State of California acting by and through the Wildlife Conservation Board of the Department of Fish and Game for conservation, restoration, or recreation purposes only, with the right to transfer the property for those uses to any other agency of the State of California.

   (2) This subdivision shall constitute the enabling legislation required by the Amendment to Declaration of Trust to empower the Controller to direct the

trustee to convey title to the trust estate under the HRH Inheritance Tax Security Trust to the State of California or an agency thereof.

(3) The conveyance of the trust estate to the Wildlife Conservation Board pursuant to this subdivision shall supersede any duty or obligation imposed upon the Controller under the Probate Code or the Revenue and Taxation Code with respect to the disposition or application of the net proceeds of the trust estate.

[Added, Chapter 739, Statutes of 2003]

21080.30. Excluded state offices

(a) For purposes of this section, "real estate transaction" means the acquisition or disposition of any interest in real property.

(b) This division does not apply to any action, approval, or authorization provided by the State Public Works Board or the Department of Finance regarding any bond issuance, capital outlay project, or real estate transaction.

[Added, Chapter 21, Statutes of 2017]

21080.32. Publicly owned transit agencies

(a) This section shall only apply to publicly owned transit agencies, but shall not apply to any publicly owned transit agency created pursuant to Section 130050.2 of the Public Utilities Code.

(b) Except as provided in Subdivision (c), and in accordance with subdivision (d), this division does not apply to actions taken on or after July 1, 1995, by a publicly owned transit agency to implement budget reductions caused by the failure of agency revenues to adequately fund agency programs and facilities.

(c) This section does not apply to any action to reduce or eliminate a transit service, facility, program, or activity that was approved or adopted as a mitigation measure in any environmental document authorized by this division or the National Environmental Policy Act (42 U.S.C. Sec. 4321 et seq.) or to any state or federal requirement that is imposed for the protection of the environment.

(d) (1) This section applies only to actions taken after the publicly owned transit agency has made a finding that there is a fiscal emergency caused by the failure of agency revenues to adequately fund agency programs and facilities, and after the publicly owned transit agency has held a public hearing to consider those actions. A publicly owned transit agency that has held such a hearing shall respond within 30 days at a regular public meeting to suggestions make by the public at the initial public hearing. Those actions shall be limited to projects defined in subdivision (a) or (b) of Section 21065 which initiate or increase fees, rates, or charges charged for any existing public service, program, or activity; or reduce or eliminate the availability of an existing publicly owned transit service, facility, program, or activity.

(2) For purpose of this subdivision, "fiscal emergency," when applied to a publicly owned transit agency, means that the agency is projected to have negative working capital within one year from the date that the agency makes the finding that there is a fiscal emergency pursuant to this section.

Working capital shall be determined by adding together all unrestricted cash, unrestricted short-term investments, and short-term unrestricted accounts receivable and then subtracting unrestricted accounts payable. Employee retirement funds, including Internal Revenue Code Section 457 deferred compensation plans and Section 401 (k) plans, health insurance reserves, bond payment reserves, workers' compensation reserves, and insurance reserves, shall not be factored into the formula for working capital.

[Added, Chapter 500, Statutes of 1996]

21080.33. Exclude emergency highway projects

This division does not apply to any emergency project undertaken, carried out, or approved by a public agency to maintain, repair, or restore an existing highway, as defined in Section 360 of the Vehicle Code, except for a highway designated as an official state scenic highway pursuant to Section 262 of the Streets and Highways Code, within the existing right-of-way of the highway, damaged as a result of fire, flood, storm, earthquake, land subsidence, gradual earth movement, or landslide, within one year of the damage. This section does not exempt from this division any project undertaken, carried out, or approved by a public agency to expand or widen a highway damaged by fire, flood, storm, earthquake, land subsidence, gradual earth movement, or landslide.

[Added, Chapter 825, Statutes of 1996]

21080.34. "Carrying out or approving a project" defined

For the purposes of Section 21069, the phrase "carrying out or approving a project" shall include the carrying out or approval of a plan for a project that expands or enlarges an existing publicly owned airport by any political subdivision, as described in Section 21661.6 of the Public Utilities Code.

[Amended & Renumbered, Chapter 303, Statutes of 2015]

21080.35. Exclusions regarding installation of solar energy systems

(a) Except as provided in subdivision (d), this division does not apply to the installation of a solar energy system on the roof of an existing building or at an existing parking lot.

(b) For the purposes of this section, the following terms mean the following:

(1) "Existing parking lot" means an area designated and used for parking of vehicles as of the time of the application for the solar energy system and for at least the previous two years.

(2) "Solar energy system" includes all associated equipment. Associated equipment consists of parts and materials that enable the generation and use of solar electricity or solar-heated water, including any monitoring and control, safety, conversion, and emergency responder equipment necessary to connect to the customer's electrical service or plumbing and any equipment, as well as any equipment necessary to connect the energy generated to the electrical grid, whether that connection is onsite or on an adjacent parcel of the building and separated only by an improved right-of-way. "Associated equipment" does not include a substation.

35

(c) (1) Associated equipment shall be located on the same parcel of the building, except that associated equipment necessary to connect the energy generated to the electrical grid may be located immediately adjacent to the parcel of the building or immediately adjacent to the parcel of the building and separated only by an improved right-of-way.

(2) Associated equipment shall not occupy more than 500 square feet of ground surface and the site of the associated equipment shall not contain plants protected by the Native Plant Protection Act (Chapter 10 (commencing with Section 1900) of Division 2 of the Fish and Game Code).

(d) This section does not apply if the associated equipment would otherwise require one of the following:

(1) An individual federal permit pursuant to Section 401 or 404 of the federal Clean Water Act (33 U.S.C. Sec. 1341 or 1344) or waste discharge requirements pursuant to the Porter-Cologne Water Quality Control Act (Division 7 (commencing with Section 13000) of the Water Code).

(2) An individual take permit for species protected under the federal Endangered Species Act of 1973 (16 U.S.C. Sec. 1531 et seq.) or the California Endangered Species Act (Chapter 1.5 (commencing with Section 2050) of Division 3 of the Fish and Game Code).

(3) A streambed alteration permit pursuant to Chapter 6 (commencing with Section 1600) of Division 2 of the Fish and Game Code.

(e) This section does not apply if the installation of a solar energy system at an existing parking lot involves either of the following:

(1) The removal of a tree required to be planted, maintained, or protected pursuant to local, state, or federal requirements, unless the tree dies and there is no requirement to replace the tree.

(2) The removal of a native tree over 25 years old.

(f) This section does not apply to any transmission or distribution facility or connection.

[Added, Chapter 469, Statutes of 2011]

21080.37. **Minor alteration exemption defined**

[Repealed, by Sunset Date, effective 1/1/20]

21080.42. **Transportation projects exempt from division**

(a) The following transportation projects are exempt from this division:

(1) U.S. Highway 101 interchange modification, adding southbound auxiliary lane and southbound mixed flow lane, from Interstate 280 to Yerba Buena Road, in Santa Clara County.

(2) Construct north and southbound high-occupancy vehicle lanes on I-805 from I-5 to Carroll Canyon Road, including construction of north-facing direct access ramps in San Diego County.

(3) State Route 99, Los Molinas rehabilitation and traffic calming, from Orange Street to Tehama Vine Road, in Tehama County.

(4) State Route 99, Island Park widening project, adding one mixed flow lane in each direction, from Ashlan Avenue to Grantlund Avenue, in Fresno County.

(5) State Route 99 median widening, adding one mixed flow lane in each direction, from State Route 120 west to 0.4 miles north of Arch Road, in Manteca in San Joaquin County.

(6) State Route 12 pavement rehabilitation and shoulder widening in San Joaquin County on Bouldin Island.

(7) State Route 91 widening, adding one mixed flow lane in each direction, from State Route 55 to Weir Canyon Road in Orange County.

(8) U.S. Highway 101 pavement rehabilitation and shoulder widening in San Luis Obispo County.

(b) An exemption provided pursuant to subdivision (a) shall not apply to a transportation project if, on or after February 1, 2009, a lead agency changes the scope of that project from the manner in which the project is described in subdivision (a).

[Added & Repealed, Chapter 6, Statutes of 2009]

21080.46.   Well ordinance exemption

(a) Without limiting any other statutory exemption or categorical exemption, this division does not apply to the adoption of an ordinance by a city, county, or city and county to limit or prohibit the drilling of new or deeper groundwater wells, or to limit or prohibit increased extractions from existing groundwater wells, through stricter conditions on the issuance of well permits or changes in the intensity of land use that would increase demand on groundwater.

(b) (1) This section shall remain operative until July 1, 2017, or so long as the state of emergency due to drought conditions declared by the Governor in the proclamation of a state of emergency issued on January 17, 2014, remains in effect, whichever is later.

(2) This section is repealed on January 1 of the year following the date on which this section becomes inoperative.

(c) Notwithstanding subdivision (a) or (b), this section does not apply to either of the following:

(1) The issuance of any permit for a new or deeper groundwater well by a city, county, or city and county.

(2) The adoption of any ordinance affecting or relating to new residential, commercial, institutional, or industrial projects or any mix of these uses, or any change in the intensity or use of land for these purposes, if that project or change in use requires approval by a city, county, or city and county. Nor does this section apply to the adoption of any ordinance that would limit or prohibit new or deeper groundwater wells, or increased extraction from existing groundwater wells, that may be needed to serve these projects.

[Added & Repealed, Chapter 27, Statutes of 2015]

21080.50. Definitions

(a) *For purposes of this section, the following definitions apply:*

  (1) *"Interim motel housing project" or "project" means the conversion of a structure with a certificate of occupancy as a motel, hotel, residential hotel, or hostel to supportive or transitional housing, and the conversion meets one or both of the following conditions:*

    (A) *It does not result in the expansion of more than 10 percent of the floor area of any individual living unit in the structure.*

    (B) *It does not result in any significant effects relating to traffic, noise, air quality, or water quality.*

  (2) *"Residential hotel" has the same meaning as defined in Section 50519 of the Health and Safety Code.*

  (3) *"Supportive housing" means housing linked to onsite or offsite supportive services and with no limit on length of stay for persons with low incomes who have one or more disabilities and may include, among other populations, adults, emancipated minors, families with children, elderly persons, young adults aging out of the foster care system, individuals exiting from institutional settings, veterans, and homeless people.*

  (4) *"Supportive services" means services that are provided on a voluntary basis to residents of supportive or transitional housing, including, but not limited to, a combination of subsidized and permanent housing services, intensive case management, medical and mental health care, substance abuse treatment, employment services, benefits advocacy, and other services or service referrals necessary to obtain and maintain housing.*

  (5) *"Transitional housing" means temporary housing linked to supportive services that is offered, usually for a period of up to 24 months, to facilitate movement to permanent housing for persons with low incomes who may have one or more disabilities, and may include, among other populations, adults, emancipated minors, families with children, elderly persons, young adults aging out of the foster care system, individuals exiting from institutional settings, veterans, and homeless people.*

(b) *This division does not apply to an interim motel housing project.*

(c) *A lead agency that determines an interim motel housing project is exempt pursuant to this section shall file a notice of exemption in accordance with subdivision (b) of Section 21152 with the Office of Planning and Research.*

(d) *This section shall remain in effect only until January 1, 2025, and as of that date is repealed.*

[Added & Repealed, Chapter 344, Statutes of 2019]

21081.   No approval if significant effect unless findings

Pursuant to the policy stated in Sections 21002 and 21002.1, no public agency shall approve or carry out a project for which an environmental impact report has been certified which identifies one or more significant effects on the environment that would occur if the project is approved or carried out unless both of the following occur:

(a) The public agency makes one or more of the following findings with respect to each significant effect:

(1) Changes or alterations have been required in, or incorporated into, the project which mitigate or avoid the significant effects on the environment.

(2) Those changes or alterations are within the responsibility and jurisdiction of another public agency and have been, or can and should be, adopted by that other agency.

(3) Specific economic, legal, social, technological, or other considerations, including considerations for the provision of employment opportunities for highly trained workers, make infeasible the mitigation measures or alternatives identified in the environmental impact report.

(b) With respect to significant effects which were subject to a finding under paragraph (3) of subdivision (a), the public agency finds that specific overriding economic, legal, social, technological, or other benefits of the project outweigh the significant effects on the environment.

[Amended, Chapter 1294, Statutes of 1994]

21081.2. Residential projects; compliance with findings regarding the impacts of the project on traffic

(a) Except as provided in subdivision (c), if a residential project, not exceeding 100 units, with a minimum residential density of 20 units per acre and within one-half mile of a transit stop, on an infill site in an urbanized area is in compliance with the traffic, circulation, and transportation policies of the general plan, applicable community plan, applicable specific plan, and applicable ordinances of the city or county with jurisdiction over the area where the project is located, and the city or county requires that the mitigation measures approved in a previously certified project area environmental impact report applicable to the project be incorporated into the project, the city or county is not required to comply with subdivision (a) of Section 21081 with respect to the making of any findings regarding the impacts of the project on traffic at intersections, or on streets, highways, or freeways.

(b) Nothing in subdivision (a) restricts the authority of a city or county to adopt feasible mitigation measures with respect to the impacts of a project on pedestrian and bicycle safety.

(c) Subdivision (a) does not apply in any of the following circumstances:

(1) The application for a proposed project is made more than five years after certification of the project area environmental impact report applicable to the project.

(2) A major change has occurred within the project area after certification of the project area environmental impact report applicable to the project.

(3) The project area environmental impact report applicable to the project was certified with overriding considerations pursuant to subdivision (b) of Section 21081 to the significant impacts on the environment with respect to traffic or transportation.

(4) The proposed project covers more than four acres.

(d) A project shall not be divided into smaller projects in order to qualify pursuant to this section.

(e) Nothing in this section relieves a city or county from the requirement to analyze the project's effects on traffic at intersections, or on streets, highways, or freeways, or from making a determination that the project may have a significant effect on traffic.

(f) For the purposes of this section, "project area environmental impact report" means an environmental impact report certified on any of the following:

(1) A general plan.

(2) A revision or update to the general plan that includes at least the land use and circulation elements.

(3) An applicable community plan.

(4) An applicable specific plan.

(5) A housing element of the general plan, if the environmental impact report analyzed the environmental effects of the density of the proposed project.

(6) A zoning ordinance.

[Added, Chapter 715, Statutes of 2006]

21081.3.   Evaluation of aesthetic effects

(a) Except as specified in subdivision (b), a lead agency is not required to evaluate the aesthetic effects of a project and aesthetic effects shall not be considered significant effects on the environment if the project involves the refurbishment, conversion, repurposing, or replacement of an existing building that meets all of the following requirements:

(1) The building is abandoned, dilapidated, or has been vacant for more than one year.

(2) The building site is immediately adjacent to parcels that are developed with qualified urban uses or at least 75 percent of the perimeter of the site adjoins parcels that are developed with qualified urban uses and the remaining 25 percent of the site adjoins parcels that previously have been developed for qualified urban uses.

(3) The project includes the construction of housing.

(4) Any new structure does not substantially exceed the height of the existing structure.

(5) The project does not create a new source of substantial light or glare.

(b) Subdivision (a) shall not apply to either of the following:

(1) A project with potentially significant aesthetic effects on an official state scenic highway established pursuant to Article 2.5 (commencing with Section 260) of Chapter 2 of Division 1 of the Streets and Highways Code.

(2) A project with potentially significant aesthetic effects on historical or cultural resources.

(c) This section does not alter, affect, or otherwise change the authority of a lead agency to consider aesthetic issues and to require the mitigation or avoidance of adverse aesthetic effect pursuant to other laws.

(d) For purposes of this section, "dilapidated" means decayed, deteriorated, or fallen into such disrepair through neglect or misuse so as to require substantial repair for safe and proper use.

(e) This section shall remain in effect only until January 1, 2024, and as of that date is repealed.

[Added & Repealed, Chapter 298, Statutes of 2018]

21081.5. Substantial evidence required for findings

In making the findings required by paragraph (3) of subdivision (a) of Section 21081, the public agency shall base its findings on substantial evidence in the record.

[Amended, Chapter 1294, Statutes of 1994]

21081.6. Public agency shall adopt monitoring program of mitigation measures and insure their enforceability

(a) When making the findings required by paragraph (1) of subdivision (a) of Section 21081 or when adopting a mitigated negative declaration pursuant to paragraph (2) of subdivision (c) of Section 21080, the following requirements shall apply:

(1) The public agency shall adopt a reporting or monitoring program for the changes made to the project or conditions of project approval, adopted in order to mitigate or avoid significant effects on the environment. The reporting or monitoring program shall be designed to ensure compliance during project implementation. For those changes which have been required or incorporated into the project at the request of a responsible agency or a public agency having jurisdiction by law over natural resources affected by the project, that agency shall, if so requested by the lead agency or a responsible agency, prepare and submit a proposed reporting or monitoring program.

(2) The lead agency shall specify the location and custodian of the documents or other material which constitute the record of proceedings upon which its decision is based.

(b) A public agency shall provide the measures to mitigate or avoid significant effects on the environment are fully enforceable through permit conditions, agreements, or other measures. Conditions of project approval may be set forth in referenced documents which address required mitigation measures or, in the case of the adoption of a plan, policy, regulation, or other public project, by incorporating the mitigation measures into the plan, policy, regulation, or project design.

(c) Prior to the close of the public review period for a draft environmental impact report or mitigated negative declaration, a responsible agency, or a public agency having jurisdiction over natural resources affected by the project, shall either submit to the lead agency complete and detailed performance objectives for mitigation measures which would address the significant effects on the environment identified by the responsible agency or agency having jurisdiction over natural resources affected by the project, or refer the lead agency to appropriate, readily available guidelines or reference documents. Any mitigation measures submitted to a lead agency by a responsible agency or an agency having jurisdiction over natural resources affected by the project shall be limited to measures which mitigate impacts to resources which are subject to the statutory authority of, and definitions applicable to, that agency. Compliance or noncompliance by a responsible agency or agency having jurisdiction over natural resources affected by a project with that requirement shall not limit the authority of the responsible agency or agency having jurisdiction over natural resources affected by a project, or the authority of the lead agency, to approve, condition, or deny projects as provided by this division or any other provision of law.

[Amended, Chapter 1294, Statutes of 1994]

21081.7. Transportation information

Transportation information resulting from the reporting or monitoring program required to be adopted by a public agency pursuant to Section 21081.6 shall be submitted to the transportation planning agency in the region where the project is located and to the Department of Transportation for a project of statewide, regional, or areawide significance according to criteria developed pursuant to Section 21083. The transportation planning agency and the Department of Transportation shall adopt guidelines for the submittal of those reporting or monitoring programs.

[Amended, Chapter 867, Statutes of 2001]

21082. Procedures for project evaluation, EIR preparation, and negative declarations

All public agencies shall adopt by ordinance, resolution, rule, or regulation, objectives, criteria, and procedures for the evaluation of projects and the preparation of environmental impact reports and negative declarations pursuant to this division. A school district, or any other district, whose boundaries are coterminous with a city, county, or city and county, may utilize the objectives, criteria, and procedures of the city, county, or city and county, as may be applicable, in which case, the school district or other district need not adopt objectives, criteria, and procedures of its own. The objectives, criteria, and procedures shall be consistent with the provisions of this division and with the guidelines adopted by the Secretary of the Resources Agency pursuant to Section 21083. Such objectives, criteria, and procedures shall be adopted by each public agency no later than 60 days after the Secretary of the Resources Agency has adopted guidelines pursuant to Section 21083.

[Amended, Chapter 1312, Statutes of 1976]

21082.1. A public agency must prepare or contract for EIRs negative declarations, mitigated negative declarations

(a) A draft environmental impact report, environmental impact report, negative declaration, or mitigated negative declaration prepared pursuant to the requirements of this division shall be prepared directly by, or under contract to, a public agency.

42

(b) This section does not prohibit, and shall not be construed as prohibiting, a person from submitting information or other comments to the public agency responsible for preparing an environmental impact report, draft environmental impact report, negative declaration, or mitigated negative declaration. The information or other comments may be submitted in any format, shall be considered by the public agency, and may be included, in whole or in part, in any report or declaration.

(c) The lead agency shall do all of the following:

(1) Independently review and analyze any report or declaration required by this division.

(2) Circulate draft documents that reflect its independent judgment.

(3) As part of the adoption of a negative declaration or a mitigated negative declaration, or certification of an environmental impact report, find that the report or declaration reflects the independent judgment of the lead agency.

(4) Submit a sufficient number of copies, in either a hard-copy or electronic form as required by the Office of Planning and Research, of the draft environmental impact report, proposed negative declaration, or proposed mitigated negative declaration to the State Clearinghouse for review and comment by state agencies, if any of the following apply:

(A) A state agency is any of the following:

(i) The lead agency.

(ii) A responsible agency.

(iii) A trustee agency.

(B) A state agency otherwise has jurisdiction by law with respect to the project.

(C) The proposed project is of sufficient statewide, regional, or areawide environmental significance as determined pursuant to the guidelines certified and adopted pursuant to Section 21083.

[Amended, Chapter 476, Statutes of 2016]

21082.2. Significant effect based on substantial evidence, not public controversy or speculation

(a) The lead agency shall determine whether a project may have a significant effect on the environment based on substantial evidence in light of the whole record.

(b) The existence of public controversy over the environmental effects of a project shall not require preparation of an environmental impact report if there is no substantial evidence in light of the whole record before the lead agency that the project may have a significant effect on the environment.

(c) Argument, speculation, unsubstantiated opinion or narrative, evidence which is clearly inaccurate or erroneous, or evidence of social or economic impacts which do not contribute to, or are not caused by, physical impacts on the environment, is not substantial evidence. Substantial evidence shall include facts, reasonable assumptions predicated upon facts, and expert opinion supported by facts.

(d) If there is substantial evidence, in light of the whole record before the lead agency, that a project may have a significant effect on the environment, an environmental impact report shall be prepared.

(e) Statements in an environmental impact report and comments with respect to an environmental impact report shall not be deemed determinative of whether the project may have a significant effect on the environment.

[Amended, Chapter 1131, Statutes of 1993]

21082.3.   California Native American tribes; identification of tribal cultural resources; processing of information

(a) Any mitigation measures agreed upon in the consultation conducted pursuant to Section 21080.3.2 shall be recommended for inclusion in the environmental document and in an adopted mitigation monitoring and reporting program, if determined to avoid or lessen the impact pursuant to paragraph (2) of subdivision (b), and shall be fully enforceable.

(b) If a project may have a significant impact on a tribal cultural resource, the lead agency's environmental document shall discuss both of the following:

(1) Whether the proposed project has a significant impact on an identified tribal cultural resource.

(2) Whether feasible alternatives or mitigation measures, including those measures that may be agreed to pursuant to subdivision (a), avoid or substantially lessen the impact on the identified tribal cultural resource.

(c) (1) Any information, including, but not limited to, the location, description, and use of the tribal cultural resources, that is submitted by a California Native American tribe during the environmental review process shall not be included in the environmental document or otherwise disclosed by the lead agency or any other public agency to the public, consistent with subdivision (r) of Section 6254 of, and Section 6254.10 of, the Government Code, and subdivision (d) of Section 15120 of Title 14 of the California Code of Regulations, without the prior consent of the tribe that provided the information. If the lead agency publishes any information submitted by a California Native American tribe during the consultation or environmental review process, that information shall be published in a confidential appendix to the environmental document unless the tribe that provided the information consents, in writing, to the disclosure of some or all of the information to the public. This subdivision does not prohibit the confidential exchange of the submitted information between public agencies that have lawful jurisdiction over the preparation of the environmental document.

(2) (A) This subdivision does not prohibit the confidential exchange of information regarding tribal cultural resources submitted by a California Native American tribe during the consultation or environmental review process among the lead agency, the California Native American tribe, the project applicant, or the project applicant's agent. Except as provided in subparagraph (B) or unless the California Native American tribe providing the information consents, in writing, to public disclosure, the project applicant or the project applicant's

44

legal advisers, using a reasonable degree of care, shall maintain the confidentiality of the information exchanged for the purposes of preventing looting, vandalism, or damage to tribal cultural resources and shall not disclose to a third party confidential information regarding tribal cultural resources.

(B) This paragraph does not apply to data or information that are or become publicly available, are already in the lawful possession of the project applicant before the provision of the information by the California Native American tribe, are independently developed by the project applicant or the project applicant's agents, or are lawfully obtained by the project applicant from a third party that is not the lead agency, a California Native American tribe, or another public agency.

(3) This subdivision does not affect or alter the application of subdivision (r) of Section 6254 of the Government Code, Section 6254.10 of the Government Code, or subdivision (d) of Section 15120 of Title 14 of the California Code of Regulations.

(4) This subdivision does not prevent a lead agency or other public agency from describing the information in general terms in the environmental document so as to inform the public of the basis of the lead agency's or other public agency's decision without breaching the confidentiality required by this subdivision.

(d) In addition to other provisions of this division, the lead agency may certify an environmental impact report or adopt a mitigated negative declaration for a project with a significant impact on an identified tribal cultural resource only if one of the following occurs:

(1) The consultation process between the California Native American tribe and the lead agency has occurred as provided in Sections 21080.3.1 and 21080.3.2 and concluded pursuant to subdivision (b) of Section 21080.3.2.

(2) The California Native American tribe has requested consultation pursuant to Section 21080.3.1 and has failed to provide comments to the lead agency, or otherwise failed to engage, in the consultation process.

(3) The lead agency has complied with subdivision (d) of Section 21080.3.1 and the California Native American tribe has failed to request consultation within 30 days.

(e) If the mitigation measures recommended by the staff of the lead agency as a result of the consultation process are not included in the environmental document or if there are no agreed upon mitigation measures at the conclusion of the consultation or if consultation does not occur, and if substantial evidence demonstrates that a project will cause a significant effect to a tribal cultural resource, the lead agency shall consider feasible mitigation pursuant to subdivision (b) of Section 21084.3.

(f) Consistent with subdivision (c), the lead agency shall publish confidential information obtained from a California Native American tribe during the consultation process in a confidential appendix to the environmental document and shall include a general description of the information, as provided in paragraph (4) of subdivision (c) in the environmental document for public review during the public comment period provided pursuant to this division.

(g) This section is not intended, and may not be construed, to limit consultation between the state and tribal governments, existing confidentiality provisions, or the protection of religious exercise to the fullest extent permitted under state and federal law.

[Amended, Chapter 303, Statutes of 2015]

21082.4. Consideration of negative impacts

In describing and evaluating a project in an environmental review document prepared pursuant to this division, the lead agency may consider specific economic, legal, social, technological, or other benefits, including regionwide or statewide environmental benefits, of a proposed project and the negative impacts of denying the project. Any benefits or negative impacts considered pursuant to this section shall be based on substantial evidence in light of the whole record.

[Added, Chapter 193, Statutes of 2018]

21083. CEQA Guidelines by Office of Planning and Research

(a) The Office of Planning and Research shall prepare and develop proposed guidelines for the implementation of this division by public agencies. The guidelines shall include objectives and criteria for the orderly evaluation of projects and the preparation of environmental impact reports and negative declarations in a manner consistent with this division.

(b) The guidelines shall specifically include criteria for public agencies to follow in determining whether or not a proposed project may have a "significant effect on the environment." The criteria shall require a finding that a project may have a "significant effect on the environment" if one or more of the following conditions exist:

(1) A proposed project has the potential to degrade the quality of the environment, curtail the range of the environment, or to achieve short-term, to the disadvantage of long-term, environmental goals.

(2) The possible effects of a project are individually limited but cumulatively considerable. As used in this paragraph, "cumulatively considerable" means that the incremental effects of an individual project are considerable when viewed in connection with the effects of past projects, the effects of other current projects, and the effects of probable future projects.

(3) The environmental effects of a project will cause substantial adverse effects on human beings, either directly or indirectly.

(c) The guidelines shall include procedures for determining the lead agency pursuant to Section 21165.

(d) The guidelines shall include criteria for public agencies to use in determining when a proposed project is of sufficient statewide, regional, or areawide environmental significance that a draft environmental impact report, a proposed negative declaration, or a proposed mitigated negative declaration shall be submitted to appropriate state agencies, through the State Clearinghouse, for review and comment prior to completion of the environmental impact report, negative declaration, or mitigated negative declaration.

(e) The Office of Planning and Research shall develop and prepare the proposed guidelines as soon as possible and shall transmit them immediately to the Secretary of the Resources Agency. The Secretary of the Resources Agency shall certify and adopt the guidelines pursuant to Chapter 3.5 (commencing with Section 11340) of Part 1 of Division 3 of Title 2 of the Government Code, which shall become effective upon the filing thereof. However, the guidelines shall not be adopted without compliance with Sections 11346.4, 11346.5, and 11346.8 of the Government Code.

(f) The Office of Planning and Research shall, at least once every two years, review the guidelines adopted pursuant to this section and shall recommend proposed changes or amendments to the Secretary of the Resources Agency. The Secretary of the Resources Agency shall certify and adopt guidelines, and any amendments thereto, at least once every two years, pursuant to Chapter 3.5 (commencing with Section 11340) of Part 1 of Division 3 of Title 2 of the Government Code, which shall become effective upon the filing thereof. However, guidelines may not be adopted or amended without compliance with Sections 11346.4, 11346.5, and 11346.8 of the Government Code.

[Amended, Chapter 689, Statutes of 2004]

21083.01. Recommendation and response to Secretary of the Natural Resources Agency

(a) On or after January 1, 2013, at the time of the next review of the guidelines prepared and developed to implement this division pursuant to subdivision (f) of Section 21083, the Office of Planning and Research, in cooperation with the Department of Forestry and Fire Protection, shall prepare, develop, and transmit to the Secretary of the Natural Resources Agency recommended proposed changes or amendments to the initial study checklist of the guidelines implementing this division for the inclusion of questions related to fire hazard impacts for projects located on lands classified as state responsibility areas, as defined in Section 4102, and on lands classified as very high fire hazard severity zones, as defined in subdivision (i) of Section 51177 of the Government Code.

(b) Upon receipt and review, the Secretary of the Natural Resources Agency shall certify and adopt the recommended proposed changes or amendments prepared and developed by the Office of Planning and Research pursuant to subdivision (a).

[Added, Chapter 311, Statutes of 2012]

21083.05. Guidelines for the mitigation of greenhouse gas emissions

The Office of Planning and Research and the Natural Resources Agency shall periodically update the guidelines for the mitigation of greenhouse gas emissions or the effects of greenhouse gas emissions as required by this division, including, but not limited to, effects associated with transportation or energy consumption, to incorporate new information or criteria established by the State Air Resources Board pursuant to Division 25.5 (commencing with Section 38500) of the Health and Safety Code.

[Amended, Chapter 548, Statutes of 2012]

21083.09.   Guidelines for the consideration of paleontological resources and tribal cultural resources

On or before July 1, 2016, the Office of Planning and Research shall prepare and develop, and the Secretary of the Natural Resources Agency shall certify and adopt, revisions to the guidelines that update Appendix G of Chapter 3 (commencing with Section 15000) of Division 6 of Title 4 of the California Code of Regulations to do both of the following:

(a) Separate the consideration of paleontological resources from tribal cultural resources and update the relevant sample questions.

(b) Add consideration of tribal cultural resources with relevant sample questions.

[Added, Chapter 532, Statutes of 2014]

21083.1.   Statutory interpretation

It is the intent of the Legislature that courts, consistent with generally accepted rules of statutory interpretation, shall not interpret this division or the state guidelines adopted pursuant to Section 21083 in a manner which imposes procedural or substantive requirements beyond those explicitly stated in this division or in the state guidelines.

[Added, Chapter 1070, Statutes of 1993]

21083.2.   Archaeological resources

(a) As part of the determination made pursuant to Section 21080.1, the lead agency shall determine whether the project may have a significant effect on archaeological resources. If the lead agency determines that the project may have a significant effect on unique archaeological resources, the environmental impact report shall address the issue of those resources. An environmental impact report, if otherwise necessary, shall not address the issue of nonunique archaeological resources. A negative declaration shall be issued with respect to a project if, but for the issue of nonunique archaeological resources, the negative declaration would be otherwise issued.

(b) If it can be demonstrated that a project will cause damage to a unique archaeological resource, the lead agency may require reasonable efforts to be made to permit any or all of these resources to be preserved in place or left in an undisturbed state. Examples of that treatment, in no order of preference, may include, but are not limited to, any of the following:

(1) Planning construction to avoid archaeological sites.

(2) Deeding archaeological sites into permanent conservation easements.

(3) Capping or covering archaeological sites with a layer of soil before building on the sites.

(4) Planning parks, greenspace, or other open space to incorporate archaeological sites.

48

(c) To the extent that unique archaeological resources are not preserved in place or not left in an undisturbed state, mitigation measures shall be required as provided in this subdivision. The project applicant shall provide a guarantee to the lead agency to pay one-half the estimated cost of mitigating the significant effects of the project on unique archaeological resources. In determining payment, the lead agency shall give due consideration to the in-kind value of project design or expenditures that are intended to permit any or all archaeological resources or California Native American culturally significant sites to be preserved in place or left in an undisturbed state. When a final decision is made to carry out or approve the project, the lead agency shall, if necessary, reduce the specified mitigation measures to those which can be funded with the money guaranteed by the project applicant plus the money voluntarily guaranteed by any other person or persons for those mitigation purposes. In order to allow time for interested persons to provide the funding guarantee referred to in this subdivision, a final decision to carry out or approve a project shall not occur sooner than 60 days after completion of the recommended special environmental impact report required by this section.

(d) Excavation as mitigation shall be restricted to those parts of the unique archaeological resource that would be damaged or destroyed by the project. Excavation as mitigation shall not be required for a unique archaeological resource if the lead agency determines that testing or studies already completed have adequately recovered the scientifically consequential information from and about the resource, if this determination is documented in the environmental impact report.

(e) In no event shall the amount paid by a project applicant for mitigation measures required pursuant to subdivision (c) exceed the following amounts:

(1) An amount equal to one-half of 1 percent of the projected cost of the project for mitigation measures undertaken within the site boundaries of a commercial or industrial project.

(2) An amount equal to three-fourths of 1 percent of the projected cost of the project for mitigation measures undertaken within the site boundaries of a housing project consisting of a single unit.

(3) If a housing project consists of more than a single unit, an amount equal to three-fourths of 1 percent of the projected cost of the project for mitigation measures undertaken within the site boundaries of the project for the first unit plus the sum of the following:

(A) Two hundred dollars ($200) per unit for any of the next 99 units.

(B) One hundred fifty dollars ($150) per unit for any of the next 400 units.

(C) One hundred dollars ($100) per unit in excess of 500 units.

(f) Unless special or unusual circumstances warrant an exception, the field excavation phase of an approved mitigation plan shall be completed within 90 days after final approval necessary to implement the physical development of the project or, if a phased project, in connection with the phased portion to which the specific mitigation measures are applicable. However, the project applicant may extend that period if he or she so elects. Nothing in this section shall nullify protections for Indian cemeteries under any other provision of law.

(g) As used in this section "unique archaeological resource" means an archaeological artifact, object, or site about which it can be clearly demonstrated that, without merely adding to the current body of knowledge, there is a high probability that it meets any of the following criteria:

(1) Contains information needed to answer important scientific research questions and that there is a demonstrable public interest in that information.

(2) Has a special and particular quality such as being the oldest of its type or the best available example of its type.

(3) Is directly associated with a scientifically recognized important prehistoric or historic event or person.

(h) As used in this section, "nonunique archaeological resource" means an archaeological artifact, object, or site which does not meet the criteria in subdivision (g). A nonunique archaeological resource need be given no further consideration, other than the simple recording of its existence by the lead agency if it so elects.

(i) As part of the objectives, criteria, and procedures required by Section 21082 or as part of conditions imposed for mitigation, a lead agency may make provisions for archaeological sites accidentally discovered during construction. These provisions may include an immediate evaluation of the find. If the find is determined to be a unique archaeological resource, contingency funding and a time allotment sufficient to allow recovering an archaeological sample or to employ one of the avoidance measures may be required under the provisions set forth in this section. Construction work may continue on other parts of the building site while archaeological mitigation takes place.

(j) This section does not apply to any project described in subdivision (a) or (b) of Section 21065 if the lead agency elects to comply with all other applicable provisions of this division. This section does not apply to any project described in subdivision (c) of Section 21065 if the applicant and the lead agency jointly elect to comply with all other applicable provisions of this division.

(k) Any additional costs to any local agency as a result of complying with this section with respect to a project of other than a public agency shall be borne by the project applicant.

(l) Nothing in this section is intended to affect or modify the requirements of Section 21084 or 21084.1.

[Amended, Chapter 375, Statutes of 1993]

21083.3. Restrict CEQA on residential zoning and community plans

(a) If a parcel has been zoned to accommodate a particular density of development or has been designated in a community plan to accommodate a particular density of development and an environmental impact report was certified for that zoning or planning action, the application of this division to the approval of any subdivision map or other project that is consistent with the zoning or community plan shall be limited to effects upon the environment which are peculiar to the parcel or to the project and which were not addressed as significant effects in the prior environmental impact report, or which substantial new information shows will be more significant than described in the prior environmental impact report.

(b) If a development project is consistent with the general plan of a local agency and an environmental impact report was certified with respect to that general plan, the application of this division to the approval of that development project shall be limited to effects on the environment which are peculiar to the parcel or to the project and which were not addressed as significant effects in the prior environmental impact report, or which substantial new information shows will be more significant than described in the prior environmental impact report.

(c) Nothing in this section affects any requirement to analyze potentially significant offsite impacts and cumulative impacts of the project not discussed in the prior environmental impact report with respect to the general plan. However, all public agencies with authority to mitigate the significant effects shall undertake or require the undertaking of any feasible mitigation measures specified in the prior environmental impact report relevant to a significant effect which the project will have on the environment or, if not, then the provisions of this section shall have no application to that effect. The lead agency shall make a finding, at a public hearing, as to whether those mitigation measures will be undertaken.

(d) An effect of a project upon the environment shall not be considered peculiar to the parcel or to the project, for purposes of this section, if uniformly applied development policies or standards have been previously adopted by the city or county, with a finding based upon substantial evidence, which need not include an environmental impact report, that the development policies or standards will substantially mitigate that environmental effect when applied to future projects, unless substantial new information shows that the policies or standards will not substantially mitigate the environmental effect.

(e) Where a community plan is the basis for application of this section, any rezoning action consistent with the community plan shall be a project subject to exemption from this division in accordance with this section. As used in this section, "community plan" means a part of the general plan of a city or county which (1) applies to a defined geographic portion of the total area included in the general plan, (2) complies with Article 5 (commencing with Section 65300) of Chapter 3 of Division 1 of Title 7 of the Government Code by including or referencing each of the mandatory elements specified in Section 65302 of the Government Code, and (3) contains specific development policies adopted for the area included in the community plan and identifies measures to implement those policies, so that the policies which will apply to each parcel can be determined.

(f) No person shall have standing to bring an action or proceeding to attack, review, set aside, void, or annul a finding of a public agency made at a public hearing pursuant to subdivision (a) with respect to the conformity of the project to the mitigation measures identified in the prior environmental impact report for the zoning or planning action, unless he or she has participated in that public hearing. However, this subdivision shall not be applicable if the local agency failed to give public notice of the hearing as required by law. For purposes of this subdivision, a person has participated in the public hearing if he or she has either submitted oral or written testimony regarding the proposed determination, finding, or decision prior to the close of the hearing.

(g) Any community plan adopted prior to January 1, 1982, which does not comply with the definitional criteria specified in subdivision (e) may be amended to comply with that criteria, in which case the plan shall be deemed a "community plan" within the meaning of subdivision (e) if (1) an environmental impact report was certified for adoption of the plan and (2) at the time of the conforming amendment, the environmental impact report has not been held inadequate by a court of this state and is not the subject of pending litigation challenging its adequacy.

[Amended, Chapter 1102, Statutes of 1992]

21083.4. Conversion of Oak Woodlands; exemptions

(a) For purposes of this section, "oak" means a native tree species in the genus Quercus, not designated as Group A or Group B commercial species pursuant to regulations adopted by the State Board of Forestry and Fire Protection pursuant to Section 4526, and that is 5 inches or more in diameter at breast height.

(b) As part of the determination made pursuant to Section 21080.1, a county shall determine whether a project within its jurisdiction may result in a conversion of oak woodlands that will have a significant effect on the environment. If a county determines that there may be a significant effect to oak woodlands, the county shall require one or more of the following oak woodlands mitigation alternatives to mitigate the significant effect of the conversion of oak woodlands:

   (1) Conserve oak woodlands, through the use of conservation easements.

   (2) (A) Plant an appropriate number of trees, including maintaining plantings and replacing dead or diseased trees.

   (B) The requirement to maintain trees pursuant to this paragraph terminates seven years after the trees are planted.

   (C) Mitigation pursuant to this paragraph shall not fulfill more than one-half of the mitigation requirement for the project.

   (D) The requirements imposed pursuant to this paragraph also may be used to restore former oak woodlands.

   (3) Contribute funds to the Oak Woodlands Conservation Fund, as established under subdivision (a) of Section 1363 of the Fish and Game Code, for the purpose of purchasing oak woodlands conservation easements, as specified under paragraph (1) of subdivision (d) of that section and the guidelines and criteria of the Wildlife Conservation Board.A project applicant that contributes funds under this paragraph shall not receive a grant from the Oak Woodlands Conservation Fund as part of the mitigation for the project.

   (4) Other mitigation measures developed by the county.

(c) Notwithstanding subdivision (d) of Section 1363 of the Fish and Game Code, a county may use a grant awarded pursuant to the Oak Woodlands Conservation Act (Article 3.5 (commencing with Section 1360) of Chapter 4 of Division 2 of the Fish and Game Code) to prepare an oak conservation element for a general plan, an oak protection ordinance, or an oak woodlands management plan, or amendments thereto, that meets the requirements of this section.

(d) The following are exempt from this section:

(1) Projects undertaken pursuant to an approved Natural Community Conservation Plan or approved subarea plan within an approved Natural Community Conservation Plan that includes oaks as a covered species or that conserves oak habitat through natural community conservation preserve designation and implementation and mitigation measures that are consistent with this section.

(2) Affordable housing projects for lower income households, as defined pursuant to Section 50079.5 of the Health and Safety Code, that are located within an urbanized area, or within a sphere of influence as defined pursuant to Section 56076 of the Government Code.

(3) Conversion of oak woodlands on agricultural land that includes land that is used to produce or process plant and animal products for commercial purposes.

(4) Projects undertaken pursuant to Section 21080.5 of the Public Resources Code.

(e) (1) A lead agency that adopts, and a project that incorporates, one or more of the measures specified in this section to mitigate the significant effects to oaks and oak woodlands shall be deemed to be in compliance with this division only as it applies to effects on oaks and oak woodlands.

(2) The Legislature does not intend this section to modify requirements of this division, other than with regard to effects on oaks and oak woodlands.

(f) This section does not preclude the application of Section 21081 to a project.

(g) This section, and the regulations adopted pursuant to this section, shall not be construed as a limitation on the power of a public agency to comply with this division or any other provision of law.

[Added, Chapter 732, Statutes of 2004]

21083.5. Use of EIRs prepared under the National Environmental Policy Act of 1969 and the Tahoe Regional Planning Compact

(a) The guidelines prepared and adopted pursuant to Section 21083 shall provide that, when an environmental impact statement has been, or will be, prepared for the same project pursuant to the requirements of the National Environmental Policy Act of 1969 (42 U.S.C. Sec. 4321 et seq.) and implementing regulations, or an environmental impact report has been, or will be, prepared for the same project pursuant to the requirements of the Tahoe Regional Planning Compact (Section 66801 of the Government Code) and implementing regulations, all or any part of that statement or report may be submitted in lieu of all or any part of an environmental impact report required by this division, if that statement or report, or the part which is used, complies with the requirements of this division and the guidelines adopted pursuant thereto.

(b) Notwithstanding subdivision (a), compliance with this division may be achieved for the adoption in a city or county general plan, without any additions or change, of all or any part of the regional plan prepared pursuant to the Tahoe Regional Planning Compact and implementing regulations by reviewing environmental documents prepared by the Tahoe Regional Planning Agency addressing the plan, providing an analysis pursuant to this division of any significant effect on the environment not addressed in the environmental documents, and proceeding in accordance with Section 21081. This subdivision does not exempt a city or county from complying with the public review and notice requirements of this division.

[Amended, Chapter 493, Statutes of 1988]

21083.6. Lead agency may waive time limits on combined impact report—impact statement

In the event that a project requires both an environmental impact report prepared pursuant to the requirements of this division and an environmental impact statement prepared pursuant to the requirements of the Naional Environmental Policy Act of 1969, an applicant may request and the lead agency may waive the time limits established pursuant to Section 21100.2 or 21151.5 if it finds that additional time is required to prepare a combined environmental impact report environmental impact statement and that the time required to prepare such a combined document would be shorter than that required to prepare each document separately.

[Added, Chapter 1200, Statutes of 1977]

21083.7. Lead agency to use environmental impact statement when both statement and report are required

(a) In the event that a project requires both an environmental impact report prepared pursuant to the requirements of this division and an environmental impact statement prepared pursuant to the requirements of the National Environmental Policy Act of 1969, the lead agency shall, whenever possible, use the environmental impact statement as such environmental impact report as provided in Section 21083.5.

(b) In order to implement this section, each lead agency to which this section is applicable shall do both of the following, as soon as possible:

(1) Consult with the federal agency required to prepare such environmental impact statement.

(2) Notify the federal agency required to prepare the environmental impact statement regarding any scoping meeting for the proposed project.

[Amended, Chapter 387, Statutes of 2000]

21083.8.1. Meaning of "reuse plan" for military base

(a) (1) For purposes of this section, "reuse plan" for a military base means an initial plan for the reuse of a military base adopted by a local government or a redevelopment agency in the form of a general plan, general plan amendment, specific plan, redevelopment plan, or other planning document, except that the reuse plan shall also consist of a statement of development policies, include a diagram or diagrams illustrating its

54

provisions, and make the designation required in paragraph (2). "Military base" or "base" means a military base or reservation either closed or realigned by, or scheduled for closure or realignment by, the federal government.

(2) The reuse plan shall designate the proposed general distribution and general location of development intensity for housing, business, industry, open space, recreation, natural resources, public buildings and grounds, roads and other transportation facilities, infrastructure, and other categories of public and private uses of land.

(b) (1) When preparing and certifying an environmental impact report for a reuse plan, including when utilizing an environmental impact statement pursuant to Section 21083.5, the determination of whether the reuse plan may have a significant effect on the environment may be made in the context of the physical conditions that were present at the time that the federal decision became final for the closure or realignment of the base. The no project alternative analyzed in the environmental impact report shall discuss the existing conditions on the base, as they exist at the time that the environmental impact report is prepared, as well as what could be reasonably expected to occur in the foreseeable future if the reuse plan were not approved, based on current plans and consistent with available infrastructure and services.

(2) For purposes of this division, all public and private activities taken pursuant to, or in furtherance of, a reuse plan shall be deemed to be a single project. However, further environmental review of any such public or private activity shall be conducted if any of the events specified in Section 21166 have occurred.

(c) Prior to preparing an environmental impact report for which a lead agency chooses to utilize the provisions of this section, the lead agency shall do all of the following:

(A) Hold a public hearing at which is discussed the federal environmental impact statement prepared for, or in the process of being prepared for, the closure of the military base. The discussion shall include the significant effects on the environment examined in the environmental impact statement, potential methods of mitigating those effects, including feasible alternatives, and the mitigative effects of federal, state, and local laws applicable to future nonmilitary activities. Prior to the close of the hearing, the lead agency may specify the baseline conditions for the reuse plan environmental impact report prepared, or in the process of being prepared, for the closure of the base. The lead agency may specify particular physical conditions that it will examine in greater detail than were examined in the environmental impact statement. Notice of the hearing shall be given as provided in Section 21092. The hearing may be continued from time to time.

(B) Identify pertinent responsible agencies and trustee agencies and consult with those agencies prior to the public hearing as to the application of their regulatory policies and permitting standards to the proposed baseline for environmental analysis, as well as to the reuse plan and planned future nonmilitary land uses of the base. The affected agencies shall have not less than 30 days prior to the public hearing to review the proposed reuse plan and to submit their comments to the lead agency.

(C) At the close of the hearing, the lead agency shall state in writing how the lead agency intends to integrate the baseline for analysis with the reuse planning and environmental review process, taking into account the adopted environmental standards of the community, including, but not limited to, the applicable general plan, specific plan, and redevelopment plan, and including other applicable provisions of adopted congestion management plans, habitat conservation or natural communities conservation plans, integrated waste management plans, and county hazardous waste management plans.

(D) At the close of the hearing, the lead agency shall state, in writing, the specific economic or social reasons, including, but not limited to, new job creation, opportunities for employment of skilled workers, availability of low- and moderate-income housing, and economic continuity, which support the selection of the baseline.

(d) (1) Nothing in this section shall in any way limit the scope of a review or determination of significance of the presence of hazardous or toxic wastes, substances, or materials including, but not limited to, contaminated soils and groundwater, nor shall the regulation of hazardous or toxic wastes, substances, or materials be constrained by prior levels of activity that existed at the time that the federal agency decision to close the military base became final.

(2) This section does not apply to any project undertaken pursuant to Chapter 6.5 (commencing with Section 25100) of, or Chapter 6.8 (commencing with Section 25300) of, Division 20 of the Health and Safety Code, or pursuant to the Porter-Cologne Water Quality Control Act (Division 7 (commencing with Section 13000) of the Water Code).

(3) This section may apply to any reuse plan environmental impact report for which a notice of preparation pursuant to subdivision (a) of Section 21092 is issued within one year from the date that the federal record of decision was rendered for the military base closure or realignment and reuse, or prior to January 1, 1997, whichever is later, if the environmental impact report is completed and certified within five years from the date that the federal record of decision was rendered.

(e) All subsequent development at the military base shall be subject to all applicable federal, state, or local laws, including, but not limited to, those relating to air quality, water quality, traffic, threatened and endangered species, noise, and hazardous or toxic wastes, substances, or materials.

[Amended, Chapter 525, Statutes of 2004]

21083.9. Lead Agency shall call scoping meeting, if Caltrans requests one

(a) Notwithstanding Section 21080.4, 21104, or 21153, a lead agency shall call at least one scoping meeting for either of the following:

(1) A proposed project that may affect highways or other facilities under the jurisdiction of the Department of Transportation if the meeting is requested by the department. The lead agency shall call the scoping meeting as soon as possible, but not later than 30 days after receiving the request from the Department of Transportation.

(2) A project of statewide, regional, or areawide significance.

(b) The lead agency shall provide notice of at least one scoping meeting held pursuant to paragraph (2) of subdivision (a) to all of the following:

(1) A county or city that borders on a county or city within which the project is located, unless otherwise designated annually by agreement between the lead agency and the county or city.

(2) A responsible agency.

(3) A public agency that has jurisdiction by law with respect to the project.

(4) A transportation planning agency or public agency required to be consulted pursuant to Section 21092.4.

(5) A public agency, organization, or individual who has filed a written request for the notice.

(c) For a public agency, organization, or individual that is required to be provided notice of a lead agency public meeting, the requirement for notice of a scoping meeting pursuant to subdivision (b) may be met by including the notice of a scoping meeting in the public meeting notice.

(d) A scoping meeting that is held in the city or county within which the project is located pursuant to the federal National Environmental Policy Act of 1969 (42 U.S.C. Sec. 4321 et seq.) and the regulations adopted pursuant to that act shall be deemed to satisfy the requirement that a scoping meeting be held for a project subject to paragraph (2) of subdivision (a) if the lead agency meets the notice requirements of subdivision (b) or subdivision (c).

(e) The referral of a proposed action to adopt or substantially amend a general plan to a city or county pursuant to paragraph (1) of subdivision (a) of Section 65352 of the Government Code may be conducted concurrently with the scoping meeting required pursuant to this section, and the city or county may submit its comments as provided pursuant to subdivision (b) of that section at the scoping meeting.

[Amended, Chapter 218, Statutes of 2012]

21084.   **Guidelines shall list classes of projects exempt from Act**

(a) The guidelines prepared and adopted pursuant to Section 21083 shall include a list of classes of projects that have been determined not to have a significant effect on the environment and that shall be exempt from this division. In adopting the guidelines, the Secretary of the Natural Resources Agency shall make a finding that the listed classes of projects referred to in this section do not have a significant effect on the environment.

(b) A project's greenhouse gas emissions shall not, in and of themselves, be deemed to cause an exemption adopted pursuant to subdivision (a) to be inapplicable if the project complies with all applicable regulations or requirements adopted to implement statewide, regional, or local plans consistent with Section 15183.5 of Title 14 of the California Code of Regulations.

(c) A project that may result in damage to scenic resources, including, but not limited to, trees, historic buildings, rock outcroppings, or similar resources, within a highway designated as an official state scenic highway, pursuant to Article 2.5 (commencing with Section 260) of Chapter 2 of Division 1 of the Streets and Highways Code, shall not be exempted from this division pursuant to subdivision (a). This subdivision does not apply to improvements as mitigation for a project for which a negative declaration has been approved or an environmental impact report has been certified.

(d) A project located on a site that is included on any list compiled pursuant to Section 65962.5 of the Government Code shall not be exempted from this division pursuant to subdivision (a).

(e) A project that may cause a substantial adverse change in the significance of a historical resource, as specified in Section 21084.1, shall not be exempted from this division pursuant to subdivision (a).

[Amended, Chapter 76, Statutes of 2013]

21084.1. Historical resources

A project that may cause a substantial adverse change in the significance of an historical resource is a project that may have a significant effect on the environment. For purposes of this section, an historical resource is a resource listed in, or determined to be eligible for listing in, the California Register of Historical Resources. Historical resources included in a local register of historical resources, as defined in subdivision (k) of Section 5020.1, or deemed significant pursuant to criteria set forth in subdivision (g) of Section 5024.1, are presumed to be historically or culturally significant for purposes of this section, unless the preponderance of the evidence demonstrates that the resource is not historically or culturally significant. The fact that a resource is not listed in, or determined to be eligible for listing in, the California Register of Historical Resources, not included in a local register of historical resources, or not deemed significant pursuant to criteria set forth in subdivision (g) of Section 5024.1 shall not preclude a lead agency from determining whether the resource may be an historical resource for purposes of this section.

[Added, Chapter 1075, Statutes of 1992]

21084.2. Tribal cultural resources

A project with an effect that may cause a substantial adverse change in the significance of a tribal cultural resource is a project that may have a significant effect on the environment.

[Added, Chapter 532, Statutes of 2014]

21084.3. Tribal cultural resources; significant adverse impacts

(a) Public agencies shall, when feasible, avoid damaging effects to any tribal cultural resource.

(b) If the lead agency determines that a project may cause a substantial adverse change to a tribal cultural resource, and measures are not otherwise identified in the consultation process provided in Section 21080.3.2, the following are examples of mitigation measures that, if feasible, may be considered to avoid or minimize the significant adverse impacts:

(1) Avoidance and preservation of the resources in place, including, but not limited to, planning and construction to avoid the resources and protect the cultural and natural context, or planning greenspace, parks, or other open space, to incorporate the resources with culturally appropriate protection and management criteria.

(2) Treating the resource with culturally appropriate dignity taking into account the tribal cultural values and meaning of the resource, including, but not limited to, the following:

(A) Protecting the cultural character and integrity of the resource.

(B) Protecting the traditional use of the resource.

(C) Protecting the confidentiality of the resource.

(3) Permanent conservation easements or other interests in real property, with culturally appropriate management criteria for the purposes of preserving or utilizing the resources or places.

(4) Protecting the resource.

[Added, Chapter 532, Statutes of 2014]

21086. Adding or deleting a class of projects

(a) A public agency may, at any time, request the addition or deletion of a class of projects, to the list designated pursuant to Section 21084. That request shall be made in writing to the Office of Planning and Research and shall include information supporting the public agency's position that the class of projects does, or does not, have a significant effect on the environment.

(b) The Office of Planning and Research shall review each request and, as soon as possible, shall submit its recommendation to the Secretary of the Resources Agency. Following the receipt of that recommendation, the Secretary of the Resources Agency may add or delete the class of projects to the list of classes of projects designated pursuant to Section 21084 that are exempt from the requirements of this division.

(c) The addition or deletion of a class of projects, as provided in this section, to the list specified in Section 21084 shall constitute an amendment to the guidelines adopted pursuant to Section 21083 and shall be adopted in the manner prescribed in Sections 21083 and 21084.

[Amended, Chapter 689, Statutes of 2004]

21088. Distributing guidelines, amendments, and completed EIRs

The Secretary of the Resources Agency shall provide for the timely distribution to all public agencies of the guidelines and any amendments or changes thereto. In addition, the Secretary of the Resources Agency may provide for publication of a bulletin to provide public notice of the guidelines, or any amendments or changes thereto, and of the completion of environmental impact reports prepared in compliance with this division.

[Added, Chapter 1154, Statutes of 1972]

21089.   Reasonable fees

(a) A lead agency may charge and collect a reasonable fee from a person proposing a project subject to this division in order to recover the estimated costs incurred by the lead agency in preparing a negative declaration or an environmental impact report for the project and for procedures necessary to comply with this division on the project. Litigation expenses, costs, and fees incurred in actions alleging noncompliance with this division under Section 21167 are not recoverable under this section.

(b) The Department of Fish and Game may charge and collect filing fees, as provided in Section 711.4 of the Fish and Game Code. Notwithstanding Section 21080.1, a finding required under Section 21081, or any project approved under a certified regulatory program authorized pursuant to Section 21080.5 is not operative, vested, or final until the filing fees required pursuant to Section 711.4 of the Fish and Game Code are paid.

(c) (1) A public agency may charge and collect a reasonable fee from members of the public for a copy of an environmental document not to exceed the cost of reproducing the environmental document. A public agency may provide the environmental document in an electronic format as provided pursuant to Section 6253.9 of the Government Code.

(2) For purposes of this subdivision, "environmental document" means an initial study, negative declaration, mitigated negative declaration, draft and final environmental impact report, a document prepared as a substitute for an environmental impact report, negative declaration, or mitigated negative declaration under a program certified pursuant to Section 21080.5, and a document prepared under the federal National Environmental Policy Act of 1969 (42 U.S.C. Sec. 4321 et seq.) and used by a state or local agency in the place of the initial study, negative declaration, mitigated negative declaration, or an environmental impact report.

[Amended, Chapter 210, Statutes of 2010]

21090.   Redevelopment plans deemed a single project; exceptions

(a) An environmental impact report for a redevelopment plan may be a master environmental impact report, program environmental impact report, or a project environmental impact report. Any environmental impact report for a redevelopment plan shall specify the type of environmental impact report that is prepared for the redevelopment plan.

(b) If the environmental impact report for a redevelopment plan is a project environmental impact report, all public and private activities or undertakings pursuant to, or in furtherance of, a redevelopment plan shall be deemed to be a single project. However, further environmental review of any public or private activity or undertaking pursuant to, or in furtherance of, a redevelopment plan for which a project environmental impact report has been certified shall be conducted if any of the events specified in Section 21166 have occurred.

[Amended, Chapter 625, Statutes of 2002]

21090.1.   Geothermal exploratory projects

For all purposes of this division, a geothermal exploratory project shall be deemed to be separate and distinct from any subsequent geothermal field development project as defined in Section 65928.5 of the Government Code.

[Added, Chapter 1271, Statutes of 1978]

21091.   Public review period for draft EIRs and proposed negative declarations

(a) The public review period for a draft environmental impact report shall not be less than 30 days. If the draft environmental impact report is submitted to the State Clearinghouse for review, the review period shall be at least 45 days, and the lead agency shall provide a sufficient number of copies of the document, in either a hard-copy or electronic form as required by the Office of Planning and Research, to the State Clearinghouse for review and comment by state agencies.

(b) The public review period for a proposed negative declaration or proposed mitigated negative declaration shall not be less than 20 days. If the proposed negative declaration or proposed mitigated negative declaration is submitted to the State Clearinghouse for review, the review period shall be at least 30 days, and the lead agency shall provide a sufficient number of copies of the document, in either a hard-copy or electronic form as required by the Office of Planning and Research, to the State Clearinghouse for review and comment by state agencies.

(c) (1) Notwithstanding subdivisions (a) and (b), if a draft environmental impact report, proposed negative declaration, or proposed mitigated negative declaration is submitted to the State Clearinghouse for review and the period of review by the State Clearinghouse is longer than the public review period established pursuant to subdivision (a) or (b), whichever is applicable, the public review period shall be at least as long as the period of review and comment by state agencies as established by the State Clearinghouse.

(2) The public review period and the state agency review period may, but are not required to, begin and end at the same time. Day one of the state agency review period shall be the date that the State Clearinghouse distributes the CEQA document to state agencies.

(3) If the submittal of a CEQA document is determined by the State Clearinghouse to be complete, the State Clearinghouse shall distribute the document within three working days from the date of receipt. The State Clearinghouse shall specify the information that will be required in order to determine the completeness of the submittal of a CEQA document.

(d) (1) The lead agency shall consider comments it receives on a draft environmental impact report, proposed negative declaration, or proposed mitigated negative declaration if those comments are received within the public review period.

(2) (A) With respect to the consideration of comments received on a draft environmental impact report, the lead agency shall evaluate any comments on environmental issues that are received from persons who have reviewed the draft and shall prepare a written response pursuant to subparagraph (B). The lead agency may also respond to comments that are received after the close of the public review period.

(B) The written response shall describe the disposition of each significant environmental issue that is raised by commenters. The responses shall be prepared consistent with Section 15088 of Title 14 of the California Code of Regulations.

(3) (A) With respect to the consideration of comments received on a draft environmental impact report, proposed negative declaration, proposed mitigated negative declaration, or notice pursuant to Section 21080.4, the lead agency shall accept comments via electronic mail and shall treat electronic mail comments as equivalent to written comments.

(B) Any law or regulation relating to written comments received on a draft environmental impact report, proposed negative declaration, proposed mitigated negative declaration, or notice received pursuant to Section 21080.4 shall also apply to electronic mail comments received for those reasons.

(e) (1) Criteria for shorter review periods by the State Clearinghouse for documents that must be submitted to the State Clearinghouse shall be set forth in the written guidelines issued by the Office of Planning and Research and made available to the public.

(2) Those shortened review periods may not be less than 30 days for a draft environmental impact report and 20 days for a negative declaration.

(3) A request for a shortened review period shall only be made in writing by the decisionmaking body of the lead agency to the Office of Planning and Research. The decisionmaking body may designate by resolution or ordinance a person authorized to request a shortened review period. A designated person shall notify the decisionmaking body of this request.

(4) A request approved by the State Clearinghouse shall be consistent with the criteria set forth in the written guidelines of the Office of Planning and Research.

(5) A shortened review period may not be approved by the Office of Planning and Research for a proposed project of statewide, regional, or areawide environmental significance as determined pursuant to Section 21083.

(6) An approval of a shortened review period shall be given prior to, and reflected in, the public notice required pursuant to Section 21092.

(f) Prior to carrying out or approving a project for which a negative declaration has been adopted, the lead agency shall consider the negative declaration together with comments that were received and considered pursuant to paragraph (1) of subdivision (d).

[Amended, Chapter 476, Statutes of 2016]

21091.5.   Extended review period of EIR's for airport construction

Notwithstanding subdivision (a) of Section 21091, or any other provision of this division, the public review period for a draft environmental impact report prepared for a proposed project involving the expansion or enlargement of a publicly owned airport requiring the acquisition of any tide and submerged lands or other lands subject to the public trust for commerce, navigation, or fisheries, or any interest therein, shall be not less than 120 days.

[Added, Chapter 534, Statutes of 2001]

21092.   Public notification prior to final adoption

(a) A lead agency that is preparing an environmental impact report or a negative declaration or making a determination pursuant to subdivision (c) of Section 21157.1 shall provide public notice of that fact within a reasonable period of time prior to certification of the environmental impact report, adoption of the negative declaration, or making the determination pursuant to subdivision (c) of Section 21157.1.

(b) (1) The notice shall specify the period during which comments will be received on the draft environmental impact report or negative declaration, and shall include the date, time, and place of any public meetings or hearings on the proposed project, a brief description of the proposed project and its location, the significant effects on the environment, if any, anticipated as a result of the project, the address where copies of the draft environmental impact report or negative declaration, and all documents referenced in the draft environmental impact report or negative declaration, are available for review, and a description of how the draft environmental impact report or negative declaration can be provided in an electronic format.

(2) This section shall not be construed in any manner that results in the invalidation of an action because of the alleged inadequacy of the notice content if there has been substantial compliance with the notice content requirements of this section.

(3) The notice required by this section shall be given to the last known name and address of all organizations and individuals who have previously requested notice, and shall also be given by at least one of the following procedures:

(A) Publication, no fewer times than required by Section 6061 of the Government Code, by the public agency in a newspaper of general circulation in the area affected by the proposed project. If more than one area will be affected, the notice shall be published in the newspaper of largest circulation from among the newspapers of general circulation in those areas.

(B) Posting of notice by the lead agency on- and off-site in the area where the project is to be located.

(C) Direct mailing to the owners and occupants of contiguous property shown on the latest equalized assessment roll.

(c) For a project involving the burning of municipal wastes, hazardous waste, or refuse-derived fuel, including, but not limited to, tires, meeting the qualifications of subdivision (d), notice shall be given to all organizations and individuals who have previously requested notice and shall also be given by at least the procedures specified in subparagraphs (A), (B), and (C) of paragraph (3) of subdivision (b). In addition, notification shall be given by direct mailing to the owners and occupants of property within one-fourth of a mile of any parcel or parcels on which is located a project subject to this subdivision.

(d) The notice requirements of subdivision (c) apply to both of the following:

(1) The construction of a new facility.

(2) The expansion of an existing facility that burns hazardous waste which would increase its permitted capacity by more than 10 percent. For purposes of this paragraph, the amount of expansion of an existing facility shall be calculated by comparing the proposed facility capacity with whichever of the following is applicable:

(A) The facility capacity approved in the facility's hazardous waste facilities permit pursuant to Section 25200 of the Health and Safety Code or its grant of interim status pursuant to Section 25200.5 of the Health and Safety Code, or the facility capacity authorized in any state or local agency permit allowing the construction or operation of a facility for the burning of hazardous waste, granted before January 1, 1990.

(B) The facility capacity authorized in the facility's original hazardous waste facilities permit, grant of interim status, or any state or local agency permit allowing the construction or operation of a facility for the burning of hazardous waste, granted on or after January 1, 1990.

(e) The notice requirements specified in subdivision (b) or (c) shall not preclude a public agency from providing additional notice by other means if the agency so desires, or from providing the public notice required by this section at the same time and in the same manner as public notice otherwise required by law for the project.

[Amended, Chapter 162, Statutes of 2012]

21092.1.   Significant new information requires re-notification

When significant new information is added to an environmental impact report after notice has been given pursuant to Section 21092 and consultation has occurred pursuant to Sections 21104 and 21153, but prior to certification, the public agency shall give notice again pursuant to Section 21092, and consult again pursuant to Sections 21104 and 21153 before certifying the environmental impact report.

[Added, Chapter 1514, Statutes of 1984]

21092.2.   Requests to receive notices

(a) The notices required pursuant to Sections 21080.4, 21083.9, 21092, 21108, 21152, and 21161 shall be mailed to every person who has filed a written request for notices with either the clerk of the governing body or, if there is no governing body, the director of the agency. If the agency offers to provide the notices by email, upon filing a written request for notices, a person may request that the notices be provided to him or her by email. The request may also be filed with any other person designated by the governing body or director to receive these requests. The agency may require requests for notices to be annually renewed. The public agency may charge a fee, except to other public agencies, that is reasonably related to the costs of providing this service.

(b) Subdivision (a) shall not be construed in any manner that results in the invalidation of an action because of the failure of a person to receive a requested notice, if there has been substantial compliance with the requirements of this section.

(c) The notices required pursuant to Sections 21080.4 and 21161 shall be provided by the State Clearinghouse to any legislator in whose district the project has an environmental impact, if the legislator requests the notice and the State Clearinghouse has received it.

[Amended, Chapter 218, Statutes of 2012]

21092.3. Posting of notices

The notices required pursuant to Sections 21080.4 and 21092 for an environmental impact report shall be posted in the office of the county clerk of each county in which the project will be located and shall remain posted for a period of 30 days. The notice required pursuant to Section 21092 for a negative declaration shall be so posted for a period of 20 days, unless otherwise required by law to be posted for 30 days. The county clerk shall post the notices within 24 hours of receipt.

[Amended, Chapter 1130, Statutes of 1993]

21092.4. Consult with transportation planning agency

(a) For a project of statewide, regional, or areawide significance, the lead agency shall consult with transportation planning agencies and public agencies that have transportation facilities within their jurisdictions that could be affected by the project. Consultation shall be conducted in the same manner as for responsible agencies pursuant to this division, and shall be for the purpose of the lead agency obtaining information concerning the project's effect on major local arterials, public transit, freeways, highways, overpasses, on-ramps, off-ramps, and rail transit service within the jurisdiction of a transportation planning agency or a public agency that is consulted by the lead agency. A transportation planning agency or public agency that provides information to the lead agency shall be notified of, and provided with copies of, environmental documents pertaining to the project.

(b) As used in this section, "transportation facilities" includes major local arterials and public transit within five miles of the project site and freeways, highways, overpasses, on-ramps, off-ramps, and rail transit service within 10 miles of the project site.

[Amended, Chapter 707, Statutes of 2008]

21092.5. Responding to comments; hearing notice

(a) At least 10 days prior to certifying an environmental impact report, the lead agency shall provide a written proposed response to a public agency on comments made by that agency which conform with the requirements of this division. Proposed responses shall conform with the legal standards established for responses to comments on draft environmental impact reports. Copies of responses or the environmental document in which they are contained, prepared in conformance with other requirements of this division and the guidelines adopted pursuant to Section 21083, may be used to meet the requirements imposed by this section.

(b) The lead agency shall notify any public agency which comments on a negative declaration, of the public hearing or hearings, if any, on the project for which the negative declaration was prepared. If notice to the commenting public agency is provided pursuant to Section 21092, the notice shall satisfy the requirement of this subdivision.

(c) Nothing in this section requires the lead agency to respond to comments not received within the comment periods specified in this division, to reopen comment periods, or to delay acting on a negative declaration or environmental impact report.

[Added, Chapter 905, Statutes of 1991]

21092.6.   Lists relating to hazardous waste

(a) The lead agency shall consult the lists compiled pursuant to Section 65962.5 of the Government Code to determine whether the project and any alternatives are located on a site which is included on any list. The lead agency shall indicate whether a site is on any list not already identified by the applicant. The lead agency shall specify the list and include the information in the statement required pursuant to subdivision (f) of Section 65962.5 of the Government Code, in the notice required pursuant to Section 21080.4, a negative declaration, and a draft environmental impact report. The requirement in this section to specify any list shall not be construed to limit compliance with this division.

(b) If a project or any alternatives are located on a site which is included on any of the lists compiled pursuant to Section 65962.5 of the Government Code and the lead agency did not accurately specify or did not specify any list pursuant to subdivision (a), the California Environmental Protection Agency shall notify the lead agency specifying any list with the site when it receives notice pursuant to Section 21080.4, a negative declaration, and a draft environmental impact report. The California Environmental Protection Agency shall not be liable for failure to notify the lead agency pursuant to this subdivision.

[Amended, Chapter 548, Statutes of 2012]

21093.   Tiering of EIRs whenever feasible

(a) The Legislature finds and declares that tiering of environmental impact reports will promote construction of needed housing and other development projects by (1) streamlining regulatory procedures, (2) avoiding repetitive discussions of the same issues in successive environmental impact reports, and (3) ensuring that environmental impact reports prepared for later projects which are consistent with a previously approved policy, plan, program, or ordinance concentrate upon environmental effects which may be mitigated or avoided in connection with the decision on each later project. The Legislature further finds and declares that tiering is appropriate when it helps a public agency to focus upon the issues ripe for decision at each level of environmental review and in order to exclude duplicative analysis of environmental effects examined in previous environmental impact reports.

(b) To achieve this purpose, environmental impact reports shall be tiered whenever feasible, as determined by the lead agency.

[Amended, Chapter 418, Statutes of 1985]

21094. **Later projects may use tiering based on reports previously prepared and certified**

(a) Where a prior environmental impact report has been prepared and certified for a program, plan, policy, or ordinance, the lead agency for a later project that meets the requirements of this section shall examine significant effects of the later project upon the environment by using a tiered environmental impact report, except that the report on the later project is not required to examine those effects that the lead agency determines were either of the following:

(1) Mitigated or avoided pursuant to paragraph (1) of subdivision (a) of Section 21081 as a result of the prior environmental impact report.

(2) Examined at a sufficient level of detail in the prior environmental impact report to enable those effects to be mitigated or avoided by site-specific revisions, the imposition of conditions, or by other means in connection with the approval of the later project.

(b) This section applies only to a later project that the lead agency determines is all of the following:

(1) Consistent with the program, plan, policy, or ordinance for which an environmental impact report has been prepared and certified.

(2) Consistent with applicable local land use plans and zoning of the city, county, or city and county in which the later project would be located.

(3) Not subject to Section 21166.

(c) For purposes of compliance with this section, an initial study shall be prepared to assist the lead agency in making the determinations required by this section. The initial study shall analyze whether the later project may cause significant effects on the environment that were not examined in the prior environmental impact report.

(d) All public agencies that propose to carry out or approve the later project may utilize the prior environmental impact report and the environmental impact report on the later project to fulfill the requirements of Section 21081.

(e) When tiering is used pursuant to this section, an environmental impact report prepared for a later project shall refer to the prior environmental impact report and state where a copy of the prior environmental impact report may be examined.

(f) This section shall become operative on January 1, 2016.

[Added, Chapter 496, Statutes of 2010]

21094.5. **Infill projects; environmental impact reports**

(a) (1) If an environmental impact report was certified for a planning level decision of a city or county, the application of this division to the approval of an infill project shall be limited to the effects on the environment that (A) are specific to the project or to the project site and were not addressed as significant effects in the prior environmental impact report or (B) substantial new information shows the effects will be more significant than described in the prior environmental impact report. A lead agency's determination pursuant to this section shall be supported by substantial evidence.

(2) An effect of a project upon the environment shall not be considered a specific effect of the project or a significant effect that was not considered significant in a prior environmental impact report, or an effect that is more significant than was described in the prior environmental impact report if uniformly applicable development policies or standards adopted by the city, county, or the lead agency, would apply to the project and the lead agency makes a finding, based upon substantial evidence, that the development policies or standards will substantially mitigate that effect.

(b) If an infill project would result in significant effects that are specific to the project or the project site, or if the significant effects of the infill project were not addressed in the prior environmental impact report, or are more significant than the effects addressed in the prior environmental impact report, and if a mitigated negative declaration or a sustainable communities environmental assessment could not be otherwise adopted, an environmental impact report prepared for the project analyzing those effects shall be limited as follows:

(1) Alternative locations, densities, and building intensities to the project need not be considered.

(2) Growth inducing impacts of the project need not be considered.

(c) This section applies to an infill project that satisfies both of the following:

(1) The project satisfies any of the following:

(A) Is consistent with the general use designation, density, building intensity, and applicable policies specified for the project area in either a sustainable communities strategy or an alternative planning strategy for which the State Air Resources Board, pursuant to subparagraph (H) of paragraph (2) of subdivision (b) of Section 65080 of the Government Code, has accepted a metropolitan planning organization's determination that the sustainable communities strategy or the alternative planning strategy would, if implemented, achieve the greenhouse gas emission reduction targets.

(B) Consists of a small walkable community project located in an area designated by a city for that purpose.

(C) Is located within the boundaries of a metropolitan planning organization that has not yet adopted a sustainable communities strategy or alternative planning strategy, and the project has a residential density of at least 20 units per acre or a floor area ratio of at least 0.75.

(2) Satisfies all applicable statewide performance standards contained in the guidelines adopted pursuant to Section 21094.5.5.

(d) This section applies after the Secretary of the Natural Resources Agency adopts and certifies the guidelines establishing statewide standards pursuant to Section 21094.5.5.

(e) For the purposes of this section, the following terms mean the following:

(1) "Infill project" means a project that meets the following conditions:

(A) Consists of any one, or combination, of the following uses:

(i) Residential.

(ii) Retail or commercial, where no more than one-half of the project area is used for parking.

(iii) A transit station.

(iv) A school.

(v) A public office building.

(B) Is located within an urban area on a site that has been previously developed, or on a vacant site where at least 75 percent of the perimeter of the site adjoins, or is separated only by an improved public right-of-way from, parcels that are developed with qualified urban uses.

(2) "Planning level decision" means the enactment or amendment of a general plan, community plan, specific plan, or zoning code.

(3) "Prior environmental impact report" means the environmental impact report certified for a planning level decision, as supplemented by any subsequent or supplemental environmental impact reports, negative declarations, or addenda to those documents.

(4) "Small walkable community project" means a project that is in an incorporated city, which is not within the boundary of a metropolitan planning organization and that satisfies the following requirements:

(A) Has a project area of approximately one-quarter mile diameter of contiguous land completely within the existing incorporated boundaries of the city.

(B) Has a project area that includes a residential area adjacent to a retail downtown area.

(C) The project has a density of at least eight dwelling units per acre or a floor area ratio for retail or commercial use of not less than 0.50.

(5) "Urban area" includes either an incorporated city or an unincorporated area that is completely surrounded by one or more incorporated cities that meets both of the following criteria:

(A) The population of the unincorporated area and the population of the surrounding incorporated cities equal a population of 100,000 or more.

(B) The population density of the unincorporated area is equal to, or greater than, the population density of the surrounding cities.

[Added, Chapter 469, Statutes of 2011]

21094.5.5.   Preparation of guidelines for infill projects

(a) On or before July 1, 2012, the Office of Planning and Research shall prepare, develop, and transmit to the Natural Resources Agency for certification and adoption guidelines for the implementation of Section 21094.5 and the Secretary of the Natural Resources Agency, on or before January 1, 2013, shall certify and adopt the guidelines.

(b) The guidelines prepared pursuant to this section shall include statewide standards for infill projects that may be amended from time to time and promote all of the following:

(1) The implementation of the land use and transportation policies in the Sustainable Communities and Climate Protection Act of 2008 (Chapter 728 of the Statutes of 2008).

(2) The state planning priorities specified in Section 65041.1 of the Government Code and in the most recently adopted Environmental Goals and Policy Report issued by the Office of Planning and Research supporting infill development.

(3) The reduction of greenhouse gas emissions under the California Global Warming Solutions Act of 2006 (Division 25.5 (commencing with Section 38500) of the Health and Safety Code).

(4) The reduction in per capita water use pursuant to Section 10608.16 of the Water Code.

(5) The creation of a transit village development district consistent with Section 65460.1 of the Government Code.

(6) Substantial energy efficiency improvements, including improvements to projects related to transportation energy.

(7) Protection of public health, including the health of vulnerable populations from air or water pollution, or soil contamination.

(c) The standards for projects on infill sites shall be updated as frequently as necessary to ensure the protection of the environment.

[Added, Chapter 469, Statutes of 2011]

21095.　Agricultural land conversions

(a) The Resources Agency, in consultation with the Office of Planning and Research, shall develop an amendment to Appendix G of the state guidelines, for adoption pursuant to Section 21083, to provide lead agencies an optional methodology to ensure that significant effects on the environment of agricultural land conversions are quantitatively and consistently considered in the environmental review process.

(b) The Department of Conservation, in consultation with the United States Department of Agriculture pursuant to Section 658.6 of Title 7 of the Code of Federal Regulations, and in consultation with the Resources Agency and the Office of Planning and Research, shall develop a state model land evaluation and site assessment system, contingent upon the availability of funding from non-General Fund sources. The department shall seek funding for that purpose from non-General Fund sources, including, but not limited to, the United States Department of Agriculture.

(c) In lieu of developing an amendment to Appendix G of the state guidelines pursuant to subdivision (a), the Resources Agency may adopt the state model

70

land evaluation and site assessment system developed pursuant to subdivision (b) as that amendment to Appendix G.

[Added, Chapter 812, Statutes of 1993]

21096. Projects adjacent to airports

(a) If a lead agency prepares an environmental impact report for a project situated within airport land use compatibility plan boundaries, or, if an airport land use compatibility has not been adopted, for a project within two nautical miles of a public airport or public use airport, the Airport Land Use Planning Handbook published by the Division of Aeronautics of the Department of Transportation, in compliance with Section 21674.5 of the Public Utilities Code and other documents, shall be utilized as technical resources to assist in the preparation of the environmental impact report as the report relates to airport-related safety hazards and noise problems.

(b) A lead agency shall not adopt a negative declaration for a project described in subdivision (a) unless the lead agency considers whether the project will result in a safety hazard or noise problem for persons using the airport or for persons residing or working in the project area.

[Amended, Chapter 438, Statutes of 2002]

21098. Notification requirements in "low-level flight path", "military impact zone", and "special use airspace"

(a) For the purposes of this section, the following terms have the following meanings:

(1) "Low-level flight path" includes any flight path for any aircraft owned, maintained, or that is under the jurisdiction of the United States Department of Defense that flies lower than 1,500 feet above ground level, as indicated in the United States Department of Defense Flight Information Publication, "Area Planning Military Training Routes: North and South America (AP/1B)" published by the United States National Imagery and Mapping Agency.

(2) "Military impact zone" includes any area, including airspace, that meets both of the following criteria:

(A) Is within two miles of a military installation, including, but not limited to, any base, military airport, camp, post, station, yard, center, homeport facility for a ship, or any other military activity center that is under the jurisdiction of the United States Department of Defense.

(B) Covers greater than 500 acres of unincorporated land, or greater than 100 acres of city incorporated land.

(3) "Military service" means any branch of the United States Armed Forces.

(4) "Special use airspace" means the area underlying the airspace that is designated for training, research, development, or evaluation for a military service, as that area is established by the United States Department of Defense Flight Information Publication, "Area Planning: Special Use Airspace: North and South America (AP/1A)" published by the United States National Imagery and Mapping Agency.

(b) If the United States Department of Defense or a military service notifies a lead agency of the contact office and address for the military service and the specific boundaries of a low-level flight path, military impact zone, or special use airspace, the lead agency shall submit notices, as required pursuant to Sections 21080.4 and 21092, to the military service if the project is within those boundaries and any of the following apply:

(1) The project includes a general plan amendment.

(2) The project is of statewide, regional, or areawide significance.

(3) The project is required to be referred to the airport land use commission, or appropriately designated body, pursuant to Article 3.5 (commencing with Section 21670) of Chapter 4 of Part 1 of Division 9 of the Public Utilities Code.

(c) The requirement to submit notices imposed by this section does not apply to any of the following:

(1) Response actions taken pursuant to Chapter 6.8 (commencing with Section 25300) of Division 20 of the Health and Safety Code.

(2) Response actions taken pursuant to Chapter 6.85 (commencing with Section 25396) of Division 20 of the Health and Safety Code.

(3) Sites subject to corrective action orders issued pursuant to Section 25187 of the Health and Safety Code.

(d) (1) The effect or potential effect that a project may have on military activities does not itself constitute an adverse effect on the environment for the purposes of this division.

(2) Notwithstanding paragraph (1), a project's impact on military activities may cause, or be associated with, adverse effects on the environment that are subject to the requirements of this division, including, but not limited to, Section 21081.

[Amended, Chapter 142, Statutes of 2019]

Chapter 2.7. Modernization of Transportation Analysis for Transit-Oriented Infill Projects

21099.   **Revisions to guidelines; transit priority areas**

(a) For purposes of this section, the following terms mean the following:

(1) "Employment center project" means a project located on property zoned for commercial uses with a floor area ratio of no less than 0.75 and that is located within a transit priority area.

(2) "Floor area ratio" means the ratio of gross building area of the development, excluding structured parking areas, proposed for the project divided by the net lot area.

(3) "Gross building area" means the sum of all finished areas of all floors of a building included within the outside faces of its exterior walls.

(4) "Infill site" means a lot located within an urban area that has been previously developed, or on a vacant site where at least 75 percent of the perimeter of the site adjoins, or is separated only by an improved public right-of-way from, parcels that are developed with qualified urban uses.

(5) "Lot" means all parcels utilized by the project.

(6) "Net lot area" means the area of a lot, excluding publicly dedicated land and private streets that meet local standards, and other public use areas as determined by the local land use authority.

(7) "Transit priority area" means an area within one-half mile of a major transit stop that is existing or planned, if the planned stop is scheduled to be completed within the planning horizon included in a Transportation Improvement Program *or applicable regional transportation plan*.

(b) (1) The Office of Planning and Research shall prepare, develop, and transmit to the Secretary of the Natural Resources Agency for certification and adoption proposed revisions to the guidelines adopted pursuant to Section 21083 establishing criteria for determining the significance of transportation impacts of projects within transit priority areas. Those criteria shall promote the reduction of greenhouse gas emissions, the development of multimodal transportation networks, and a diversity of land uses. In developing the criteria, the office shall recommend potential metrics to measure transportation impacts that may include, but are not limited to, vehicle miles traveled, vehicle miles traveled per capita, automobile trip generation rates, or automobile trips generated. The office may also establish criteria for models used to analyze transportation impacts to ensure the models are accurate, reliable, and consistent with the intent of this section.

(2) Upon certification of the guidelines by the Secretary of the Natural Resources Agency pursuant to this section, automobile delay, as described solely by level of service or similar measures of vehicular capacity or traffic congestion, shall not be considered a significant impact on the environment pursuant to this division, except in locations specifically identified in the guidelines, if any.

(3) This subdivision does not relieve a public agency of the requirement to analyze a project's potentially significant transportation impacts related to air quality, noise, safety, or any other impact associated with transportation. The methodology established by these guidelines shall not create a presumption that a project will not result in significant impacts related to air quality, noise, safety, or any other impact associated with transportation. Notwithstanding the foregoing, the adequacy of parking for a project shall not support a finding of significance pursuant to this section.

(4) This subdivision does not preclude the application of local general plan policies, zoning codes, conditions of approval, thresholds, or any other planning requirements pursuant to the police power or any other authority.

(5) On or before July 1, 2014, the Office of Planning and Research shall circulate a draft revision prepared pursuant to paragraph (1).

(c) (1) The Office of Planning and Research may adopt guidelines pursuant to Section 21083 establishing alternative metrics to the metrics used for traffic levels of service for transportation impacts outside transit priority areas. The alternative metrics may include the retention of traffic levels of service, where appropriate and as determined by the office.

(2) This subdivision shall not affect the standard of review that would apply to the new guidelines adopted pursuant to this section.

(d) (1) Aesthetic and parking impacts of a residential, mixed-use residential, or employment center project on an infill site within a transit priority area shall not be considered significant impacts on the environment.

(2) (A) This subdivision does not affect, change, or modify the authority of a lead agency to consider aesthetic impacts pursuant to local design review ordinances or other discretionary powers provided by other laws or policies.

(B) For the purposes of this subdivision, aesthetic impacts do not include impacts on historical or cultural resources.

(e) This section does not affect the authority of a public agency to establish or adopt thresholds of significance that are more protective of the environment.

[Amended, Chapter 466, Statutes of 2019]

Chapter 3. State Agencies, Boards and Commissions

21100. **Requires preparation and certification of EIRs; cumulative impact reports**

(a) All lead agencies shall prepare, or cause to be prepared by contract, and certify the completion of, an environmental impact report on any project which they propose to carry out or approve that may have a significant effect on the environment. Whenever feasible, a standard format shall be used for environmental impact reports.

(b) The environmental impact report shall include a detailed statement setting forth all of the following:

(1) All significant effects on the environment of the proposed project.

(2) In a separate section:

(A) Any significant effects on the environment that cannot be avoided if the project is implemented.

(B) Any significant effect on the environment that would be irreversible if the project is implemented.

(3) Mitigation measures proposed to minimize the significant effects on the environment, including, but not limited to, measures to reduce the wasteful, inefficient, and unnecessary consumption of energy.

(4) Alternatives to the proposed project.

(5) The growth-inducing impacts of the proposed project.

(c) The report shall also contain a statement briefly indicating the reasons for determining that various effects on the environment of a project are not significant and consequently have not been discussed in detail in the environmental impact report.

(d) For purposes of this section, any significant effect on the environment shall be limited to substantial, or potentially substantial, adverse changes in physical conditions which exist within the area as defined in Section 21060.5.

(e) Previously approved land use documents, including, but not limited to, general plans, specific plans, and local coastal plans, may be used in cumulative impact analysis.

[Amended, Chapter 1230, Statutes of 1994]

21100.1.   Information not required for some EIRs

The information described in subparagraph (B) of paragraph (2) of subdivision (b) of Section 21100 shall be required only in environmental impact reports prepared in connection with the following:

(a) The adoption, amendment, or enactment of a plan, policy, or ordinance of a public agency.

(b) The adoption by local agency formation commission of a resolution making determinations.

(c) A project which will be subject to the requirement for preparing an environmental impact statement pursuant to the requirements of the National Environmental Policy Act of 1969.

[Amended, Chapter 1230, Statutes of 1994]

21100.2.   State agency time limits for EIRs and negative declarations; report preparation under contract

(a) (1) For projects described in subdivision (c) of Section 21065, each state agency shall establish, by resolution or order, time limits that do not exceed the following:

(A) One year for completing and certifying environmental impact reports.

(B) One hundred eighty days for completing and adopting negative declarations.

(2) The time limits specified in paragraph (1) shall apply only to those circumstances in which the state agency is the lead agency for a project. These resolutions or orders may establish different time limits for different types or classes of projects, but all limits shall be measured from the date on which an application requesting approval of the project is received and accepted as complete by the state agency.

(3) No application for a project may be deemed incomplete for lack of a waiver of time periods prescribed in state regulations.

(4) The resolutions or orders required by this section may provide for a reasonable extension of the time period in the event that compelling circumstances justify additional time and the project applicant consents thereto.

(b) If a draft environmental impact report, environmental impact report, or focused environmental impact report is prepared under a contract to a state agency, the contract shall be executed within 45 days from the date on which the state agency sends a notice of preparation pursuant to Section 21080.4. The state agency may take longer to execute the contract if the project applicant and the state agency mutually agree to an extension of the time limit provided by this subdivision.

(c) This section shall become operative January 1, 2018.

[Added, Chapter 487, Statutes of 2012]

21101. Federal projects

In regard to any proposed federal project in this state which may have a significant effect on the environment and on which the state officially comments, the state officials responsible for such comments shall include in their report a detailed statement setting forth the matters specified in Section 21100 prior to transmitting the comments of the state to the federal government. No report shall be transmitted to the federal government unless it includes such a detailed statement as to the matters specified in Section 21100.

21102. Exempts feasibility and planning studies from funding requests by state agency

No state agency, board, or commission shall request funds, nor shall any state agency, board, or commission which authorizes expenditures of funds, other than funds appropriated in the Budget Act, authorize funds for expenditure for any project, other than a project involving only feasibility or planning studies for possible future actions which the agency, board, or commission has not approved, adopted or funded, which may have a significant effect on the environment unless such request or authorization is accompanied by an environmental impact report.

Feasibility and planning studies exempted by this section from the preparation of an environmental impact report shall nevertheless include consideration of environmental factors.

[Amended, Chapter 1154, Statutes of 1972]

21104. Lead agency shall consult with certain agencies and may consult with person who has special expertise

(a) Prior to completing an environmental impact report, the state lead agency shall consult with, and obtain comments from, each responsible agency, trustee agency, any public agency that has jurisdiction by law with respect to the project, and any city or county that borders on a city or county within which the project is located unless otherwise designated annually by agreement between the state lead agency and the city or county, and may consult with any person who has special expertise with respect to any environmental impact involved. In the case of a project described in subdivision (c) of Section 21065, the state lead agency shall, upon the request of the applicant, provide for early consultation to identify the range of actions, alternatives, mitigation measures, and significant effects to be analyzed in depth in the environmental impact report. The state lead agency may consult with persons identified by the applicant who the applicant believes will be concerned with the environmental effects of the project and may consult with members of the public who have made a written request to be consulted on the project. A request by the applicant for early consultation shall be made not later than 30 days after the determination required by Section 21080.1 with respect to the project.

(b) The state lead agency shall consult with, and obtain comments from, the State Air Resources Board in preparing an environmental impact report on a highway or freeway project, as to the air pollution impact of the potential vehicular use of the highway or freeway.

(c) A responsible agency or other public agency shall only make substantive comments regarding those activities involved in a project that are within an area of expertise of the agency or that are required to be carried out or approved by the agency. Those comments shall be supported by specific documentation.

[Amended, Chapter 744, Statutes of 2004]

21104.2.   Department of Fish and Game consultation on any endangered or threatened species

The state lead agency shall consult with, and obtain written findings from, the Department of Fish and Game in preparing an environmental impact report on a project, as to the impact of the project on the continued existence of any endangered species or threatened species pursuant to Article 4 (commencing with Section 2090) of Chapter 1.5 of Division 3 of the Fish and Game Code.

[Added, Chapter 1240, Statutes of 1984]

21105.   State lead agency review and budgetary process to include EIR

The state lead agency shall include the environmental impact report as a part of the regular project report used in the existing review and budgetary process. It shall be available to the Legislature. It shall also be available for inspection by any member of the general public, who may secure a copy thereof by paying for the actual cost of such a copy. It shall be filed by the state lead agency with the appropriate local planning agency of any city, county, or city and county which will be affected by the project.

[Amended, Chapter 1200, Statutes of 1977]

21106.   States funds for environmental protection

All state agencies, boards, and commissions shall request in their budgets the funds necessary to protect the environment in relation to problems caused by their activities.

21108.   State agency files notice of determination

(a) If a state agency approves or determines to carry out a project that is subject to this division, the state agency shall file *a* notice of determination with the Office of Planning and Research. The notice shall identify the person or persons in subdivision (b) or (c) of Section 21065, as reflected in the agency's record of proceedings, and indicate the determination of the state agency whether the project will, or will not, have a significant effect on the environment and shall indicate whether an environmental impact report has been prepared pursuant to this division.

(b) If a state agency determines that a project is not subject to this division pursuant to subdivision (b) of Section 21080 or Section 21172, and the state agency approves or determines to carry out the project, the state agency or the person specified in subdivision (b) or (c) of Section 21065 may file *a* notice of *exemption* with the Office of Planning and Research. A notice filed pursuant to this subdivision shall identify the person or persons in subdivision (b) or (c) of Section 21065, as reflected in the agency's record of proceedings. A notice filed pursuant to this subdivision by a person specified in subdivision (b) or (c) of Section 21065 shall have a certificate of determination attached to it issued by the state agency responsible for making the determination that the project is not subject to this division pursuant to subdivision (b) of Section 21080 or pursuant to Section 21172. The certificate of determination may be in the form of a certified copy of an existing document or record of the state agency.

(c) A notice filed pursuant to this section shall be available for public inspection, and a list of these notices shall be posted on a weekly basis in the Office of Planning and Research. Each list shall remain posted for a period of 30 days. The Office of Planning and Research shall retain each notice for not less than 12 months.

[Amended, Chapter 466, Statutes of 2019]

Chapter 4. Local Agencies

21150. Funding for feasibility and or planning studies

State agencies, boards, and commissions, responsible for allocating state or federal funds on a project-by-project basis to local agencies for any project which may have a significant effect on the environment, shall require from the responsible local governmental agency a detailed statement setting forth the matters specified in Section 21100 prior to the allocation of any funds other than funds solely for projects involving only feasibility or planning studies for possible future actions which the agency, board, or commission has not approved, adopted, or funded.

[Amended, Chapter 1154, Statutes of 1972]

21151. EIRs by local agencies: appeals permitted

(a) All local agencies shall prepare, or cause to be prepared by contract, and certify the completion of, an environmental impact report on any project that they intend to carry out or approve which may have a significant effect on the environment. When a report is required by Section 65402 of the Government Code, the environmental impact report may be submitted as a part of that report.

(b) For purposes of this section, any significant effect on the environment shall be limited to substantial, or potentially substantial, adverse changes in physical conditions which exist within the area as defined in Section 21060.5.

(c) If a nonelected decisionmaking body of a local lead agency certifies an environmental impact report, approves a negative declaration or mitigated negative declaration, or determines that a project is not subject to this division, that certification, approval, or determination may be appealed to the agency's elected decisionmaking body, if any.

[Amended, Chapter 1121, Statutes of 2002]

21151.1. Waste burning activities; exemptions

(a) Notwithstanding paragraph (6) of subdivision (b) of Section 21080, or Section 21080.5 or 21084, or any other provision of law, except as provided in this section, a lead agency shall prepare or cause to be prepared by contract, and certify the completion of, an environmental impact report or, if appropriate, a modification, addendum, or supplement to an existing environmental impact report, for a project involving any of the following:

    (1) The burning of municipal wastes, hazardous waste, or refuse-derived fuel, including, but not limited to, tires, if the project is either of the following:

        (A) The construction of a new facility.

        (B) The expansion of an existing facility that burns hazardous waste that would increase its permitted capacity by more than 10 percent.

    (2) The initial issuance of a hazardous waste facilities permit to a land disposal facility, as defined in subdivision (d) of Section 25199.1 of the Health and Safety Code.

    (3) The initial issuance of a hazardous waste facilities permit pursuant to Section 25200 of the Health and Safety Code to an offsite large treatment facility, as defined pursuant to subdivision (d) of Section 25205.1 of the Health and Safety Code.

    (4) A base reuse plan as defined in Section 21083.8.1. The Legislature hereby finds that no reimbursement is required pursuant to Section 6 of Article XIII B of the California Constitution for an environmental impact report for a base reuse plan if an environmental impact report is otherwise required for that base reuse plan pursuant to any other provision of this division.

(b) For purposes of clause (ii) of subparagraph (A) of paragraph (1) of subdivision (a), the amount of expansion of an existing facility shall be calculated by comparing the proposed facility capacity with whichever of the following is applicable:

    (1) The facility capacity authorized in the facility's hazardous waste facilities permit pursuant to Section 25200 of the Health and Safety Code or its grant of interim status pursuant to Section 25200.5 of the Health and Safety Code, or the facility capacity authorized in a state or local agency permit allowing the construction or operation of a facility for the burning of hazardous waste, granted before January 1, 1990.

    (2) The facility capacity authorized in the facility's original hazardous waste facilities permit, grant of interim status, or a state or local agency permit allowing the construction or operation of a facility for the burning of hazardous waste, granted on or after January 1, 1990.

(c) For purposes of paragraphs (2) and (3) of subdivision (a), the initial issuance of a hazardous waste facilities permit does not include the issuance of a closure or postclosure permit pursuant to Chapter 6.5 (commencing with Section 25100) of Division 20 of the Health and Safety Code.

(d) Paragraph (1) of subdivision (a) does not apply to a project that does any of the following:

(1) Exclusively burns digester gas produced from manure or any other solid or semisolid animal waste.

(2) Exclusively burns methane gas produced from a disposal site, as defined in Section 40122, that is used only for the disposal of solid waste, as defined in Section 40191.

(3) Exclusively burns forest, agricultural, wood, or other biomass wastes.

(4) Exclusively burns hazardous waste in an incineration unit that is transportable and that is either at a site for not longer than three years or is part of a remedial or removal action. For purposes of this paragraph, "transportable" means any equipment which performs a "treatment" as defined in Section 66216 of Title 22 of the California Code of Regulations, and that is transported on a vehicle as defined in Section 66230 of Title 22 of the California Code of Regulations, as those sections read on June 1, 1991.

(5) Exclusively burns refinery waste in a flare on the site of generation.

(6) Exclusively burns in a flare methane gas produced at a municipal sewage treatment plant.

(7) Exclusively burns hazardous waste, or exclusively burns hazardous waste as a supplemental fuel, as part of a research, development, or demonstration project that, consistent with federal regulations implementing the Resource Conservation and Recovery Act of 1976, as amended (42 U.S.C. Sec. 6901 et seq.), has been determined to be innovative and experimental by the Department of Toxic Substances Control and that is limited in type and quantity of waste to that necessary to determine the efficacy and performance capabilities of the technology or process. However, a facility that operated as a research, development, or demonstration project and for which an application is thereafter submitted for a hazardous waste facility permit for operation other than as a research, development, or demonstration project shall be considered a new facility for the burning of hazardous waste and shall be subject to subdivision (a) of Section 21151.1.

(8) Exclusively burns soils contaminated only with petroleum fuels or the vapors from these soils.

(9) Exclusively treats less than 3,000 pounds of hazardous waste per day in a thermal processing unit operated in the absence of open flame, and submits a worst-case health risk assessment of the technology to the Department of Toxic Substances Control for review and distribution to the interested public. This assessment shall be prepared in accordance with guidelines set forth in the Air Toxics Assessment Manual of the California Air Pollution Control Officers Association.

(10) Exclusively burns less than 1,200 pounds per day of medical waste, as defined in Section 117690 of the Health and Safety Code, on hospital sites.

(11) Exclusively burns chemicals and fuels as part of firefighter training.

(12) Exclusively conducts open burns of explosives subject to the requirements of the air pollution control district or air quality management district and in compliance with OSHA and Cal-OSHA regulations.

(13) Exclusively conducts onsite burning of less than 3,000 pounds per day of fumes directly from a manufacturing or commercial process.

(14) Exclusively conducts onsite burning of hazardous waste in an industrial furnace that recovers hydrogen chloride from the flue gas if the hydrogen chloride is subsequently sold, distributed in commerce, or used in a manufacturing process at the site where the hydrogen chloride is recovered, and the burning is in compliance with the requirements of the air pollution control district or air quality management district and the Department of Toxic Substances Control.

(e) Paragraph (1) of subdivision (a) does not apply to a project for which the State Energy Resources Conservation and Development Commission has assumed jurisdiction under Chapter 6 (commencing with Section 25500) of Division 15.

(f) Paragraphs (2) and (3) of subdivision (a) do not apply if the facility only manages hazardous waste that is identified or listed pursuant to Section 25140 or 25141 of the Health and Safety Code on or after January 1, 1992, but not before that date, or only conducts activities that are regulated pursuant to Chapter 6.5 (commencing with Section 25100) of Division 20 of the Health and Safety Code on or after January 1, 1992, but not before that date.

(g) This section does not exempt a project from any other requirement of this division.

(h) For purposes of this section, offsite facility means a facility that serves more than one generator of hazardous waste.

[Amended, Chapter 548, Statutes of 2012]

21151.2.   School site review

To promote the safety of pupils and comprehensive community planning the governing board of each school district before acquiring title to property for a new school site or for an addition to a present school site, shall give the planning commission having jurisdiction notice in writing of the proposed acquisition. The planning commission shall investigate the proposed site and within 30 days after receipt of the notice shall submit to the governing board a written report of the investigation and its recommendations concerning acquisition of the site. The governing board shall not acquire title to the property until the report of the planning commission has been received. If the report does not favor the acquisition of the property for a school site, or for an addition to a present school site, the governing board of the school district shall not acquire title to the property until 30 days after the commission's report is received.

[Added, Chapter 1452, Statutes of 1987]

21151.4.   Hazardous materials near schools

(a) An environmental impact report shall not be certified or a negative declaration shall not be approved for any project involving the construction or alteration of a facility within one-fourth of a mile of a school that might reasonably be anticipated to emit hazardous air emissions, or that would handle an extremely hazardous substance or a mixture containing extremely hazardous substances in a quantity equal to or greater than the state threshold quantity specified pursuant to subdivision (j) of Section 25532 of the Health and Safety Code, that may pose a health or safety hazard to persons who would attend or would be employed at the school, unless both of the following occur:

(1) The lead agency preparing the environmental impact report or negative declaration has consulted with the school district having jurisdiction regarding the potential impact of the project on the school.

(2) The school district has been given written notification of the project not less than 30 days prior to the proposed certification of the environmental impact report or approval of the negative declaration.

(b) As used in this section, the following definitions apply:

(1) "Extremely hazardous substance" means an extremely hazardous substance as defined pursuant to paragraph (2) of subdivision (g) of Section 25532 of the Health and Safety Code.

(2) "Hazardous air emissions" means emissions into the ambient air of air contaminants that have been identified as a toxic air contaminant by the State Air Resources Board or by the air pollution control officer for the jurisdiction in which the project is located. As determined by the air pollution control officer, hazardous air emissions also means emissions into the ambient air of a substance identified in subdivisions (a) to (f), inclusive, of Section 44321 of the Health and Safety Code.

[Amended, Chapter 148, Statutes of 2008]

21151.5. Local agency time limits for, EIRs, negative declarations and report preparation contracts

(a) (1) For projects described in subdivision (c) of Section 21065, each local agency shall establish, by ordinance or resolution, time limits that do not exceed the following:

(A) One year for completing and certifying environmental impact reports.

(B) One hundred eighty days for completing and adopting negative declarations.

(2) The time limits specified in paragraph (1) shall apply only to those circumstances in which the local agency is the lead agency for a project. These ordinances or resolutions may establish different time limits for different types or classes of projects and different types of environmental impact reports, but all limits shall be measured from the date on which an application requesting approval of the project is received and accepted as complete by the local agency.

(3) No application for a project may be deemed incomplete for lack of a waiver of time periods prescribed by local ordinance or resolution.

(4) The ordinances or resolutions required by this section may provide for a reasonable extension of the time period in the event that compelling

circumstances justify additional time and the project applicant consents thereto.

(b) If a draft environmental impact report, environmental impact report, or focused environmental impact report is prepared under a contract to a local agency, the contract shall be executed within 45 days from the date on which the local agency sends a notice of preparation pursuant to Section 21080.4. The local agency may take longer to execute the contract if the project applicant and the local agency mutually agree to an extension of the time limit provided by this subdivision.

[Amended, Chapter 808, Statutes of 1996]

21151.7.   Open pit mining operations

Notwithstanding any other provision of law, a lead agency shall prepare or cause to be prepared by contract, and certify the completion of, an environmental impact report for any open-pit mining operation that is subject to the permit requirements or reclamation plan requirements of the Surface Mining and Reclamation Act of 1975 (Chapter 9 (commencing with Section 2710) of Division 2) and utilizes a cyanide heap-leaching process for the purpose of producing gold or other metallic minerals.

[Amended, Chapter 1154, Statutes of 2002]

21151.8.   Schoolsites and hazardous substances

(a) An environmental impact report shall not be certified or a negative declaration shall not be approved for a project involving the purchase of a schoolsite or the construction of a new elementary or secondary school by a school district unless all of the following occur:

(1) The environmental impact report or negative declaration includes information that is needed to determine if the property proposed to be purchased, or to be constructed upon, is any of the following:

(A) The site of a current or former hazardous waste disposal site or solid waste disposal site and, if so, whether the wastes have been removed.

(B) A hazardous substance release site identified by the Department of Toxic Substances Control in a current list adopted pursuant to Section 25356 of the Health and Safety Code for removal or remedial action pursuant to Chapter 6.8 (commencing with Section 25300) of Division 20 of the Health and Safety Code.

(C) A site that contains one or more pipelines, situated underground or aboveground, that carries hazardous substances, extremely hazardous substances, or hazardous wastes, unless the pipeline is a natural gas line that is used only to supply natural gas to that school or neighborhood, or other nearby schools.

(D) A site that is within 500 feet of the edge of the closest traffic lane of a freeway or other busy traffic corridor.

(2) (A) The school district, as the lead agency, in preparing the environmental impact report or negative declaration has notified in writing and consulted with the administering agency in which the proposed

schoolsite is located, pursuant to Section 2735.3 of Title 19 of the California Code of Regulations, and with any air pollution control district or air quality management district having jurisdiction in the area, to identify both permitted and nonpermitted facilities within that district's authority, including, but not limited to, freeways and busy traffic corridors, large agricultural operations, and railyards, within one-fourth of a mile of the proposed schoolsite, that might reasonably be anticipated to emit hazardous emissions or handle hazardous or extremely hazardous substances or waste. The notification by the school district, as the lead agency, shall include a list of the locations for which information is sought.

(B) Each administering agency, air pollution control district, or air quality management district receiving written notification from a lead agency to identify facilities pursuant to subparagraph (A) shall provide the requested information and provide a written response to the lead agency within 30 days of receiving the notification. The environmental impact report or negative declaration shall be conclusively presumed to comply with subparagraph (A) as to the area of responsibility of an agency that does not respond within 30 days.

(C) If the school district, as a lead agency, has carried out the consultation required by subparagraph (A), the environmental impact report or the negative declaration shall be conclusively presumed to comply with subparagraph (A), notwithstanding any failure of the consultation to identify an existing facility or other pollution source specified in subparagraph (A).

(3) The governing board of the school district makes one of the following written findings:

(A) Consultation identified no facilities of this type or other significant pollution sources specified in paragraph (2).

(B) The facilities or other pollution sources specified in paragraph (2) exist, but one of the following conditions applies:

    (i) The health risks from the facilities or other pollution sources do not and will not constitute an actual or potential endangerment of public health to persons who would attend or be employed at the proposed school.

    (ii) Corrective measures required under an existing order by another agency having jurisdiction over the facilities or other pollution sources will, before the school is occupied, result in the mitigation of all chronic or accidental hazardous air emissions to levels that do not constitute an actual or potential endangerment of public health to persons who would attend or be employed at the proposed school. If the governing board makes a finding pursuant to this clause, it shall also make a subsequent finding, prior to occupancy of the school, that the emissions have been so mitigated.

      (iii) For a schoolsite with a boundary that is within 500 feet of the edge of the closest traffic lane of a freeway or other busy traffic corridor, the governing board of the school district determines, through analysis pursuant to paragraph (2) of subdivision (b) of Section 44360 of the Health and Safety Code, based on appropriate air dispersion modeling, and after considering any potential mitigation measures, that the air quality at the proposed site is such that neither short-term nor long-term exposure poses significant health risks to pupils.

   (C) The facilities or other pollution sources specified in paragraph (2) exist, but conditions in clause (i), (ii), or (iii) of subparagraph (B) cannot be met, and the school district is unable to locate an alternative site that is suitable due to a severe shortage of sites that meet the requirements in subdivision (a) of Section 17213 of the Education Code. If the governing board makes this finding, the governing board shall adopt a statement of overriding considerations pursuant to Section 15093 of Title 14 of the California Code of Regulations.

(b) As used in this section, the following definitions shall apply:

   (1) "Hazardous substance" means any substance defined in Section 25316 of the Health and Safety Code.

   (2) "Extremely hazardous substances" means an extremely hazardous substance as defined pursuant to paragraph (2) of subdivision (g) of Section 25532 of the Health and Safety Code.

   (3) "Hazardous waste" means any waste defined in Section 25117 of the Health and Safety Code.

   (4) "Hazardous waste disposal site" means any site defined in Section 25114 of the Health and Safety Code.

   (5) "Hazardous air emissions" means emissions into the ambient air of air contaminants that have been identified as a toxic air contaminant by the State Air Resources Board or by the air pollution control officer for the jurisdiction in which the project is located. As determined by the air pollution control officer, hazardous air emissions also means emissions into the ambient air from any substances identified in subdivisions (a) to (f), inclusive, of Section 44321 of the Health and Safety Code.

   (6) "Administering agency" means an agency authorized pursuant to Section 25502 of the Health and Safety Code to implement and enforce Chapter 6.95 (commencing with Section 25500) of Division 20 of the Health and Safety Code.

   (7) "Handle" means handle as defined in Article 1 (commencing with Section 25500) of Chapter 6.95 of Division 20 of the Health and Safety Code.

   (8) "Facilities" means any source with a potential to use, generate, emit, or discharge hazardous air pollutants, including, but not limited to, pollutants that meet the definition of a hazardous substance, and whose process or operation is identified as an emission source pursuant to the most recent list of source categories published by the California Air Resources Board.

(9) "Freeway or other busy traffic corridors" means those roadways that, on an average day, have traffic in excess of 50,000 vehicles in a rural area, as defined in Section 50101 of the Health and Safety Code, and 100,000 vehicles in an urban area, as defined in Section 50104.7 of the Health and Safety Code.

[Amended, Chapter 148, Statutes of 2008]

21151.9. Projects that are subject to this division

Whenever a city or county determines that a project, as defined in Section 10912 of the Water Code, is subject to this division, it shall comply with Part 2.10 (commencing with Section 10910) of Division 6 of the Water Code.

[Amended, Chapter 643, Statutes of 2001]

21152. File notices with County Clerk

(a) If a local agency approves or determines to carry out a project that is subject to this division, the local agency shall file *a* notice of determination within five working days after the approval or determination becomes final, with the county clerk of each county in which the project will be located. The notice shall identify the person or persons in subdivision (b) or (c) of Section 21065, as reflected in the agency's record of proceedings, and indicate the determination of the local agency whether the project will, or will not, have a significant effect on the environment and shall indicate whether an environmental impact report has been prepared pursuant to this division. The notice shall also include certification that the final environmental impact report, if one was prepared, together with comments and responses, is available to the general public.

(b) If a local agency determines that a project is not subject to this division pursuant to subdivision (b) of Section 21080 or pursuant to Section 21172, and the local agency approves or determines to carry out the project, the local agency or the person specified in subdivision (b) or (c) of Section 21065 may file a notice of *exemption* with the county clerk of each county in which the project will be located. A notice filed pursuant to this subdivision shall identify the person or persons in subdivision (b) or (c) of Section 21065, as reflected in the agency's record of proceedings. A notice filed pursuant to this subdivision by a person specified in subdivision (b) or (c) of Section 21065 shall have a certificate of determination attached to it issued by the local agency responsible for making the determination that the project is not subject to this division pursuant to subdivision (b) of Section 21080 or Section 21172. The certificate of determination may be in the form of a certified copy of an existing document or record of the local agency.

(c) A notice filed pursuant to this section shall be available for public inspection, and shall be posted within 24 hours of receipt in the office of the county clerk. A notice shall remain posted for a period of 30 days. Thereafter, the clerk shall return the notice to the local agency with a notation of the period it was posted. The local agency shall retain the notice for not less than 12 months.

[Amended, Chapter 466, Statutes of 2019]

21152.1.   Notice Requirement; OPR

(a) When a local agency determines that a project is not subject to this division pursuant to Section 21159.22, 21159.23, or 21159.24, and it approves or determines to carry out that project, the local agency or the person specified in subdivision (b) or (c) of Section 21065, shall file *a* notice of *exemption* with the Office of Planning and Research.

(b) All notices filed pursuant to this section shall be available for public inspection, and a list of these notices shall be posted on a weekly basis in the Office of Planning and Research. Each list shall remain posted for a period of 30 days.

(c) Failure to file the notice required by this section does not affect the validity of a project.

(d) Nothing in this section affects the time limitations contained in Section 21167.

[Amended, Chapter 466, Statutes of 2019]

21153.   Consultations with agencies and applicants

(a) Prior to completing an environmental impact report, every local lead agency shall consult with, and obtain comments from, each responsible agency, trustee agency, any public agency that has jurisdiction by law with respect to the project, and any city or county that borders on a city or county within which the project is located unless otherwise designated annually by agreement between the local lead agency and the city or county, and may consult with any person who has special expertise with respect to any environmental impact involved. In the case of a project described in subdivision (c) of Section 21065, the local lead agency shall, upon the request of the project applicant, provide for early consultation to identify the range of actions, alternatives, mitigation measures, and significant effects to be analyzed in depth in the environmental impact report. The local lead agency may consult with persons identified by the project applicant who the applicant believes will be concerned with the environmental effects of the project and may consult with members of the public who have made written request to be consulted on the project. A request by the project applicant for early consultation shall be made not later than 30 days after the date that the determination required by Section 21080.1 was made with respect to the project. The local lead agency may charge and collect a fee from the project applicant in an amount that does not exceed the actual costs of the consultations.

(b) In the case of a project described in subdivision (a) of Section 21065, the lead agency may provide for early consultation to identify the range of actions, alternatives, mitigation measures, and significant effects to be analyzed in depth in the environmental impact report. At the request of the lead agency, the Office of Planning and Research shall ensure that each responsible agency, and any public agency that has jurisdiction by law with respect to the project, is notified regarding any early consultation.

(c) A responsible agency or other public agency shall only make substantive comments regarding those activities involved in a project that are within an area of expertise of the agency or that are required to be carried out or approved by the agency. Those comments shall be supported by specific documentation.

[Amended, Chapter 744, Statutes of 2004]

21154. State ordered projects

Whenever any state agency, board, or commission issues an order which requires a local agency to carry out a project which may have a significant effect on the environment, any environmental impact report which the local agency may prepare shall be limited to consideration of those factors and alternatives which will not conflict with such order.

[Added, Chapter 1154, Statutes of 1972]

Chapter 4.2. Implementation of the Sustainable Communities Strategy

21155. Purpose and definitions

(a) This chapter applies only to a transit priority project that is consistent with the general use designation, density, building intensity, and applicable policies specified for the project area in either a sustainable communities strategy or an alternative planning strategy, for which the State Air Resources Board, pursuant to subparagraph (H) of paragraph (2) of subdivision (b) of Section 65080 of the Government Code, has accepted a metropolitan planning organization's determination that the sustainable communities strategy or the alternative planning strategy would, if implemented, achieve the greenhouse gas emission reduction targets.

(b) For purposes of this chapter, a transit priority project shall (1) contain at least 50 percent residential use, based on total building square footage and, if the project contains between 26 percent and 50 percent nonresidential uses, a floor area ratio of not less than 0.75; (2) provide a minimum net density of at least 20 dwelling units per acre; and (3) be within one-half mile of a major transit stop or high-quality transit corridor included in a regional transportation plan. A major transit stop is as defined in Section 21064.3, except that, for purposes of this section, it also includes major transit stops that are included in the applicable regional transportation plan. For purposes of this section, a high-quality transit corridor means a corridor with fixed route bus service with service intervals no longer than 15 minutes during peak commute hours. A project shall be considered to be within one-half mile of a major transit stop or high-quality transit corridor if all parcels within the project have no more than 25 percent of their area farther than one-half mile from the stop or corridor and if not more than 10 percent of the residential units or 100 units, whichever is less, in the project are farther than one-half mile from the stop or corridor.

[Added, Chapter 728, Statutes of 2008]

21155.1. Transit project; applicability requirements

If the legislative body finds, after conducting a public hearing, that a transit priority project meets all of the requirements of subdivisions (a) and (b) and one of the requirements of subdivision (c), the transit priority project is declared to be a sustainable communities project and shall be exempt from this division.

(a) The transit priority project complies with all of the following environmental criteria:

    (1) The transit priority project and other projects approved prior to the approval of the transit priority project but not yet built can be adequately served by existing utilities, and the transit priority project applicant has paid, or has committed to pay, all applicable in-lieu or development fees.

    (2) (A) The site of the transit priority project does not contain wetlands or riparian areas and does not have significant value as a wildlife habitat, and the transit priority project does not harm any species protected by the federal Endangered Species Act of 1973 (16 U.S.C. Sec. 1531 et seq.), the Native Plant Protection Act (Chapter 10 (commencing with Section 1900) of Division 2 of the Fish and Game Code), or the California Endangered Species Act (Chapter 1.5 (commencing with Section 2050) of Division 3 of the Fish and Game Code), and the project does not cause the destruction or removal of any species protected by a local ordinance in effect at the time the application for the project was deemed complete.

        (B) For the purposes of this paragraph, "wetlands" has the same meaning as in the United States Fish and Wildlife Service Manual, Part 660 FW 2 (June 21, 1993).

        (C) For the purposes of this paragraph:

            (i) "Riparian areas" means those areas transitional between terrestrial and aquatic ecosystems and that are distinguished by gradients in biophysical conditions, ecological processes, and biota. A riparian area is an area through which surface and subsurface hydrology connect waterbodies with their adjacent uplands. A riparian area includes those portions of terrestrial ecosystems that significantly influence exchanges of energy and matter with aquatic ecosystems. A riparian area is adjacent to perennial, intermittent, and ephemeral streams, lakes, and estuarine-marine shorelines.

           (ii) "Wildlife habitat" means the ecological communities upon which wild animals, birds, plants, fish, amphibians, and invertebrates depend for their conservation and protection.

           (iii) Habitat of "significant value" includes wildlife habitat of national, statewide, regional, or local importance; habitat for species protected by the federal Endangered Species Act of 1973 (16 U.S.C. Sec. 1531, et seq.), the California Endangered Species Act (Chapter 1.5 (commencing with Section 2050) of Division 3 of the Fish and Game Code), or the Native Plant Protection Act (Chapter 10 (commencing with Section 1900) of Division 2 of the Fish and Game Code); habitat identified as candidate, fully protected, sensitive, or species of special status by local, state, or federal agencies; or habitat essential to the movement of resident or migratory wildlife.

(3) The site of the transit priority project is not included on any list of facilities and sites compiled pursuant to Section 65962.5 of the Government Code.

(4) The site of the transit priority project is subject to a preliminary endangerment assessment prepared by an environmental assessor to determine the existence of any release of a hazardous substance on the site and to determine the potential for exposure of future occupants to significant health hazards from any nearby property or activity.

  (A) If a release of a hazardous substance is found to exist on the site, the release shall be removed or any significant effects of the release shall be mitigated to a level of insignificance in compliance with state and federal requirements.

  (B) If a potential for exposure to significant hazards from surrounding properties or activities is found to exist, the effects of the potential exposure shall be mitigated to a level of insignificance in compliance with state and federal requirements.

(5) The transit priority project does not have a significant effect on historical resources pursuant to Section 21084.1.

(6) The transit priority project site is not subject to any of the following:

  (A) A wildland fire hazard, as determined by the Department of Forestry and Fire Protection, unless the applicable general plan or zoning ordinance contains provisions to mitigate the risk of a wildland fire hazard.

  (B) An unusually high risk of fire or explosion from materials stored or used on nearby properties.

  (C) Risk of a public health exposure at a level that would exceed the standards established by any state or federal agency.

  (D) Seismic risk as a result of being within a delineated earthquake fault zone, as determined pursuant to Section 2622, or a seismic hazard zone, as determined pursuant to Section 2696, unless the applicable general plan or zoning ordinance contains provisions to mitigate the risk of an earthquake fault or seismic hazard zone.

  (E) Landslide hazard, flood plain, flood way, or restriction zone, unless the applicable general plan or zoning ordinance contains provisions to mitigate the risk of a landslide or flood.

(7) The transit priority project site is not located on developed open space.

  (A) For the purposes of this paragraph, "developed open space" means land that meets all of the following criteria:

    (i) Is publicly owned, or financed in whole or in part by public funds.

    (ii) Is generally open to, and available for use by, the public.

    (iii) Is predominantly lacking in structural development other than structures associated with open spaces, including, but not limited to, playgrounds, swimming pools, ballfields, enclosed child play areas, and picnic facilities.

(B) For the purposes of this paragraph, "developed open space" includes land that has been designated for acquisition by a public agency for developed open space, but does not include lands acquired with public funds dedicated to the acquisition of land for housing purposes.

(8) The buildings in the transit priority project are 15 percent more energy efficient than required by Chapter 6 of Title 24 of the California Code of Regulations and the buildings and landscaping are designed to achieve 25 percent less water usage than the average household use in the region.

(b) The transit priority project meets all of the following land use criteria:

(1) The site of the transit priority project is not more than eight acres in total area.

(2) The transit priority project does not contain more than 200 residential units.

(3) The transit priority project does not result in any net loss in the number of affordable housing units within the project area.

(4) The transit priority project does not include any single level building that exceeds 75,000 square feet.

(5) Any applicable mitigation measures or performance standards or criteria set forth in the prior environmental impact reports, and adopted in findings, have been or will be incorporated into the transit priority project.

(6) The transit priority project is determined not to conflict with nearby operating industrial uses.

(7) The transit priority project is located within one-half mile of a rail transit station or a ferry terminal included in a regional transportation plan or within one-quarter mile of a high-quality transit corridor included in a regional transportation plan.

(c) The transit priority project meets at least one of the following three criteria:

(1) The transit priority project meets both of the following:

(A) At least 20 percent of the housing will be sold to families of moderate income, or not less than 10 percent of the housing will be rented to families of low income, or not less than 5 percent of the housing is rented to families of very low income.

(B) The transit priority project developer provides sufficient legal commitments to the appropriate local agency to ensure the continued availability and use of the housing units for very low, low-, and moderate-income households at monthly housing costs with an affordable housing cost or affordable rent, as defined in Section 50052.5 or 50053 of the Health and Safety Code, respectively, for the period required by the applicable financing. Rental units shall be affordable for at least 55 years. Ownership units shall be subject to resale restrictions or equity sharing requirements for at least 30 years.

(2) The transit priority project developer has paid or will pay in-lieu fees pursuant to a local ordinance in an amount sufficient to result in the development of an equivalent number of units that would otherwise be required pursuant to paragraph (1).

(3) The transit priority project provides public open space equal to or greater than five acres per 1,000 residents of the project.

[Amended, Chapter 39, Statutes of 2012]

21155.2.   Transit project review

(a) A transit priority project that has incorporated all feasible mitigation measures, performance standards, or criteria set forth in the prior applicable environmental impact reports and adopted in findings made pursuant to Section 21081, shall be eligible for either the provisions of subdivision (b) or (c).

(b) A transit priority project that satisfies the requirements of subdivision (a) may be reviewed through a sustainable communities environmental assessment as follows:

(1) An initial study shall be prepared to identify all significant or potentially significant impacts of the transit priority project, other than those which do not need to be reviewed pursuant to Section 21159.28 based on substantial evidence in light of the whole record. The initial study shall identify any cumulative effects that have been adequately addressed and mitigated pursuant to the requirements of this division in prior applicable certified environmental impact reports. Where the lead agency determines that a cumulative effect has been adequately addressed and mitigated, that cumulative effect shall not be treated as cumulatively considerable for the purposes of this subdivision.

(2) The sustainable communities environmental assessment shall contain measures that either avoid or mitigate to a level of insignificance all potentially significant or significant effects of the project required to be identified in the initial study.

(3) A draft of the sustainable communities environmental assessment shall be circulated for public comment for a period of not less than 30 days. Notice shall be provided in the same manner as required for an environmental impact report pursuant to Section 21092.

(4) Prior to acting on the sustainable communities environmental assessment, the lead agency shall consider all comments received.

(5) A sustainable communities environmental assessment may be approved by the lead agency after conducting a public hearing, reviewing the comments received, and finding that:

(A) All potentially significant or significant effects required to be identified in the initial study have been identified and analyzed.

(B) With respect to each significant effect on the environment required to be identified in the initial study, either of the following apply:

(i) Changes or alterations have been required in or incorporated into the project that avoid or mitigate the significant effects to a level of insignificance.

(ii) Those changes or alterations are within the responsibility and jurisdiction of another public agency and have been, or can and should be, adopted by that other agency.

(6) The legislative body of the lead agency shall conduct the public hearing or a planning commission may conduct the public hearing if local ordinances allow a direct appeal of approval of a document prepared pursuant to this division to the legislative body subject to a fee not to exceed five hundred dollars ($500).

(7) The lead agency's decision to review and approve a transit priority project with a sustainable communities environmental assessment shall be reviewed under the substantial evidence standard.

(c) A transit priority project that satisfies the requirements of subdivision (a) may be reviewed by an environmental impact report that complies with all of the following:

(1) An initial study shall be prepared to identify all significant or potentially significant effects of the transit priority project other than those that do not need to be reviewed pursuant to Section 21159.28 based upon substantial evidence in light of the whole record. The initial study shall identify any cumulative effects that have been adequately addressed and mitigated pursuant to the requirements of this division in prior applicable certified environmental impact reports. Where the lead agency determines that a cumulative effect has been adequately addressed and mitigated, that cumulative effect shall not be treated as cumulatively considerable for the purposes of this subdivision.

(2) An environmental impact report prepared pursuant to this subdivision need only address the significant or potentially significant effects of the transit priority project on the environment identified pursuant to paragraph (1). It is not required to analyze off-site alternatives to the transit priority project. It shall otherwise comply with the requirements of this division.

[Added, Chapter 728, Statutes of 2008]

21155.3. Applicable traffic mitigation projects

(a) The legislative body of a local jurisdiction may adopt traffic mitigation measures that would apply to transit priority projects. These measures shall be adopted or amended after a public hearing and may include requirements for the installation of traffic control improvements, street or road improvements, and contributions to road improvement or transit funds, transit passes for future residents, or other measures that will avoid or mitigate the traffic impacts of those transit priority projects.

(b) (1) A transit priority project that is seeking a discretionary approval is not required to comply with any additional mitigation measures required by paragraph (1) or (2) of subdivision (a) of Section 21081, for the traffic impacts of that project on intersections, streets, highways, freeways, or mass transit, if the local jurisdiction issuing that discretionary approval has adopted traffic mitigation measures in accordance with this section.

(2) Paragraph (1) does not restrict the authority of a local jurisdiction to adopt feasible mitigation measures with respect to the effects of a project on public health or on pedestrian or bicycle safety.

(c) The legislative body shall review its traffic mitigation measures and update them as needed at least every five years.

[Added, Chapter 728, Statutes of 2008]

21155.4. Exemptions

(a) Except as provided in subdivision (b), a residential, employment center, as defined in paragraph (1) of subdivision (a) of Section 21099, or mixed-use development project, including any subdivision, or any zoning, change that meets all of the following criteria is exempt from the requirements of this division:

(1) The project is proposed within a transit priority area, as defined in subdivision (a) of Section 21099.

(2) The project is undertaken to implement and is consistent with a specific plan for which an environmental impact report has been certified.

(3) The project is consistent with the general use designation, density, building intensity, and applicable policies specified for the project area in either a sustainable communities strategy or an alternative planning strategy for which the State Air Resources Board, pursuant to subparagraph (H) of paragraph (2) of subdivision (b) of Section 65080 of the Government Code, has accepted a metropolitan planning organization's determination that the sustainable communities strategy or the alternative planning strategy would, if implemented, achieve the greenhouse gas emissions reduction targets.

(b) Further environmental review shall be conducted only if any of the events specified in Section 21166 have occurred.

[Added, Chapter 386, Statutes of 2013]

Chapter 4.3. Housing Sustainability Districts

21155.10. Environmental impact reports

A lead agency shall prepare an environmental impact report when designating a housing sustainability district pursuant to Section 66201 of the Government Code to identify and mitigate, to the extent feasible, environmental impacts resulting from the designation. The environmental impact report shall identify mitigation measures that may be undertaken by housing projects in the housing sustainability district to mitigate the environmental impacts identified by the environmental impact report.

[Added, Chapter 371, Statutes of 2017]

21155.11. Conditions for exemption

This division does not apply to a housing project undertaken in a housing sustainability district designated by a local government if all of the following are met:

(a) The lead agency has certified an environmental impact report for the housing sustainability district, and the Department of Housing and Community Development has approved the housing sustainability district pursuant to

Section 66202 of the Government Code, within 10 years of the lead agency's review of the housing project.

(b) The housing project meets the conditions specified in the designation for the housing sustainability district.

(c) The housing project is required to implement appropriate mitigation measures identified in the environmental impact report prepared pursuant to Section 21155.10 to mitigate environmental impacts identified by that environmental impact report.

[Added, Chapter 371, Statutes of 2017]

Chapter 4.5. Streamlined Environmental Review

Article 1. Findings

21156.　　Legislative intent

It is the intent of the Legislature in enacting this chapter that a master environmental impact report shall evaluate the cumulative impacts, growth inducing impacts, and irreversible significant effects on the environment of subsequent projects to the greatest extend feasible. The Legislature further intends that the environmental review of subsequent projects be substantially reduced to the extent that the project impacts have been reviewed and appropriate mitigation measures are set forth in a certified master environmental impact report.

[Added, Chapter 1130, Statutes of 1993]

Article 2. Master Environmental Impact Report

21157.　　Master EIRs; when permitted; scope

(a) A master environmental impact report may be prepared for any one of the following projects:

(1) A general plan, element, general plan amendment, or specific plan.

(2) A project that consists of smaller individual projects that will be carried out in phases.

(3) A rule or regulation that will be implemented by subsequent projects.

(4) A project that will be carried out or approved pursuant to a development agreement.

(5) A public or private project that will be carried out or approved pursuant to, or in furtherance of, a redevelopment plan.

(6) A state highway project or mass transit project that will be subject to multiple stages of review or approval.

(7) A regional transportation plan or congestion management plan.

(8) A plan proposed by a local agency for the reuse of a federal military base or reservation that has been closed or that is proposed for closure.

(9) Regulations adopted by the Fish and Game Commission for the regulation of hunting and fishing.

(10) A plan for district projects to be undertaken by a school district, that also complies with applicable school facilities requirements, including, but not limited to, the requirements of Chapter 12.5 (commencing with Section 17070.10) of Part 10 of, and Article 1 (commencing with Section 17210) of Chapter 1 of Part 10.5 of, Division 1 of Title 1 of Education Code.

(b) When a lead agency prepares a master environmental impact report, the document shall include all of the following:

(1) A detailed statement as required by Section 21100.

(2) A description of anticipated subsequent projects that would be within the scope of the master environmental impact report, that contains sufficient information with regard to the kind, size, intensity, and location of the subsequent projects, including, but not limited to, all of the following:

(A) The specific type of project anticipated to be undertaken.

(B) The maximum and minimum intensity of any anticipated subsequent project, such as the number of residences in a residential development, and, with regard to a public works facility, its anticipated capacity and service area.

(C) The anticipated location and alternative locations for any development projects.

(D) A capital outlay or capital improvement program, or other scheduling or implementing device that governs the submission and approval of subsequent projects.

(3) A description of potential impacts of anticipated subsequent projects for which there is not sufficient information reasonably available to support a full assessment of potential impacts in the master environmental impact report. This description shall not be construed as a limitation on the impacts which may be considered in a focused environmental impact report.

(c) Lead agencies may develop and implement a fee program in accordance with applicable provisions of law to generate the revenue necessary to prepare a master environmental impact report.

[Amended, Chapter 882, Statutes of 2006]

21157.1.   Subsequent projects following a master EIR

The preparation and certification of a master environmental impact report, if prepared and certified consistent with this division, may allow for the limited review of subsequent projects that were described in the master environmental impact report as being within the scope of the report, in accordance with the following requirements:

(a) The lead agency for a subsequent project shall be the lead agency or any responsible agency identified in the master environmental impact report.

(b) The lead agency shall prepare an initial study on any proposed subsequent project. This initial study shall analyze whether the subsequent project may cause any significant effect on the environment that was not examined in the master environmental impact report and whether the subsequent project was described in the master environmental impact report as being within the scope of the report.

(c) If the lead agency, based on the initial study, determines that a proposed subsequent project will have no additional significant effect on the environment, as defined in subdivision (d) of Section 21158, that was not identified in the master environmental impact report and that no new or additional mitigation measures or alternatives may be required, the lead agency shall make a written finding based upon the information contained in the initial study that the subsequent project is within the scope of the project covered by the master environmental impact report. No new environmental document nor findings pursuant to Section 21081 shall be required by this division. Prior to approving or carrying out the proposed subsequent project, the lead agency shall provide notice of this fact pursuant to Section 21092 and incorporate all feasible mitigation measures or feasible alternatives set forth in the master environmental impact report which are appropriate to the project. Whenever a lead agency approves or determines to carry out any subsequent project pursuant to this section, it shall file a notice pursuant to Section 21108 or 21152.

(d) Where a lead agency cannot make the findings required in subdivision (c), the lead agency shall prepare, pursuant to Section 21157.7, either a mitigated negative declaration or environmental impact report.

[Amended, Chapter 1294, Statutes of 1994]

21157.5. Mitigated negative declaration may be required for projects following master EIR

(a) A proposed mitigated negative declaration shall be prepared for any proposed subsequent project if both of the following occur:

(1) An initial study has identified potentially new or additional significant effects on the environment that were not analyzed in the master environmental impact report.

(2) Feasible mitigation measures or alternatives will be incorporated to revise the proposed subsequent project, before the negative declaration is released for public review, in order to avoid the effects or mitigate the effects to a point where clearly no significant effect on the environment will occur.

(b) If there is substantial evidence in light of the whole record before the lead agency that the proposed subsequent project may have a significant effect on the environment and a mitigated negative declaration is not prepared, the lead agency shall prepare an environmental impact report or a focused environmental impact report pursuant to Section 21158.

[Added, Chapter 1130, Statutes of 1993]

21157.6. 5-year time limit; adequacy of environmental review

(a) The master environmental impact report shall not be used for the purposes of this chapter if either of the following has occurred:

(1) The certification of the master environmental impact report occurred more than five years prior to the filing of an application for the subsequent project.

(2) The filing of an application for the subsequent project occurs following the certification of the master environmental impact report, and the approval of a project that was not described in the master environmental impact report, may affect the adequacy of the environmental review in the master environmental impact report for any subsequent project.

(b) A master environmental impact report that was certified more than five years prior to the filing of an application for the subsequent project may be used for purposes of this chapter to review a subsequent project that was described in the master environmental impact report if the lead agency reviews the adequacy of the master environmental impact report and does either of the following:

(1) Finds that no substantial changes have occurred with respect to the circumstances under which the master environmental impact report was certified or that no new information, which was not known and could not have been known at the time that the master environmental impact report was certified as complete, has become available.

(2) Prepares an initial study and, pursuant to the findings of the initial study, does either of the following:

(A) Certifies a subsequent or supplemental environmental impact report that has been either incorporated into the previously certified master environmental impact report or references any deletions, additions, or any other modifications to the previously certified master environmental impact report.

(B) Approves a mitigated negative declaration that addresses substantial changes that have occurred with respect to the circumstances under which the master environmental impact report was certified or the new information that was not known and could not have been known at the time the master environmental impact report was certified.

[Amended, Chapter 684, Statutes of 2004]

21157.7.   Preparation of master environmental impact report for Highway 99 improvements and subsequent projects

(a) For purposes of this section, a master environmental impact report is a document prepared in accordance with subdivision (c) for the projects described in subdivision (b) that, upon certification, is followed by review of subsequent projects as provided in Sections 21157.1 and 21157.5.

(b) A master environmental impact report may be prepared for a plan adopted by the Department of Transportation for improvements to regional segments of Highway 99 funded pursuant to subdivision (b) of Section 8879.23 of the Government Code, to streamline, coordinate, and improve environmental review.

(c) The report shall include all of the following:

(1) A detailed statement as required by Section 21100.

(2) A description of the anticipated highway improvements along Highway 99 that would be within the scope of the master environmental impact report, that contains sufficient information about all phases of the Highway 99 construction activities, including, but not limited to, all of the following:

(A) The specific types of improvements that will be undertaken.

(B) The anticipated location and alternative locations for any of the Highway 99 improvements, including overpasses, bridges, railroad crossings, and interchanges.

(C) A capital outlay or capital improvement program, or other scheduling or implementing device that governs the construction activities associated with the Highway 99 improvements.

(d) The Department of Transportation may communicate, coordinate, and consult with the Resources Agency, Wildlife Conservation Board, Department of Fish and Game, Department of Conservation, and other appropriate federal, state, or local governments, including interested stakeholders, to consider and implement mitigation requirements on a regional basis for the projects described in subdivision (b). This may include both of the following:

(1) Identification of priority areas for mitigation, using information from these agencies and departments as well as from other sources.

(2) Utilization of existing conservation programs of the agencies or departments identified in this subdivision, if mitigation under those programs for improvements under this section does not supplant mitigation for a project.

(e) The Department of Transportation may execute an agreement, memorandum of understanding, or other similar instrument to memorialize its understanding of any communication, coordination, or implementation activities with other state agencies for the purposes of meeting mitigation requirements on a regional basis.

(f) Notwithstanding any other provision of law, nothing in this section is intended to interfere with or prevent the existing authority of an agency or department to carry out its programs, projects, or responsibilities to identify, review, approve, deny, or implement any mitigation requirements, and nothing in this section shall be construed as a limitation on mitigation requirements for the project, or a limitation on compliance with requirements under this division or any other provision of law.

(g) Notwithstanding Section 21157.6, the master environmental impact report shall not be used for the purposes of this section, if the certification of the master environmental impact report occurred more than seven years prior to the filing of an application for the subsequent project.

[Amended, Chapter 503, Statutes of 2007]

Article 3. Focused Environmental Impact Report

21158. When to use focused EIRs; scope

(a) A focused environmental impact report is an environmental impact report on a subsequent project identified in a master environmental impact report. A focused environmental impact report may be utilized only if the lead agency finds that the analysis in the master environmental impact report of cumulative impacts, growth inducing impacts, and irreversible significant effects on the environment is adequate for the subsequent project. The focused environmental impact report shall incorporate, by reference, the master environmental impact report and analyze only the subsequent project's additional significant effects on the environment, as defined in subdivision (d), and any new or additional mitigation measures or alternatives that were not identified and analyzed by the master environmental impact report.

(b) The focused environmental impact report need not examine those effects which the lead agency finds were one of the following:

(1) Mitigated or avoided pursuant to paragraph (1) of subdivision (a) of Section 21081 as a result of mitigation measures identified in the master environmental impact report which will be required as part of the approval of the subsequent project.

(2) Examined at a sufficient level of detail in the master environmental impact report to enable those significant environmental effects to be mitigated or avoided by specific revisions to the project, the imposition of conditions, or by other means in connection with the approval of the subsequent project.

(3) Subject to a finding pursuant to paragraph (2) of subdivision (a) of Section 21081.

(c) A focused environmental impact report on any subsequent project shall analyze any significant effects on the environment where substantial new or additional information shows that the adverse environmental impact may be more significant than was described in the master environmental impact report. The substantial new or additional information may also show that mitigation measures or alternatives identified in the master environmental impact report, which were previously determined to be infeasible, are feasible and will avoid or reduce the significant effects on the environment of the subsequent project to a level of insignificance.

(d) For purposes of this chapter, "additional significant effects on the environment" are those project specific effects on the environment which were not addressed as significant effects on the environment in the master environmental impact report.

(e) Nothing in this chapter is intended to limit or abridge the ability of a lead agency to focus upon the issues that are ripe for decision at each level of environmental review, or to exclude duplicative analysis of environmental effects examined in previous environmental impact reports pursuant to Section 21093.

[Amended, Chapter 1294, Statutes of 1994]

21158.1.   Focused EIRs and regulatory programs

When a lead agency is required to prepare an environmental impact report pursuant to subdivision (d) of Section 21157.1 or is authorized to prepare a focused environmental impact report pursuant to Section 21158, the lead agency may not rely on subdivision (a) of Section 21080.5 for that purpose even though the lead agency's regulatory program is otherwise certified in accordance with Section 21080.5.

[Added, Chapter 444, Statutes of 1996]

21158.5   Focused EIRs and small projects

(a) Where a project consists of multiple-family residential development of not more than 100 units or a residential and commercial or retail mixed-use development of not more than 100,000 square feet which complies with all of the following, a focused environmental impact report shall be prepared, notwithstanding that the project was not identified in a master environmental impact report:

  (1) Is consistent with a general plan, specific plan, community plan, or zoning ordinance for which an environmental impact report was prepared within five years of the certification of the focused environmental impact report.

  (2) The lead agency cannot make the finding described in subdivision (c) of Section 21157.1, a negative declaration or mitigated negative declaration cannot be prepared pursuant to Section 21080, 21157.5, or 21158, and Section 21166 does not apply.

  (3) Meets one or more of the following conditions:

    (A) The parcel on which the project is to be developed is surrounded by immediately contiguous urban development.

    (B) The parcel on which the project is to be developed has been previously developed with urban uses.

    (C) The parcel on which the project is to be developed is within one-half mile of an existing rail transit station.

(b) A focused environmental impact report prepared pursuant to this section shall be limited to a discussion of potentially significant effects on the environment specific to the project, or which substantial new information shows will be more significant than described in the prior environmental impact report. No discussion shall be required of alternatives to the project, cumulative impacts of the project, or the growth inducing impacts of the project.

[Added, Chapter 1130, Statutes of 1993]

Article 4. Expedited Environmental Review for Environmental Mandated Projects

21159.   Rapid review of regulations on pollution control equipment

(a) An agency listed in Section 21159.4 shall perform, at the time of the adoption of a rule or regulation requiring the installation of pollution control equipment, or a performance standard or treatment requirement, including a rule or regulation that requires the installation of pollution control equipment or a performance standard or treatment requirement pursuant to the California Global Warming Solutions Act of 2006 (Division 25.5 (commencing with Section 38500) of the Health and Safety Code), an environmental analysis of the reasonably foreseeable methods of compliance. In the preparation of this analysis, the agency may utilize numerical ranges or averages where specific

101

data is not available; however, the agency shall not be required to engage in speculation or conjecture. The environmental analysis shall, at minimum, include all of the following:

(1) An analysis of the reasonably foreseeable environmental impacts of the methods of compliance.

(2) An analysis of reasonably foreseeable feasible mitigation measures.

(3) An analysis of reasonably foreseeable alternative means of compliance with the rule or regulation.

(4) For a rule or regulation that requires the installation of pollution control equipment adopted pursuant to the California Global Warming Solutions Act of 2006 (Division 25.5 (commencing with Section 38500) of the Health and Safety Code), the analysis shall also include reasonably foreseeable greenhouse gas emission impacts of compliance with the rule or regulation.

(b) The preparation of an environmental impact report at the time of adopting a rule or regulation pursuant to this division shall be deemed to satisfy the requirements of this section.

(c) The environmental analysis shall take into account a reasonable range of environmental, economic, and technical factors, population and geographic areas, and specific sites.

(d) This section does not require the agency to conduct a project-level analysis.

(e) For purposes of this article, the term "performance standard" includes process or raw material changes or product reformulation.

(f) This section is not intended, and may not be used, to delay the adoption of any rule or regulation for which an analysis is required to be performed pursuant to this section.

[Amended, Chapter 195, Statutes of 2010]

21159.1.   Focused EIRs and installing pollution control equipment

(a) A focused environmental impact report may be utilized if a project meets all of the following requirements:

(1) The project consists solely of the installation of either of the following:

(A) Pollution control equipment required by a rule or regulation of an agency listed in subdivision (a) of Section 21159.4 and other components necessary to complete the installation of that equipment.

(B) Pollution control equipment and other components necessary to complete the installation of that equipment that reduces greenhouse gases required by a rule or regulation of an agency listed in Section 21159.4 pursuant to the California Global Warming Solutions Act of 2006 (Division 25.5 (commencing with Section 38500) of the Health and Safety Code).

(2) The agency certified an environmental impact report on the rule or regulation or reviewed it pursuant to a certified regulatory program, and, in either case, the review included an assessment of growth inducing impacts and cumulative impacts of, and alternatives to, the project.

(3) The environmental review required by paragraph (2) was completed within five years of certification of the focused environmental impact report.

(4) An environmental impact report is not required pursuant to Section 21166.

(b) The discussion of significant effects on the environment in the focused environmental impact report shall be limited to project-specific potentially significant effects on the environment of the project that were not discussed in the environmental analysis of the rule or regulation required pursuant to subdivision (a) of Section 21159. A discussion of growth-inducing impacts or cumulative impacts shall not be required in the focused environmental impact report, and the discussion of alternatives shall be limited to a discussion of alternative means of compliance, if any, with the rule or regulation.

[Amended, Chapter 195, Statutes of 2010]

21159.2. Compliance with performance standard or treatment requirement

(a) If a project consists solely of compliance with a performance standard or treatment requirement imposed by an agency listed in Section 21159.4, the lead agency for the compliance project shall, to the greatest extent feasible, utilize the environmental analysis required pursuant to subdivision (a) of Section 21159 in the preparation of a negative declaration, mitigated negative declaration, or environmental impact report on the compliance project or in otherwise fulfilling its responsibilities under this division. The use of numerical averages or ranges in an environmental analysis shall not relieve a lead agency of its obligations under this division to identify and evaluate the environmental effects of a compliance project.

(b) If the lead agency determines that an environmental impact report on the compliance project is required, the lead agency shall prepare an environmental impact report which addresses only the project-specific issues related to the compliance project or other issues that were not discussed in sufficient detail in the environmental analysis to enable the lead agency to fulfill its responsibilities under Section 21100 or 21151, as applicable. The mitigation measures imposed by the lead agency for the project shall relate only to the significant effects on the environment to be mitigated. The discussion of alternatives shall be limited to a discussion of alternative means of compliance, if any, with the rule or regulation.

[Added, Chapter 1130, Statutes of 1993]

21159.3. EIR deadlines

In the preparation of any environmental impact report pursuant to Section 21159.1 or 21159.2, the following deadlines shall apply:

(a) A lead agency shall determine whether an environmental impact report should be prepared within 30 days of its determination that the application for the project is complete.

(b) If the environmental impact report will be prepared under contract to the lead agency pursuant to Section 21082.1, the lead agency shall issue a request for proposals for preparation of the environmental impact report as soon as it has enough information to prepare a request for proposals, and in any event, not later than 30 days after the time for response to the notice of preparation has expired. The contract shall be awarded within 30 days of the response date for the request for proposals.

[Added, Chapter 1130, Statutes of 1993]

21159.4. Affected state agencies

(a) This article shall apply to all of the following agencies:

(1) The State Air Resources Board.

(2) A district as defined in Section 39025 of the Health and Safety Code.

(3) The State Water Resources Control Board.

(4) A California regional water quality control board.

(5) The Department of Toxic Substances Control.

(6) The Department of Resources Recycling and Recovery.

(b) This article shall apply to the State Energy Resources Conservation and Development Commission and the California Public Utilities Commission for rules and regulations requiring the installation of pollution control equipment adopted pursuant to the California Global Warming Solutions Act of 2006 (Division 25.5 (commencing with Section 38500) of the Health and Safety Code.)

[Amended, Chapter 195, Statutes of 2010]

Article 5. Public Assistance Program

21159.9. Public education program; data base for EIR preparation; repository of electronic documents

The Office of Planning and Research shall implement a public assistance and information program to ensure efficient and effective implementation of this division and to do both of the following:

(a) Establish a public education and training program for planners, developers, and other interested parties to assist them in implementing this division.

(b) (1) Establish and maintain a database for the collection, storage, retrieval, and dissemination of environmental documents, notices of exemption, notices of preparation, notices of determination, and notices of completion provided to the Office of Planning and Research. The database shall be available online to the public through the Internet. The Office of Planning and Research may coordinate with another state agency to host and maintain the online database.

(2) The Office of Planning and Research may phase in the submission of electronic documents and use of the database by state and local public agencies.

(3) (A) Pursuant to Section 9795 of the Government Code, the Office of Planning and Research shall, no later than July 1, 2017, submit to the Legislature a report describing how it plans to implement this subdivision, and shall provide an additional report to the Legislature

no later than July 1, 2019, describing the status of the implementation of this subdivision.

(B) Pursuant to Section 10231.5 of the Government Code, this paragraph is inoperative on July 1, 2023.

[Amended, Chapter 476, Statutes of 20161]

Article 6. Special Review of Housing Projects

21159.20.   "Census-defined place", "community-level environmental review", "low-income households" defined

For the purposes of this article, the following terms have the following meanings:

(a) "Census-defined place" means a specific unincorporated land area within boundaries determined by the United States Census Bureau in the most recent decennial census.

(b) "Community-level environmental review" means either of the following:

(1) An environmental impact report certified on any of the following:

(A) A general plan.

(B) A revision or update to the general plan that includes at least the land use and circulation elements.

(C) An applicable community plan.

(D) An applicable specific plan.

(E) A housing element of the general plan, if the environmental impact report analyzed the environmental effects of the density of the proposed project.

(2) Pursuant to this division and the implementing guidelines adopted pursuant to this division that govern subsequent review following a program environmental impact report, or pursuant to Section 21157.1, 21157.5, or 21166, a negative declaration or mitigated negative declaration was adopted as a subsequent environmental review document, following and based upon an environmental impact report on any of the projects listed in subparagraphs (A), (C), or (D) of paragraph (1).

(c) "Low-income households" means households of persons and families of very low and low income, as defined in Sections 50093 and 50105 of the Health and Safety Code.

(d) "Low- and moderate-income households" means households of persons and families of low or moderate income, as defined in Section 50093 of the Health and Safety Code.

[Added, Chapter 1039, Statutes of 2002]

21159.21   Exemption for qualified housing projects

A housing project qualifies for an exemption from this division pursuant to Section 21159.22, 21159.23, or 21159.24 if it meets the criteria in the applicable section and all of the following criteria:

(a) The project is consistent with any applicable general plan, specific plan, and local coastal program, including any mitigation measures required by a plan or program, as that plan or program existed on the date that the application was deemed complete and with any applicable zoning ordinance, as that zoning ordinance existed on the date that the application was deemed complete, except that a project shall not be deemed to be inconsistent with the zoning designation for the site if that zoning designation is inconsistent with the general plan only because the project site has not been rezoned to conform with a more recently adopted general plan.

(b) Community-level environmental review has been adopted or certified.

(c) The project and other projects approved prior to the approval of the project can be adequately served by existing utilities, and the project applicant has paid, or has committed to pay, all applicable in-lieu or development fees.

(d) The site of the project does not contain wetlands, does not have any value as a wildlife habitat, and the project does not harm any species protected by the federal Endangered Species Act of 1973 (16 U.S.C. Sec. 1531 et seq.) or by the Native Plant Protection Act (Chapter 10 (commencing with Section 1900) of Division 2 of the Fish and Game Code), the California Endangered Species Act (Chapter 1.5 (commencing with Section 2050) of Division 3 of the Fish and Game Code), and the project does not cause the destruction or removal of any species protected by a local ordinance in effect at the time the application for the project was deemed complete. For the purposes of this subdivision, "wetlands" has the same meaning as in Section 328.3 of Title 33 of the Code of Federal Regulations and "wildlife habitat" means the ecological communities upon which wild animals, birds, plants, fish, amphibians, and invertebrates depend for their conservation and protection.

(e) The site of the project is not included on any list of facilities and sites compiled pursuant to Section 65962.5 of the Government Code.

(f) The site of the project is subject to a preliminary endangerment assessment prepared by an environmental assessor to determine the existence of any release of a hazardous substance on the site and to determine the potential for exposure of future occupants to significant health hazards from any nearby property or activity.

    (1) If a release of a hazardous substance is found to exist on the site, the release shall be removed, or any significant effects of the release shall be mitigated to a level of insignificance in compliance with state and federal requirements.

    (2) If a potential for exposure to significant hazards from surrounding properties or activities is found to exist, the effects of the potential exposure shall be mitigated to a level of insignificance in compliance with state and federal requirements.

(g) The project does not have a significant effect on historical resources pursuant to Section 21084.1.

(h) The project site is not subject to any of the following:

(1) A wildland fire hazard, as determined by the Department of Forestry and Fire Protection, unless the applicable general plan or zoning ordinance contains provisions to mitigate the risk of a wildland fire hazard.

(2) An unusually high risk of fire or explosion from materials stored or used on nearby properties.

(3) Risk of a public health exposure at a level that would exceed the standards established by any state or federal agency.

(4) Within a delineated earthquake fault zone, as determined pursuant to Section 2622, or a seismic hazard zone, as determined pursuant to Section 2696, unless the applicable general plan or zoning ordinance contains provisions to mitigate the risk of an earthquake fault or seismic hazard zone.

(5) Landslide hazard, flood plain, flood way, or restriction zone, unless the applicable general plan or zoning ordinance contains provisions to mitigate the risk of a landslide or flood.

(i) (1) The project site is not located on developed open space.

(2) For the purposes of this subdivision, "developed open space" means land that meets all of the following criteria:

(A) Is publicly owned, or financed in whole or in part by public funds.

(B) Is generally open to, and available for use by, the public.

(C) Is predominantly lacking in structural development other than structures associated with open spaces, including, but not limited to, playgrounds, swimming pools, ballfields, enclosed child play areas, and picnic facilities.

(3) For the purposes of this subdivision, "developed open space" includes land that has been designated for acquisition by a public agency for developed open space, but does not include lands acquired by public funds dedicated to the acquisition of land for housing purposes.

(j) The project site is not located within the boundaries of a state conservancy.

[Amended, Chapter 39, Statutes of 2012]

21159.22   Exemption for agricultural employee housing

(a) This division does not apply to any development project that meets the requirements of subdivision (b), and meets either of the following criteria:

(1) Consists of the construction, conversion, or use of residential housing for agricultural employees, and meets all of the following criteria:

(A) Is affordable to lower income households, as defined in Section 50079.5 of the Health and Safety Code.

(B) Lacks public financial assistance.

(C) The developer of the development project provides sufficient legal commitments to the appropriate local agency to ensure the continued availability and use of the housing units for lower income households for a period of at least 15 years.

(2) Consists of the construction, conversion, or use of residential housing for agricultural employees and meets all of the following criteria:

(A) Is housing for very low, low-, or moderate-income households as defined in paragraph (2) of subdivision (h) of Section 65589.5 of the Government Code.

(B) Public financial assistance exists for the development project.

(C) The developer of the development project provides sufficient legal commitments to the appropriate local agency to ensure the continued availability and use of the housing units for low- and moderate-income households for a period of at least 15 years.

(b) (1) If the development project is proposed within incorporated city limits or within a census defined place with a minimum population density of at least 5,000 persons per square mile, it is located on a project site that is adjacent, on at least two sides, to land that has been developed, and consists of not more than 45 units, or is housing for a total of 45 or fewer agricultural employees if the housing consists of dormitories, barracks, or other group living facilities.

(2) If the development project is located on a project site zoned for general agricultural use, and consists of not more than 20 units, or is housing for a total of 20 or fewer agricultural employees if the housing consists of dormitories, barracks, or other group living facilities.

(3) The project satisfies the criteria in Section 21159.21.

(4) The development project is not more than five acres in area, except that a project site located in an area with a population density of at least 1,000 persons per square mile shall not be more than two acres in area.

(c) Notwithstanding subdivision (a), if a project satisfies the criteria described in subdivisions (a) and (b), but does not satisfy the criteria described in paragraph (1) of subdivision (b), this division does not apply to the project if the project meets all of the following criteria:

(1) Is located within either an incorporated city or a census-defined place.

(2) The population density of the incorporated city or census-defined place has a population density of at least 1,000 persons per square mile.

(3) The project site is adjacent on at least two sides to land that has been developed and the project consists of not more than 45 units, or the project consist of dormitories, barracks, or other group housing facilities for a total of 45 or fewer agricultural employees.

(d) Notwithstanding subdivision (c), this division shall apply to a project that meets the criteria described in subdivision (c) if a public agency that is carrying out or approving the project determines that there is a reasonable possibility that the project, if completed, would have a significant effect on the environment due to unusual circumstances or that the cumulative impacts of successive projects of the same type in the same area, over time, would be significant.

For the purposes of this section, "agricultural employee" has the same meaning as defined by subdivision (b) of Section 1140.4 of the Labor Code.

[Added, Chapter 1039, Statutes of 2002]

(a) This division does not apply to any development project that consists of the construction, conversion, or use of residential housing consisting of 100 or fewer that is affordable to low-income households if both of the following criteria are met:

    (1) The developer of the development project provides sufficient legal commitments to the appropriate local agency to ensure the continued availability and use of the housing units for lower income households, as defined in Section 50079.5 of the Health and Safety Code, for a period of at least 30 years, at monthly housing costs, as determined pursuant to Section 50053 of the Health and Safety Code.

    (2) The development project meets all of the following requirements:

        (A) The project satisfies the criteria described in Section 21159.21.

        (B) The project site meets one of the following conditions:

            (i) Has been previously developed for qualified urban uses.

            (ii) The parcels immediately adjacent to the site are developed with qualified urban uses, or at least 75 percent of the perimeter of the site adjoins parcels that are developed with qualified urban uses and the remaining 25 percent of the perimeter of the site adjoins parcels that have previously been developed for qualified urban uses, and the site has not been developed for urban uses and no parcel within the site has been created within 10 years prior to the proposed development of the site.

        (C) The project site is not more than five acres in area.

        (D) The project site is located within an urbanized area or within a census-defined place with a population density of at least 5,000 persons per square mile or, if the project consists of 50 or fewer units, within an incorporated city with a population density of at least 2,500 persons per square mile and a total population of at least 25,000 persons.

(b) Notwithstanding subdivision (a), if a project satisfies all of the criteria described in subdivision (a) except subparagraph (D) of paragraph (2) of that subdivision, this division does not apply to the project if the project is located within either an incorporated city or a census defined place with a population density of at least 1,000 persons per square mile.

(c) Notwithstanding subdivision (b), this division applies to a project that meets the criteria of subdivision (b), if there is a reasonable possibility that the project would have a significant effect on the environment or the residents of the project due to unusual circumstances or due to the related or cumulative impacts of reasonably foreseeable projects in the vicinity of the project.

(d) For the purposes of this section, "residential" means a use consisting of either of the following:

    (1) Residential units only.

    (2) Residential units and primarily neighborhood-serving goods, services, or retail uses that do not exceed 15 percent of the total floor area of the project.

[Added, Chapter 1039, Statutes of 2002]

21159.24   Division not applicable to certain projects; exceptions

(a) Except as provided in subdivision (b), this division does not apply to a project if all of the following criteria are met:

(1) The project is a residential project on an infill site.

(2) The project is located within an urbanized area.

(3) The project satisfies the criteria of Section 21159.21.

(4) Within five years of the date that the application for the project is deemed complete pursuant to Section 65943 of the Government Code, community-level environmental review was certified or adopted.

(5) The site of the project is not more than four acres in total area.

(6) The project does not contain more than 100 residential units.

(7) Either of the following criteria are met:

(A) (i) At least 10 percent of the housing is sold to families of moderate income, or not less than 10 percent of the housing is rented to families of low income, or not less than 5 percent of the housing is rented to families of very low income.

(ii) The project developer provides sufficient legal commitments to the appropriate local agency to ensure the continued availability and use of the housing units for very low, low-, and moderate-income households at monthly housing costs determined pursuant to paragraph (3) of subdivision (h) of Section 65589.5 of the Government Code.

(B) The project developer has paid or will pay in-lieu fees pursuant to a local ordinance in an amount sufficient to result in the development of an equivalent number of units that would otherwise be required pursuant to subparagraph (A).

(8) The project is within one-half mile of a major transit stop.

(9) The project does not include any single level building that exceeds 100,000 square feet.

(10) The project promotes higher density infill housing. A project with a density of at least 20 units per acre shall be conclusively presumed to promote higher density infill housing. A project with a density of at least 10 units per acre and a density greater than the average density of the residential properties within 1,500 feet shall be presumed to promote higher density housing unless the preponderance of the evidence demonstrates otherwise.

(b) Notwithstanding subdivision (a), this division shall apply to a development project that meets the criteria described in subdivision (a), if any of the following occur:

(1) There is a reasonable possibility that the project will have a project-specific, significant effect on the environment due to unusual circumstances.

(2) Substantial changes with respect to the circumstances under which the project is being undertaken that are related to the project have occurred since community-level environmental review was certified or adopted.

(3) New information becomes available regarding the circumstances under which the project is being undertaken and that is related to the project, that was not known, and could not have been known, at the time that community-level environmental review was certified or adopted.

(c) If a project satisfies the criteria described in subdivision (a), but is not exempt from this division as a result of satisfying the criteria described in subdivision (b), the analysis of the environmental effects of the project in the environmental impact report or the negative declaration shall be limited to an analysis of the project-specific effect of the projects and any effects identified pursuant to paragraph (2) or (3) of subdivision (b).

(d) For the purposes of this section, "residential" means a use consisting of either of the following:

(1) Residential units only.

(2) Residential units and primarily neighborhood-serving goods, services, or retail uses that do not exceed 25 percent of the total building square footage of the project.

[Amended, Chapter 549, Statutes of 2014]

21159.25. Limited exemption for certain multi-family residential and mixed-use housing projects

(a) For purposes of this section, the following definitions apply:

(1) "Residential or mixed-use housing project" means a project consisting of multifamily residential uses only or a mix of multifamily residential and nonresidential uses, with at least two-thirds of the square footage of the development designated for residential use.

(2) "Substantially surrounded" means at least 75 percent of the perimeter of the project site adjoins, or is separated only by an improved public right-of-way from, parcels that are developed with qualified urban uses. The remainder of the perimeter of the site adjoins, or is separated only by an improved public right-of-way from, parcels that have been designated for qualified urban uses in a zoning, community plan, or general plan for which an environmental impact report was certified.

(b) Without limiting any other statutory exemption or categorical exemption, this division does not apply to a residential or mixed-use housing project if all of the following conditions described in this section are met:

(1) The project is consistent with the applicable general plan designation and all applicable general plan policies as well as with applicable zoning designation and regulations.

(2) (A) The public agency approving or carrying out the project determines, based upon substantial evidence, that the density of the residential portion of the project is not less than the greater of the following:

(i) The average density of the residential properties that adjoin, or are separated only by an improved public right-of-way from, the perimeter of the project site, if any.

      (ii) The average density of the residential properties within 1,500 feet of the project site.

      (iii) Six dwelling units per acre.

   (B) The residential portion of the project is a multifamily housing development that contains six or more residential units.

(3) The proposed development occurs within an unincorporated area of a county on a project site of no more than five acres substantially surrounded by qualified urban uses.

(4) The project site has no value as habitat for endangered, rare, or threatened species.

(5) Approval of the project would not result in any significant effects relating to transportation, noise, air quality, greenhouse gas emissions, or water quality.

(6) The site can be adequately served by all required utilities and public services.

(7) The project is located on a site that is a legal parcel or parcels wholly within the boundaries of an urbanized area or urban cluster, as designated by the United States Census Bureau.

(c) Subdivision (b) does not apply to a residential or mixed-use housing project if any of the following conditions exist:

(1) The cumulative impact of successive projects of the same type in the same place over time is significant.

(2) There is a reasonable possibility that the project will have a significant effect on the environment due to unusual circumstances.

(3) The project may result in damage to scenic resources, including, but not limited to, trees, historic buildings, rock outcroppings, or similar resources, within a highway officially designated as a state scenic highway.

(4) The project is located on a site which is included on any list compiled pursuant to Section 65962.5 of the Government Code.

(5) The project may cause a substantial adverse change in the significance of a historical resource.

(d) If the lead agency determines that a project is not subject to this division pursuant to this section and it determines to approve or carry out the project, the lead agency shall file a notice with the Office of Planning and Research and with the county clerk in the county in which the project will be located in the manner specified in subdivisions (b) and (c) of Section 21152.

(e) This section shall remain in effect only until January 1, 2025, and as of that date is repealed.

[Amended, Chapter 497, Statutes of 2019]

21159.26.   Density reductions not a mitigation measure

With respect to a project that includes a housing development, a public agency may not reduce the proposed number of housing units as a mitigation measure or project alternative for a particular significant effect on the environment if it determines that

112

there is another feasible specific mitigation measure or project alternative that would provide a comparable level of mitigation. This section does not affect any other requirement regarding the residential density of that project.

[Added, Chapter 1039, Statutes of 2002]

21159.27.   Projects may not be divided

A project may not be divided into smaller projects to qualify for one or more exemptions pursuant to this article.

[Added, Chapter 1039, Statutes of 2002]

21159.28.   Residential streamlining

(a) If a residential or mixed-use residential project is consistent with the use designation, density, building intensity, and applicable policies specified for the project area in either a sustainable communities strategy or an alternative planning strategy, for which the State Air Resources Board pursuant to subparagraph (I) of paragraph (2) of subdivision (b) of Section 65080 of the Government Code has accepted the metropolitan planning organization's determination that the sustainable communities strategy or the alternative planning strategy would, if implemented, achieve the greenhouse gas emission reduction targets and if the project incorporates the mitigation measures required by an applicable prior environmental document, then any findings or other determinations for an exemption, a negative declaration, a mitigated negative declaration, a sustainable communities environmental assessment, an environmental impact report, or addenda prepared or adopted for the project pursuant to this division shall not be required to reference, describe, or discuss (1) growth inducing impacts; or (2) any project specific or cumulative impacts from cars and light-duty truck trips generated by the project on global warming or the regional transportation network.

(b) Any environmental impact report prepared for a project described in subdivision (a) shall not be required to reference, describe, or discuss a reduced residential density alternative to address the effects of car and light-duty truck trips generated by the project.

(c) "Regional transportation network," for purposes of this section, means all existing and proposed transportation system improvements, including the state transportation system, that were included in the transportation and air quality conformity modeling, including congestion modeling, for the final regional transportation plan adopted by the metropolitan planning organization, but shall not include local streets and roads. Nothing in the foregoing relieves any project from a requirement to comply with any conditions, exactions, or fees for the mitigation of the project's impacts on the structure, safety, or operations of the regional transportation network or local streets and roads.

(d) A residential or mixed-use residential project is a project where at least 75 percent of the total building square footage of the project consists of residential use or a project that is a transit priority project as defined in Section 21155.

[Added, Chapter 728, Statutes of 2008]

Chapter 5. Submission of Information

21160. **Information required to evaluate project; "trade secrets" limitation**

Whenever any person applies to any public agency for a lease, permit, license, certificate, or other entitlement for use, the public agency may require that person to submit data and information which may be necessary to enable the public agency to determine whether the proposed project may have a significant effect on the environment or to prepare an environmental impact report.

If any or all of the information so submitted is a "trade secret" as defined in Section 6254.7 of the Government Code by those submitting that information, it shall not be included in the impact report or otherwise disclosed by any public agency. This section shall not be construed to prohibit the exchange of properly designated trade secrets between public agencies who have lawful jurisdiction over the preparation of the impact report.

[Added, Chapter 1154, Statutes of 1972]

21161. **Filing notice of completion with OP&R**

Whenever a public agency has completed an environmental *document*, it shall cause a notice of completion of that report to be filed with the Office of Planning and Research. The notice of completion shall briefly identify the project and shall indicate that an environmental *document* has been prepared. The notice of completion shall identify the project location by latitude and longitude. Failure to file the notice required by this section shall not affect the validity of a project.

[Amended, Chapter 466, Statutes of 2019]

Chapter 5.5. No Place Like Home Projects

21163. **"No Place Like Home project"**

For purposes of this chapter, "No Place Like Home project" means a permanent supportive housing project that meets the criteria for funding pursuant to the No Place Like Home Program (Part 3.9 (commencing with Section 5849.1) of Division 5 of the Welfare and Institutions Code) and for which a public agency applies for, or receives, funding from the Department of Housing and Community Development.

[Added & Repealed, Chapter 346, Statutes of 2019]

21163.1. **Applicability**

A decision by a public agency to seek funding from, or the Department of Housing and Community Development's awarding of funds pursuant to, the No Place Like Home Program (Part 3.9 (commencing with Section 5849.1) of Division 5 of the Welfare and Institutions Code) does not constitute a "project" for purposes of this division.

[Added & Repealed, Chapter 346, Statutes of 2019]

21163.2.   Environmental review: record of proceeding

If a No Place Like Home project is not eligible for approval as a use by right pursuant to Article 11 (commencing with Section 65650) of Chapter 3 of Division 1 of Title 7 of the Government Code and is subject to this division, the development applicant may request, within 10 days after the lead agency determines the type of environmental documentation required for the project pursuant to this division, that the lead agency prepare and certify the record of proceeding for the environmental review of the No Place Like Home project in accordance with Section 21186.

[Added & Repealed, Chapter 346, Statutes of 2019]

21163.3.   Notice requirements

(a) (1) If a local agency approves or determines to carry out a No Place Like Home project that is subject to this division, the local agency shall file notice of that approval or determination in accordance with the requirements of subdivision (a) of Section 21152, except that the notice shall be filed within two working days after the approval or determination becomes final.

(2) If a local agency approves or determines to carry out a No Place Like Home project that is not subject to this division, the local agency shall file a notice of exemption in accordance with the requirements of subdivision (b) of Section 21152, except that the notice shall be filed within two working days after the approval or determination becomes final.

(b) Notwithstanding Section 21167, an action or proceeding to attack, review, set aside, void, or annul the acts or decision of a public agency on the grounds of noncompliance with this division for a No Place Like Home project shall commence within 30 days from the date of the filing of the notice required pursuant to subdivision (a).

(c) If the local agency fails to comply with the applicable timing requirements set forth in subdivision (a), an action or proceeding to attack, review, set aside, void, or annul the acts or decision of a public agency on the grounds of noncompliance with this division for a No Place Like Home project shall commence within 30 days from the date of the local agency's late filing of the notice required pursuant to subdivision (a) or 90 days from the date that the notice was required to be filed pursuant to subdivision (a), whichever is earlier.

[Added & Repealed, Chapter 346, Statutes of 2019]

21163.4.   Notification to the Legislature

(a) (1) The Department of Housing and Community Development shall notify the Speaker of the Assembly and the President pro Tempore of the Senate when the funding provided pursuant to the No Place Like Home Program (Part 3.9 (commencing with Section 5849.1) of Division 5 of the Welfare and Institutions Code) is fully allocated and disbursed. Notification from the Department of Housing and Community Development pursuant to

this subdivision shall be printed in the journal of each of the respective houses of the Legislature.

(2) **The Department of Housing and Community Development shall post a copy of the notification provided pursuant to this subdivision on its internet website.**

(b) **This chapter shall remain in effect only until January 1 of the year following notification from the Department of Housing and Community Development pursuant to subdivision (a), and as of that date is repealed.**

[Added & Repealed, Chapter 346, Statutes of 2019]

Chapter 6. Limitations

21165. **Local agency required to make determination. Office of Planning and Research to designate lead agency if dispute**

(a) When a project is to be carried out or approved by two or more public agencies, the determination of whether the project may have a significant effect on the environment shall be made by the lead agency, and that agency shall prepare, or cause to be prepared by contract, the environmental impact report for the project, if a report is required by this division. In the event that a dispute arises as to which is the lead agency, any of the disputing public agencies, or in the case of a project described in subdivision (c) of Section 21065 the applicant for such project, may submit the question to the Office of Planning and Research, and the Office of Planning and Research shall designate, within 21 days of receiving the request, the lead agency, giving due consideration to the capacity of that agency to adequately fulfill the requirements of this division.

(b) For the purposes of this section, a "dispute" means a contested, active difference of opinion between two or more public agencies as to which of those agencies shall prepare any necessary environmental document. A dispute exists where each of those agencies claims that it either has or does not have the obligation to prepare that environmental document. The Office of Planning and Research shall not designate a lead agency in the absence of such a dispute.

[Amended, Chapter 267, Statutes of 2005]

21166. **Lead agency prohibition to require subsequent reports for a certified project unless specific events. Cites events**

When an environmental impact report has been prepared for a project pursuant to this division, no subsequent or supplemental environmental impact report shall be required by the lead agency or by any responsible agency, unless one or more of the following events occurs:

(a) Substantial changes are proposed in the project which will require major revisions of the environmental impact report.

(b) Substantial changes occur with respect to the circumstances under which the project is being undertaken which will require major revisions in the environmental impact report.

(c) New information, which was not known and could not have been known at the time the environmental impact report was certified as complete, becomes available.

[Amended, Chapter 1200, Statutes of 1977]

21166.1.   Geographic area or group project report no basis for inadequate determination of individual project

The decision of a lead agency to prepare an environmental impact report with respect to environmental impacts within a geographic area or for a group of projects shall not be a basis for determining that an environmental document prepared for an individual project within that area or group is inadequate.

[Added, Chapter 1514, Statutes of 1984]

21167.   Procedure for action against public agency as grounds of noncompliance. Cites requirements

An action or proceeding to attack, review, set aside, void, or annul the following acts or decisions of a public agency on the grounds of noncompliance with this division shall be commenced as follows:

(a) An action or proceeding alleging that a public agency is carrying out or has approved a project that may have a significant effect on the environment without having determined whether the project may have a significant effect on the environment shall be commenced within 180 days from the date of the public agency's decision to carry out or approve the project, or, if a project is undertaken without a formal decision by the public agency, within 180 days from the date of commencement of the project.

(b) An action or proceeding alleging that a public agency has improperly determined whether a project may have a significant effect on the environment shall be commenced within 30 days from the date of the filing of the notice required by subdivision (a) of Section 21108 or subdivision (a) of Section 21152.

(c) An action or proceeding alleging that an environmental impact report does not comply with this division shall be commenced within 30 days from the date of the filing of the notice required by subdivision (a) of Section 21108 or subdivision (a) of Section 21152 by the lead agency.

(d) An action or proceeding alleging that a public agency has improperly determined that a project is not subject to this division pursuant to subdivision (b) of Section 21080 or Section 21172 shall be commenced within 35 days from the date of the filing by the public agency, or person specified in subdivision (b) or (c) of Section 21065, of the notice authorized by subdivision (b) of Section 21108 or subdivision (b) of Section 21152. If the notice has not been filed, the action or proceeding shall be commenced within 180 days from the date of the public agency's decision to carry out or approve the project, or, if a project is undertaken without a formal decision by the public agency, within 180 days from the date of commencement of the project.

(e) An action or proceeding alleging that another act or omission of a public agency does not comply with this division shall be commenced within 30 days from the date of the filing of the notice required by subdivision (a) of Section 21108 or subdivision (a) of Section 21152.

(f) If a person has made a written request to the public agency for a copy of the notice specified in Section 21108 or 21152 prior to the date on which the agency approves or determines to carry out the project, then not later than five days from the date of the agency's action, the public agency shall deposit a written copy of the notice addressed to that person in the United States mail, first-class postage prepaid. The date upon which this notice is mailed shall not affect the time periods specified in subdivisions (b), (c), (d), and (e).

[Amended, Chapter 744, Statutes of 2004]

21167.1.   Preference over other civil actions; deadline for appeals court hearings; judges with CEQA expertise; severance from other actions

(a) In all actions or proceedings brought pursuant to Sections 21167, 21168, and 21168.5, including the hearing of an action or proceeding on appeal from a decision of a lower court, all courts in which the action or proceeding is pending shall give the action or proceeding preference over all other civil actions, in the matter of setting the action or proceeding for hearing or trial, and in hearing or trying the action or proceeding, so that the action or proceeding shall be quickly heard and determined. The court shall regulate the briefing schedule so that, to the extent feasible, the court shall commence hearings on an appeal within one year of the date of the filing of the appeal.

(b) To ensure that actions or proceedings brought pursuant to Sections 21167, 21168, and 21168.5 may be quickly heard and determined in the lower courts, the superior courts in all counties with a population of more than 200,000 shall designate one or more judges to develop expertise in this division and related land use and environmental laws, so that those judges will be available to hear, and quickly resolve, actions or proceedings brought pursuant to Sections 21167, 21168, and 21168.5.

(c) In an action or proceeding filed pursuant to this chapter that is joined with any other cause of action, the court, upon a motion by any party, may grant severance of the actions. In determining whether to grant severance, the court shall consider such matters as judicial economy, administrative economy, and prejudice to any party.

[Amended, Chapter 538, Statutes of 2006]

21167.2.   Missed deadline by agency equals CEQA compliance

If no action or proceeding alleging that an environmental impact report does not comply with the provisions of this division is commenced during the period prescribed in subdivision (c) of Section 21167, the environmental impact report shall be conclusively presumed to comply with the provisions of this division for purposes of its use by responsible agencies, unless the provisions of Section 21166 are applicable.

[Added, Chapter 1200, Statutes of 1977]

21167.3. Conditional approvals pending decision on noncompliance

(a) If an action or proceeding alleging that an environmental impact report or a negative declaration does not comply with the provisions of this division is commenced during the period described in subdivision (b) or (c) of Section 21167, and if an injunction or stay is issued prohibiting the project from being carried out or approved pending final determination of the issue of such compliance, responsible agencies shall assume that the environmental impact report or the negative declaration for the project does comply with the provisions of this division and shall issue a conditional approval or disapproval of such project according to the timetable for agency action in Article 5 (commencing with Section 65950) of Chapter 4.5 of Division 1 of Title 7 of the Government Code. A conditional approval shall constitute permission to proceed with a project when and only when such action or proceeding results in a final determination that the environmental impact report or negative declaration does comply with the provisions of this division.

(b) In the event that an action or proceeding is commenced as described in subdivision (a) but no injunction or similar relief is sought and granted, responsible agencies shall assume that the environmental impact report or negative declaration for the project does comply with the provisions of this division and shall approve or disapprove the project according to the timetable for agency action in Article 5 (commencing with Section 65950) of Chapter 4.5 of Division 1 of Title 7 of the Government Code. Such approval shall constitute permission to proceed with the project at the applicant's risk pending final determination of such action or proceeding.

[Amended, Chapter 131, Statutes of 1980]

21167.4. Time limit for hearing on noncompliance; briefing schedule

(a) In any action or proceeding alleging noncompliance with this division, the petitioner shall request a hearing within 90 days from the date of filing the petition or shall be subject to dismissal on the court's own motion or on the motion of any party interested in the action or proceeding.

(b) The petitioner shall serve a notice of the request for a hearing on all parties at the time that the petitioner files the request for a hearing.

(c) Upon the filing of a request by the petitioner for a hearing and upon application by any party, the court shall establish a briefing schedule and a hearing date. In the absence of good cause, briefing shall be completed within 90 days from the date that the request for a hearing is filed, and the hearing, to the extent feasible, shall be held within 30 days thereafter. Good cause may include, but shall not be limited to, the conduct of discovery, determination of the completeness of the record of proceedings, the complexity of the issues, and the length of the record of proceedings and the timeliness of its production. The parties may stipulate to a briefing schedule or hearing date that differs from the schedule set forth in this subdivision if the stipulation is approved by the court.

(d) This section shall become operative on January 1, 2016.

[Added, Chapter 496, Statutes of 2010]

21167.5.   File proof of service with pleading

Proof of prior service by mail upon the public agency carrying out or approving the project of a written notice of the commencement of any action or proceeding described in Section 21167 identifying the project shall be filed concurrently with the initial pleading in such action or proceeding.

[Added, Chapter 1154, Statutes of 1972]

21167.6.   Procedure in actions brought for noncompliance, record of proceedings; excepts PUC

Notwithstanding any other law, in all actions or proceedings brought pursuant to Section 21167, except as provided in Section 21167.6.2 or those involving the Public Utilities Commission, all of the following shall apply:

(a) At the time that the action or proceeding is filed, the plaintiff or petitioner shall file a request that the respondent public agency prepare the record of proceedings relating to the subject of the action or proceeding. The request, together with the complaint or petition, shall be served personally upon the public agency not later than 10 business days from the date that the action or proceeding was filed.

(b) (1) The public agency shall prepare and certify the record of proceedings not later than 60 days from the date that the request specified in subdivision (a) was served upon the public agency. Upon certification, the public agency shall lodge a copy of the record of proceedings with the court and shall serve on the parties notice that the record of proceedings has been certified and lodged with the court. The parties shall pay any reasonable costs or fees imposed for the preparation of the record of proceedings in conformance with any law or rule of court.

(2) The plaintiff or petitioner may elect to prepare the record of proceedings or the parties may agree to an alternative method of preparation of the record of proceedings, subject to certification of its accuracy by the public agency, within the time limit specified in this subdivision.

(c) The time limit established by subdivision (b) may be extended only upon the stipulation of all parties who have been properly served in the action or proceeding or upon order of the court. Extensions shall be liberally granted by the court when the size of the record of proceedings renders infeasible compliance with that time limit. There is no limit on the number of extensions that may be granted by the court, but no single extension shall exceed 60 days unless the court determines that a longer extension is in the public interest.

(d) If the public agency fails to prepare and certify the record within the time limit established in paragraph (1) of subdivision (b), or any continuances of that time limit, the plaintiff or petitioner may move for sanctions, and the court may, upon that motion, grant appropriate sanctions.

(e) The record of proceedings shall include, but is not limited to, all of the following items:

(1) All project application materials.

(2) All staff reports and related documents prepared by the respondent public agency with respect to its compliance with the substantive and procedural requirements of this division and with respect to the action on the project.

(3) All staff reports and related documents prepared by the respondent public agency and written testimony or documents submitted by any person relevant to any findings or statement of overriding considerations adopted by the respondent agency pursuant to this division.

(4) Any transcript or minutes of the proceedings at which the decisionmaking body of the respondent public agency heard testimony on, or considered any environmental document on, the project, and any transcript or minutes of proceedings before any advisory body to the respondent public agency that were presented to the decisionmaking body prior to action on the environmental documents or on the project.

(5) All notices issued by the respondent public agency to comply with this division or with any other law governing the processing and approval of the project.

(6) All written comments received in response to, or in connection with, environmental documents prepared for the project, including responses to the notice of preparation.

(7) All written evidence or correspondence submitted to, or transferred from, the respondent public agency with respect to compliance with this division or with respect to the project.

(8) Any proposed decisions or findings submitted to the decisionmaking body of the respondent public agency by its staff, or the project proponent, project opponents, or other persons.

(9) The documentation of the final public agency decision, including the final environmental impact report, mitigated negative declaration, or negative declaration, and all documents, in addition to those referenced in paragraph (3), cited or relied on in the findings or in a statement of overriding considerations adopted pursuant to this division.

(10) Any other written materials relevant to the respondent public agency's compliance with this division or to its decision on the merits of the project, including the initial study, any drafts of any environmental document, or portions thereof, that have been released for public review, and copies of studies or other documents relied upon in any environmental document prepared for the project and either made available to the public during the public review period or included in the respondent public agency's files on the project, and all internal agency communications, including staff notes and memoranda related to the project or to compliance with this division.

(11) The full written record before any inferior administrative decisionmaking body whose decision was appealed to a superior administrative decisionmaking body prior to the filing of litigation.

(f) In preparing the record of proceedings, the party preparing the record shall strive to do so at reasonable cost in light of the scope of the record.

(g) The clerk of the superior court shall prepare and certify the clerk's transcript on appeal not later than 60 days from the date that the notice designating the papers or records to be included in the clerk's transcript was filed with the superior court, if the party or parties pay any costs or fees for the preparation of the clerk's transcript imposed in conformance with any law or rules of court. Nothing in this subdivision precludes an election to proceed by appendix, as provided in Rule 8.124 of the California Rules of Court.

(h) Extensions of the period for the filing of any brief on appeal may be allowed only by stipulation of the parties or by order of the court for good cause shown. Extensions for the filing of a brief on appeal shall be limited to one 30-day extension for the preparation of an opening brief, and one 30-day extension for the preparation of a responding brief except that the court may grant a longer extension or additional extensions if it determines that there is a substantial likelihood of settlement that would avoid the necessity of completing the appeal.

(i) At the completion of the filing of briefs on appeal, the appellant shall notify the court of the completion of the filing of briefs, whereupon the clerk of the reviewing court shall set the appeal for hearing on the first available calendar date.

[Amended, Chapter 476, Statutes of 2016]

21167.6.2. Concurrent preparation of the record of proceeding

(a) (1) Notwithstanding Section 21167.6, upon the written request of a project applicant received no later than 30 days after the date that the lead agency makes a determination pursuant to subdivision (a) of Section 21080.1, Section 21094.5, or Chapter 4.2 (commencing with Section 21155) and with the consent of the lead agency as provided in subdivision (e), the lead agency shall prepare and certify the record of proceedings in the following manner:

(A) The lead agency for the project shall prepare the record of proceedings pursuant to this division concurrently with the administrative process.

(B) All documents and other materials placed in the record of proceedings shall be posted on, and be downloadable from, an Internet Web site maintained by the lead agency commencing with the date of the release of the draft environmental document for the project. If the lead agency cannot maintain an Internet Web site with the information required pursuant to this section, the lead agency shall provide a link on the agency's Internet Web site to that information.

(C) The lead agency shall make available to the public in a readily accessible electronic format the draft environmental document for the project, and all other documents submitted to, cited by, or relied on by the lead agency, in the preparation of the draft environmental document for the project.

(D) A document prepared by the lead agency or submitted by the applicant after the date of the release of the draft environmental document for the project that is a part of the record of the proceedings shall be made available to the public in a readily accessible electronic format within 5 business days after the document is released or received by the lead agency.

(E) The lead agency shall encourage written comments on the project to be submitted in a readily accessible electronic format, and shall make any comment available to the public in a readily accessible electronic format within 5 business days of its receipt.

(F) Within 7 business days after the receipt of any comment that is not in an electronic format, the lead agency shall convert that comment into a readily accessible electronic format and make it available to the public in that format.

(G) The lead agency shall certify the record of proceedings within 30 days after the filing of the notice required pursuant to Section 21108 or 21152.

(2) This subdivision does not require the disclosure or posting of any trade secret as defined in Section 6254.7 of the Government Code, information about the location of archaeological sites or sacred lands, or any other information that is subject to the disclosure restrictions of Section 6254 of the Government Code.

(b) Any dispute regarding the record of proceedings prepared pursuant to this section shall be resolved by the court in an action or proceeding brought pursuant to subdivision (b) or (c) of Section 21167.

(c) The content of the record of proceedings shall be as specified in subdivision (e) of Section 21167.6.

(d) The negative declaration, mitigated negative declaration, draft and final environmental impact report, or other environmental document shall include a notice in no less than 12-point type stating the following:

"THIS DOCUMENT IS SUBJECT TO SECTION 21167.6.2 OF THE PUBLIC RESOURCES CODE, WHICH REQUIRES THE RECORD OF PROCEEDINGS FOR THIS PROJECT TO BE PREPARED CONCURRENTLY WITH THE ADMINISTRATIVE PROCESS; DOCUMENTS PREPARED BY, OR SUBMITTED TO, THE LEAD AGENCY TO BE POSTED ON THE LEAD AGENCY'S INTERNET WEB SITE; AND THE LEAD AGENCY TO ENCOURAGE WRITTEN COMMENTS ON THE PROJECT TO BE SUBMITTED TO THE LEAD AGENCY IN A READILY ACCESSIBLE ELECTRONIC FORMAT."

(e) (1) The lead agency shall respond to a request by the project applicant within 10 business days from the date that the request pursuant to subdivision (a) is received by the lead agency.

(2) A project applicant and the lead agency may mutually agree, in writing, to extend the time period for the lead agency to respond pursuant to paragraph (1), but they shall not extend that period beyond the commencement of the public review period for the proposed negative declaration, mitigated negative declaration, draft environmental impact report, or other environmental document.

(3) The request to prepare a record of proceedings pursuant to this section shall be deemed denied if the lead agency fails to respond within 10 business days of receiving the request or within the time period agreed upon pursuant to paragraph (2), whichever ends later.

(f) The written request of the applicant submitted pursuant to subdivision (a) shall include an agreement to pay all of the lead agency's costs of preparing and certifying the record of proceedings pursuant to this section and complying with the requirements of this section, in a manner specified by the lead agency.

(g) The costs of preparing the record of proceedings pursuant to this section and complying with the requirements of this section are not recoverable costs pursuant to Section 1032 of the Code of Civil Procedure.

(h) Pursuant to subdivision (f) and Section 21089, the lead agency may charge and collect a reasonable fee from the person making the request pursuant to subdivision (a) to recover the costs incurred by the lead agency in preparing the record of proceedings pursuant to this section.

[Added, Chapter 476, Statutes of 2016]

21167.6.5. Notification requirements

(a) The petitioner or plaintiff shall name, as a real party in interest, the person or persons identified by the public agency in its notice filed pursuant to subdivision (a) or (b) of Section 21108 or Section 21152 or, if no notice is filed, the person or persons in subdivision (b) or (c) of Section 21065, as reflected in the agency's record of proceedings for the project that is the subject of an action or proceeding brought pursuant to Section 21167, 21168, or 21168.5, and shall serve the petition or complaint on that real party in interest, by personal service, mail, facsimile, or any other method permitted by law, not later than 20 business days following service of the petition or complaint on the public agency.

(b) The public agency shall provide the petitioner or plaintiff, not later than 10 business days following service of the petition or complaint on the public agency, with a list of responsible agencies and a public agency having jurisdiction over a natural resource affected by the project.

(c) The petitioner or plaintiff shall provide the responsible agencies, and a public agency having jurisdiction over a natural resource affected by the project, with notice of the action or proceeding within 15 days of receipt of the list described in subdivision (b).

(d) Failure to name potential persons, other than those real parties in interest described in subdivision (a), is not grounds for dismissal pursuant to Section 389 of the Code of Civil Procedure.

(e) This section is not intended to affect an existing right of a party to intervene in the action.

An uncodified provision in AB 320, Chapter 570 of 2011 provided that:

"Section 21167.6.5. of the Public Resources Code as amended by this act does not apply to a proceeding for judicial review filed pursuant to Chapter 6 (commencing with Section 21165) of Division 13 of the Public Resources Code that is pending on or before December 31, 2011, or to an action or proceeding that seeks to attack, review, void, or set aside an act or decision of a public agency for which a notice of determination or notice of exemption was filed on or before December 31, 2011, and the applicable law in effect on that date shall continue to apply to that proceeding."

[Amended, Chapter 162, Statutes of 2012]

21167.7.   File pleading with Attorney General

Every person who brings an action pursuant to Section 21167 shall comply with the requirements of Section 388 of the Code of Civil Procedure. Every such person shall also furnish pursuant to Section 388 of the Code of Civil Procedure a copy of any amended or supplemental pleading filed by such person in such action to the Attorney General. No relief, temporary or permanent, shall be granted until a copy of the pleading has been furnished to the Attorney General in accordance with such requirements.

[Amended, Chapter 664, Statutes of 2002]

21167.8.   Settlement procedure and requirements

(a) Not later than 20 days from the date of service upon a public agency of a petition or complaint brought pursuant to Section 21167, the public agency shall file with the court a notice setting forth the time and place at which all parties shall meet and attempt to settle the litigation. The meeting shall be scheduled and held not later than 45 days from the date of service of the petition or complaint upon the public agency. The notice of the settlement meeting shall be served by mail upon the counsel for each party. If the public agency does not know the identity of counsel for any party, the notice shall be served by mail upon the party for whom counsel is not known.

(b) At the time and place specified in the notice filed with the court, the parties shall meet and confer regarding anticipated issues to be raised in the litigation and shall attempt in good faith to settle the litigation and the dispute which forms the basis of the litigation. The settlement meeting discussions shall be comprehensive in nature and shall focus on the legal issues raised by the parties concerning the project that is the subject of the litigation.

(c) The settlement meeting may be continued from time to time without postponing or otherwise delaying other applicable time limits in the litigation. The settlement meeting is intended to be conducted concurrently with any judicial proceedings.

(d) If the litigation is not settled, the court, in its discretion, may, or at the request of any party, shall, schedule a further settlement conference before a judge of the superior court. If the petition or complaint is later heard on its merits, the judge hearing the matter shall not be the same judge conducting the settlement conference, except in counties that have only one judge of the superior court.

(e) The failure of any party, who was notified pursuant to subdivision (a), to participate in the litigation settlement process, without good cause, may result in an imposition of sanctions by the court.

(f) Not later than 30 days from the date that notice of certification of the record of proceedings was filed and served in accordance with Section 21167.6, the petitioner or plaintiff shall file and serve on all other parties a statement of issues which the petitioner or plaintiff intends to raise in any brief or at any hearing or trial. Not later than 10 days from the date on which the respondent or real party in interest has been served with the statement of issues from the petitioner or plaintiff, each respondent and real party in interest shall file and serve on all other parties a statement of issues which that party intends to raise in any brief or at any hearing or trial.

125

(g) This section shall become operative on January 1, 2016.

[Added, Chapter 496, Statutes of 2010]

21167.9. Mediation

Any action brought in the superior court relating to this division may be subject to a mediation proceeding conducted pursuant to Chapter 9.3 (commencing with Section 66030) of Division 1 of Title 7 of the Government Code.

[Added, Chapter 699, Statutes of 2010]

21168. Court review of agency decisions must comply with CCP; limited court discretion; statement of issues to be raised at trial

Any action or proceeding to attack, review, set aside, void or annul a determination, finding, or decision of a public agency, made as a result of a proceeding in which by law a hearing is required to be given, evidence is required to be taken and discretion in the determination of facts is vested in a public agency, on the grounds of noncompliance with the provisions of this division shall be in accordance with the provisions of Section 1094.5 of the Code of Civil Procedure.

In any such action, the court shall not exercise its independent judgment on the evidence but shall only determine whether the act or decision is supported by substantial evidence in the light of the whole record.

[Amended, Chapter 1312, Statutes of 1976]

21168.5. Court review of decision limited to prejudicial abuse of discretion

In any action or proceeding, other than an action or proceeding under Section 21168, to attack, review, set aside, void or annul a determination, finding, or decision of a public agency on the grounds of noncompliance with this division, the inquiry shall extend only to whether there was a prejudicial abuse of discretion. Abuse of discretion is established if the agency has not proceeded in a manner required by law or if the determination or decision is not supported by substantial evidence.

[Amended, Chapter 1312, Statutes of 1976]

21168.6. Action against PUC goes to the Supreme Court

In any action or proceeding under Sections 21168 or 21168.5 against the Public Utilities Commission the writ of mandate shall lie only from the Supreme Court to such commission.

[Added, Chapter 1154, Statutes of 1972]

21168.6.5. Convention Center Modernization and Farmers Field Project: conditions for project approval

(a) For the purposes of this section, the following definitions shall apply:

(1) "Applicant" means a private entity or its affiliates that proposes the project and its successors, heirs, and assignees.

(2) "Initial project approval" means any actions, activities, ordinances, resolutions, agreements, approvals, determinations, findings, or decisions taken, adopted, or approved by the lead agency required to allow the

126

applicant to commence the construction of the project, as determined by the lead agency.

(3) "Project" means a project that substantially conforms to the project description for the Convention Center Modernization and Farmers Field Project set forth in the notice of preparation released by the City of Los Angeles on March 17, 2011.

(4) "Stadium" means, except as the context indicates otherwise, the stadium built pursuant to the project for football and other spectator events.

(5) "Subsequent project approval" means any actions, activities, ordinances, resolutions, agreements, approvals, determinations, findings, or decisions by the lead agency required for, or in furtherance of, the project that are taken, adopted, or approved following the initial project approvals until the project obtains certificates of occupancy.

(6) "Trip ratio" means the total annual number of private automobiles arriving at the stadium for spectator events divided by the total annual number of spectators at the events.

(b) (1) This section does not apply to the project and shall become inoperative on the date of the release of the draft environmental impact report and is repealed on January 1 of the following year, if the applicant fails to notify the lead agency prior to the release of the draft environmental impact report for public comment that the applicant is electing to proceed pursuant to this section.

(2) The lead agency shall notify the Secretary of State if the applicant fails to notify the lead agency of its election to proceed pursuant to this section.

(c) (1) (A) Notwithstanding any other law, the procedures set forth in subdivision (d) shall apply to any action or proceeding brought to attack, review, set aside, void, or annul the certification of the environmental impact report for the project or the granting of any initial project approvals.

(B) Notwithstanding any other law, the procedures set forth in subdivision (j) shall apply to any action or proceeding brought to attack, review, set aside, void, or annul any subsequent project approvals.

(2) Notwithstanding any other law, the procedure set forth in subdivision (f) shall apply to the certification of the environmental impact report for the project and to any initial project approvals.

(d) (1) An action or proceeding to attack, set aside, void, or annul a determination, finding, or decision of the lead agency certifying the environmental impact report or granting one or more initial project approvals shall be commenced by filing a petition for a writ of mandate with the Second District Court of Appeal and shall be served on the respondent and the real party in interest within 30 days of the filing by the lead agency of the notice required by subdivision (a) of Section 21152.

(2) The petitioner shall file and serve the opening brief in support of the petition for writ of mandate within 40 days of the filing of the petition for a writ of mandate.

(3) The respondent and real party in interest shall file and serve any brief in opposition to the petition for writ of mandate within 25 days of the filing of the opening brief.

(4) The petitioner shall file and serve the reply brief within 20 days of the filing of the last opposition brief to the petitioner's opening brief.

(5) Except as provided in paragraph (6), parties to the action shall comply with all applicable California Rules of Court in the filing of the petition for writ of mandate and the briefs.

(6) (A) Rule 8.220 of the California Rules of Court shall not apply to the time periods set forth in paragraphs (2) to (4), inclusive.

    (B) If a petitioner fails to file the opening brief pursuant to paragraph (2), the Court of Appeal shall dismiss the petition.

    (C) If the respondents and real party in interest fail to file the brief in opposition pursuant to paragraph (3), the Court of Appeal shall decide the petition for writ of mandate based on the record, the opening brief, and any oral argument by the petitioner.

(7) Except upon a showing of extraordinary good cause, the Court of Appeal shall not grant any extensions of time to the deadlines specified in this subdivision. Any extension shall be limited to the minimum amount the Court of Appeal deems to be necessary.

(8) The Court of Appeal may, on its motion or upon request from a party, appoint a special master to assist the Court of Appeal in conducting the expedited judicial review required pursuant to this subdivision. If the Court of Appeal appoints a special master, the applicant shall pay all reasonable costs for the special master, not to exceed one hundred fifty thousand dollars ($150,000). If the Court of Appeal determines that the cost of the special master may exceed one hundred fifty thousand dollars ($150,000), it may request that additional funds be provided by the applicant and, if the applicant agrees to provide the funding, shall use the funds to pay the additional costs of the special master.

(9) The Court of Appeal shall hold a hearing and issue a decision on all petitions for writ of mandate filed pursuant to this subdivision within 60 days of the filing of the last timely reply brief.

(10)(A) A petition for review of the decision rendered by the Court of Appeal shall be filed with the Supreme Court and served on all parties to the petition for writ of mandate within 15 days of the decision.

    (B) Any opposition to the petition for review shall be filed and served within 15 days of the filing of the petition for review.

    (C) The Supreme Court shall render a decision on the petition for review within 30 days after the filing of the petition for review or within 15 days after the filing of the opposition to the petition for review, whichever is earlier.

(11)All briefs and notices filed pursuant to this subdivision shall be electronically served on parties pursuant to Rule 8.71 of the California

Rules of Court. Each party to the petition shall provide an electronic service address at which the party agrees to accept the service.

(12) (A) No provision of law that is inconsistent or conflicts with this subdivision shall apply to a petition for a writ of mandate subject to this subdivision, including, but not limited to, any of the following:

(i) Section 21167.4.

(ii) Subdivisions (a) through (d), inclusive, and (g) through (i), inclusive, of Section 21167.6.

(iii) Subdivision (f) of Section 21167.8.

(iv) Section 21167.6.5.

(v) Sections 66031 through 66035, inclusive, of the Government Code.

(B) Except as provided in this section, including subparagraph (A), the requirements of this division are fully applicable to the project.

(e) (1) The draft and final environmental impact report shall include a notice in not less than 12-point type stating the following:

THIS EIR IS SUBJECT TO SECTION 21168.6.5 OF THE PUBLIC RESOURCES CODE, WHICH PROVIDES, AMONG OTHER THINGS, THAT THE LEAD AGENCY NEED NOT CONSIDER CERTAIN COMMENTS FILED AFTER THE CLOSE OF THE PUBLIC COMMENT PERIOD FOR THE DRAFT EIR. ANY JUDICIAL ACTION CHALLENGING THE CERTIFICATION OF THE EIR OR THE APPROVAL OF THE PROJECT DESCRIBED IN THE EIR IS SUBJECT TO THE PROCEDURES SET FORTH IN SECTION 21168.6.5 OF THE PUBLIC RESOURCES CODE AND MUST BE FILED WITH THE SECOND DISTRICT COURT OF APPEAL. A COPY OF SECTION 21168.6.5 OF THE PUBLIC RESOURCES CODE IS INCLUDED IN THE APPENDIX TO THIS EIR.

(2) The draft environmental impact report and final environmental impact report shall contain, as an appendix, the full text of this section.

(f) (1) Within 10 days after the release of the draft environmental impact report, the lead agency shall conduct an informational workshop to inform the public of the key analyses and conclusions of that report.

(2) Within 10 days before the close of the public comment period, the lead agency shall hold a public hearing to receive testimony on the draft environmental impact report. A transcript of the hearing shall be included as an appendix to the final environmental impact report.

(3) (A) Within five days following the close of the public comment period, a commenter on the draft environmental impact report may submit to the lead agency a written request for nonbinding mediation. The lead agency and applicant shall participate in nonbinding mediation with all commenters who submitted timely comments on the draft environmental impact report and who requested the mediation. Mediation conducted pursuant to this paragraph shall end no later than 35 days after the close of the public comment period.

(B)   A request for mediation shall identify all areas of dispute raised in the comment submitted by the commenter that are to be mediated.

(C)   The lead agency shall select one or more mediators who shall be retired judges or recognized experts with at least five years experience in land use and environmental law or science, or mediation. The applicant shall bear the costs of mediation.

(D)   A mediation session shall be conducted on each area of dispute with the parties requesting mediation on that area of dispute.

(E)   The lead agency shall adopt, as a condition of approval, any measures agreed upon by the lead agency, the applicant, and any commenter who requested mediation. A commenter who agrees to a measure pursuant to this subparagraph shall not raise the issue addressed by that measure as a basis for a petition for writ of mandate challenging the lead agency's decision to certify the environmental impact report or to grant one or more initial project approvals.

(4)   The lead agency need not consider written comments submitted after the close of the public comment period, unless those comments address any of the following:

(A)   New issues raised in the response to comments by the lead agency.

(B)   New information released by the public agency subsequent to the release of the draft environmental impact report, such as new information set forth or embodied in a staff report, proposed permit, proposed resolution, ordinance, or similar documents.

(C)   Changes made to the project after the close of the public comment period.

(D)   Proposed conditions for approval, mitigation measures, or proposed findings required by Section 21081 or a proposed reporting and monitoring program required by paragraph (1) of subdivision (a) of Section 21081.6, where the lead agency releases those documents subsequent to the release of the draft environmental impact report.

(E)   New information that was not reasonably known and could not have been reasonably known during the public comment period.

(5)   (A)   The lead agency shall file the notice required by subdivision (a) of Section 21152 within five days after the last initial project approval.

(B)   If the notice required by subdivision (a) of Section 21152 is filed after June 1, 2013, this section shall become inoperative as of June 1, 2013, and is repealed as of January 1, 2014.

(C)   In the event this section is repealed pursuant to subparagraph (B), the lead agency shall notify the Secretary of State.

(g)   (1)   For a petition for writ of mandate filed pursuant to this section, the lead agency shall prepare and certify the record of the proceedings in accordance with this subdivision and in accordance with Rule 3.1365 of the California Rules of Court. The applicant shall pay the lead agency for all costs of preparing and certifying the record of proceedings.

(2) No later than the date of the release of the draft environmental impact report, the lead agency shall make available to the public in a readily accessible electronic format the draft environmental impact report and all other documents submitted to or relied on by the lead agency in the preparation of the draft environmental impact report. A document prepared by the lead agency or submitted by the applicant after the date of the release of the draft environmental impact report that is a part of the record of the proceedings shall be made available to the public in a readily accessible electronic format within five business days after the document is prepared or received by the lead agency.

(3) The lead agency shall encourage written comments on the project to be submitted in a readily accessible electronic format, and shall make any such comment available to the public in a readily accessible electronic format within five days of its receipt.

(4) Within seven business days after the receipt of any comment that is not in an electronic format, the lead agency shall convert that comment into a readily accessible electronic format and make it available to the public in that format.

(5) The lead agency shall indicate in the record of the proceedings comments received that were not considered by the lead agency pursuant to paragraph (4) of subdivision (f) and need not include the content of the comments as a part of the record.

(6) Within five days after the filing of the notice required by subdivision (a) of Section 21152, the lead agency shall certify the record of the proceedings for the approval or determination and shall provide an electronic copy of the record to a party that has submitted a written request for a copy. The lead agency may charge and collect a reasonable fee for the electronic copy, which shall not exceed the reasonable cost of reproducing that copy.

(7) Within 10 days after being served with a petition for a writ of mandate pursuant to paragraph (1) of subdivision (d), the lead agency shall lodge a copy of the certified record of proceedings with the Court of Appeal.

(8) Any dispute over the content of the record of the proceedings shall be resolved by the Court of Appeal. Unless the Court of Appeal directs otherwise, a party disputing the content of the record shall file a motion to augment the record at the time it files its initial brief.

(9) The contents of the record of proceedings shall be as set forth in subdivision (e) of Section 21167.6.

(h) It is the intent of the Legislature that the project minimize traffic congestion and air quality impacts that may result from private automobile trips to the stadium through the requirements of this division as supplemented, pursuant to subdivision (i), by the implementation of measures that will do both of the following:

(1) Achieve and maintain carbon neutrality by reducing to zero the net emissions of greenhouse gases, as defined in subdivision (g) of Section 38505 of the Health and Safety Code, from private automobile trips to the stadium.

131

(2) Achieve and maintain a trip ratio that is no more than 90 percent of the trip ratio at any other stadium serving a team in the National Football League.

(i) (1) As a condition of approval of the project subject to this section, the lead agency shall require the applicant to implement measures that will meet the requirements of this division and paragraph (1) of subdivision (h) by the end of the first season during which a National Football League team has played at the stadium. To maximize public health, environmental, and employment benefits, the lead agency shall place the highest priority on feasible measures that will reduce greenhouse gas emissions on the stadium site and in the neighboring communities of the stadium. Offset credits shall be employed by the applicant only after feasible local emission reduction measures have been implemented. The applicant shall, to the extent feasible, place the highest priority on the purchase of offset credits that produce emission reductions within the city or the boundaries of the South Coast Air Quality Management District.

(2) To ensure that the stadium achieves a trip ratio that is no more than 90 percent of the trip ratio at any other stadium serving a team in the National Football League, the applicant shall implement the necessary measures as follows:

(A) Not later than the date of the certification of the environmental impact report for the project, the lead agency shall develop and adopt a protocol to implement this subdivision pursuant to this division and subdivision (h), including, but not limited to, criteria and guidelines that will be used to determine the trip ratio.

(B) Following the conclusion of the second, third, fourth, and fifth seasons during which a National Football League team has played at the stadium, the applicant shall prepare a report to the lead agency that describes the measures it has undertaken to reduce trips based on the protocol developed and adopted pursuant to subparagraph (A), the trip ratio at the stadium, and the results of those measures. The report shall also include a summary of publicly available data and other data gathered by the applicant regarding average vehicle ridership, nonpassenger automobile modes of arrival, and trip reduction measures undertaken at other stadiums serving a team in the National Football League.

(C) Following the lead agency's review of the report submitted following the fourth season, the lead agency shall determine whether adequate data is available to determine whether the trip ratio at stadium events is more than 90 percent of the trip ratio at any other stadiums serving a National Football League team. If the lead agency concludes that adequate data does not exist, the lead agency shall take necessary steps to collect, or cause to be collected, the data reasonably necessary to make the determination. The applicant shall pay the reasonable costs of collecting the data pursuant to subdivision (a) of Section 21089.

(D) Following the lead agency's review of the report submitted following the fifth season, the lead agency shall determine the trip ratio at stadium events and the lowest trip ratio at any other stadium serving a

National Football League team. If the trip ratio at the stadium is more than 90 percent of the trip ratio at the other stadium with the lowest trip ratio, the lead agency shall, within six months following the receipt of the report, require the applicant to implement additional feasible measures that the lead agency determines pursuant to subparagraph (E) will be sufficient for the stadium to achieve the target specified in paragraph (2) of subdivision (h).

(E) Any trip reduction measure used at other stadiums serving a National Football League team shall be presumed to be feasible unless a preponderance of the evidence demonstrates that the measure is infeasible. The lead agency's decision whether to adopt any mitigation measures pursuant to subparagraph (D) other than those used at another stadium serving a National Football League team shall be governed by the substantial evidence test. This subparagraph does not require the applicant to bear the cost of improving the capacity or performance of transit facilities other than the following:

(i) Temporarily expanding the capacity of a public transit line, as needed, to serve stadium events.

(ii) Providing private charter buses or other similar services, as needed, to serve stadium events.

(iii) Paying its fair share of the cost of measures that expand the capacity of a public fixed or light rail station that is used by spectators attending stadium events.

(F) Any action or proceeding to attack, review, set aside, void, or annul a determination, finding, or decision of the lead agency regarding the additional mitigation measures pursuant to subparagraph (D) shall be commenced within 30 days following the lead agency's filing of the notice required by subdivision (a) of Section 21152 and shall be governed by this division. The procedures set forth in subdivision (d) shall not apply to that action or proceeding. Notwithstanding any other law, compliance or noncompliance with this paragraph shall not result in the stadium being required to cease or limit operations.

(G) If the lead agency requires the applicant to implement additional measures pursuant to subparagraph (D), the applicant shall submit the report described in subparagraph (B) to the lead agency following the conclusion of each subsequent season until the lead agency determines that the applicant has achieved a trip ratio at the stadium that is not more than 90 percent of the trip ratio at any other stadium serving a National Football League team for two consecutive seasons or until the applicant submits the required report following the conclusion of the 10th season, whichever occurs earlier. Nothing in this subparagraph affects the ongoing obligations of the applicant pursuant to subdivision (h) and this subdivision.

(H) All obligations of the applicant set forth in this subdivision or imposed upon the applicant by the lead agency pursuant to this subdivision shall run with the land.

(3) This subdivision and subdivision (h) shall not serve as a basis for any action or proceeding to attack, set aside, void, or annul a determination, finding, or decision of the lead agency in certifying the environmental impact report for the project or in granting the initial or subsequent project approvals.

(4) The obligations imposed pursuant to this subdivision and subdivision (h) supplement, and do not replace, mitigation measures otherwise imposed on the project pursuant to this division.

(j) (1) An action or proceeding to attack, set aside, void, or annul a determination, finding, or decision of the lead agency granting a subsequent project approval shall be subject to the requirements of Chapter 6 (commencing with Section 21165).

(2) (A) In granting relief in an action or proceeding brought pursuant to this subdivision, the court shall not stay or enjoin the construction or operation of the project unless the court finds either of the following:

(i) The continued construction or operation of the project presents an imminent threat to the public health and safety.

(ii) The project site contains unforeseen important Native American artifacts or unforeseen important historical, archaeological, or ecological values that would be materially, permanently, and adversely affected by the continued construction or operation of the project.

(B) If the court finds that clause (i) or (ii) is satisfied, the court shall only enjoin those specific project activities that present an imminent threat to public health and safety or that materially, permanently, and adversely affect unforeseen important Native American artifacts or unforeseen important historical, archaeological, or ecological values.

(k) The provisions of this section are severable. If any provision of this section or its application is held invalid, that invalidity shall not affect other provisions or applications that can be given effect without the invalid provision or application.

[Added & Repealed, Chapter 353, Statutes of 2011]

21168.6.6. Judicial review streamlining for environmental leadership development projects; entertainment and sports center in the City of Sacramento

(a) For the purposes of this section, the following definitions shall have the following meanings:

(1) "Applicant" means a private entity or its affiliates that proposes the project and its successors, heirs, and assignees.

(2) "City" means the City of Sacramento.

(3) "Downtown arena" means the following components of the entertainment and sports center project from demolition and site preparation through operation:

(A) An arena facility that will become the new home to the City of Sacramento's National Basketball Association (NBA) team that does both of the following:

    (i) Receives Leadership in Energy and Environmental Design (LEED) gold certification for new construction within one year of completion of the first NBA season.

    (ii) Minimizes operational traffic congestion and air quality impacts through either or both project design and the implementation of feasible mitigation measures that will do all of the following:

        (I) Achieve and maintain carbon neutrality or better by reducing to at least zero the net emissions of greenhouse gases, as defined in subdivision (g) of Section 38505 of the Health and Safety Code, from private automobile trips to the downtown arena as compared to the baseline as verified by the Sacramento Metropolitan Air Quality Management District.

        (II) Achieve a per attendee reduction in greenhouse gas emissions from automobiles and light trucks compared to per attendee greenhouse gas emissions associated with the existing arena during the 2012-13 NBA season that will exceed the carbon reduction targets for 2020 and 2035 achieved in the sustainable communities strategy prepared by the Sacramento Area Council of Governments for the Sacramento region pursuant to Chapter 728 of the Statutes of 2008.

        (III) Achieve and maintain vehicle-miles-traveled per attendee for NBA events at the downtown arena that is no more than 85 percent of the baseline.

(B) Associated public spaces.

(C) Facilities and infrastructure for ingress, egress, and use of the arena facility.

(4) "Entertainment and sports center project" or "project" means a project that substantially conforms to the project description for the entertainment and sports center project set forth in the notice of preparation released by the City of Sacramento on April 12, 2013.

(b) (1) The city may prosecute an eminent domain action for 545 and 600 K Street, Sacramento, California, and surrounding publicly accessible areas and rights-of-way within 200 feet of 600 K Street, Sacramento, California, through order of possession pursuant to the Eminent Domain Law (Title 7 (commencing with Section 1230.010) of Part 3 of the Code of Civil Procedure) prior to completing the environmental review under this division.

(2) Paragraph (1) shall not apply to any other eminent domain actions prosecuted by the City of Sacramento or to eminent domain actions based on a finding of blight.

(c) Notwithstanding any other law, the procedures established pursuant to subdivision (d) shall apply to an action or proceeding brought to attack, review, set aside, void, or annul the certification of the environmental impact report for the project or the granting of any project approvals.

(d) On or before July 1, 2014, the Judicial Council shall adopt a rule of court to establish procedures applicable to actions or proceedings brought to attack, review, set aside, void, or annul the certification of the environmental impact report for the project or the granting of any project approvals that require the actions or proceedings, including any potential appeals therefrom, be resolved, to the extent feasible, within 270 days of certification of the record of proceedings pursuant to subdivision (f).

(e) (1) The draft and final environmental impact report shall include a notice in not less than 12-point type stating the following:

THIS EIR IS SUBJECT TO SECTION 21168.6.6 OF THE PUBLIC RESOURCES CODE, WHICH PROVIDES, AMONG OTHER THINGS, THAT THE LEAD AGENCY NEED NOT CONSIDER CERTAIN COMMENTS FILED AFTER THE CLOSE OF THE PUBLIC COMMENT PERIOD FOR THE DRAFT EIR. ANY JUDICIAL ACTION CHALLENGING THE CERTIFICATION OF THE EIR OR THE APPROVAL OF THE PROJECT DESCRIBED IN THE EIR IS SUBJECT TO THE PROCEDURES SET FORTH IN SECTION 21168.6.6 OF THE PUBLIC RESOURCES CODE. A COPY OF SECTION 21168.6.6 OF THE PUBLIC RESOURCES CODE IS INCLUDED IN THE APPENDIX TO THIS EIR.

(2) The draft environmental impact report and final environmental impact report shall contain, as an appendix, the full text of this section.

(3) Within 10 days after the release of the draft environmental impact report, the lead agency shall conduct an informational workshop to inform the public of the key analyses and conclusions of that report.

(4) Within 10 days before the close of the public comment period, the lead agency shall hold a public hearing to receive testimony on the draft environmental impact report. A transcript of the hearing shall be included as an appendix to the final environmental impact report.

(5) (A) Within five days following the close of the public comment period, a commenter on the draft environmental impact report may submit to the lead agency a written request for nonbinding mediation. The lead agency and applicant shall participate in nonbinding mediation with all commenters who submitted timely comments on the draft environmental impact report and who requested the mediation. Mediation conducted pursuant to this paragraph shall end no later than 35 days after the close of the public comment period.

(B) A request for mediation shall identify all areas of dispute raised in the comment submitted by the commenter that are to be mediated.

(C) The lead agency shall select one or more mediators who shall be retired judges or recognized experts with at least five years experience in land use and environmental law or science, or mediation. The applicant shall bear the costs of mediation.

(D) A mediation session shall be conducted on each area of dispute with the parties requesting mediation on that area of dispute.

(E) The lead agency shall adopt, as a condition of approval, any measures agreed upon by the lead agency, the applicant, and any commenter who requested mediation. A commenter who agrees to a measure pursuant to this subparagraph shall not raise the issue addressed by that measure as a basis for an action or proceeding challenging the lead agency's decision to certify the environmental impact report or to grant one or more initial project approvals.

(6) The lead agency need not consider written comments submitted after the close of the public comment period, unless those comments address any of the following:

(A) New issues raised in the response to comments by the lead agency.

(B) New information released by the public agency subsequent to the release of the draft environmental impact report, such as new information set forth or embodied in a staff report, proposed permit, proposed resolution, ordinance, or similar documents.

(C) Changes made to the project after the close of the public comment period.

(D) Proposed conditions for approval, mitigation measures, or proposed findings required by Section 21081 or a proposed reporting and monitoring program required by paragraph (1) of subdivision (a) of Section 21081.6, where the lead agency releases those documents subsequent to the release of the draft environmental impact report.

(E) New information that was not reasonably known and could not have been reasonably known during the public comment period.

(7) The lead agency shall file the notice required by subdivision (a) of Section 21152 within five days after the last initial project approval.

(f) (1) The lead agency shall prepare and certify the record of the proceedings in accordance with this subdivision and in accordance with Rule 3.1365 of the California Rules of Court. The applicant shall pay the lead agency for all costs of preparing and certifying the record of proceedings.

(2) No later than three business days following the date of the release of the draft environmental impact report, the lead agency shall make available to the public in a readily accessible electronic format the draft environmental impact report and all other documents submitted to or relied on by the lead agency in the preparation of the draft environmental impact report. A document prepared by the lead agency or submitted by the applicant after the date of the release of the draft environmental impact report that is a part of the record of the proceedings shall be made available to the public in a readily accessible electronic format within five business days after the document is prepared or received by the lead agency.

(3) Notwithstanding paragraph (2), documents submitted to or relied on by the lead agency that were not prepared specifically for the project and are copyright protected are not required to be made readily accessible in an electronic format. For those copyright protected documents, the lead

agency shall make an index of these documents available in an electronic format no later than the date of the release of the draft environmental impact report, or within five business days if the document is received or relied on by the lead agency after the release of the draft environmental impact report. The index must specify the libraries or lead agency offices in which hardcopies of the copyrighted materials are available for public review.

(4) The lead agency shall encourage written comments on the project to be submitted in a readily accessible electronic format, and shall make any such comment available to the public in a readily accessible electronic format within five days of its receipt.

(5) Within seven business days after the receipt of any comment that is not in an electronic format, the lead agency shall convert that comment into a readily accessible electronic format and make it available to the public in that format.

(6) The lead agency shall indicate in the record of the proceedings comments received that were not considered by the lead agency pursuant to paragraph (6) of subdivision (e) and need not include the content of the comments as a part of the record.

(7) Within five days after the filing of the notice required by subdivision (a) of Section 21152, the lead agency shall certify the record of the proceedings for the approval or determination and shall provide an electronic copy of the record to a party that has submitted a written request for a copy. The lead agency may charge and collect a reasonable fee from a party requesting a copy of the record for the electronic copy, which shall not exceed the reasonable cost of reproducing that copy.

(8) Within 10 days after being served with a complaint or a petition for a writ of mandate, the lead agency shall lodge a copy of the certified record of proceedings with the superior court.

(9) Any dispute over the content of the record of the proceedings shall be resolved by the superior court. Unless the superior court directs otherwise, a party disputing the content of the record shall file a motion to augment the record at the time it files its initial brief.

(10) The contents of the record of proceedings shall be as set forth in subdivision (e) of Section 21167.6.

(g) (1) As a condition of approval of the project subject to this section, the lead agency shall require the applicant, with respect to any measures specific to the operation of the downtown arena, to implement those measures that will meet the requirements of this division by the end of the first NBA regular season or June of the first NBA regular season, whichever is later, during which an NBA team has played at the downtown arena.

(2) To maximize public health, environmental, and employment benefits, the lead agency shall place the highest priority on feasible measures that will reduce greenhouse gas emissions on the downtown arena site and in the neighboring communities of the downtown arena. Mitigation measures that shall be considered and implemented, if feasible and necessary, to achieve

the standards set forth in subclauses (I) to (III), inclusive, of clause (ii) of subparagraph (A) of paragraph (3) of subdivision (a), including, but not limited to:

(A) Temporarily expanding the capacity of a public transit line, as needed, to serve downtown arena events.

(B) Providing private charter buses or other similar services, as needed, to serve downtown arena events.

(C) Paying its fair share of the cost of measures that expand the capacity of a public fixed or light rail station that is used by spectators attending downtown arena events.

(3) Offset credits shall be employed by the applicant only after feasible local emission reduction measures have been implemented. The applicant shall, to the extent feasible, place the highest priority on the purchase of offset credits that produce emission reductions within the city or the boundaries of the Sacramento Metropolitan Air Quality Management District.

(h) (1) (A) In granting relief in an action or proceeding brought pursuant to this section, the court shall not stay or enjoin the construction or operation of the downtown arena unless the court finds either of the following:

(i) The continued construction or operation of the downtown arena presents an imminent threat to the public health and safety.

(ii) The downtown arena site contains unforeseen important Native American artifacts or unforeseen important historical, archaeological, or ecological values that would be materially, permanently, and adversely affected by the continued construction or operation of the downtown arena unless the court stays or enjoins the construction or operation of the downtown arena.

(B) If the court finds that clause (i) or (ii) is satisfied, the court shall only enjoin those specific activities associated with the downtown arena that present an imminent threat to public health and safety or that materially, permanently, and adversely affect unforeseen important Native American artifacts or unforeseen important historical, archaeological, or ecological values.

(2) An action or proceeding to attack, set aside, void, or annul a determination, finding, or decision of the lead agency granting a subsequent project approval shall be subject to the requirements of Chapter 6 (commencing with Section 21165).

(3) Where an action or proceeding brought pursuant to this section challenges aspects of the project other than the downtown arena and those portions or specific project activities are severable from the downtown arena, the court may enter an order as to aspects of the project other than the downtown arena that includes one or more of the remedies set forth in Section 21168.9.

(i) The provisions of this section are severable. If any provision of this section or its application is held invalid, that invalidity shall not affect other provisions or applications that can be given effect without the invalid provision or application.

(j) (1) This section does not apply to the project and shall become inoperative on the date of the release of the draft environmental impact report and is repealed on January 1 of the following year, if the applicant fails to notify the lead agency prior to the release of the draft environmental impact report for public comment that the applicant is electing to proceed pursuant to this section.

(2) The lead agency shall notify the Secretary of State if the applicant fails to notify the lead agency of its election to proceed pursuant to this section.

[Added & Repealed, Chapter 386, Statutes of 2013]

21168.6.7. Oakland Sports and Mixed-use project, procedures; expedited judicial review

(a) For purposes of this section, the following definitions apply:

(1) "Applicant" means a public or private entity or its affiliates that proposes the project and its successors, heirs, and assignees.

(2) "City of Oakland's Bird Safety Measures" means bird safe ordinance guidelines added in June 2013 by City of Oakland's planning staff to the city's standard building permit requirements to reduce bird collisions and other negative impacts to wildlife.

(3) "Oakland Sports and Mixed-Use Project" or "project" means the following components of a sports center and mixed-use project located at the Howard Terminal site in the City of Oakland, from demolition and site preparation through operation:

(A) A baseball park that will become the new home to the Oakland Athletics and adjacent residential, retail, commercial, cultural, entertainment, or recreational uses developed by the Oakland Athletics, and that meets all of the following:

(i) The baseball park receives Leadership in Energy and Environmental Design (LEED) Gold certification for new construction within one year after completion of the first baseball season and each new nonresidential building receives LEED Gold certification for new construction within one year after completion of the applicable nonresidential building. Any residential building shall achieve sustainability standards of at least a LEED Gold level or the comparable GreenPoint rating, including meeting sustainability standards for access to quality transit.

(ii) The project does not result in any net additional emissions of greenhouse gases, including greenhouse gas emissions from employee transportation, as determined by the State Air Resources Board pursuant to Division 25.5 (commencing with Section 38500) of the Health and Safety Code. To maximize public health, environmental, and employment benefits, the lead agency shall require measures that will reduce the emissions of

140

greenhouse gases in the project area and in the neighboring communities of the baseball park. Not less than 50 percent of the greenhouse gas emissions reductions necessary to achieve the requirements of this clause, excluding the greenhouse gas emissions from residential uses of the project, shall be from local, direct greenhouse gas emissions reduction measures that give consideration to criteria air pollutant and toxic air contaminant emissions reductions, including, but not limited to, any of the following:

(I) Project design features or onsite reduction measures, or both design features and onsite reduction measures.

(II) Off-site reduction measures in the neighboring communities.

The applicant may obtain offset credits for up to 50 percent of the greenhouse gas emissions reductions necessary to achieve the requirement of this clause. The applicant shall, to the extent feasible, place the highest priority on the purchase of offset credits that produce emission reductions within the City of Oakland or the boundaries of the Bay Area Air Quality Management District. Any offset credits shall be verified by a third party accredited by the State Air Resources Board. In no event shall offset credits be used from a project located outside the United States.

(iii) The project has a transportation management plan or transportation demand management program, or both, that achieves a 20-percent reduction in the number of vehicle trips collectively by attendees, employees, visitors, and customers as compared to operations absent the transportation management plan or transportation demand management program, or both that plan and program. The plan or program for the baseball park shall achieve the 20-percent reduction within one-year after the completion of the first baseball season. The plan or program for the nonbaseball-park portion of the project shall achieve the 20-percent reduction within one year after the completion of that portion. The transportation management plan or transportation demand program shall include a menu of options designed to reduce the number of vehicle trips, including temporarily expanding the capacity of a public transit line, as appropriate, to serve the baseball park events, and participation in a transportation management association that will determine a range of services and programs designed to meet the 20-percent reduction, including providing incentives for transit usage and carpools, bicycle parking and support, signage, and real-time transit information.

(iv) The project is located within a priority development area identified in the sustainable communities strategy Plan Bay Area

2040 adopted by the Metropolitan Transportation Commission and the Association of Bay Area Governments.

    (v) The project is subject to a comprehensive package of community benefits approved by the Port of Oakland or City Council of the City of Oakland, as applicable, which may include local employment and job training programs, local business and small business policies, public access and open space, affordable housing, transportation infrastructure, increased frequency of public transit, and transit accessibility and sustainable and healthy development measures for the surrounding community.

  (B) Associated public spaces.

  (C) Facilities and infrastructure for ingress, egress, and use of the baseball park and mixed-use development.

(b) As a condition of approval of the project, the lead agency shall require the applicant, with respect to any measures specific to the operation of the baseball park, to implement measures that will meet the requirements of this division by the end of the first baseball season.

(c) Rules 3.2220 to 3.2237, inclusive, of the California Rules of Court, as may be amended by the Judicial Council, shall apply to any action or proceeding brought to attack, review, set aside, void, or annul the certification or adoption of any environmental impact report for the project that is certified pursuant to subdivision (d) or the granting of any project approvals, to require the action or proceeding, including any potential appeals therefrom, to be resolved, to the extent feasible, within 270 days of the filing of the certified record of proceedings with the court. On or before September 1, 2019, the Judicial Council shall amend the California Rules of Court, as necessary, to implement this subdivision.

(d) The Governor may certify the project for streamlining pursuant to this section if it complies with all of the following conditions:

  (1) The project creates high-wage, highly skilled jobs that pay prevailing wages and living wages, provides construction jobs and permanent jobs for Californians, and helps reduce unemployment. For purposes of this subdivision, "jobs that pay prevailing wages" means that all construction workers employed in the execution of the project will receive at least the general prevailing rate of per diem wages for the type of work and geographic area, as determined by the Director of Industrial Relations pursuant to Sections 1773 and 1773.9 of the Labor Code. If the project is certified for streamlining, the project applicant shall include this requirement in all contracts for the performance of the work.

  (2) (A) If the project is certified pursuant to this section, contractors and subcontractors shall pay to all construction workers employed in the execution of the project at least the general prevailing rate of per diem wages.

    (B) Except as provided in subparagraph (C), the obligation of the contractors and subcontractors to pay prevailing wages pursuant to subparagraph (A) may be enforced by the Labor Commissioner through the issuance of a civil wage and penalty assessment pursuant to Section 1741 of the Labor Code, which may be reviewed pursuant to Section 1742 of the Labor Code within 18 months after the completion of the project, or by an underpaid worker through an administrative complaint or civil action. If a civil wage and penalty assessment is issued, the contractor, subcontractor, and surety on a bond or bonds issued to secure the payment of wages covered by the assessment shall be liable for liquidated damages pursuant to Section 1742.1 of the Labor Code.

(C) Subparagraph (B) does not apply if all contractors and subcontractors performing work on the project are subject to a project labor agreement that requires the payment of prevailing wages to all construction workers employed in the execution of the project and provides for enforcement of that obligation through an arbitration procedure. For purposes of this subparagraph, "project labor agreement" has the same meaning as set forth in paragraph (1) of subdivision (b) of Section 2500 of the Public Contract Code.

(3) The project applicant demonstrates compliance with clauses (i) to (iii), inclusive, of subparagraph (A) of paragraph (3) of subdivision (a) and mitigation measures, to the extent feasible, to reduce any additional greenhouse gas emissions from the project, including greenhouse gas emissions from employee transportation.

(4) The project applicant demonstrates compliance with the requirements of Chapter 12.8 (commencing with Section 42649) and Chapter 12.9 (commencing with Section 42649.8) of Part 3 of Division 30, as applicable.

(5) The project applicant has entered into a binding and enforceable agreement that all mitigation measures required pursuant to this division and any other environmental measures required by this section to certify the project under this chapter shall be conditions of approval of the project, and those conditions will be fully enforceable by the lead agency or another agency designated by the lead agency. In the case of environmental mitigation measures and any other environmental measures required by this section, the applicant agrees, as an ongoing obligation, that those measures will be monitored and enforced by the lead agency for the life of the obligation.

(6) The project applicant agrees to pay for any additional costs incurred by the courts in hearing and deciding any case brought pursuant to this section, including payment of the costs for the appointment of a special master if deemed appropriate by the court, in a form and manner specified by the Judicial Council, as provided in the rules of court adopted by the Judicial Council.

(7) The project applicant agrees to pay the costs of preparing the record of proceedings for the project concurrent with review and consideration of the project pursuant to this division, in a form and manner specified by the lead agency for the project.

(8) Project design and implementation will comply with the City of Oakland's Bird Safety Measures, adopted in 2013. Nighttime programming will apply

best management practice strategies to avoid and reduce potential collision hazards for migratory and resident birds, to the extent feasible.

(9) The project meets the requirements of clauses (iv) and (v) of subparagraph (A) of paragraph (3) of subdivision (a).

(e) (1) Prior to certifying the project, the Governor shall make a determination that each of the conditions specified in subdivision (d) has been met. These findings are not subject to judicial review.

(2) The guidelines issued pursuant to Chapter 6.5 (commencing with Section 21178) apply to the implementation of this section, to the extent those guidelines are applicable and do not conflict with specific requirements of this section.

(f) (1) The draft and final environmental impact report shall include a notice in not less than 12-point type stating the following:

THIS ENVIRONMENTAL IMPACT REPORT IS SUBJECT TO SECTION 21168.6.7 OF THE PUBLIC RESOURCES CODE, WHICH PROVIDES, AMONG OTHER THINGS, THAT THE LEAD AGENCY NEED NOT CONSIDER CERTAIN COMMENTS FILED AFTER THE CLOSE OF THE PUBLIC COMMENT PERIOD, IF ANY, FOR THE DRAFT ENVIRONMENTAL IMPACT REPORT. ANY JUDICIAL ACTION CHALLENGING THE CERTIFICATION OR ADOPTION OF THE ENVIRONMENTAL IMPACT REPORT OR THE APPROVAL OF THE PROJECT DESCRIBED IN SECTION 21168.6.7 OF THE PUBLIC RESOURCES CODE IS SUBJECT TO THE PROCEDURES SET FORTH IN THAT SECTION. A COPY OF SECTION 21168.6.7 OF THE PUBLIC RESOURCES CODE IS INCLUDED IN THE APPENDIX TO THIS ENVIRONMENTAL IMPACT REPORT.

(2) The draft environmental impact report and final environmental impact report shall contain, as an appendix, the full text of this section.

(3) Within 10 days after the release of the draft environmental impact report, the lead agency shall conduct an informational workshop to inform the public of the key analyses and conclusions of that document.

(4) Within 10 days before the close of the public comment period, the lead agency shall hold a public hearing to receive testimony on the draft environmental impact report. A transcript of the hearing shall be included as an appendix to the final environmental impact report.

(5) (A) Within five days following the close of the public comment period, a commenter on the draft environmental impact report may submit to the lead agency a written request for nonbinding mediation. The lead agency and applicant shall participate in nonbinding mediation with all commenters who submitted timely comments on the draft environmental impact report and who requested the mediation. Mediation conducted pursuant to this paragraph shall end no later than 35 days after the close of the public comment period.

(B) A request for mediation shall identify all areas of dispute raised in the comment submitted by the commenter that are to be mediated.

(C) The lead agency shall select one or more mediators who shall be retired judges or recognized experts with at least five years' experience in land use and environmental law or science, or mediation. The applicant shall bear the costs of mediation.

(D) A mediation session shall be conducted on each area of dispute with the parties requesting mediation on that area of dispute.

(E) The lead agency shall adopt, as a condition of approval, any measures agreed upon by the lead agency, the applicant, and any commenter who requested mediation. A commenter who agrees to a measure pursuant to this subparagraph shall not raise the issue addressed by that measure as a basis for an action or proceeding challenging the lead agency's decision to certify or to adopt the environmental impact report or to grant project approval.

(6) The lead agency need not consider written comments submitted after the close of the public comment period, unless those comments address any of the following:

(A) New issues raised in the response to comments by the lead agency.

(B) New information released by the public agency subsequent to the release of the draft environmental impact report, such as new information set forth or embodied in a staff report, proposed permit, proposed resolution, ordinance, or similar documents.

(C) Changes made to the project after the close of the public comment period.

(D) Proposed conditions for approval, mitigation measures, or proposed findings required by Section 21081 or a proposed reporting and monitoring program required by paragraph (1) of subdivision (a) of Section 21081.6, if the lead agency releases those documents subsequent to the release of the draft environmental impact report.

(E) New information that was not reasonably known and could not have been reasonably known during the public comment period.

(7) The lead agency shall file the notice required by subdivision (a) of Section 21152 within five days after the last initial project approval.

(g) (1) The lead agency shall prepare and certify the record of the proceedings in accordance with this subdivision and in accordance with Rule 3.1365 of the California Rules of Court. The applicant shall pay the lead agency for all costs of preparing and certifying the record of proceedings.

(2) No later than three business days following the date of the release of the draft environmental impact report, the lead agency shall make available to the public in a readily accessible electronic format the draft environmental impact report and all other documents submitted to or relied on by the lead agency in the preparation of the draft environmental impact report. A document prepared by the lead agency or submitted by the applicant after the date of the release of the draft environmental impact report that is a part of the record of the proceedings shall be made available to the public in a readily accessible electronic format within five business days after the document is prepared or received by the lead agency.

(3) Notwithstanding paragraph (2), documents submitted to or relied on by the lead agency that were not prepared specifically for the project and are copyright protected are not required to be made readily accessible in an electronic format. For those copyright protected documents, the lead agency shall make an index of the documents available in an electronic format no later than the date of the release of the draft environmental impact report, or within five business days if the document is received or relied on by the lead agency after the release of the draft environmental impact report. The index shall specify the libraries or lead agency offices in which hardcopies of the copyrighted materials are available for public review.

(4) The lead agency shall encourage written comments on the project to be submitted in a readily accessible electronic format, and shall make any such comments available to the public in a readily accessible electronic format within five days of their receipt.

(5) Within seven business days after the receipt of any comment that is not in an electronic format, the lead agency shall convert that comment into a readily accessible electronic format and make it available to the public in that format.

(6) The lead agency shall indicate in the record of the proceedings comments received that were not considered by the lead agency pursuant to paragraph (6) of subdivision (f) and need not include the content of the comments as a part of the record.

(7) Within five days after the filing of the notice required by subdivision (a) of Section 21152, the lead agency shall certify the record of the proceedings for the approval or determination and shall provide an electronic copy of the record to a party that has submitted a written request for a copy. The lead agency may charge and collect a reasonable fee from a party requesting a copy of the record for the electronic copy, which shall not exceed the reasonable cost of reproducing that copy.

(8) Within 10 days after being served with a complaint or a petition for a writ of mandate, the lead agency shall lodge a copy of the certified record of proceedings with the superior court.

(9) Any dispute over the content of the record of the proceedings shall be resolved by the superior court. Unless the superior court directs otherwise, a party disputing the content of the record shall file a motion to augment the record at the time it files its initial brief.

(10) The contents of the record of proceedings shall be as set forth in subdivision (e) of Section 21167.6.

[Added, Chapter 959, Statutes of 2018]

21168.6.8. City of Inglewood Sports and Entertainment project, procedures; expedited judicial review

(a) For the purposes of this section, the following definitions apply:

(1) "Applicant" means a private or public entity or its affiliates that proposes to implement and operate all or any portion of the project and its successors, heirs, and assignees.

(2) "Arena" means an 18,000 to 20,000 seat arena built as part of the project for National Basketball Association (NBA) basketball games and other spectator events.

(3) "Project" means a project located within the project area consisting of the arena plus practice and athletic training facility, and related parking and access, infrastructure construction or relocation, and landscaping, up to approximately 75,000 square feet of associated office space, up to approximately 30,000 square feet of sports medicine clinic space, up to approximately 70,000 square feet of ancillary retail, restaurant, community space, and similar uses, and a hotel, provided that the project meets all of the following:

(A) Receives Leadership in Energy and Environmental Design (LEED) gold certification for new construction within one year of the completion of the first NBA season.

(B) (i) Requires a transportation demand management program that, upon full implementation, will achieve and maintain a 15-percent reduction in the number of vehicle trips, collectively, by attendees, employees, visitors, and customers as compared to operations absent the transportation demand management program.

(ii) To accelerate and maximize vehicle trip reduction, each measure in the transportation demand management program shall be implemented as soon as feasible, so that no less than a 7.5-percent reduction in vehicle trips is achieved and maintained by the end of the first NBA season during which an NBA team has played at the arena.

(iii) A 15-percent reduction in vehicle trips shall be achieved and maintained as soon as feasible, but not later than January 1, 2030. The applicant shall verify achievement to the lead agency and the Office of Planning and Research.

(iv) If the applicant fails to verify achievement of the reduction required by clause (iii), the lead agency shall impose additional feasible measures to reduce vehicle trips by 17 percent, or, if there is a rail transit line with a stop within one-quarter mile of the arena, 20 percent, by January 1, 2035.

(C) Is located on an infill site.

(D) Is consistent with the general use designation, density, building intensity, and applicable policies specified for the project area in either a sustainable communities strategy or an alternative planning strategy for which the State Air Resources Board, pursuant to subparagraph (H) of paragraph (2) of subdivision (b) of Section 65080 of the Government Code, has accepted a metropolitan planning organization's determination that the sustainable communities strategy or the alternative planning strategy would, if implemented, achieve the greenhouse gas emission reduction targets.

(4) "Project approval" means any action, activity, ordinance, resolution, agreement, approval, determination, finding, or decision taken, adopted, or approved by the lead agency required to allow the applicant to commence the construction of the project, as determined by the lead agency.

(5) "Project area" means real property in the City of Inglewood consisting of approximately 35 acres, including without limitation areas generally described as follows:

(A) Assessor identification numbers 4032-001-005, 4032-001-006, 4032-001-033, 4032-001-035, 4032-001-039, 4032-001-048, 4032-001-049, 4032-001-900 to 4032-001-913, inclusive, 4032-002-913 to 4032-002-917, inclusive, 4032-003-912, 4032-003-914, 4032-003-915, 4032-004-913, 4032-004-914, 4032-007-035, 4032-007-900 to 4032-007-905, inclusive, 4032-008-001, 4032-008-002, 4032-008-006, 4032-008-034, 4032-008-035, 4032-008-900 to 4032-008-905, inclusive, 4032-008-907, 4032-008-908, 4034-004-026, 4034-004-900 to 4034-004-913, inclusive, and 4034-005-900 to 4034-005-912, inclusive.

(B) West 101st Street from its intersection with South Prairie Avenue westerly to a line approximately 488 feet west of the western boundary of South Prairie Avenue, and West 102nd Street from its intersection with South Prairie Avenue easterly to a line approximately 883 feet east of the eastern boundary of South Prairie Avenue.

(C) Adjacent areas or air space to be used for access.

(6) "Transportation demand management program" means a specific program of strategies, incentives, and tools to be implemented, with specific annual status reporting obligations in accordance with paragraph (5) of subdivision (b), to reduce vehicle trips by providing opportunities for event attendees and employees to choose sustainable travel options such as transit, bicycle riding, or walking. A specific program of strategies, incentives, and tools includes, but is not limited to, the following:

(A) Provision of shuttles, charter buses, or similar services from a major transit stop to serve arena events.

(B) Provision of onsite electric vehicle charging stations in excess of applicable requirements.

(C) Provision of dedicated parking for car-share or zero-emission vehicles, or both types of vehicle, in excess of applicable requirements.

(D) Provision of bicycle parking in excess of applicable requirements.

(E) Inclusion of a transit facility with area dedicated to shuttle bus staging, ride share, bicycle parking, and other modalities intended to reduce the use of single occupant vehicles.

(b) The Governor may certify the project for streamlining pursuant to this section if all the following conditions are met:

(1) The project will result in a minimum investment of one hundred million dollars ($100,000,000) in California upon completion of construction.

(2) (A) (i) The project creates high-wage, highly skilled jobs that pay prevailing wages and living wages, employs a skilled and trained workforce, as defined in subdivision (d) of Section 2601 of the Public Contract Code, provides construction jobs and permanent jobs for Californians, and helps reduce unemployment. For purposes of this subdivision, "jobs that pay prevailing wages" means that all construction workers employed in the execution of the project will receive at least the general prevailing rate of per diem wages for the type of work and geographic area, as determined by the Director of Industrial Relations pursuant to Sections 1773 and 1773.9 of the Labor Code. If the project is certified for streamlining, the project applicant shall include this requirement in all contracts for the performance of the work.

(ii) Clause (i) does not apply to a contractor or subcontractor performing the work on the project that is subject to a project labor agreement requiring the payment of prevailing wages to all construction workers employed in the execution of the project and providing for enforcement of that obligation through an arbitration procedure. For purposes of this clause, "project labor agreement" has the same meaning as set forth in paragraph (1) of subdivision (b) of Section 2500 of the Public Contract Code.

(B) (i) If the project is certified pursuant to this subdivision, contractors and subcontractors shall pay to all construction workers employed in the execution of the project at least the general prevailing rate of per diem wages.

(ii) Except as provided in clause (iii), the obligation of the contractors and subcontractors to pay prevailing wages pursuant to subparagraph (A) may be enforced by the Labor Commissioner through the issuance of a civil wage and penalty assessment pursuant to Section 1741 of the Labor Code, which may be reviewed pursuant to Section 1742 of the Labor Code, within 18 months after the completion of the project, or by an underpaid worker through an administrative complaint or civil action. If a civil wage and penalty assessment is issued, the contractor, subcontractor, and surety on a bond or bonds issued to secure the payment of wages covered by the assessment shall be liable for liquidated damages pursuant to Section 1742.1 of the Labor Code.

(iii) Clause (ii) does not apply if all contractors and subcontractors performing work on the project are subject to a project labor agreement that requires the payment of prevailing wages to all construction workers employed in the execution of the project and provides for enforcement of that obligation through an arbitration procedure. For purposes of this subparagraph, "project labor agreement" has the same meaning as set forth in paragraph (1) of subdivision (b) of Section 2500 of the Public Contract Code.

(3) The project does not result in any net additional emission of greenhouse gases, including greenhouse gas emissions from employee transportation, as determined by the State Air Resources Board pursuant to Division 25.5 (commencing with Section 38500) of the Health and Safety Code. The State Air Resources Board is encouraged to make its determination no later than 120 calendar days after receiving an application for review of the methodology and calculations of the project's greenhouse gas emissions.

(4) The project applicant demonstrates compliance with the requirements of Chapters 12.8 (commencing with Section 42649) and 12.9 (commencing with Section 42649.8) of Part 3 of Division 30, as applicable.

(5) The project applicant has entered into a binding and enforceable agreement that all mitigation measures required pursuant to this division and any other environmental measures required by this section to certify the project under this section shall be conditions of approval of the project, and those conditions will be fully enforceable by the lead agency or another agency designated by the lead agency. In the case of environmental mitigation measures and any other environmental measures required by this section, the applicant agrees, as an ongoing obligation, that those measures will be monitored and enforced by the lead agency for the life of the obligation. The project applicant shall submit to the lead agency an annual status report on the implementation of the environmental mitigation measures and any other environmental measures required by this section.

(6) The project applicant agrees to pay any additional costs incurred by the courts in hearing and deciding any case subject to this section, including payment of the costs for the appointment of a special master if deemed appropriate by the court, in a form and manner specified by the Judicial Council, as provided in the Rules of Court adopted by the Judicial Council.

(7) The project applicant agrees to pay the costs of preparing the record of proceedings for the project concurrent with review and consideration of the project pursuant to this division, in a form and manner specified by the lead agency for the project.

(c) (1) The Governor may certify the project for streamlining pursuant to this section if it complies with the conditions specified in subdivision (b).

(2) (A) Prior to certifying the project, the Governor shall make a determination that each of the conditions specified in subdivision (b) has been met. These findings are not subject to judicial review.

(B) (i) If the Governor determines that the project is eligible for streamlining pursuant to this section, he or she shall submit that determination, and any supporting information, to the Joint Legislative Budget Committee for review and concurrence or nonconcurrence.

(ii) Within 30 days of receiving the determination, the Joint Legislative Budget Committee shall concur or nonconcur in writing on the determination.

(iii) If the Joint Legislative Budget Committee fails to concur or nonconcur on a determination by the Governor within 30 days of the submittal, the project is deemed to be certified.

(3) The guidelines issued pursuant to Chapter 6.5 (commencing with Section 21178) apply for the implementation of this section to the extent the guidelines are applicable and do not conflict with specific requirements of this section, including the transportation demand management program specified in subparagraph (B) of paragraph (3) of subdivision (a).

(d) (1) Within 10 days of the Governor certifying the project pursuant to this section, the lead agency shall, at the applicant's expense, issue a public notice in no less than 12-point type stating the following:

"THE APPLICANT HAS ELECTED TO PROCEED UNDER SECTION 21168.6.8 OF THE PUBLIC RESOURCES CODE, WHICH PROVIDES, AMONG OTHER THINGS, THAT ANY JUDICIAL ACTION CHALLENGING THE CERTIFICATION OF THE EIR OR THE APPROVAL OF THE PROJECT DESCRIBED IN THE EIR IS SUBJECT TO THE PROCEDURES SET FORTH IN SECTION 21186.6.8 OF THE PUBLIC RESOURCES CODE. A COPY OF SECTION 21168.6.8 OF THE PUBLIC RESOURCES CODE IS INCLUDED BELOW

(2) The public notice shall be distributed by the lead agency as required for public notices issued pursuant to paragraph (3) of subdivision (b) of Section 21092.

(e) Notwithstanding any other law, the procedures set forth in subdivision (f) shall apply to any action or proceeding brought to attack, review, set aside, void, or annul the certification of any environmental impact report for the project that is certified pursuant to this section or the granting of any project approvals.

(f) Rules 3.2220 to 3.2237, inclusive, of the California Rules of Court, as may be amended by the Judicial Council, shall apply to any action or proceeding brought to attack, review, set aside, void, or annul the certification of any environmental impact report for the project or granting of any project approvals to require the actions or proceeding, including any potential appeals therefrom, to be resolved, to the extent feasible, within 270 days of the filing of the certified record of proceedings with the court. On or before July 1, 2019, the Judicial Council shall amend the California Rules of Court, as necessary, to implement this subdivision.

(g) Notwithstanding any other law, the preparation and certification of the record of proceedings for the certified project shall be performed in the following manner:

(1) The lead agency for the project shall prepare the record of proceedings pursuant to this division concurrently with the administrative process.

(2) All documents and other materials placed in the record of proceedings shall be posted on, and be downloadable from, an Internet Web site maintained by the lead agency commencing with the date of the release of the draft environmental impact report.

(3) The lead agency shall make available to the public in a readily accessible electronic format the draft environmental impact report and all other

documents submitted to, or relied on by, the lead agency in the preparation of the draft environmental impact report.

(4) A document prepared by the lead agency or submitted by the applicant after the date of the release of the draft environmental impact report that is a part of the record of the proceedings shall be made available to the public in a readily accessible electronic format within five business days after the document is released or received by the lead agency.

(5) The lead agency shall encourage written comments on the project to be submitted in a readily accessible electronic format, and shall make any comment available to the public in a readily accessible electronic format within five days of its receipt.

(6) Within 14 business days after the receipt of any comment that is not in an electronic format, the lead agency shall convert that comment into a readily accessible electronic format and make it available to the public in that format.

(7) Notwithstanding paragraphs (2) to (6), inclusive, documents submitted to or relied on by the lead agency that were not prepared specifically for the project and are copyright protected are not required to be made readily accessible in an electronic format. For those copyright-protected documents, the lead agency shall make an index of these documents available in an electronic format no later than the date of the release of the draft environmental impact report, or within five business days if the document is received or relied on by the lead agency after the release of the draft environmental impact report. The index shall specify the libraries or lead agency offices in which hardcopies of the copyrighted materials are available for public review.

(8) The lead agency shall certify the final record of proceedings within five days after the filing of the notice required by subdivision (a) of Section 21152.

(9) Any dispute arising from the record of proceedings shall be resolved by the superior court. Unless the superior court directs otherwise, a party disputing the content of the record shall file a motion to augment the record at the time it files its initial brief.

(10) The contents of the record of proceedings shall be as set forth in subdivision (e) of Section 21167.6.

(h) The provisions of this section are severable. If any provision of this section or its application is held invalid, that invalidity shall not affect other provisions or applications that can be given effect without the invalid provision or application.

(i) (1) If the lead agency fails to certify an environmental impact report for the project before January 1, 2025, this section shall become inoperative and is repealed as of that date.

(2) The lead agency shall notify the Secretary of State if it fails to certified the environmental impact report for the project before January 1, 2025.

(j) (1) As a condition of approval of the project, the lead agency shall require the applicant, with respect to any measures specific to the operation of the

152

arena, to implement measures that will meet the requirements of this division by the end of the first NBA regular season or June of the first NBA regular season, whichever is later, during which an NBA team has played at the arena.

(2) To maximize public health, environmental, and employment benefits, the lead agency shall require measures that will reduce the emissions of greenhouse gases in the project area and in the neighboring communities of the arena.

(3) Not less than 50 percent of the greenhouse gas emissions reductions necessary to achieve the requirement of paragraph (3) of subdivision (b) shall be from local, direct greenhouse gas emissions reduction measures, including, but not limited to, any of the following:

(A) Project design features or onsite reduction measures, or both design features and onsite reduction measures, that include, but are not limited to, any of the following:

(i) Implementing project design features that enable the arena to exceed the building energy efficiency standards set forth in Part 6 of Title 24 of the California Code of Regulations, except for 50 percent of emissions reductions attributable to design features necessary to meet the LEED gold certification requirement.

(ii) Requiring a transportation demand management program to reduce single-occupancy vehicular travel and vehicle miles traveled.

(iii) Providing onsite renewable energy generation, including a solar roof on the arena with a minimum peak generation capacity of 500 kilowatts.

(iv) Providing solar-ready roofs.

(v) Providing cool roofs and "cool parking" promoting cool surface treatment for new parking facilities.

(B) Off-site reduction measures in the neighboring communities, including, but not limited to, any of the following:

(i) Temporarily expanding the capacity of a public transit line, as appropriate, to serve arena events.

(ii) Paying its fair share of the cost of measures that expand the capacity of public transit, if appropriate, that is used by spectators attending arena events.

(iii) Providing funding to an off-site mitigation project consisting of replacing buses, trolleys, or other transit vehicles with zero-emission vehicles.

(iv) Providing off-site safety or other improvements for bicycles, pedestrians, and transit connections.

(v) Providing zero-emission transit buses to serve arena events and to meet other local transit needs, including senior and public school transportation services.

(vi) Undertaking or funding building retrofits to improve the energy efficiency of existing buildings.

(4) The applicant may obtain offset credits for up to 50 percent of the greenhouse gas emissions reductions necessary to achieve the requirements of paragraph (3) of subdivision (b). The applicant shall, to the extent feasible, place the highest priority on the purchase of offset credits that produce emission reductions within the City of Inglewood or the boundaries of the South Coast Air Quality Management District. Any offset credits shall be verified by a third party accredited by the State Air Resources Board. Offset credits generated by a project located outside the United States shall not be used pursuant to this paragraph.

(k) As a condition of approval of the project, the lead agency shall require the applicant, in consultation with the South Coast Air Quality Management District, to implement measures that will achieve criteria pollutant and toxic air contaminant reductions over and above any emission reductions required by other laws or regulations in communities surrounding the project consistent with emission reduction measures that may be identified for those communities pursuant to Section 44391.2 of the Health and Safety Code.

(1) At a minimum, these measures shall achieve reductions of a minimum of 400 tons of oxides of nitrogen and 10 tons of PM2.5, as defined in Section 39047.2 of the Health and Safety Code, over 10 years following the commencement of construction of the project. Of these amounts, reductions of a minimum of 130 tons of oxides of nitrogen and 3 tons of PM2.5 shall be achieved within the first year following commencement of construction of the project. The reductions required pursuant to this paragraph are in addition to any other requirements imposed by other laws.

(2) If the project applicant can demonstrate and verify to the South Coast Air Quality Management District that it has invested at least thirty million dollars ($30,000,000) to achieve the requirements of this subdivision, the requirements of this subdivision shall be deemed met, so long as one-half of the reductions set forth in paragraph (1) are met.

(3) Greenhouse gas emissions reductions achieved pursuant to this subdivision shall count toward the applicant's obligations under paragraph (3) of subdivision (j).

(l) This section does not apply to a project that proposes the construction of a new gambling establishment, as defined in Section 19805 of the Business and Professions Code or Section 337 of the Penal Code.

[Added and Repealed, Chapter 961, Statutes of 2018]

21168.7.　　Judicial review

Sections 21168 and 21168.5 are declaratory of existing law with respect to the judicial review of determinations or decisions of public agencies made pursuant to this division.

[Added, Chapter 1154, Statutes of 1972]

21168.9. **Requirements of court order for noncompliance**

(a) If a court finds, as a result of a trial, hearing, or remand from an appellate court, that any determination, finding, or decision of a public agency has been made without compliance with this division, the court shall enter an order that includes one or more of the following:

(1) A mandate that the determination, finding, or decision be voided by the public agency, in whole or in part.

(2) If the court finds that a specific project activity or activities will prejudice the consideration or implementation of particular mitigation measures or alternatives to the project, a mandate that the public agency and any real parties in interest suspend any or all specific project activity or activities, pursuant to the determination, finding, or decision, that could result in an adverse change or alteration to the physical environment, until the public agency has taken any actions that may be necessary to bring the determination, finding, or decision into compliance with this division.

(3) A mandate that the public agency take specific action as may be necessary to bring the determination, finding, or decision into compliance with this division.

(b) Any order pursuant to subdivision (a) shall include only those mandates which are necessary to achieve compliance with this division and only those specific project activities in noncompliance with this division. The order shall be made by the issuance of a peremptory writ of mandate specifying what action by the public agency is necessary to comply with this division. However, the order shall be limited to that portion of a determination, finding, or decision or the specific project activity or activities found to be in noncompliance only if a court finds that (1) the portion or specific project activity or activities are severable, (2) severance will not prejudice complete and full compliance with this division, and (3) the court has not found the remainder of the project to be in noncompliance with this division. The trial court shall retain jurisdiction over the public agency's proceedings by way of a return to the peremptory writ until the court has determined that the public agency has complied with this division.

(c) Nothing in this section authorizes a court to direct any public agency to exercise its discretion in any particular way. Except as expressly provided in this section, nothing in this section is intended to limit the equitable powers of the court.

[Amended, Chapter 1131, Statutes of 1993]

21169. **Exempts previously approved projects**

Any project defined in subdivision (c) of Section 21065 undertaken, carried out or approved on or before the effective date of this section and the issuance by any public agency of any lease, permit, license, certificate or other entitlement for use executed or issued on or before the effective date of this section notwithstanding a failure to comply with this division, if otherwise legal and valid, is hereby confirmed, validated and declared legally effective. Any project undertaken by a person which was supported in whole or part through contracts with one or more public agencies on or before the effective date of this section, notwithstanding a failure to comply with this division, if otherwise legal and valid, is hereby confirmed, validated and declared legally effective. [This section was enacted on December 5, 1972]

[Added, Chapter 1154, Statutes of 1972]

21170.   Limits exemptions for projects prior to Act

(a) Section 21169 shall not operate to confirm, validate or give legal effect to any project the legality of which was being contested in a judicial proceeding in which proceeding the pleadings, prior to the effective date of this section, alleged facts constituting a cause of action for, or raised the issue of, a violation of this division and which was pending and undetermined on the effective date of this section; provided, however, that Section 21169 shall operate to confirm, validate or give legal effect to any project to which this subdivision applies if, prior to the commencement of judicial proceedings and in good faith and in reliance upon the issuance by a public agency of any lease, permit, license, certificate or other entitlement for use, substantial construction has been performed and substantial liabilities for construction and necessary materials have been incurred.

(b) Section 21169 shall not operate to confirm, validate or give legal effect to any project which had been determined in any judicial proceeding, on or before the effective date of this section to be illegal, void or ineffective because of noncompliance with this division. [This section was enacted on December 5, 1972]

[Added, Chapter 1154, Statutes of 1972]

21171.   Effective date of Act regarding issuance of a lease, permit, license, certificate or other entitlement

This division, except for Section 21169, shall not apply to the issuance of any lease, permit, license, certificate or other entitlement for use for any project defined in subdivision (c) of Section 21065 or to any project undertaken by a person which is supported in whole or in part through contracts with one or more public agencies until the 121st day after the effective date of this section. This section shall not apply to any project to which Section 21170 is applicable or to any successor project which is the same as, or substantially identical to, such a project.

This section shall not prohibit or prevent a public agency, prior to the 121st day after the effective date of this section, from considering environmental factors in connection with the approval or disapproval of a project and from imposing reasonable fees in connection therewith. [This section was enacted on December 5, 1972]

[Added, Chapter 1154, Statutes of 1972]

21173.   Provision invalidation does not invalidate CEQA

If any provision of this division or the application thereof to any person or circumstances is held invalid, such invalidity shall not effect other provisions or applications of this division which can be given effect without the invalid provision or application thereof, and to this end the provisions of this division are severable.

[Added, Chapter 1154, Statutes of 1972]

21174.   CEQA does not limit public agency authority

No provision of this division is a limitation or restriction on the power or authority of any public agency in the enforcement or administration of any provision of law which it is specifically permitted or required to enforce or administer, including, but not limited to, the powers and authority granted to the California Coastal Commission pursuant to Division 20 (commencing with Section 30000). To the extent of any inconsistency or conflict between the provisions of the California Coastal Act of 1976 (Division 20 (commencing with Section 30000)) and the provisions of this division, the provisions of Division 20 (commencing with Section 30000) shall control.

[Amended, Chapter 285, Statutes of 1991]

21177.   Only persons who presented data to the agency may sue

(a) An action or proceeding shall not be brought pursuant to Section 21167 unless the alleged grounds for noncompliance with this division were presented to the public agency orally or in writing by any person during the public comment period provided by this division or *before* the close of the public hearing on the project before the issuance of the notice of determination.

(b) A person shall not maintain an action or proceeding unless that person objected to the approval of the project orally or in writing during the public comment period provided by this division or *before* the close of the public hearing on the project before the filing of notice of determination pursuant to Sections 21108 and 21152.

(c) This section does not preclude any organization formed after the approval of a project from maintaining an action pursuant to Section 21167 if a member of that organization has complied with subdivision (b).

(d) This section does not apply to the Attorney General.

(e) This section does not apply to any alleged grounds for noncompliance with this division for which there was no public hearing or other opportunity for members of the public to raise those objections orally or in writing *before* the approval of the project, or if the public agency failed to give the notice required by law.

[Amended, Chapter 466, Statutes of 2019]

Chapter 6.5. Jobs And Economic Improvement Through Environmental Leadership Act Of 2011

21178.   Legislative intent

The Legislature finds and declares all of the following:

(a) The California Environmental Quality Act (Division 13 (commencing with Section 21000) of the Public Resources Code) requires that the environmental impacts of development projects be identified and mitigated.

(b) The act also guarantees the public an opportunity to review and comment on the environmental impacts of a project and to participate meaningfully in the development of mitigation measures for potentially significant environmental impacts.

(c) There are large projects under consideration in various regions of the state that would replace old and outmoded facilities with new job-creating facilities to meet those regions' needs while also establishing new, cutting-edge environmental benefits to those regions.

(d) These projects are privately financed or financed from revenues generated from the projects themselves and do not require taxpayer financing.

(e) These projects further will generate thousands of full-time jobs during construction and thousands of additional permanent jobs once they are constructed and operating.

(f) These projects also present an unprecedented opportunity to implement nation-leading innovative measures that will significantly reduce traffic, air quality, and other significant environmental impacts, and fully mitigate the greenhouse gas emissions resulting from passenger vehicle trips attributed to the project.

(g) These pollution reductions will be the best in the nation compared to other comparable projects in the United States.

(h) The purpose of this chapter is to provide unique and unprecedented streamlining benefits under the California Environmental Quality Act for projects that provide the benefits described above for a limited period of time to put people to work as soon as possible.

[Amended, Chapter 210, Statutes of 2016]

21180.   Definitions

For the purposes of this chapter, the following terms shall have the following meanings:

(a) "Applicant" means a public or private entity or its affiliates, or a person or entity that undertakes a public works project, that proposes a project and its successors, heirs, and assignees.

(b) "Environmental leadership development project," "leadership project," or "project" means a project as described in Section 21065 that is one the following:

(1) A residential, retail, commercial, sports, cultural, entertainment, or recreational use project that is certified as LEED gold or better by the United States Green Building Council and, where applicable, that achieves a 15-percent greater standard for transportation efficiency than for comparable projects. These projects must be located on an infill site. For a project that is within a metropolitan planning organization for which a sustainable communities strategy or alternative planning strategy is in effect, the infill project shall be consistent with the general use designation, density, building intensity, and applicable policies specified for the project area in either a sustainable communities strategy or an alternative planning strategy, for which the State Air Resources Board, pursuant to subparagraph (H) of paragraph (2) of subdivision (b) of Section 65080 of the Government Code, has accepted a metropolitan planning organization's determination that the sustainable communities strategy or the alternative planning strategy would, if implemented, achieve the greenhouse gas emission reduction targets.

158

(2) A clean renewable energy project that generates electricity exclusively through wind or solar, but not including waste incineration or conversion.

(3) A clean energy manufacturing project that manufactures products, equipment, or components used for renewable energy generation, energy efficiency, or for the production of clean alternative fuel vehicles.

(c) "Transportation efficiency" means the number of vehicle trips by employees, visitors, or customers of the residential, retail, commercial, sports, cultural, entertainment, or recreational use project divided by the total number of employees, visitors, and customers.

[Amended, Chapter 522, Statutes of 2017]

21181.   Exceptions

This chapter does not apply to a project if the Governor does not certify the project as an environmental leadership development project eligible for streamlining pursuant to this chapter prior to January 1, 2020.

[Amended, Chapter 522, Statutes of 2017]

21182.   Request to Governor

A person proposing to construct a leadership project may apply to the Governor for certification that the leadership project is eligible for streamlining provided by this chapter. The person shall supply evidence and materials that the Governor deems necessary to make a decision on the application. Any evidence or materials shall be made available to the public at least 15 days before the Governor certifies a project pursuant to this chapter.

[Added & Repealed, Chapter 900, Statutes of 2011]

21183.   Governor's criteria for review

The Governor may certify a leadership project for streamlining pursuant to this chapter if all the following conditions are met:

(a) The project will result in a minimum investment of one hundred million dollars ($100,000,000) in California upon completion of construction.

(b) (1) The project creates high-wage, highly skilled jobs that pay prevailing wages and living wages and provide construction jobs and permanent jobs for Californians, and helps reduce unemployment. For purposes of this subdivision, "jobs that pay prevailing wages" means that all construction workers employed in the execution of the project will receive at least the general prevailing rate of per diem wages for the type of work and geographic area, as determined by the Director of Industrial Relations pursuant to Sections 1773 and 1773.9 of the Labor Code. If the project is certified for streamlining, the project applicant shall include this requirement in all contracts for the performance of the work.

(2) (A) If the project is certified pursuant to this chapter, contractors and subcontractors shall pay to all construction workers employed in the execution of the project at least the general prevailing rate of per diem wages.

(B) Except as provided in subparagraph (C), the obligation of the contractors and subcontractors to pay prevailing wages pursuant to subparagraph (A) may be enforced by the Labor Commissioner through the issuance of a civil wage and penalty assessment pursuant to Section 1741 of the Labor Code, which may be reviewed pursuant to Section 1742 of the Labor Code, within 18 months after the completion of the project, or by an underpaid worker through an administrative complaint or civil action. If a civil wage and penalty assessment is issued, the contractor, subcontractor, and surety on a bond or bonds issued to secure the payment of wages covered by the assessment shall be liable for liquidated damages pursuant to Section 1742.1 of the Labor Code.

(C) Subparagraph (B) does not apply if all contractors and subcontractors performing work on the project are subject to a project labor agreement that requires the payment of prevailing wages to all construction workers employed in the execution of the project and provides for enforcement of that obligation through an arbitration procedure. For purposes of this subparagraph, "project labor agreement" has the same meaning as set forth in paragraph (1) of subdivision (b) of Section 2500 of the Public Contract Code.

(c) The project does not result in any net additional emission of greenhouse gases, including greenhouse gas emissions from employee transportation, as determined by the State Air Resources Board pursuant to Division 25.5 (commencing with Section 38500) of the Health and Safety Code.

(d) The project applicant demonstrates compliance with the requirements of Chapters 12.8 (commencing with Section 42649) and 12.9 (commencing with Section 42649.8) of Part 3 of Division 30, as applicable.

(e) The project applicant has entered into a binding and enforceable agreement that all mitigation measures required pursuant to this division to certify the project under this chapter shall be conditions of approval of the project, and those conditions will be fully enforceable by the lead agency or another agency designated by the lead agency. In the case of environmental mitigation measures, the applicant agrees, as an ongoing obligation, that those measures will be monitored and enforced by the lead agency for the life of the obligation.

(f) The project applicant agrees to pay the costs of the Court of Appeal in hearing and deciding any case, including payment of the costs for the appointment of a special master if deemed appropriate by the court, in a form and manner specified by the Judicial Council, as provided in the Rules of Court adopted by the Judicial Council pursuant to Section 21185.

(g) The project applicant agrees to pay the costs of preparing the record of proceedings for the project concurrent with review and consideration of the project pursuant to this division, in a form and manner specified by the lead agency for the project.

[Amended, Chapter 522, Statutes of 2017]

21184.   Governor's certification

(a) The Governor may certify a project for streamlining pursuant to this chapter if it complies with the conditions specified in Section 21183.

(b) (1) Prior to certifying a project, the Governor shall make a determination that each of the conditions specified in Section 21183 has been met. These findings are not subject to judicial review.

(2) (A) If the Governor determines that a leadership project is eligible for streamlining pursuant to this chapter, he or she shall submit that determination, and any supporting information, to the Joint Legislative Budget Committee for review and concurrence or nonconcurrence.

(B) Within 30 days of receiving the determination, the Joint Legislative Budget Committee shall concur or nonconcur in writing on the determination.

(C) If the Joint Legislative Budget Committee fails to concur or nonconcur on a determination by the Governor within 30 days of the submittal, the leadership project is deemed to be certified.

(c) The Governor may issue guidelines regarding application and certification of projects pursuant to this chapter. Any guidelines issued pursuant to this subdivision are not subject to the rulemaking provisions of the Administrative Procedure Act (Chapter 3.5 (commencing with Section 11340) of Part 1 of Division 3 of Title 2 of the Government Code).

[Added & Repealed, Chapter 900, Statutes of 2011]

21184.5.   Multifamily residential projects; unbundled parking

(a) Notwithstanding any other law, except as provided in subdivision (b), a multifamily residential project certified under this chapter shall provide unbundled parking, such that private vehicle parking spaces are priced and rented or purchased separately from dwelling units.

(b) Subdivision (a) shall not apply if the dwelling units are subject to affordability restrictions in law that prescribe rent or sale prices, and the cost of parking spaces cannot be unbundled from the cost of dwelling units.

[Added, Chapter 210, Statutes of 2016]

21185.   Appealing Governor's certification

On or before July 1, 2014, the Judicial Council shall adopt a rule of court to establish procedures applicable to actions or proceedings brought to attack, review, set aside, void, or annul the certification of the environmental impact report for an environmental leadership development project certified by the Governor pursuant to this chapter or the granting of any project approvals that require the actions or proceedings, including any potential appeals therefrom, be resolved, to the extent feasible, within 270 days of the filing of the certified record of proceedings with the court.

[Amended, Chapter 522, Statutes of 2017]

21186. Requirements of Governor's certification

Notwithstanding any other law, the preparation and certification of the record of proceedings for a leadership project certified by the Governor shall be performed in the following manner:

(a) The lead agency for the project shall prepare the record of proceedings pursuant to this division concurrently with the administrative process.

(b) All documents and other materials placed in the record of proceedings shall be posted on, and be downloadable from, an Internet Web site maintained by the lead agency commencing with the date of the release of the draft environmental impact report.

(c) The lead agency shall make available to the public in a readily accessible electronic format the draft environmental impact report and all other documents submitted to, or relied on by, the lead agency in the preparation of the draft environmental impact report.

(d) A document prepared by the lead agency or submitted by the applicant after the date of the release of the draft environmental impact report that is a part of the record of the proceedings shall be made available to the public in a readily accessible electronic format within five business days after the document is released or received by the lead agency.

(e) The lead agency shall encourage written comments on the project to be submitted in a readily accessible electronic format, and shall make any comment available to the public in a readily accessible electronic format within five days of its receipt.

(f) Within seven business days after the receipt of any comment that is not in an electronic format, the lead agency shall convert that comment into a readily accessible electronic format and make it available to the public in that format.

(g) Notwithstanding paragraphs (b) to (f), inclusive, documents submitted to or relied on by the lead agency that were not prepared specifically for the project and are copyright protected are not required to be made readily accessible in an electronic format. For those copyright-protected documents, the lead agency shall make an index of these documents available in an electronic format no later than the date of the release of the draft environmental impact report, or within five business days if the document is received or relied on by the lead agency after the release of the draft environmental impact report. The index must specify the libraries or lead agency offices in which hardcopies of the copyrighted materials are available for public review.

(h) The lead agency shall certify the final record of proceedings within five days of its approval of the project.

(i) Any dispute arising from the record of proceedings shall be resolved by the superior court. Unless the superior court directs otherwise, a party disputing the content of the record shall file a motion to augment the record at the time it files its initial brief.

(j) The contents of the record of proceedings shall be as set forth in subdivision (e) of Section 21167.6.

[Amended, Chapter 522, Statutes of 2017]

21187. EIR statement

Within 10 days of the Governor certifying an environmental leadership development project pursuant to this section, the lead agency shall, at the applicant's expense, issue a public notice in no less than 12-point type stating the following:

"THE APPLICANT HAS ELECTED TO PROCEED UNDER CHAPTER 6.5 (COMMENCING WITH SECTION 21178) OF THE PUBLIC RESOURCES CODE, WHICH PROVIDES, AMONG OTHER THINGS, THAT ANY JUDICIAL ACTION CHALLENGING THE CERTIFICATION OF THE EIR OR THE APPROVAL OF THE PROJECT DESCRIBED IN THE EIR IS SUBJECT TO THE PROCEDURES SET FORTH IN SECTIONS 21185 TO 21186, INCLUSIVE, OF THE PUBLIC RESOURCES CODE. A COPY OF CHAPTER 6.5 (COMMENCING WITH SECTION 21178) OF THE PUBLIC RESOURCES CODE IS INCLUDED BELOW."

The public notice shall be distributed by the lead agency as required for public notices issued pursuant to paragraph (3) of subdivision (b) of Section 21092.

[Amended, Chapter 386, Statutes of 2013]

21188. Severability of provisions

The provisions of this chapter are severable. If any provision of this chapter or its application is held to be invalid, that invalidity shall not affect any other provision or application that can be given effect without the invalid provision or application.

[Added & Repealed, Chapter 900, Statutes of 2011]

21189. Duty to comply

Except as otherwise provided expressly in this chapter, nothing in this chapter affects the duty of any party to comply with this division.

[Added & Repealed, Chapter 900, Statutes of 2011]

21189.1. Failure to certify an EIR on a related project

If, prior to January 1, 2021, a lead agency fails to approve a project certified by the Governor pursuant to this chapter, then the certification expires and is no longer valid.

[Amended, Chapter 522, Statutes of 2017]

21189.2. Judicial Council review of this chapter

The Judicial Council shall report to the Legislature on or before January 1, 2017, on the effects of this chapter on the administration of justice.

[Amended, Chapter 913, Statutes of 2014]

21189.3. Sunset date

This chapter shall remain in effect until January 1, 2021, and as of that date is repealed unless a later enacted statute extends or repeals that date.

[Amended, Chapter 522, Statutes of 2017]

Chapter 6.7. Judicial Review of Capitol Building Annex and State Office Building Projects

21189.50.   Definition

As used in this chapter, the following definitions shall apply:

(a) "Capitol building annex project" means any work of construction of a state capitol building annex or restoration, rehabilitation, renovation, or reconstruction of the State Capitol Building Annex described in Section 9105 of the Government Code that is performed pursuant to Article 5.2 (commencing with Section 9112) of Chapter 1.5 of Part 1 of Division 2 of Title 2 of the Government Code.

(b) "Annex project related work" means all work closely related to the Capitol building annex project, including, but not limited to, any visitor's center or parking facility constructed pursuant to Section 9112 of the Government Code.

(c) "State office building project" means any work of construction, restoration, rehabilitation, renovation, or reconstruction of a state office building that is performed pursuant to Article 5.6 (commencing with Section 9125) of Chapter 1.5 of Part 1 of Division 2 of Title 2 of the Government Code.

[Amended, Chapter 40, Statutes of 2018]

21189.51.   Authority to adopt procedures; certification of the EIR

(a) On or before July 1, 2017, the Judicial Council shall adopt a rule of court to establish procedures applicable to actions or proceedings brought to attack, review, set aside, void, or annul the certification of the environmental impact report for a capitol building annex project or the granting of any project approvals that require the actions or proceedings, including any potential appeals therefrom, be resolved, to the extent feasible, within 270 days of certification of the record of proceedings pursuant to Section 21189.52.

(b) On or before July 1, 2019, the Judicial Council shall adopt a rule of court to establish procedures applicable to actions or proceedings brought to attack, review, set aside, void, or annul the certification of the environmental impact report for annex project related work or a state office building or the granting of any project approvals with respect to either that work or building that require the actions or proceedings, including any potential appeals therefrom, be resolved, to the extent feasible, within 270 days of certification of the record of proceedings pursuant to Section 21189.52.

[Amended, Chapter 40, Statutes of 2018]

21189.52.   Preparation and certification of record of proceedings

(a) The lead agency shall prepare and certify the record of the proceedings in accordance with this section and in accordance with Rule 3.1365 of the California Rules of Court.

(b) No later than three business days following the date of the release of the draft environmental impact report, the lead agency shall make available to the public in a readily accessible electronic format the draft environmental impact report and all other documents submitted to or relied on by the lead agency in the preparation of the draft environmental impact report. A document prepared by the lead agency after the date of the release of the draft environmental impact report that is a part of the record of the proceedings shall be made available to the public in a readily accessible electronic format within five business days after the document is prepared or received by the lead agency.

(c) Notwithstanding subdivision (b), documents submitted to or relied on by the lead agency that were not prepared specifically for the capitol building annex project, annex project related work, or the state office building project, as applicable, and are copyright protected are not required to be made readily accessible in an electronic format. For those copyright protected documents, the lead agency shall make an index of these documents available in an electronic format no later than the date of the release of the draft environmental impact report, or within five business days if the document is received or relied on by the lead agency after the release of the draft environmental impact report. The index must specify the libraries or lead agency offices in which hard copies of the copyrighted materials are available for public review.

(d) The lead agency shall encourage written comments on the capitol building annex project, annex project related work, and the state office building project, to be submitted in a readily accessible electronic format, and shall make any such comment available to the public in a readily accessible electronic format within five days of its receipt.

(e) Within seven business days after the receipt of any comment that is not in an electronic format, the lead agency shall convert that comment into a readily accessible electronic format and make it available to the public in that format.

(f) The lead agency shall indicate in the record of the proceedings comments received that were not considered by the lead agency pursuant to subdivision (d) of Section 21189.55 and need not include the content of the comments as a part of the record.

(g) Within five days after the filing of the notice required by subdivision (a) of Section 21152, the lead agency shall certify the record of the proceedings for the approval or determination and shall provide an electronic copy of the record to a party that has submitted a written request for a copy. The lead agency may charge and collect a reasonable fee from a party requesting a copy of the record for the electronic copy, which shall not exceed the reasonable cost of reproducing that copy.

(h) Within 10 days after being served with a complaint or a petition for a writ of mandate, the lead agency shall lodge a copy of the certified record of proceedings with the superior court.

(i) Any dispute over the content of the record of the proceedings shall be resolved by the superior court. Unless the superior court directs otherwise, a party disputing the content of the record shall file a motion to augment the record at the time it files its initial brief.

(j) The contents of the record of proceedings shall be as set forth in subdivision (e) of Section 21167.6.

[Amended, Chapter 40, Statutes of 2018]

21189.53.   Granting relief

(a) In granting relief in an action or proceeding brought pursuant to this chapter, the court shall not enjoin the capitol building annex project, annex project related work, or the state office building project unless the court finds either of the following:

   (1) The continuation of the capitol building annex project, annex project related work, or the state office building project presents an imminent threat to the public health and safety.

   (2) The capitol building annex project, annex project related work, or the state office building project site contains unforeseen important Native American artifacts or unforeseen important historical, archaeological, or ecological values that would be materially, permanently, and adversely affected by the continuation of the capitol building annex project, annex project related work, or the state office building project unless the court stays or enjoins the capitol building annex project.

(b) If the court finds that either paragraph (1) or (2) of subdivision (a) is satisfied, the court shall only enjoin those specific activities associated with the capitol building annex project, annex project related work, or the state office building project, as applicable, that present an imminent threat to public health and safety or that materially, permanently, and adversely affect unforeseen important Native American artifacts or unforeseen important historical, archaeological, or ecological values.

[Amended, Chapter 40, Statutes of 2018]

21189.54.   EIR notice requirements

(a) The draft and final environmental impact report shall include a notice in not less than 12-point type stating the following:

THIS EIR IS SUBJECT TO CHAPTER 6.7 (COMMENCING WITH SECTION 21189.50) OF DIVISION 13 OF THE PUBLIC RESOURCES CODE, WHICH PROVIDES, AMONG OTHER THINGS, THAT THE LEAD AGENCY NEED NOT CONSIDER CERTAIN COMMENTS FILED AFTER THE CLOSE OF THE PUBLIC COMMENT PERIOD FOR THE DRAFT EIR. ANY JUDICIAL ACTION CHALLENGING THE CERTIFICATION OF THE EIR OR THE APPROVAL OF THE PROJECT DESCRIBED IN THE EIR IS SUBJECT TO THE PROCEDURES SET FORTH IN SECTIONS 21189.51 TO 21189.53, INCLUSIVE, OF THE PUBLIC RESOURCES CODE. A COPY OF CHAPTER 6.7 (COMMENCING WITH SECTION 21189.50) OF DIVISION 13 OF THE PUBLIC RESOURCES CODE IS INCLUDED IN THE APPENDIX TO THIS EIR.

(b) The draft environmental impact report and final environmental impact report shall contain, as an appendix, the full text of this chapter.

[Added, Chapter 31, Statutes of 2016]

21189.55.   Informational public workshop

(a) Within 10 days after the release of the draft environmental impact report, the lead agency shall conduct an informational workshop to inform the public of the key analyses and conclusions of that report.

(b) Within 10 days before the close of the public comment period, the lead agency shall hold a public hearing to receive testimony on the draft environmental impact report. A transcript of the hearing shall be included as an appendix to the final environmental impact report.

(c) (1) Within five days following the close of the public comment period, a commenter on the draft environmental impact report may submit to the lead agency a written request for nonbinding mediation. The lead agency shall participate in nonbinding mediation with all commenters who submitted timely comments on the draft environmental impact report and who requested the mediation. Mediation conducted pursuant to this paragraph shall end no later than 35 days after the close of the public comment period.

(2) A request for mediation shall identify all areas of dispute raised in the comment submitted by the commenter that are to be mediated.

(3) The lead agency shall select one or more mediators who shall be retired judges or recognized experts with at least five years experience in land use and environmental law or science, or mediation.

(4) A mediation session shall be conducted on each area of dispute with the parties requesting mediation on that area of dispute.

(5) The lead agency shall adopt, as a condition of approval, any measures agreed upon by the lead agency and any commenter who requested mediation. A commenter who agrees to a measure pursuant to this subparagraph shall not raise the issue addressed by that measure as a basis for an action or proceeding challenging the lead agency's decision to certify the environmental impact report or to grant one or more initial project approvals.

(d) The lead agency need not consider written comments submitted after the close of the public comment period, unless those comments address any of the following:

(1) New issues raised in the response to comments by the lead agency.

(2) New information released by the public agency subsequent to the release of the draft environmental impact report, such as new information set forth or embodied in a staff report, proposed permit, proposed resolution, ordinance, or similar documents.

(3) Changes made to the project after the close of the public comment period.

(4) Proposed conditions for approval, mitigation measures, or proposed findings required by Section 21081 or a proposed reporting and monitoring program required by paragraph (1) of subdivision (a) of Section 21081.6, where the lead agency releases those documents subsequent to the release of the draft environmental impact report.

(5) New information that was not reasonably known and could not have been reasonably known during the public comment period.

[Added, Chapter 31, Statutes of 2016]

21189.56.   Severability of provisions

The provisions of this chapter are severable. If any provision of this chapter or its application is held to be invalid, that invalidity shall not affect any other provision or application that can be given effect without the invalid provision or application.

[Added, Chapter 31, Statutes of 2016]

21189.57.   Duty to comply

Except as otherwise provided expressly in this chapter, nothing in this chapter affects the duty of any party to comply with this division.

[Added, Chapter 31, Statutes of 2016]

Guidelines
for
California Environmental
Quality Act

as amended December 1, 2019

§15000–15387

California Code of Regulations

Title 14, Chapter 3

State of California

Notice

The CEQA Guidelines are subject to change throughout the year.

**There were no changes made to the
CEQA Guidelines during 2019**

Notes

The section titles in the CEQA Guidelines
are part of the CEQA Guidelines. The
Guidelines are subject to change during
the year.

Article 1. General

15000. Authority.

The regulations contained in this chapter are prescribed by the Secretary for Resources to be followed by all state and local agencies in California in the implementation of the California Environmental Quality Act. These Guidelines have been developed by the Office of Planning and Research for adoption by the Secretary for Resources in accordance with Section 2108-3. Additional information may be obtained by writing:

Secretary for Resources
Room 1311, 1416 Ninth Street
Sacramento, CA 95814

These Guidelines are binding on all public agencies in California.

15001. Short Title.

These Guidelines may be cited as the "State CEQA Guidelines." Existing references to the "State EIR Guidelines" shall be construed to be references to the "State CEQA Guidelines."

15002. General Concepts.

(a) Basic Purposes of CEQA. The basic purposes of CEQA are to:

  (1) Inform governmental decision makers and the public about the potential, significant environmental effects of proposed activities.

  (2) Identify ways that environmental damage can be avoided or significantly reduced.

  (3) Prevent significant, avoidable damage to the environment by requiring changes in projects through the use of alternatives or mitigation measures when the governmental agency finds the changes to be feasible.

  (4) Disclose to the public the reasons why a governmental agency approved the project in the manner the agency chose if significant environmental effects are involved.

(b) Governmental Action. CEQA applies to governmental action. This action may involve:

  (1) Activities directly undertaken by a governmental agency,

  (2) Activities financed in whole or in part by a governmental agency, or

  (3) Private activities which require approval from a governmental agency.

(c) Private Action. Private action is not subject to CEQA unless the action involves governmental participation, financing or approval.

(d) Project. A "project" is an activity subject to CEQA. The term "project" has been interpreted to mean far more than the ordinary dictionary definition of the term. See Section 15378.

(e) Time for Compliance. A governmental agency is required to comply with CEQA procedures when the agency proposes to carry out or approve the activity. See Section 15004.

(f) Environmental Impact Reports and Negative Declarations. An environmental impact report (EIR) is the public document used by the governmental agency to analyze the significant environmental effects of a proposed project, to identify alternatives, and to disclose possible ways to reduce or avoid the possible environmental damage.

(1) An EIR is prepared when the public agency finds substantial evidence that the project may have a significant effect on the environment. See Section 15064 (a) (1).

(2) When the agency finds that there is no substantial evidence that a project may have a significant environmental effect, the agency will prepare a "Negative Declaration" instead of an EIR. See Section 15070.

(g) Significant Effect on the Environment. A significant effect on the environment is defined as a substantial adverse change in the physical conditions which exist in the area affected by the proposed project. See Section 15382. Further, when an EIR identifies a significant effect, the government agency approving the project must make findings on whether the adverse environmental effects have been substantially reduced or if not, why not. See Section 15091.

(h) Methods for Protecting the Environment. CEQA requires more than merely preparing environmental documents. The EIR by itself does not control the way in which a project can be built or carried out. Rather, when an EIR shows that a project could cause substantial adverse changes in the environment, the governmental agency must respond to the information by one or more of the following methods:

(1) Changing a proposed project;

(2) Imposing conditions on the approval of the project;

(3) Adopting plans or ordinances to control a broader class of projects to avoid the adverse changes;

(4) Choosing an alternative way of meeting the same need;

(5) Disapproving the project;

(6) Finding that changes in, or alterations, the project are not feasible.

(7) Finding that the unavoidable, significant environmental damage is acceptable as provided in Section 15093.

(i) Discretionary Action. CEQA applies in situations where a governmental agency can use its judgment in deciding whether and how to carry out or approve a project. A project subject to such judgmental controls is called a "discretionary project". See Section 15357.

(1) Where the law requires a governmental agency to act on a project in a set way without allowing the agency to use its own judgment, the project is called "ministerial," and CEQA does not apply. See Section 15369.

(2) Whether an agency has discretionary or ministerial controls over a project depends on the authority granted by the law providing the controls over the activity. Similar projects may be subject to discretionary controls in one city or county and only ministerial controls in another. See Section 15268.

(j) Public Involvement. Under CEQA, an agency must solicit and respond to comments from the public and from other agencies concerned with the project. See Sections 15073, 15086, 15087 and 15088.

(k) Three Step Process. An agency will normally take up to three separate steps in deciding which document to prepare for a project subject to CEQA.

(1) In the first step the lead agency examines the project to determine whether the project is subject to CEQA at all. If the project is exempt, the process does not need to proceed any farther. The agency may prepare a notice of exemption. See Sections 15061 and 15062.

(2) If the project is not exempt, the lead agency takes the second step and conducts an initial study (Section 15063) to determine whether the project may have a significant effect on the environment. If the initial study shows that there is no substantial evidence that the project may have a significant effect, the lead agency prepares a negative declaration. See Sections 15070 et seq.

(3) If the initial study shows that the project may have a significant effect, the lead agency takes the third step and prepares an EIR. See Sections 15080 et seq.

(l) Certified Equivalent Programs. A number of environmental regulatory programs have been certified by the Secretary of the Resources Agency as involving essentially the same consideration of environmental issues as is provided by use of EIRs and negative declarations. Certified programs are exempt from preparing EIRs and negative declarations but use other documents instead. Certified programs are discussed in Article 17 and are listed in Section 15251.

(m) This section is intended to present the general concepts of CEQA in a simplified and introductory manner. If there are any conflicts between the short statement of a concept in this section and the provisions of other sections of these guidelines, the other sections shall prevail.

15003. Policies.

In addition to the policies declared by the Legislature concerning environmental protection and administration of CEQA in Sections 21000, 21001, 21002, and 21002.1 of the Public Resources Code, the courts of this state have declared the following policies to be implicit in CEQA:

(a) The EIR requirement is the heart of CEQA. (County of Inyo v. Yorty, 32 Cal. App. 3d 795.)

(b) The EIR serves not only to protect the environment but also to demonstrate to the public that it is being protected. (County of Inyo v. Yorty, 32 Cal. App. 3d 795.)

(c) The EIR is to inform other governmental agencies and the public generally of the environmental impact of a proposed project. (No Oil, Inc. v. City of Los Angeles, 13 C. 3d 68.)

(d) The EIR is to demonstrate to an apprehensive citizenry that the agency has, in fact, analyzed and considered the ecological implications of its action. (People ex rel. Department of Public Works v. Bosio, 47 Cal. App. 3d 495.)

(e) The EIR process will enable the public to determine the environmental and economic values of their elected and appointed officials thus allowing for appropriate action come election day should a majority of the voters disagree. (People v. County of Kern, 39 Cal. App. 3d 830.)

(f) CEQA was intended to be interpreted in such a manner as to afford the fullest possible protection to the environment within the reasonable scope of the statutory language. (Friends of Mammoth v. Board of Supervisors, 8 Cal. 3d 247.)

(g) The purpose of CEQA is not to generate paper, but to compel government at all levels to make decisions with environmental consequences in mind. (Bozung v. LAFCO (1975) 13 Cal.3d 263)

(h) The lead agency must consider the whole of an action, not simply its constituent parts, when determining whether it will have a significant environmental effect. (Citizens Assoc. for Sensible Development of Bishop Area v. County of Inyo (1985) 172 Cal.App.3d 151)

(i) CEQA does not require technical perfection in an EIR, but rather adequacy, completeness, and a good-faith effort at full disclosure. A court does not pass upon the correctness of an EIR's environmental conclusions, but only determines if the EIR is sufficient as an informational document. (Kings County Farm Bureau v. City of Hanford (1990) 221 Cal. App.3d 692)

(j) CEQA requires that decisions be informed and balanced. It must not be subverted into an instrument for the oppression and delay of social, economic, or recreational development or advancement. (Laurel Heights Improvement Assoc. v. Regents of U.C. (1993) 6 Cal.4th 1112 and Citizens of Goleta Valley v. Board of Supervisors (1990) 52 Cal.3d 553)

15004.   **Time of Preparation.**

(a) Before granting any approval of a project subject to CEQA, every lead agency or responsible agency shall consider a final EIR or negative declaration or another document authorized by these guidelines to be used in the place of an EIR or negative declaration. See the definition of "approval" in Section 15352.

(b) Choosing the precise time for CEQA compliance involves a balancing of competing factors. EIRs and negative declarations should be prepared as early as feasible in the planning process to enable environmental considerations to influence project program and design and yet late enough to provide meaningful information for environmental assessment.

(1) With public projects, at the earliest feasible time, project sponsors shall incorporate environmental considerations into project conceptualization, design, and planning. CEQA compliance should be completed prior to acquisition of a site for a public project.

(2) To implement the above principles, public agencies shall not undertake actions concerning the proposed public project that would have a significant adverse effect or limit the choice of alternatives or mitigation measures, before completion of CEQA compliance. For example, agencies shall not:

(A) Formally make a decision to proceed with the use of a site for facilities which would require CEQA review, regardless of whether the agency has made any final purchase of the site for these facilities, except that agencies may designate a preferred site for CEQA review and may enter into land acquisition agreements when the agency has conditioned the agency's future use of the site on CEQA compliance.

(B) Otherwise take any action which gives impetus to a planned or foreseeable project in a manner that forecloses alternatives or mitigation measures that would ordinarily be part of CEQA review of that public project.

(3) With private projects, the Lead Agency shall encourage the project proponent to incorporate environmental considerations into project conceptualization, design, and planning at the earliest feasible time.

(4) While mere interest in, or inclination to support, a project does not constitute approval, a public agency entering into preliminary agreements regarding a project prior to approval shall not, as a practical matter, commit the agency to the project. For example, an agency shall not grant any vested development entitlements prior to compliance with CEQA. Further, any such pre-approval agreement should, for example:

(A) Condition the agreement on compliance with CEQA;

(B) Not bind any party, or commit to any definite course of action, prior to CEQA compliance;

(C) Not restrict the lead agency from considering any feasible mitigation measures and alternatives, including the "no project" alternative; and

(D) Not restrict the lead agency from denying the project.

(c) The environmental document preparation and review should be coordinated in a timely fashion with the existing planning, review, and project approval processes being used by each public agency. These procedures, to the maximum extent feasible, are to run concurrently, not consecutively. When the lead agency is a state agency, the environmental document shall be included as part of the regular project report if such a report is used in its existing review and budgetary process.

[Amended effective December 28, 2018]

15005. Terminology.

The following words are used to indicate whether a particular subject in the Guidelines is mandatory, advisory, or permissive:

(a) "Must" or "shall" identifies a mandatory element which all public agencies are required to follow.

(b) "Should" identifies guidance provided by the Secretary for Resources based on policy considerations contained in CEQA, in the legislative history of the statute, or in federal court decisions which California courts can be expected to follow. Public agencies are advised to follow this guidance in the absence of compelling, countervailing considerations.

(c) "May" identifies a permissive element which is left fully to the discretion of the public agencies involved.

15006.   Reducing Delay and Paperwork.

Public agencies should reduce delay and paperwork by:

(a) Integrating the CEQA process into early planning. (15004(c))

(b) Ensuring the swift and fair resolution of lead agency disputes. (15053)

(c) Identifying projects which fit within categorical exemptions and are therefore exempt from CEQA processing. (15300.4)

(d) Using initial studies to identify significant environmental issues and to narrow the scope of EIRs. (15063)

(e) Using a negative declaration when a project not otherwise exempt will not have a significant effect on the environment. (15070)

(f) Using a previously prepared EIR when it adequately addresses the proposed project. (15153)

(g) Consulting with state and local responsible agencies before and during preparation of an environmental impact report so that the document will meet the needs of all the agencies which will use it. (15083)

(h) Urging applicants, either before or after the filing of an application, to revise projects to eliminate possible significant effects on the environment, thereby enabling the project to qualify for a negative declaration rather than an environmental impact report. (15063(c)(2))

(i) Integrating CEQA requirements with other environmental review and consulting requirements. (Public Resources Code Section 21080.5)

(j) Eliminating duplication with federal procedures by providing for joint preparation of environmental documents with federal agencies and by adopting completed federal NEPA documents. (15227)

(k) Emphasizing consultation before an environmental impact report is prepared, rather than submitting adversary comments on a completed document. (15082(b))

(l) Combining environmental documents with other documents such as general plans. (15166)

(m) Eliminating repetitive discussions of the same issues by using environmental impact reports on programs, policies, or plans and tiering from reports of broad scope to those of narrower scope. (15152)

(n) Reducing the length of environmental impact reports by means such as setting appropriate page limits. (15141)

(o) Preparing analytic rather than encyclopedic environmental impact reports. (15142)

(p) Mentioning only briefly issues other than significant ones in EIRs. (15143)

(q) Writing environmental impact reports in plain language. (15140)

(r) Following a clear format for environmental impact reports. (15120)

(s) Emphasizing the portions of the environmental impact report that are useful to decision-makers and the public and reducing emphasis on background material. (15143)

(t) Using incorporation by reference. (15150)

(u) Making comments on environmental impact reports as specific as possible. (15204)

15007.   Amendments.

(a) These guidelines will be amended from time to time to match new developments relating to CEQA.

(b) Amendments to the guidelines apply prospectively only. New requirements in amendments will apply to steps in the CEQA process not yet undertaken by the date when agencies must comply with the amendments.

(c) If a document meets the content requirements in effect when the document is set out for public review, the document shall not need to be revised to conform to any new content requirements in guideline amendments taking effect before the document is finally approved.

(d) Public agencies shall comply with new requirements in amendments to the guidelines beginning with the earlier of the following two dates:

(1) The effective date of the agency's procedures amended to conform to the new guideline amendments; or

(2) The 120th day after the effective date of the guideline amendments.

(e) Public agencies may implement any permissive or advisory elements of the guidelines beginning with the effective date of the guideline amendments.

Article 2. General Responsibilities

15020.   General.

Each public agency is responsible for complying with CEQA and these Guidelines. A public agency must meet its own responsibilities under CEQA and shall not rely on comments from other public agencies or private citizens as a substitute for work CEQA requires the lead agency to accomplish. For example, a lead agency is responsible for the adequacy of its environmental documents. The lead agency shall not knowingly release a deficient document hoping that public comments will correct defects in the document.

15021.   Duty to Minimize Environmental Damage and Balance Competing Public Objectives.

(a) CEQA establishes a duty for public agencies to avoid or minimize environmental damage where feasible.

(1) In regulating public or private activities, agencies are required to give major consideration to preventing environmental damage.

(2) A public agency should not approve a project as proposed if there are feasible alternatives or mitigation measures available that would substantially lessen any significant effects that the project would have on the environment.

(b) In deciding whether changes in a project are feasible, an agency may consider specific economic, environmental, legal, social, and technological factors.

(c) The duty to prevent or minimize environmental damage is implemented through the findings required by Section 15091.

(d) CEQA recognizes that in determining whether and how a project should be approved, a public agency has an obligation to balance a variety of public objectives, including economic, environmental, and social factors and in particular the goal of providing a decent home and satisfying living environment for every Californian. An agency shall prepare a statement of overriding considerations as described in Section 15093 to reflect the ultimate balancing of competing public objectives when the agency decides to approve a project that will cause one or more significant effects on the environment.

15022.   Public Agency Implementing Procedures.

(a) Each public agency shall adopt objectives, criteria, and specific procedures consistent with CEQA and these Guidelines for administering its responsibilities under CEQA, including the orderly evaluation of projects and preparation of environmental documents. The implementing procedures should contain at least provisions for:

(1) Identifying the activities that are exempt from CEQA. These procedures should contain:

(A) Provisions for evaluating a proposed activity to determine if there is no possibility that the activity may have a significant effect on the environment.

(B) A list of projects or permits over which the public agency has only ministerial authority.

(C) A list of specific activities which the public agency has found to be within the categorical exemptions established by these guidelines.

(2) Conducting initial studies.

(3) Preparing negative declarations.

(4) Preparing draft and final EIRs.

(5) Consulting with and obtaining comments from other public agencies and members of the public with regard to the environmental effects of projects.

(6) Assuring adequate opportunity and time for public review and comment on the Draft EIR or Negative Declaration.

(7) Evaluating and responding to comments received on environmental documents.

(8) Assigning responsibility for determining the adequacy of an EIR or negative declaration.

(9) Reviewing and considering environmental documents by the person or decisionmaking body who will approve or disapprove a project.

(10) Filing documents required or authorized by CEQA and these Guidelines.

(11) Providing adequate comments on environmental documents which are submitted to the public agency for review.

(12) Assigning responsibility for specific functions to particular units of the public agency.

(13) Providing time periods for performing functions under CEQA.

(b) Any district, including a school district, need not adopt objectives, criteria, and procedures of its own if it uses the objectives, criteria, and procedures of another public agency whose boundaries are coterminous with or entirely encompass the district.

(c) Public agencies should revise their implementing procedures to conform to amendments to these guidelines within 120 days after the effective date of the amendments. During the period while the public agency is revising its procedures, the agency must conform to any statutory changes in the California Environmental Quality Act that have become effective regardless of whether the public agency has revised its formally adopted procedures to conform to the statutory changes.

(d) In adopting procedures to implement CEQA, a public agency may adopt the State CEQA Guidelines through incorporation by reference. The agency may then adopt only those specific procedures or provisions described in subsection (a) which are necessary to tailor the general provisions of the guidelines to the specific operations of the agency. A public agency may also choose to adopt a complete set of procedures identifying in one document all the necessary requirements.

15023.   Office of Planning and Research (OPR).

(a) From time to time OPR shall review the State CEQA Guidelines and shall make recommendations for amendments to the Secretary for Resources.

(b) OPR shall receive and evaluate proposals for adoption, amendment, or repeal of categorical exemptions and shall make recommendations on the proposals to the Secretary for Resources. People making suggestions concerning categorical exemptions shall submit their recommendations to OPR with supporting information to show that the class of projects in the proposal either will or will not have a significant effect on the environment.

(c) The State Clearinghouse in the Office of Planning and Research shall be responsible for distributing environmental documents to State agencies, departments, boards, and commissions for review and comment.

(d) Upon request of a Lead Agency or a project applicant, OPR shall provide assistance in identifying the various responsible agencies and any federal agencies which have responsibility for carrying out or approving a proposed project.

(e) OPR shall ensure that state responsible agencies provide the necessary information to lead agencies in response to notices of preparation within at most 30 days after receiving a notice of preparation.

(f) OPR shall resolve disputes as to which agency is the lead agency for a project.

(g) OPR shall receive and file all notices of completion, determination, and exemption.

(h) OPR shall establish and maintain a database for the collection, storage, retrieval, and dissemination of notices of exemption, notices of preparation, notices of determination, and notices of completion provided to the office. This database of notice information shall be available through the Internet.

[Amended effective September 7, 2004]

15024. Secretary for Resources.

(a) The Guidelines shall be adopted by the Secretary for Resources. The Secretary shall make a finding that each class of projects given a categorical exemption will not have a significant effect on the environment.

(b) The Secretary may issue amendments to these Guidelines.

(c) The Secretary shall certify state environmental regulatory programs which meet the standards for certification in Section 21080.5, Public Resources Code.

(d) The Secretary shall receive and file notices required by certified state environmental regulatory programs.

15025. Delegation of Responsibilities.

(a) A public agency may assign specific functions to its staff to assist in administering CEQA. Functions which may be delegated include but are not limited to:

(1) Determining whether a project is exempt.

(2) Conducting an initial study and deciding whether to prepare a draft EIR or negative declaration.

(3) Preparing a negative declaration or EIR.

(4) Determining that a negative declaration has been completed within a period of 180 days.

(5) Preparing responses to comments on environmental documents.

(6) Filing of notices.

(b) The decisionmaking body of a public agency shall not delegate the following functions:

(1) Reviewing and considering a final EIR or approving a negative declaration prior to approving a project.

(2) The making of findings as required by Sections 15091 and 15093.

(c) Where an advisory body such as a planning commission is required to make a recommendation on a project to the decisionmaking body, the advisory body shall also review and consider the EIR or negative declaration in draft or final form.

[Amended effective November 1, 2005]

Article 3. Authorities Granted to Public Agencies by CEQA

15040. Authority Provided by CEQA.

(a) CEQA is intended to be used in conjunction with discretionary powers granted to public agencies by other laws.

(b) CEQA does not grant an agency new powers independent of the powers granted to the agency by other laws.

(c) Where another law grants an agency discretionary powers, CEQA supplements those discretionary powers by authorizing the agency to use the discretionary powers to mitigate or avoid significant effects on the environment when it is feasible to do so with respect to projects subject to the powers of the agency. Prior to January 1, 1983, CEQA provided implied authority for an agency to use its discretionary powers to mitigate or avoid significant effects on the environment. Effective January 1, 1983, CEQA provides express authority to do so.

(d) The exercise of the discretionary powers may take forms that had not been expected before the enactment of CEQA, but the exercise must be within the scope of the power.

(e) The exercise of discretionary powers for environmental protection shall be consistent with express or implied limitations provided by other laws.

15041.   Authority to Mitigate.

Within the limitations described in Section 15040,

(a) A lead agency for a project has authority to require feasible changes in any or all activities involved in the project in order to substantially lessen or avoid significant effects on the environment, consistent with applicable constitutional requirements such as the "nexus" and "rough proportionality" standards established by case law (Nollan v. California Coastal Commission (1987) 483 U.S. 825, Dolan V. City of Tigard, (1994) 512 U.S. 374, Ehrlich v. City of Culver City, (1996) 12 Cal. 4th 854.).

(b) When a public agency acts as a responsible agency for a project, the agency shall have more limited authority than a lead agency. The responsible agency may require changes in a project to lessen or avoid only the effects, either direct or indirect, of that part of the project which the agency will be called on to carry out or approve.

(c) With respect to a project which includes housing development, a lead or responsible agency shall not reduce the proposed number of housing units as a mitigation measure or alternative to lessen a particular significant effect on the environment if that agency determines that there is another feasible, specific mitigation measure or alternative that would provide a comparable lessening of the significant effect.

15042.   Authority to Disapprove Projects.

A public agency may disapprove a project if necessary in order to avoid one or more significant effects on the environment that would occur if the project were approved as proposed. A lead agency has broader authority to disapprove a project than does a responsible agency. A responsible agency may refuse to approve a project in order to avoid direct or indirect environmental effects of that part of the project which the responsible agency would be called on to carry out or approve. For example, an air quality management district acting as a responsible agency would not have authority to disapprove a project for water pollution effects that were unrelated to the air quality aspects of the project regulated by the district.

15043.   Authority to Approve Projects Despite Significant Effects.

A public agency may approve a project even though the project would cause a significant effect on the environment if the agency makes a fully informed and publicly disclosed decision that:

(a) There is no feasible way to lessen or avoid the significant effect (see Section 15091); and

(b) Specifically identified expected benefits from the project outweigh the policy of reducing or avoiding significant environmental impacts of the project. (See Section 15093.)

15044.   Authority to Comment.

Any person or entity other than a responsible agency may submit comments to a lead agency concerning any environmental effects of a project being considered by the lead agency.

15045.   Fees.

(a) For a project to be carried out by any person or entity other than the lead agency, the lead agency may charge and collect a reasonable fee from the person or entity proposing the project in order to recover the estimated costs incurred in preparing environmental documents and for procedures necessary to comply with CEQA on the project. Litigation expenses, costs and fees incurred in actions alleging noncompliance with CEQA are not recoverable under this section.

(b) Public agencies may charge and collect a reasonable fee from members of the public for a copy of an environmental document not to exceed the actual cost of reproducing a copy.

Article 4. Lead Agency

15050.   Lead Agency Concept.

(a) Where a project is to be carried out or approved by more than one public agency, one public agency shall be responsible for preparing an EIR or negative declaration for the project. This agency shall be called the lead agency.

(b) Except as provided in subdivision (c), the decisionmaking body of each responsible agency shall consider the lead agency's EIR or negative declaration prior to acting upon or approving the project. Each responsible agency shall certify that its decisionmaking body reviewed and considered the information contained in the EIR or negative declaration on the project.

(c) The determination of the lead agency of whether to prepare an EIR or a negative declaration shall be final and conclusive for all persons, including responsible agencies, unless:

(1) The decision is successfully challenged as provided in Section 21167 of the Public Resources Code,

(2) Circumstances or conditions change as provided in Section 15162, or

(3) A responsible agency becomes a lead agency under Section 15052.

[Amended effective November 1, 2005]

15051.   Criteria for Identifying the Lead Agency.

Where two or more public agencies will be involved with a project, the determination of which agency will be the lead agency shall be governed by the following criteria:

(a) If the project will be carried out by a public agency, that agency shall be the lead agency even if the project would be located within the jurisdiction of another public agency.

(b) If the project is to be carried out by a nongovernmental person or entity, the lead agency shall be the public agency with the greatest responsibility for supervising or approving the project as a whole.

    (1) The lead agency will normally be the agency with general governmental powers, such as a city or county, rather than an agency with a single or limited purpose such as an air pollution control district or a district which will provide a public service or public utility to the project.

    (2) Where a city prezones an area, the city will be the appropriate lead agency for any subsequent annexation of the area and should prepare the appropriate environmental document at the time of the prezoning. The local agency formation commission shall act as a responsible agency.

(c) Where more than one public agency equally meet the criteria in subdivision (b), the agency which will act first on the project in question will normally be the lead agency.

(d) Where the provisions of subdivisions (a), (b), and (c) leave two or more public agencies with a substantial claim to be the lead agency, the public agencies may by agreement designate an agency as the lead agency. An agreement may also provide for cooperative efforts by two or more agencies by contract, joint exercise of powers, or similar devices.

[Amended effective December 28, 2018]

15052.   Shift in Lead Agency Designation.

(a) Where a responsible agency is called on to grant an approval for a project subject to CEQA for which another public agency was the appropriate lead agency, the responsible agency shall assume the role of the lead agency when any of the following conditions occur:

    (1) The lead agency did not prepare any environmental documents for the project, and the statute of limitations has expired for a challenge to the action of the appropriate lead agency.

    (2) The lead agency prepared environmental documents for the project, but the following conditions occur:

        (A) A subsequent EIR is required pursuant to Section 15162,

        (B) The lead agency has granted a final approval for the project, and

        (C) The statute of limitations for challenging the lead agency's action under CEQA has expired.

183

(3) The lead agency prepared inadequate environmental documents without consulting with the responsible agency as required by Sections 15072 or 15082, and the statute of limitations has expired for a challenge to the action of the appropriate lead agency.

(b) When a responsible agency assumes the duties of a lead agency under this section, the time limits applicable to a lead agency shall apply to the actions of the agency assuming the lead agency duties.

15053.   Designation of Lead Agency by the Office of Planning and Research.

(a) If there is a dispute over which of several agencies should be the lead agency for a project, the disputing agencies should consult with each other in an effort to resolve the dispute prior to submitting it to the Office of Planning and Research. If an agreement cannot be reached, any of the disputing public agencies, or the applicant if a private project is involved, may submit the dispute to the Office of Planning and Research for resolution.

(b) For purposes of this section, a "dispute" means a contested, active difference of opinion between two or more public agencies as to which of those agencies shall prepare any necessary environmental document. A dispute exists where each of those agencies claims that it either has or does not have the obligation to prepare that environmental document.

(c) The Office of Planning and Research shall designate a lead agency within 21 days after receiving a completed request to resolve a dispute. The Office of Planning and Research shall not designate a lead agency in the absence of a dispute.

(d) Regulations adopted by the Office of Planning and Research for resolving Lead Agency disputes may be found in Title 14, California Code of Regulations, Sections 16000 et seq.

(e) Designation of a lead agency by the Office of Planning and Research shall be based on consideration of the criteria in Section 15051 as well as the capacity of the agency to adequately fulfill the requirements of CEQA.

[Amended effective July 27, 2007]

Article 5. Preliminary Review of Projects and Conduct of Initial Study

15060.   Preliminary Review.

(a) A lead agency is allowed 30 days to review for completeness applications for permits or other entitlements for use. While conducting this review for completeness, the agency should be alert for environmental issues that might require preparation of an EIR or that may require additional explanation by the applicant. Accepting an application as complete does not limit the authority of the lead agency to require the applicant to submit additional information needed for environmental evaluation of the project. Requiring such additional information after the application is complete does not change the status of the application.

(b) Except as provided in section 15111, the lead agency shall begin the formal environmental evaluation of the project after accepting an application as complete and determining that the project is subject to CEQA.

(c) Once an application is deemed complete, a lead agency must first determine whether an activity is subject to CEQA before conducting an initial study. An activity is not subject to CEQA if:

   (1) The activity does not involve the exercise of discretionary powers by a public agency:

   (2) The activity will not result in a direct or reasonably foreseeable indirect physical change in the environment: or

   (3) The activity is not a project as defined in Section 15378.

(d) If the lead agency can determine that an EIR will be clearly required for a project, the agency may skip further initial review of the project and begin work directly on the EIR process described in Article 9, commencing with Section 15080. In the absence of an initial study, the lead agency shall still focus the EIR on the significant effects of the project and indicate briefly its reasons for determining that other effects would not be significant or potentially significant.

15060.5.   Preapplication Consultation.

(a) For a potential project involving the issuance of a lease, permit, license, certificate, or other entitlement for use by one or more public agencies, the lead agency shall, upon the request of a potential applicant and prior to the filing of a formal application, provide for consultation with the potential applicant to consider the range of actions, potential alternatives, mitigation measures, and any potential significant effects on the environment of the potential project.

(b) The lead agency may include in the consultation one or more responsible agencies, trustee agencies, and other public agencies who in the opinion of the lead agency may have an interest in the proposed project. The lead agency may consult the Office of Permit Assistance in the Trade and Commerce Agency for help in identifying interested agencies.

15061.   Review for Exemption.

(a) Once a lead agency has determined that an activity is a project subject to CEQA, a lead agency shall determine whether the project is exempt from CEQA.

(b) A project is exempt from CEQA if:

   (1) The project is exempt by statute (see, e.g. Article 18, commencing with Section 15260).

   (2) The project is exempt pursuant to a categorical exemption (see Article 19, commencing with Section 15300) and the application of that categorical exemption is not barred by one of the exceptions set forth in Section 15300.2.

   (3) The activity is covered by the common sense exemption that CEQA applies only to projects, which have the potential for causing a significant effect on the environment. Where it can be seen with certainty that there is no possibility that the activity in question may have a significant effect on the environment, the activity is not subject to CEQA.

(4) The project will be rejected or disapproved by a public agency. (See Section 15270(b)).

(5) The project is exempt pursuant to the provisions of Article 12.5 of this Chapter.

(c) Each public agency should include in its implementing procedures a listing of the projects often handled by the agency that the agency determined to be exempt. This listing should be used in preliminary review.

(d) After determining that a project is exempt, the agency may prepare a notice of exemption as provided in Section 15062. Although the notice may be kept with the project application at this time, the notice shall not be filed with the Office of Planning and Research or the county clerk until the project has been approved.

(e) When a non-elected official or decisionmaking body of a local lead agency decides that a project is exempt from CEQA, and the public agency approves or determines to carry out the project, the decision that the project is exempt may be appealed to the local lead agency's elected decisionmaking body, if one exists. A local lead agency may establish procedures governing such appeals.

[Amended effective December 28, 2018]

15062. Notice of Exemption.

(a) When a public agency decides that a project is exempt from CEQA pursuant to Section 15061, and the public agency approves or determines to carry out the project, the agency may file a notice of exemption. The notice shall be filed, if at all, after approval of the project. Such a notice shall include:

(1) A brief description of the project,

(2) The location of the project (either by street address and cross street for a project in an urbanized area or by attaching a specific map, preferably a copy of a U.S.G.S. 15' or 7-1/2' topographical map identified by quadrangle name).

(3) A finding that the project is exempt from CEQA, including a citation to the State Guidelines section or statute under which it is found to be exempt,

(4) A brief statement of reasons to support the finding, and

(5) The applicant's name, if any.

(6) If different from the applicant, the identity of the person undertaking the project which is supported, in whole or in part, through contracts, grants, subsidies, loans, or other forms of assistance from one or more public agencies, or the identity of the person receiving a lease, permit, license, certificate, or other entitlement for use from one or more public agencies.

(b) A notice of exemption may be filled out and may accompany the project application through the approval process. The notice shall not be filed with the county clerk or OPR until the project has been approved.

(c) When a public agency approves an applicant's project, either the agency or the applicant may file a notice of exemption.

(1) When a state agency files this notice, the notice of exemption shall be filed with the Office of Planning and Research. A form for this notice is provided

in Appendix E. A list of all such notices shall be posted on a weekly basis at the Office of Planning and Research, 1400 Tenth Street, Sacramento, California. The list shall remain posted for at least 30 days. The Office of Planning and Research shall retain each notice for not less than 12 months.

(2) When a local agency files this notice, the notice of exemption shall be filed with the county clerk of each county in which the project will be located. Copies of all such notices will be available for public inspection and such notices shall be posted within 24 hours of receipt in the office of the county clerk. Each notice shall remain posted for a period of 30 days. Thereafter, the clerk shall return the notice to the local agency with a notation of the period it was posted. The local agency shall retain the notice for not less than 12 months.

(3) All public agencies are encouraged to make postings pursuant to this section available in electronic format on the Internet. Such electronic postings are in addition to the procedures required by these guidelines and the Public Resources Code.

(4) When an applicant files this notice, special rules apply.

   (A) The notice filed by an applicant is filed in the same place as if it were filed by the agency granting the permit. If the permit was granted by a state agency, the notice is filed with the Office of Planning and Research. If the permit was granted by a local agency, the notice is filed with the county clerk of the county or counties in which the project will be located.

   (B) The notice of exemption filed by an applicant shall contain the information required in subdivision (a) together with a certified document issued by the public agency stating that the agency has found the project to be exempt. The certified document may be a certified copy of an existing document or record of the public agency.

   (C) A notice filed by an applicant is subject to the same posting and time requirements as a notice filed by a public agency.

(d) The filing of a Notice of Exemption and the posting on the list of notices start a 35 day statute of limitations period on legal challenges to the agency's decision that the project is exempt from CEQA. If a Notice of Exemption is not filed, a 180-day statute of limitations will apply.

(e) When a local agency determines that a project is not subject to CEQA under sections 15193, 15194, or 15195, and it approves or determines to carry out that project, the local agency or person seeking project approval shall file a notice with OPR identifying the section under which the exemption is claimed.

[Amended effective December 28, 2018]

15063.   Initial Study.

(a) Following preliminary review, the lead agency shall conduct an initial study to determine if the project may have a significant effect on the environment. If the lead agency can determine that an EIR will clearly be required for the project, an initial study is not required but may still be desirable.

(1) All phases of project planning, implementation, and operation must be considered in the initial study of the project.

(2) To meet the requirements of this section, the lead agency may use an environmental assessment or a similar analysis prepared pursuant to the National Environmental Policy Act.

(3) An initial study may rely upon expert opinion supported by facts, technical studies or other substantial evidence to document its findings. However, an initial study is neither intended nor required to include the level of detail included in an EIR.

(4) The lead agency may use any of the arrangements or combination of arrangements described in Section 15084(d) to prepare an initial study. The initial study sent out for public review must reflect the independent judgment of the Lead Agency.

(b) Results.

(1) If the agency determines that there is substantial evidence that any aspect of the project, either individually or cumulatively, may cause a significant effect on the environment, regardless of whether the overall effect of the project is adverse or beneficial, the lead agency shall do one of the following:

(A) Prepare an EIR or

(B) Use a previously prepared EIR which the lead agency determines would adequately analyze the project at hand, or

(C) Determine, pursuant to a program EIR, tiering, or another appropriate process, which of a project's effects were adequately examined by an earlier EIR or negative declaration. Another appropriate process may include, for example, a master EIR, a master environmental assessment, approval of housing and neighborhood commercial facilities in urban areas, approval of residential projects pursuant to a specific plan as described in section 15182, approval of residential projects consistent with a community plan, general plan or zoning as described in section 15183, or an environmental document prepared under a State certified regulatory program. The lead agency shall then ascertain which effects, if any, should be analyzed in a later EIR or negative declaration.

(2) The lead agency shall prepare a negative declaration if there is no substantial evidence that the project or any of its aspects may cause a significant effect on the environment.

(c) Purposes. The purposes of an initial study are to:

(1) Provide the lead agency with information to use as the basis for deciding whether to prepare an EIR or negative declaration;

(2) Enable an applicant or lead agency to modify a project, mitigating adverse impacts before an EIR is prepared, thereby enabling the project to qualify for a negative declaration;

(3) Assist the preparation of an EIR, if one is required, by:

(A) Focusing the EIR on the effects determined to be significant,

(B) Identifying the effects determined not to be significant,

(C) Explaining the reasons for determining that potentially significant effects would not be significant, and

(D) Identifying whether a program EIR, tiering, or another appropriate process can be used for analysis of the project's environmental effects.

(4) Facilitate environmental assessment early in the design of a project;

(5) Provide documentation of the factual basis for the finding in a negative declaration that a project will not have a significant effect on the environment;

(6) Eliminate unnecessary EIRs;

(7) Determine whether a previously prepared EIR could be used with the project.

(d) Contents. An initial study shall contain in brief form:

(1) A description of the project including the location of the project;

(2) An identification of the environmental setting;

(3) An identification of environmental effects by use of a checklist, matrix, or other method, provided that entries on a checklist or other form are briefly explained to indicate that there is some evidence to support the entries. The brief explanation may be either through a narrative or a reference to another information source such as an attached map, photographs, or an earlier EIR or negative declaration. A reference to another document should include, where appropriate, a citation to the page or pages where the information is found.

(4) A discussion of ways to mitigate the significant effects identified, if any;

(5) An examination of whether the project would be consistent with existing zoning, plans, and other applicable land use controls;

(6) The name of the person or persons who prepared or participated in the initial study.

(e) Submission of Data. If the project is to be carried out by a private person or private organization, the lead agency may require such person or organization to submit data and information which will enable the lead agency to prepare the initial study. Any person may submit any information in any form to assist a lead agency in preparing an initial study.

(f) Format. Sample forms for an applicant's project description and a review form for use by the lead agency are contained in Appendices G and H. When used together, these forms would meet the requirements for an initial study, provided that the entries on the checklist are briefly explained pursuant to subdivision (d)(3). These forms are only suggested, and public agencies are free to devise their own format for an initial study. A previously prepared EIR may also be used as the initial study for a later project.

(g) Consultation. As soon as a lead agency has determined that an initial study will be required for the project, the lead agency shall consult informally with all responsible agencies and all trustee agencies responsible for resources affected by the project to obtain the recommendations of those agencies as to whether an EIR or a negative declaration should be prepared. During or immediately after preparation of an initial study for a private project, the lead agency may consult with the applicant to determine if the applicant is willing to modify the project to reduce or avoid the significant effects identified in the initial study.

[Amended effective December 28, 2018]

15064.   Determining the Significance of the Environmental Effects Caused by a Project.

(a) Determining whether a project may have a significant effect plays a critical role in the CEQA process.

(1) If there is substantial evidence, in light of the whole record before a lead agency, that a project may have a significant effect on the environment, the agency shall prepare a draft EIR.

(2) When a final EIR identifies one or more significant effects, the lead agency and each responsible agency shall make a finding under Section 15091 for each significant effect and may need to make a statement of overriding considerations under Section 15093 for the project.

(b) (1) The determination of whether a project may have a significant effect on the environment calls for careful judgment on the part of the public agency involved, based to the extent possible on scientific and factual data. An iron clad definition of significant effect is not always possible because the significance of an activity may vary with the setting. For example, an activity which may not be significant in an urban area may be significant in a rural area.

(2) Thresholds of significance, as defined in Section 15064.7(a), may assist lead agencies in determining whether a project may cause a significant impact. When using a threshold, the lead agency should briefly explain how compliance with the threshold means that the project's impacts are less than significant. Compliance with the threshold does not relieve a lead agency of the obligation to consider substantial evidence indicating that the project's environmental effects may still be significant.

(c) In determining whether an effect will be adverse or beneficial, the lead agency shall consider the views held by members of the public in all areas affected as expressed in the whole record before the lead agency. Before requiring the preparation of an EIR, the lead agency must still determine whether environmental change itself might be substantial.

(d) In evaluating the significance of the environmental effect of a project, the lead agency shall consider direct physical changes in the environment which may be caused by the project and reasonably foreseeable indirect physical changes in the environment which may be caused by the project.

(1) A direct physical change in the environment is a physical change in the environment which is caused by and immediately related to the project. Examples of direct physical changes in the environment are the dust, noise, and traffic of heavy equipment that would result from construction of a sewage treatment plant and possible odors from operation of the plant.

(2) An indirect physical change in the environment is a physical change in the environment which is not immediately related to the project, but which is caused indirectly by the project. If a direct physical change in the environment in turn causes another change in the environment, then the other change is an indirect physical change in the environment. For example, the construction of a new sewage treatment plant may facilitate population growth in the service area due to the increase in sewage treatment capacity and may lead to an increase in air pollution.

(3) An indirect physical change is to be considered only if that change is a reasonably foreseeable impact which may be caused by the project. A change which is speculative or unlikely to occur is not reasonably foreseeable.

(e) Economic and social changes resulting from a project shall not be treated as significant effects on the environment. Economic or social changes may be used, however, to determine that a physical change shall be regarded as a significant effect on the environment. Where a physical change is caused by economic or social effects of a project, the physical change may be regarded as a significant effect in the same manner as any other physical change resulting from the project. Alternatively, economic and social effects of a physical change may be used to determine that the physical change is a significant effect on the environment. If the physical change causes adverse economic or social effects on people, those adverse effects may be used as a factor in determining whether the physical change is significant. For example, if a project would cause overcrowding of a public facility and the overcrowding causes an adverse effect on people, the overcrowding would be regarded as a significant effect.

(f) The decision as to whether a project may have one or more significant effects shall be based on substantial evidence in the record of the lead agency.

(1) If the lead agency determines there is substantial evidence in the record that the project may have a significant effect on the environment, the lead agency shall prepare an EIR (Friends of B Street v. City of Hayward (1980) 106 Cal. App. 3d 988). Said another way, if a lead agency is presented with a fair argument that a project may have a significant effect on the environment, the lead agency shall prepare an EIR even though it may also be presented with other substantial evidence that the project will not have a significant effect (No Oil, Inc. v. City of Los Angeles (1974) 13 Cal. 3d 68).

(2) If the lead agency determines there is substantial evidence in the record that the project may have a significant effect on the environment but the lead agency determines that revisions in the project plans or proposals made by, or agreed to by, the applicant would avoid the effects or mitigate the effects to a point where clearly no significant effect on the environment would occur and there is no substantial evidence in light of the whole record before the public agency that the project, as revised, may have a significant effect on the environment then a mitigated negative declaration shall be prepared.

(3) If the lead agency determines there is no substantial evidence that the project may have a significant effect on the environment, the lead agency

shall prepare a negative declaration (Friends of B Street v. City of Hayward (1980) 106 Cal. App. 3d 988).

(4) The existence of public controversy over the environment effects of a project will not require preparation of an EIR if there is no substantial evidence before the agency that the project may have a significant effect on the environment.

(5) Argument, speculation, unsubstantiated opinion or narrative, or evidence that is clearly inaccurate or erroneous, or evidence that is not credible, shall not constitute substantial evidence. Substantial evidence shall include facts, reasonable assumptions predicated upon facts, and expert opinion supported by facts.

(6) Evidence of economic and social impacts that do not contribute to or are not caused by physical changes in the environment is not substantial evidence that the project may have a significant effect on the environment.

(7) The provisions of sections 15162, 15163, and 15164 apply when the project being analyzed is a change to, or further approval for, a project for which an EIR or negative declaration was previously certified or adopted (e.g. a tentative subdivision, conditional use permit). Under case law, the fair argument standard does not apply to determinations of significance pursuant to sections 15162, 15163, and 15164.

(g) After application of the principles set forth above in Section 15064(f), and in marginal cases where it is not clear whether there is substantial evidence that a project may have a significant effect on the environment, the lead agency shall be guided by the following principle: If there is disagreement among expert opinion supported by facts over the significance of an effect on the environment, the Lead Agency shall treat the effect as significant and shall prepare an EIR.

(h) (1) When assessing whether a cumulative effect requires an EIR, the lead agency shall consider whether the cumulative impact is significant and whether the effects of the project are cumulatively considerable. An EIR must be prepared if the cumulative impact may be significant and the project's incremental effect, though individually limited, is cumulatively considerable. "Cumulatively considerable" means that the incremental effects of an individual project are significant when viewed in connection with the effects of past projects, the effects of other current projects, and the effects of probable future projects.

(2) A lead agency may determine in an initial study that a project's contribution to a significant cumulative impact will be rendered less than cumulatively considerable and thus is not significant. When a project might contribute to a significant cumulative impact, but the contribution will be rendered less than cumulatively considerable through mitigation measures set forth in a mitigated negative declaration, the initial study shall briefly indicate and explain how the contribution has been rendered less than cumulatively considerable.

(3) A lead agency may determine that a project's incremental contribution to a cumulative effect is not cumulatively considerable if the project will

comply with the requirements in a previously approved plan or mitigation program (including, but not limited to, water quality control plan, air quality attainment or maintenance plan, integrated waste management plan, habitat conservation plan, natural community conservation plan, plans or regulations for the reduction of greenhouse gas emissions) that provides specific requirements that will avoid or substantially lessen the cumulative problem within the geographic area in which the project is located. Such plans or programs must be specified in law or adopted by the public agency with jurisdiction over the affected resources through a public review process to implement, interpret, or make specific the law enforced or administered by the public agency. When relying on a plan, regulation or program, the lead agency should explain how implementing the particular requirements in the plan, regulation or program ensure that the project's incremental contribution to the cumulative effect is not cumulatively considerable. If there is substantial evidence that the possible effects of a particular project are still cumulatively considerable notwithstanding that the project complies with the specified plan or mitigation program addressing the cumulative problem, an EIR must be prepared for the project.

(4) The mere existence of significant cumulative impacts caused by other projects alone shall not constitute substantial evidence that the proposed project's incremental effects are cumulatively considerable.

[Amended effective December 28, 2018]

15064.3.   Determining the Significance of Transportation Impacts.

(a) Purpose.

This section describes specific considerations for evaluating a project's transportation impacts. Generally, vehicle miles traveled is the most appropriate measure of transportation impacts. For the purposes of this section, "vehicle miles traveled" refers to the amount and distance of automobile travel attributable to a project. Other relevant considerations may include the effects of the project on transit and non-motorized travel. Except as provided in subdivision (b)(2) below (regarding roadway capacity), a project's effect on automobile delay shall not constitute a significant environmental impact.

(b) Criteria for Analyzing Transportation Impacts.

(1) Land Use Projects. Vehicle miles traveled exceeding an applicable threshold of significance may indicate a significant impact. Generally, projects within one-half mile of either an existing major transit stop or a stop along an existing high quality transit corridor should be presumed to cause a less than significant transportation impact. Projects that decrease vehicle miles traveled in the project area compared to existing conditions should be presumed to have a less than significant transportation impact.

(2) Transportation Projects. Transportation projects that reduce, or have no impact on, vehicle miles traveled should be presumed to cause a less than significant transportation impact. For roadway capacity projects, agencies have discretion to determine the appropriate measure of transportation impact consistent with CEQA and other applicable requirements. To the

extent that such impacts have already been adequately addressed at a programmatic level, such as in a regional transportation plan EIR, a lead agency may tier from that analysis as provided in Section 15152 .

(3) Qualitative Analysis. If existing models or methods are not available to estimate the vehicle miles traveled for the particular project being considered, a lead agency may analyze the project's vehicle miles traveled qualitatively. Such a qualitative analysis would evaluate factors such as the availability of transit, proximity to other destinations, etc. For many projects, a qualitative analysis of construction traffic may be appropriate.

(4) Methodology. A lead agency has discretion to choose the most appropriate methodology to evaluate a project's vehicle miles traveled, including whether to express the change in absolute terms, per capita, per household or in any other measure. A lead agency may use models to estimate a project's vehicle miles traveled, and may revise those estimates to reflect professional judgment based on substantial evidence. Any assumptions used to estimate vehicle miles traveled and any revisions to model outputs should be documented and explained in the environmental document prepared for the project. The standard of adequacy in Section 15151 shall apply to the analysis described in this section.

(c) Applicability.

The provisions of this section shall apply prospectively as described in section 15007. A lead agency may elect to be governed by the provisions of this section immediately. Beginning on July 1, 2020, the provisions of this section shall apply statewide.

[Added effective December 28, 2018]

15064.4. Determining the Significance of Impacts from Greenhouse Gas Emissions.

(a) The determination of the significance of greenhouse gas emissions calls for a careful judgment by the lead agency consistent with the provisions in section 15064. A lead agency shall make a good-faith effort, based to the extent possible on scientific and factual data, to describe, calculate or estimate the amount of greenhouse gas emissions resulting from a project. A lead agency shall have discretion to determine, in the context of a particular project, whether to:

(1) Quantify greenhouse gas emissions resulting from a project; and/or

(2) Rely on a qualitative analysis or performance based standards.

(b) In determining the significance of a project's greenhouse gas emissions, the lead agency should focus its analysis on the reasonably foreseeable incremental contribution of the project's emissions to the effects of climate change. A project's incremental contribution may be cumulatively considerable even if it appears relatively small compared to statewide, national or global emissions. The agency's analysis should consider a timeframe that is appropriate for the project. The agency's analysis also must reasonably reflect evolving scientific knowledge and state regulatory schemes. A lead agency should consider the following factors, among others, when determining the significance of impacts from greenhouse gas emissions on the environment:

(1) The extent to which the project may increase or reduce greenhouse gas emissions as compared to the existing environmental setting;

(2) Whether the project emissions exceed a threshold of significance that the lead agency determines applies to the project.

(3) The extent to which the project complies with regulations or requirements adopted to implement a statewide, regional, or local plan for the reduction or mitigation of greenhouse gas emissions (see, e.g., section 15183.5(b)). Such requirements must be adopted by the relevant public agency through a public review process and must reduce or mitigate the project's incremental contribution of greenhouse gas emissions. If there is substantial evidence that the possible effects of a particular project are still cumulatively considerable notwithstanding compliance with the adopted regulations or requirements, an EIR must be prepared for the project. In determining the significance of impacts, the lead agency may consider a project's consistency with the State's long-term climate goals or strategies, provided that substantial evidence supports the agency's analysis of how those goals or strategies address the project's incremental contribution to climate change and its conclusion that the project's incremental contribution is not cumulatively considerable.

(c) A lead agency may use a model or methodology to estimate greenhouse gas emissions resulting from a project. The lead agency has discretion to select the model or methodology it considers most appropriate to enable decision makers to intelligently take into account the project's incremental contribution to climate change. The lead agency must support its selection of a model or methodology with substantial evidence. The lead agency should explain the limitations of the particular model or methodology selected for use.

[Amended effective December 28, 2018]

15064.5. Determining the Significance of Impacts to Archeological and Historical Resources.

(a) For purposes of this section, the term "historical resources" shall include the following:

(1) A resource listed in, or determined to be eligible by the State Historical Resources Commission, for listing in the California Register of Historical Resources (Pub. Res. Code §5024.1, Title 14 CCR, Section 4850 et seq.).

(2) A resource included in a local register of historical resources, as defined in section 5020.1(k) of the Public Resources Code or identified as significant in an historical resource survey meeting the requirements section 5024.1(g) of the Public Resources Code, shall be presumed to be historically or culturally significant. Public agencies must treat any such resource as significant unless the preponderance of evidence demonstrates that it is not historically or culturally significant.

(3) Any object, building, structure, site, area, place, record, or manuscript which a lead agency determines to be historically significant or significant in the architectural, engineering, scientific, economic, agricultural, educational, social, political, military, or cultural annals of California may be considered to be an historical resource, provided the lead agency's

determination is supported by substantial evidence in light of the whole record. Generally, a resource shall be considered by the lead agency to be "historically significant" if the resource meets the criteria for listing on the California Register of Historical Resources (Pub. Res. Code §5024.1, Title 14 CCR, Section 4852) including the following:

(A) Is associated with events that have made a significant contribution to the broad patterns of California's history and cultural heritage;

(B) Is associated with the lives of persons important in our past;

(C) Embodies the distinctive characteristics of a type, period, region, or method of construction, or represents the work of an important creative individual, or possesses high artistic values; or

(D) Has yielded, or may be likely to yield, information important in prehistory or history.

(4) The fact that a resource is not listed in, or determined to be eligible for listing in the California Register of Historical Resources, not included in a local register of historical resources (pursuant to section 5020.1(k) of the Public Resources Code), or identified in an historical resources survey (meeting the criteria in section 5024.1(g) of the Public Resources Code) does not preclude a lead agency from determining that the resource may be an historical resource as defined in Public Resources Code sections 5020.1(j) or 5024.1.

(b) A project with an effect that may cause a substantial adverse change in the significance of an historical resource is a project that may have a significant effect on the environment.

(1) Substantial adverse change in the significance of an historical resource means physical demolition, destruction, relocation, or alteration of the resource or its immediate surroundings such that the significance of an historical resource would be materially impaired.

(2) The significance of an historical resource is materially impaired when a project:

(A) Demolishes or materially alters in an adverse manner those physical characteristics of an historical resource that convey its historical significance and that justify its inclusion in, or eligibility for, inclusion in the California Register of Historical Resources; or

(B) Demolishes or materially alters in an adverse manner those physical characteristics that account for its inclusion in a local register of historical resources pursuant to section 5020.1(k) of the Public Resources Code or its identification in an historical resources survey meeting the requirements of section 5024.1(g) of the Public Resources Code, unless the public agency reviewing the effects of the project establishes by a preponderance of evidence that the resource is not historically or culturally significant; or

(C) Demolishes or materially alters in an adverse manner those physical characteristics of a historical resource that convey its historical significance and that justify its eligibility for inclusion in the California

Register of Historical Resources as determined by a lead agency for purposes of CEQA.

(3) Generally, a project that follows the Secretary of the Interior's Standards for the Treatment of Historic Properties with Guidelines for Preserving, Rehabilitating, Restoring, and Reconstructing Historic Buildings or the Secretary of the Interior's Standards for Rehabilitation and Guidelines for Rehabilitating Historic Buildings (1995), Weeks and Grimmer, shall be considered as mitigated to a level of less than a significant impact on the historical resource.

(4) A lead agency shall identify potentially feasible measures to mitigate significant adverse changes in the significance of an historical resource. The lead agency shall ensure that any adopted measures to mitigate or avoid significant adverse changes are fully enforceable through permit conditions, agreements, or other measures.

(5) When a project will affect state-owned historical resources, as described in Public Resources Code Section 5024, and the lead agency is a state agency, the lead agency shall consult with the State Historic Preservation Officer as provided in Public Resources Code Section 5024.5. Consultation should be coordinated in a timely fashion with the preparation of environmental documents.

(c) CEQA applies to effects on archaeological sites.

(1) When a project will impact an archaeological site, a lead agency shall first determine whether the site is an historical resource, as defined in subdivision (a).

(2) If a lead agency determines that the archaeological site is an historical resource, it shall refer to the provisions of Section 21084.1 of the Public Resources Code, and this section, Section 15126.4 of the Guidelines, and the limits contained in Section 21083.2 of the Public Resources Code do not apply.

(3) If an archaeological site does not meet the criteria defined in subdivision (a), but does meet the definition of a unique archeological resource in Section 21083.2 of the Public Resources Code, the site shall be treated in accordance with the provisions of section 21083.2. The time and cost limitations described in Public Resources Code Section 21083.2 (c-f) do not apply to surveys and site evaluation activities intended to determine whether the project location contains unique archaeological resources.

(4) If an archaeological resource is neither a unique archaeological nor an historical resource, the effects of the project on those resources shall not be considered a significant effect on the environment. It shall be sufficient that both the resource and the effect on it are noted in the Initial Study or EIR, if one is prepared to address impacts on other resources, but they need not be considered further in the CEQA process.

(d) When an initial study identifies the existence of, or the probable likelihood, of Native American human remains within the project, a lead agency shall work with the appropriate Native Americans as identified by the Native American Heritage Commission as provided in Public Resources Code Section 5097.98.

The applicant may develop an agreement for treating or disposing of, with appropriate dignity, the human remains and any items associated with Native American burials with the appropriate Native Americans as identified by the Native American Heritage Commission." Action implementing such an agreement is exempt from:

(1) The general prohibition on disinterring, disturbing, or removing human remains from any location other than a dedicated cemetery (Health and Safety Code Section 7050.5).

(2) The requirements of CEQA and the Coastal Act.

(e) In the event of the accidental discovery or recognition of any human remains in any location other than a dedicated cemetery, the following steps should be taken:

(1) There shall be no further excavation or disturbance of the site or any nearby area reasonably suspected to overlie adjacent human remains until:

(A) The coroner of the county in which the remains are discovered must be contacted to determine that no investigation of the cause of death is required, and

(B) If the coroner determines the remains to be Native American:

1. The coroner shall contact the Native American Heritage Commission within 24 hours.

2. The Native American Heritage Commission shall identify the person or persons it believes to be the most likely descended from the deceased Native American.

3. The most likely descendent may make recommendations to the landowner or the person responsible for the excavation work, for means of treating or disposing of, with appropriate dignity, the human remains and any associated grave goods as provided in Public Resources Code Section 5097.98, or

(2) Where the following conditions occur, the landowner or his authorized representative shall rebury the Native American human remains and associated grave goods with appropriate dignity on the property in a location not subject to further subsurface disturbance.

(A) The Native American Heritage Commission is unable to identify a most likely descendent or the most likely descendent failed to make a recommendation within 24 hours after being notified by the commission.

(B) The descendant identified fails to make a recommendation; or

(C) The landowner or his authorized representative rejects the recommendation of the descendant, and the mediation by the Native American Heritage Commission fails to provide measures acceptable to the landowner.

(f) As part of the objectives, criteria, and procedures required by Section 21082 of the Public Resources Code, a lead agency should make provisions for historical or unique archaeological resources accidentally discovered during construction. These provisions should include an immediate evaluation of the find by a

198

qualified archaeologist. If the find is determined to be an historical or unique archaeological resource, contingency funding and a time allotment sufficient to allow for implementation of avoidance measures or appropriate mitigation should be available. Work could continue on other parts of the building site while historical or unique archaeological resource mitigation takes place.

[Amended effective November 1, 2005]

15064.7.   Thresholds of Significance.

(a) A threshold of significance is an identifiable quantitative, qualitative or performance level of a particular environmental effect, non-compliance with which means the effect will normally be determined to be significant by the agency and compliance with which means the effect normally will be determined to be less than significant.

(b) Each public agency is encouraged to develop and publish thresholds of significance that the agency uses in the determination of the significance of environmental effects. Thresholds of significance to be adopted for general use as part of the lead agency's environmental review process must be adopted by ordinance, resolution, rule, or regulation, and developed through a public review process and be supported by substantial evidence. Lead agencies may also use thresholds on a case-by-case basis as provided in Section 15064(b)(2).

(c) When adopting or using thresholds of significance, a lead agency may consider thresholds of significance previously adopted or recommended by other public agencies or recommended by experts, provided the decision of the lead agency to adopt such thresholds is supported by substantial evidence.

(d) Using environmental standards as thresholds of significance promotes consistency in significance determinations and integrates environmental review with other environmental program planning and regulation. Any public agency may adopt or use an environmental standard as a threshold of significance. In adopting or using an environmental standard as a threshold of significance, a public agency shall explain how the particular requirements of that environmental standard reduce project impacts, including cumulative impacts, to a level that is less than significant, and why the environmental standard is relevant to the analysis of the project under consideration. For the purposes of this subdivision, an "environmental standard" is a rule of general application that is adopted by a public agency through a public review process and that is all of the following:

(1) a quantitative, qualitative or performance requirement found in an ordinance, resolution, rule, regulation, order, plan or other environmental requirement;

(2) adopted for the purpose of environmental protection;

(3) addresses the environmental effect caused by the project; and,

(4) applies to the project under review.

[Amended effective December 28, 2018]

15065.   **Mandatory Findings of Significance.**

(a) A lead agency shall find that a project may have a significant effect on the environment and thereby require an EIR to be prepared for the project where there is substantial evidence, in light of the whole record, that any of the following conditions may occur:

  (1) The project has the potential to substantially degrade the quality of the environment; substantially reduce the habitat of a fish or wildlife species; cause a fish or wildlife population to drop below self-sustaining levels; threaten to eliminate a plant or animal community; substantially reduce the number or restrict the range of an endangered, rare or threatened species; or eliminate important examples of the major periods of California history or prehistory.

  (2) The project has the potential to achieve short-term environmental goals to the disadvantage of long-term environmental goals.

  (3) The project has possible environmental effects that are individually limited but cumulatively considerable. "Cumulatively considerable" means that the incremental effects of an individual project are significant when viewed in connection with the effects of past projects, the effects of other current projects, and the effects of probable future projects.

  (4) The environmental effects of a project will cause substantial adverse effects on human beings, either directly or indirectly.

(b) (1) Where, prior to the commencement of public review of an environmental document, a project proponent agrees to mitigation measures or project modifications that would avoid any significant effect on the environment specified by subdivision (a) or would mitigate the significant effect to a point where clearly no significant effect on the environment would occur, a lead agency need not prepare an environmental impact report solely because, without mitigation, the environmental effects at issue would have been significant.

  (2) Furthermore, where a proposed project has the potential to substantially reduce the number or restrict the range of an endangered, rare or threatened species, the lead agency need not prepare an EIR solely because of such an effect, if:

    (A) the project proponent is bound to implement mitigation requirements relating to such species and habitat pursuant to an approved habitat conservation plan or natural community conservation plan;

    (B) the state or federal agency approved the habitat conservation plan or natural community conservation plan in reliance on an environmental impact report or environmental impact statement; and

    (C) 1. such requirements avoid any net loss of habitat and net reduction in number of the affected species, or

         2. such requirements preserve, restore, or enhance sufficient habitat to mitigate the reduction in habitat and number of the affected species to below a level of significance.

(c) Following the decision to prepare an EIR, if a lead agency determines that any of the conditions specified by subdivision (a) will occur, such a determination shall apply to:

(1) the identification of effects to be analyzed in depth in the environmental impact report or the functional equivalent thereof,

(2) the requirement to make detailed findings on the feasibility of alternatives or mitigation measures to substantially lessen or avoid the significant effects on the environment,

(3) when found to be feasible, the making of changes in the project to substantially lessen or avoid the significant effects on the environment, and

(4) where necessary, the requirement to adopt a statement of overriding considerations.

[Amended effective March 18, 2010]

Article 6. Negative Declaration Process

15070.   **Decision to Prepare a Negative or Mitigated Negative Declaration.**

A public agency shall prepare or have prepared a proposed negative declaration or mitigated negative declaration for a project subject to CEQA when:

(a) The initial study shows that there is no substantial evidence, in light of the whole record before the agency, that the project may have a significant effect on the environment, or

(b) The initial study identified potentially significant effects, but:

(1) Revisions in the project plans or proposals made by or agreed to by the applicant before a proposed mitigated negative declaration and initial study are released for public review would avoid the effects or mitigate the effects to a point where clearly no significant effects would occur, and

(2) There is no substantial evidence, in light of the whole record before the agency, that the project as revised may have a significant effect on the environment.

15071.   Contents.

A negative declaration circulated for public review shall include:

(a) A brief description of the project, including a commonly used name for the project, if any;

(b) The location of the project, preferably shown on a map, and the name of the project proponent;

(c) A proposed finding that the project will not have a significant effect on the environment;

(d) An attached copy of the initial study documenting reasons to support the finding; and

(e) Mitigation measures, if any, included in the project to avoid potentially significant effects.

15072. Notice of Intent to Adopt a Negative Declaration or Mitigated Negative Declaration.

(a) A lead agency shall provide a notice of intent to adopt a negative declaration or mitigated negative declaration to the public, responsible agencies, trustee agencies, and the county clerk of each county within which the proposed project is located, sufficiently prior to adoption by the lead agency of the negative declaration or mitigated negative declaration to allow the public and agencies the review period provided under Section 15105.

(b) The lead agency shall mail a notice of intent to adopt a negative declaration or mitigated negative declaration to the last known name and address of all organizations and individuals who have previously requested such notice in writing and shall also give notice of intent to adopt a negative declaration or mitigated negative declaration by at least one of the following procedures to allow the public the review period provided under Section 15105:

  (1) Publication at least one time by the lead agency in a newspaper of general circulation in the area affected by the proposed project. If more than one area is affected, the notice shall be published in the newspaper of largest circulation from among the newspapers of general circulation in those areas.

  (2) Posting of notice by the lead agency on and off site in the area where the project is to be located.

  (3) Direct mailing to the owners and occupants of property contiguous to the project. Owners of such property shall be identified as shown on the latest equalized assessment roll.

(c) The alternatives for providing notice specified in subdivision (b) shall not preclude a lead agency from providing additional notice by other means if the agency so desires, nor shall the requirements of this section preclude a lead agency from providing the public notice at the same time and in the same manner as public notice required by any other laws for the project.

(d) The county clerk of each county within which the proposed project is located shall post such notices in the office of the county clerk within 24 hours of receipt for a period of at least 20 days.

(e) For a project of statewide, regional, or areawide significance, the lead agency shall also provide notice to transportation planning agencies and public agencies which have transportation facilities within their jurisdictions which could be affected by the project as specified in Section 21092.4(a) of the Public Resources Code. "Transportation facilities" includes: major local arterials and public transit within five miles of the project site and freeways, highways and rail transit service within 10 miles of the project site. The lead agency should also consult with public transit agencies with facilities within one-half mile of the proposed project.

(f) If the United States Department of Defense or any branch of the United States Armed Forces has given a lead agency written notification of the specific boundaries of a low-level flight path, military impact zone, or special use airspace and provided the lead agency with written notification of the military contact office and address for the military service pursuant to subdivision (b) of

202

Section 15190.5, then the lead agency shall include the specified military contact office in the list of organizations and individuals receiving a notice of intent to adopt a negative declaration or a mitigated negative declaration pursuant to this section for projects that meet the criteria set forth in subdivision (c) of Section 15190.5. The lead agency shall send the specified military contact office such notice of intent sufficiently prior to adoption by the lead agency of the negative declaration or mitigated negative declaration to allow the military service the review period provided under Section 15105.

(g) A notice of intent to adopt a negative declaration or mitigated negative declaration shall specify the following:

(1) A brief description of the proposed project and its location.

(2) The starting and ending dates for the review period during which the lead agency will receive comments on the proposed negative declaration or mitigated negative declaration. This shall include starting and ending dates for the review period. If the review period has been is shortened pursuant to Section 15105, the notice shall include a statement to that effect.

(3) The date, time, and place of any scheduled public meetings or hearings to be held by the lead agency on the proposed project, when known to the lead agency at the time of notice.

(4) The address or addresses where copies of the proposed negative declaration or mitigated negative declaration including the revisions developed under Section 15070(b) and all documents incorporated by reference in the proposed negative declaration or mitigated negative declaration are available for review. This location or locations shall be readily accessible to the public during the lead agency's normal working hours.

(5) The presence of the site on any of the lists enumerated under Section 65962.5 of the Government Code including, but not limited to lists of hazardous waste facilities, land designated as hazardous waste property, and hazardous waste disposal sites, and the information in the Hazardous Waste and Substances Statement required under subdivision (f) of that section.

(6) Other information specifically required by statute or regulation for a particular project or type of project.

[Amended effective December 28, 2018]

15073. **Public Review of a Proposed Negative Declaration or Mitigated Negative Declaration.**

(a) The lead agency shall provide a public review period pursuant to Section 15105 of not less than 20 days. When a proposed negative declaration or mitigated negative declaration and initial study are submitted to the State Clearinghouse for review by state agencies, the public review period shall not be less than 30 days, unless a shorter period is approved by the State Clearinghouse under Section 15105(d).

(b) When a proposed negative declaration or mitigated negative declaration and initial study have been submitted to the State Clearinghouse for review by state agencies, the public review period shall be at least as long as the review period established by the State Clearinghouse. The public review period and the state agency review period may, but are not required to, begin and end at the same time. Day one of the state review period shall be the date that the State Clearinghouse distributes the document to state agencies.

(c) A copy of the proposed negative declaration or mitigated negative declaration and the initial study shall be attached to the notice of intent to adopt the proposed declaration that is sent to every responsible agency and trustee agency concerned with the project and every other public agency with jurisdiction by law over resources affected by the project.

(d) Where one or more state agencies will be a responsible agency or a trustee agency or will exercise jurisdiction by law over natural resources affected by the project, or where the project is of statewide, regional, or areawide environmental significance, the lead agency shall send copies of the proposed negative declaration or mitigated negative declaration to the State Clearinghouse for distribution to the state agencies.

(e) The lead agency shall notify in writing any public agency which comments on a proposed negative declaration or mitigated negative declaration of any public hearing to be held for the project for which the document was prepared. A notice provided to a public agency pursuant to Section 15072 satisfies this requirement.

[Amended effective July 27, 2007]

15073.5.   Recirculation of a Negative Declaration Prior to Adoption.

(a) A lead agency is required to recirculate a negative declaration when the document must be substantially revised after public notice of its availability has previously been given pursuant to Section 15072, but prior to its adoption. Notice of recirculation shall comply with Sections 15072 and 15073.

(b) A "substantial revision" of the negative declaration shall mean:

(1) A new, avoidable significant effect is identified and mitigation measures or project revisions must be added in order to reduce the effect to insignificance, or

(2) The lead agency determines that the proposed mitigation measures or project revisions will not reduce potential effects to less than significance and new measures or revisions must be required.

(c) Recirculation is not required under the following circumstances:

(1) Mitigation measures are replaced with equal or more effective measures pursuant to Section 15074.1.

(2) New project revisions are added in response to written or verbal comments on the project's effects identified in the proposed negative declaration which are not new avoidable significant effects.

(3) Measures or conditions of project approval are added after circulation of the negative declaration which are not required by CEQA, which do not create new significant environmental effects and are not necessary to mitigate an avoidable significant effect.

(4) New information is added to the negative declaration which merely clarifies, amplifies, or makes insignificant modifications to the negative declaration.

(d) If during the negative declaration process there is substantial evidence in light of the whole record, before the lead agency that the project, as revised, may have a significant effect on the environment which cannot be mitigated or avoided, the lead agency shall prepare a draft EIR and certify a final EIR prior to approving the project. It shall circulate the draft EIR for consultation and review pursuant to Sections 15086 and 15087, and advise reviewers in writing that a proposed negative declaration had previously been circulated for the project.

15074. Consideration and Adoption of a Negative Declaration or Mitigated Negative Declaration.

(a) Any advisory body of a public agency making a recommendation to the decisionmaking body shall consider the proposed negative declaration or mitigated negative declaration before making its recommendation.

(b) Prior to approving a project, the decisionmaking body of the lead agency shall consider the proposed negative declaration or mitigated negative declaration together with any comments received during the public review process. The decisionmaking body shall adopt the proposed negative declaration or mitigated negative declaration only if it finds on the basis of the whole record before it (including the initial study and any comments received), that there is no substantial evidence that the project will have a significant effect on the environment and that the negative declaration or mitigated negative declaration reflects the lead agency's independent judgment and analysis.

(c) When adopting a negative declaration or mitigated negative declaration, the lead agency shall specify the location and custodian of the documents or other material which constitute the record of proceedings upon which its decision is based.

(d) When adopting a mitigated negative declaration, the lead agency shall also adopt a program for reporting on or monitoring the changes which it has either required in the project or made a condition of approval to mitigate or avoid significant environmental effects.

(e) A lead agency shall not adopt a negative declaration or mitigated negative declaration for a project within the boundaries of a comprehensive airport land use plan or, if a comprehensive airport land use plan has not been adopted, for a project within two nautical miles of a public airport or public use airport, without first considering whether the project will result in a safety hazard or noise problem for persons using the airport or for persons residing or working in the project area.

(f) When a non-elected official or decisionmaking body of a local lead agency adopts a negative declaration or mitigated negative declaration, that adoption may be appealed to the agency's elected decisionmaking body, if one exists. For example, adoption of a negative declaration for a project by a city's planning commission may be appealed to the city council. A local lead agency may establish procedures governing such appeals.

[Amended effective July 27, 2007]

15074.1. Substitution of Mitigation Measures in a Proposed Mitigated Negative Declaration.

(a) As a result of the public review process for a proposed mitigated negative declaration, including any administrative decisions or public hearings conducted on the project prior to its approval, the lead agency may conclude that certain mitigation measures identified in the mitigated negative declaration are infeasible or otherwise undesirable. Prior to approving the project, the lead agency may, in accordance with this section, delete those mitigation measures and substitute for them other measures which the lead agency determines are equivalent or more effective.

(b) Prior to deleting and substituting for a mitigation measure, the lead agency shall do both of the following:

(1) Hold a public hearing on the matter. Where a public hearing is to be held in order to consider the project, the public hearing required by this section may be combined with that hearing. Where no public hearing would otherwise be held to consider the project, then a public hearing shall be required before a mitigation measure may be deleted and a new measure adopted in its place.

(2) Adopt a written finding that the new measure is equivalent or more effective in mitigating or avoiding potential significant effects and that it in itself will not cause any potentially significant effect on the environment.

(c) No recirculation of the proposed mitigated negative declaration pursuant to Section 15072 is required where the new mitigation measures are made conditions of, or are otherwise incorporated into, project approval in accordance with this section.

(d) "Equivalent or more effective" means that the new measure will avoid or reduce the significant effect to at least the same degree as, or to a greater degree than, the original measure and will create no more adverse effect of its own than would have the original measure.

15075. Notice of Determination on a Project for Which a Proposed Negative or Mitigated Negative Declaration Has Been Approved.

(a) The lead agency shall file a notice of determination within 5 working days after deciding to carry out or approve the project. For projects with more than one phase, the lead agency shall file a notice of determination for each phase requiring a discretionary approval.

(b) The notice of determination shall include:

(1) An identification of the project including the project title as identified on the proposed negative declaration, its location, and the State Clearinghouse identification number for the proposed negative declaration if the notice of determination is filed with the State Clearinghouse.

206

(2) A brief description of the project.

(3) The agency's name, the applicant's name, if any, and the date on which the agency approved the project.

(4) The determination of the agency that the project will not have a significant effect on the environment.

(5) A statement that a negative declaration or a mitigated negative declaration was adopted pursuant to the provisions of CEQA.

(6) A statement indicating whether mitigation measures were made a condition of the approval of the project, and whether a mitigation monitoring plan/program was adopted.

(7) The address where a copy of the negative declaration or mitigated negative declaration may be examined.

(8) The identity of the person undertaking a project which is supported, in whole or in part, through contracts, grants, subsidies, loans, or other forms of assistance from one or more public agencies or the identity of the person receiving a lease, permit, license, certificate, or other entitlement for use from one or more public agencies.

(c) If the lead agency is a state agency, the lead agency shall file the notice of determination with the Office of Planning and Research within 5 working days after approval of the project by the lead agency.

(d) If the lead agency is a local agency, the local agency shall file the notice of determination with the county clerk of the county or counties in which the project will be located within five working days after approval of the project by the lead agency. If the project requires a discretionary approval from any state agency, the local lead agency shall also, within five working days of this approval, file a copy of the notice of determination with the Office of Planning and Research.

(e) A notice of determination filed with the county clerk shall be available for public inspection and shall be posted by the county clerk within 24 hours of receipt for a period of at least 30 days. Thereafter, the clerk shall return the notice to the local lead agency with a notation of the period during which it was posted. The local lead agency shall retain the notice for not less than 12 months.

(f) A notice of determination filed with the Office of Planning and Research shall be available for public inspection and shall be posted for a period of at least 30 days. The Office of Planning and Research shall retain each notice for not less than 12 months.

(g) The filing of the notice of determination pursuant to subdivision (c) above for state agencies and the filing and posting of the notice of determination pursuant to subdivisions (d) and (e) above for local agencies, start a 30-day statute of limitations on court challenges to the approval under CEQA.

(h) A sample Notice of Determination is provided in Appendix D. Each public agency may devise its own form, but the minimum content requirements of subdivision (b) above shall be met.

Public agencies are encouraged to make copies of all notices filed pursuant to this section available in electronic format on the Internet. Such electronic notices are in addition to the posting requirements of these guidelines and the Public Resources Code.

[Amended effective December 28, 2018]

Article 7. EIR Process

15080. General.

To the extent possible, the EIR process should be combined with the existing planning, review, and project approval process used by each public agency.

15081. Decision to Prepare an EIR.

The EIR process starts with the decision to prepare an EIR. This decision will be made either during preliminary review under Section 15060 or at the conclusion of an initial study after applying the standards described in Section 15064.

15081.5. EIRs Required by Statute.

(a) A lead agency shall prepare or have prepared an EIR for the following types of projects. An initial study may be prepared to help identify the significant effects of the project.

(1) The burning of municipal wastes, hazardous wastes, or refuse-derived fuel, including but not limited to tires, if the project is either:

(A) The construction of a new facility; or

(B) The expansion of an existing facility that burns hazardous waste that would increase its permitted capacity by more than 10 percent. This does not apply to any project exclusively burning hazardous waste for which a determination to prepare a negative declaration, or mitigated negative declaration or environmental impact report was made prior to July 14, 1989. The amount of expansion of an existing facility is calculated pursuant to subdivision (b) of Section 21151.1 of the Public Resources Code.

(C) Subdivision (1) of the subdivision does not apply to:

1. Projects for which the State Energy Resources Conservation and Development Commission has assumed jurisdiction pursuant to Chapter 6 (commencing with Section 25500) of Division 15 of the Public Resources Code.

2. Any of the types of burn or thermal processing projects listed in subdivision (d) of Section 21151.1 of the Public Resources Code.

(2) The initial issuance of a hazardous waste facilities permit to a land disposal facility, as defined in subdivision (d) of Section 25199.1 of the Health and Safety Code. Preparation of an EIR is not mandatory if the facility only manages hazardous waste which is identified or listed pursuant to Section 25140 or Section 25141 of the Health and Safety Code on or after January 1, 1992; or only conducts activities which are regulated pursuant to Chapter 6.5 (commencing with Section 25100) of Division 20 of the Health and Safety Code on or after January 1, 1992. "Initial issuance" does not include the issuance of a closure or post closure permit pursuant to Chapter 6.5

(commencing with Section 25100) of Division 20 of the Health and Safety Code.

(3) The initial issuance of a hazardous waste facility permit pursuant to Section 25200 of the Health and Safety Code to an off-site large treatment facility, as defined pursuant to subdivision (d) of Section 25205.1 of that code. Preparation of an EIR is not mandatory if the facility only manages hazardous waste which is identified or listed pursuant to Section 25140 or Section 25141 of the Health and Safety Code on or after January 1, 1992; or only conducts activities which are regulated pursuant to Chapter 6.5 (commencing with Section 25100) of Division 20 of the Health and Safety Code on or after January 1, 1992. "Initial issuance" does not include the issuance of a closure or post closure permit pursuant to Chapter 6.5 (commencing with Section 25 100) of Division 20 of the Health and Safety Code.

(4) Any open pit mining operation which is subject to the permit requirements of the Surface Mining and Reclamation Act (beginning at Section 2710 of the Public Resources Code) and which utilizes a cyanide heap-leaching process for the purpose of extracting gold or other precious metals.

(5) An initial base reuse plan as defined in Section 15229.

(b) A lead agency shall prepare or have prepared an EIR for the selection of a California Community College, California State University, University of California, or California Maritime Academy campus location and approval of a long range development plan for that campus.

(1) The EIR for a long range development plan for a campus shall include an analysis of, among other significant impacts, those environmental effects relating to changes in enrollment levels.

(2) Subsequent projects within the campus may be addressed in environmental analyses tiered on the EIR prepared for the long range development plan.

[Amended effective November 1, 2005]

15082.   Notice of Preparation and Determination of Scope of EIR.

(a) Notice of Preparation. Immediately after deciding that an environmental impact report is required for a project, the lead agency shall send a notice of preparation stating that an environmental impact report will be prepared to the Office of Planning and Research and each responsible and trustee agency and file with the county clerk of each county in which the project will be located. This notice shall also be sent to every federal agency involved in approving or funding the project. If the United States Department of Defense or any branch of the United States Armed Forces has given the lead agency written notification of the specific boundaries of a low-level flight path, military impact zone, or special use airspace and provided the lead agency with written notification of the military contact office and address for the military service pursuant to subdivision (b) of Section 15190.5, then the lead agency shall include the specified military contact office in the list of organizations and individuals receiving a notice of preparation of an EIR pursuant to this section for projects that meet the criteria set forth in subdivision (c) of Section 15190.5.

(1) The notice of preparation shall provide the responsible and trustee agencies, the Office of Planning and Research and county clerk with sufficient information describing the project and the potential environmental effects to enable the responsible agencies to make a meaningful response. At a minimum, the information shall include:

(A) Description of the project,

(B) Location of the project (either by street address and cross street, for a project in an urbanized area, or by attaching a specific map, preferably a copy of a U.S.G.S. 15' or 7 1/2' topographical map identified by quadrangle name), and

(C) Probable environmental effects of the project.

(2) A sample notice of preparation is shown in Appendix I. Public agencies are free to devise their own formats for this notice. A copy of the initial study may be sent with the notice to supply the necessary information.

(3) To send copies of the notice of preparation, the lead agency shall use either certified mail or any other method of transmittal that provides it with a record that the notice was received.

(4) The lead agency may begin work on the draft EIR immediately without awaiting responses to the notice of preparation. The draft EIR in preparation may need to be revised or expanded to conform to responses to the notice of preparation. A lead agency shall not circulate a draft EIR for public review before the time period for responses to the notice of preparation has expired.

(b) Response to Notice of Preparation. Within 30 days after receiving the notice of preparation under subdivision (a), each responsible and trustee agency and the Office of Planning and Research shall provide the lead agency with specific detail about the scope and content of the environmental information related to the responsible or trustee agency's area of statutory responsibility that must be included in the draft EIR.

(1) The response at a minimum shall identify:

(A) The significant environmental issues and reasonable alternatives and mitigation measures that the responsible or trustee agency, or the Office of Planning and Research will need to have explored in the draft EIR; and

(B) Whether the agency will be a responsible agency or trustee agency for the project.

(2) If a responsible or trustee agency, or the Office of Planning and Research fails by the end of the 30-day period to provide the lead agency with either a response to the notice or a well- justified request for additional time, the lead agency may presume that none of those entities have a response to make.

(3) A generalized list of concerns not related to the specific project shall not meet the requirements of this section for a response.

(c) Meetings. In order to expedite the consultation, the lead agency, a responsible agency, a trustee agency, the Office of Planning and Research or a project applicant may request one or more meetings between representatives of the agencies involved to assist the lead agency in determining the scope and content of the environmental information that the responsible or trustee agency may require. Such meetings shall be convened by the lead agency as soon as possible, but no later than 30 days after the meetings were requested. On request, the Office of Planning and Research will assist in convening meetings that involve state agencies.

(1) For projects of statewide, regional or areawide significance pursuant to Section 15206, the lead agency shall conduct at least one scoping meeting. A scoping meeting held pursuant to the National Environmental Policy Act, 42 USC 4321 et seq. (NEPA) in the city or county within which the project is located satisfies this requirement if the lead agency meets the notice requirements of subsection (c)(2) below.

(2) The lead agency shall provide notice of the scoping meeting to all of the following:

(A) any county or city that borders on a county or city within which the project is located, unless otherwise designated annually by agreement between the lead agency and the county or city;

(B) any responsible agency

(C) any public agency that has jurisdiction by law with respect to the project;

(D) any organization or individual who has filed a written request for the notice.

(3) A lead agency shall call at least one scoping meeting for a proposed project that may affect highways or other facilities under the jurisdiction of the Department of Transportation if the meeting is requested by the department. The lead agency shall call the scoping meeting as soon as possible but not later than 30 days after receiving the request from the Department of Transportation.

(d) Office of Planning and Research. The Office of Planning and Research will ensure that the state responsible and trustee agencies reply to the lead agency within 30 days of receipt of the notice of preparation by the state responsible and trustee agencies.

(e) Identification Number. When the notice of preparation is submitted to the State Clearinghouse, the state identification number issued by the Clearinghouse shall be the identification number for all subsequent environmental documents on the project. The identification number should be referenced on all subsequent correspondence regarding the project, specifically on the title page of the draft and final EIR and on the notice of determination.

[Amended effective December 28, 2018]

15083.   Early Public Consultation.

Prior to completing the draft EIR, the lead agency may also consult directly with any person or organization it believes will be concerned with the environmental effects of the project. Many public agencies have found that early consultation solves many potential problems that would arise in more serious forms later in the review process. This early consultation may be called scoping. Scoping will be necessary when preparing an EIR/EIS jointly with a federal agency.

(a) Scoping has been helpful to agencies in identifying the range of actions, alternatives, mitigation measures, and significant effects to be analyzed in depth in an EIR and in eliminating from detailed study issues found not to be important.

(b) Scoping has been found to be an effective way to bring together and resolve the concerns of affected federal, state, and local agencies, the proponent of the action, and other interested persons including those who might not be in accord with the action on environmental grounds.

(c) Where scoping is used, it should be combined to the extent possible with consultation under Section 15082.

15084.   Preparing the Draft EIR.

(a) The draft EIR shall be prepared directly by or under contract to the lead agency. The required contents of a draft EIR are discussed in Article 9 beginning with Section 15120.

(b) The lead agency may require the project applicant to supply data and information both to determine whether the project may have a significant effect on the environment and to assist the lead agency in preparing the draft EIR. The requested information should include an identification of other public agencies which will have jurisdiction by law over the project.

(c) Any person, including the applicant, may submit information or comments to the lead agency to assist in the preparation of the draft EIR. The submittal may be presented in any format, including the form of a draft EIR. The lead agency must consider all information and comments received. The information or comments may be included in the draft EIR in whole or in part.

(d) The lead agency may choose one of the following arrangements or a combination of them for preparing a draft EIR.

(1) Preparing the draft EIR directly with its own staff.

(2) Contracting with another entity, public or private, to prepare the draft EIR.

(3) Accepting a draft prepared by the applicant, a consultant retained by the applicant, or any other person.

(4) Executing a third party contract or memorandum of understanding with the applicant to govern the preparation of a draft EIR by an independent contractor.

(5) Using a previously prepared EIR.

(e) Before using a draft prepared by another person, the lead agency shall subject the draft to the agency's own review and analysis. The draft EIR which is sent out for public review must reflect the independent judgment of the lead agency. The lead agency is responsible for the adequacy and objectivity of the draft EIR.

15085. Notice of Completion.

(a) As soon as the draft EIR is completed, a notice of completion must be filed with the Office of Planning and Research in a printed hard copy or in electronic form on a diskette or by electronic mail transmission.

(b) The notice of completion shall include:

    (1) A brief description of the project,

    (2) The proposed location of the project (either by street address and cross street, for a project in an urbanized area, or by attaching a specific map, preferably a copy of a U.S.G.S. 15' or 7-1/2' topographical map identified by quadrangle name).

    (3) An address where copies of the draft EIR are available, and

    (4) The review period during which comments will be received on the draft EIR.

(c) A sample form for the notice of completion is included in Appendix L.

(d) Where the EIR will be reviewed through the state review process handled by the State Clearinghouse, the notice of completion cover form required by the State Clearinghouse will serve as the notice of completion (see Appendix C).

(e) Public agencies are encouraged to make copies of notices of completion filed pursuant to this section available in electronic format on the Internet.

[Amended effective November 1, 2005]

15086. Consultation Concerning Draft EIR.

(a) The lead agency shall consult with and request comments on the draft EIR from:

    (1) Responsible agencies,

    (2) Trustee agencies with resources affected by the project, and

    (3) Any other state, federal, and local agencies which have jurisdiction by law with respect to the project or which exercise authority over resources which may be affected by the project, including water agencies consulted pursuant to section 15083.5.

    (4) Any city or county which borders on a city or county within which the project is located.

    (5) For a project of statewide, regional, or areawide significance, the transportation planning agencies and public agencies which have transportation facilities within their jurisdictions which could be affected by the project. "Transportation facilities" includes: major local arterials and public transit within five miles of the project site, and freeways, highways and rail transit service within 10 miles of the project site. The lead agency should also consult with public transit agencies with facilities within one-half mile of the proposed project.

    (6) For a state lead agency when the EIR is being prepared for a highway or freeway project, the California Air Resources Board as to the air pollution impact of the potential vehicular use of the highway or freeway and if a non-attainment area, the local air quality management district for a determination of conformity with the air quality management plan.

(7) For a subdivision project located within one mile of a facility of the State Water Resources Development System, the California Department of Water Resources.

(b) The lead agency may consult directly with:

(1) Any person who has special expertise with respect to any environmental impact involved.

(2) Any member of the public who has filed a written request for notice with the lead agency or the clerk of the governing body.

(3) Any person identified by the applicant whom the applicant believes will be concerned with the environmental effects of the project.

(c) A responsible agency or other public agency shall only make substantive comments regarding those activities involved in the project that are within an area of expertise of the agency or which are required to be carried out or approved by the responsible agency. Those comments shall be supported by specific documentation.

(d) Prior to the close of the public review period, a responsible agency or trustee agency which has identified what that agency considers to be significant environmental effects shall advise the lead agency of those effects. As to those effects relevant to its decision, if any, on the project, the responsible or trustee agency shall either submit to the lead agency complete and detailed performance objectives for mitigation measures addressing those effects or refer the lead agency to appropriate, readily available guidelines or reference documents concerning mitigation measures. If the responsible or trustee agency is not aware of mitigation measures that address identified effects, the responsible or trustee agency shall so state.

[Amended effective December 28, 2018]

15087.   Public Review of Draft EIR.

(a) The lead agency shall provide public notice of the availability of a draft EIR at the same time as it sends a notice of completion to the Office of Planning and Research. If the United States Department of Defense or any branch of the United States Armed Forces has given the lead agency written notification of the specific boundaries of a low-level flight path, military impact zone, or special use airspace and provided the lead agency with written notification of the contact office and address for the military service pursuant to subdivision (b) of Section 15190.5, then the lead agency shall include the specified military contact office in the list of organizations and individuals receiving a notice of availability of a draft EIR pursuant to this section for projects that meet the criteria set forth in subdivision (c) of Section 15190.5. The public notice shall be given as provided under Section 15105 (a sample form is provided in Appendix L). Notice shall be mailed to the last known name and address of all organizations and individuals who have previously requested such notice in writing, and shall also be given by at least one of the following procedures:

(1) Publication at least one time by the public agency in a newspaper of general circulation in the area affected by the proposed project. If more than one area is affected, the notice shall be published in the newspaper of largest

circulation from among the newspapers of general circulation in those areas.

(2) Posting of notice by the public agency on and off the site in the area where the project is to be located.

(3) Direct mailing to the owners and occupants of property contiguous to the parcel or parcels on which the project is located. Owners of such property shall be identified as shown on the latest equalized assessment roll.

(b) The alternatives for providing notice specified in subdivision (a) shall not preclude a public agency from providing additional notice by other means if such agency so desires, nor shall the requirements of this section preclude a public agency from providing the public notice required by this section at the same time and in the same manner as public notice otherwise required by law for the project.

(c) The notice shall disclose the following:

(1) A brief description of the proposed project and its location.

(2) The starting and ending dates for the review period during which the lead agency will receive comments, and the manner in which the lead agency will receive those comments. If the review period is shortened, the notice shall disclose that fact.

(3) The date, time, and place of any scheduled public meetings or hearings to be held by the lead agency on the proposed project when known to the lead agency at the time of notice.

(4) A list of the significant environmental effects anticipated as a result of the project, to the extent which such effects are known to the lead agency at the time of the notice.

(5) The address where copies of the EIR and all documents incorporated by reference in the EIR will be available for public review. This location shall be readily accessible to the public during the lead agency's normal working hours.

(6) The presence of the site on any of the lists of sites enumerated under Section 65962.5 of the Government Code including, but not limited to lists of hazardous waste facilities, land designated as hazardous waste property, hazardous waste disposal sites and others, and the information in the Hazardous Waste and Substances Statement required under subdivision (f) of that Section.

(d) The notice required under this section shall be posted in the office of the county clerk of each county in which the project will be located for a period of at least 30 days. The county clerk shall post such notices within 24 hours or receipt.

(e) In order to provide sufficient time for public review, the review period for a draft EIR shall be as provided in Section 15105. The review period shall be combined with the consultation required under Section 15086. When a draft EIR has been submitted to the State Clearinghouse, the public review period shall be at least as long as the review period established by the State Clearinghouse. The public review period and the state agency review period may, but are not required to, begin and end at the same time. Day one of the state review period shall be the date that the State Clearinghouse distributes the document to state agencies.

(f) Public agencies shall use the State Clearinghouse to distribute draft EIRs to state agencies for review and should use areawide clearinghouses to distribute the documents to regional and local agencies.

(g) To make copies of EIRs available to the public, lead agencies should furnish copies of draft EIRs to public library systems serving the area involved. Copies should also be available in offices of the lead agency.

(h) Public agencies should compile listings of other agencies, particularly local agencies, which have jurisdiction by law and/or special expertise with respect to various projects and project locations. Such listings should be a guide in determining which agencies should be consulted with regard to a particular project.

(i) Public hearings may be conducted on the environmental documents, either in separate proceedings or in conjunction with other proceedings of the public agency. Public hearings are encouraged, but not required as an element of the CEQA process.

[Amended effective December 28, 2018]

15088.   Evaluation of and Response to Comments.

(a) The lead agency shall evaluate comments on environmental issues received from persons who reviewed the draft EIR and shall prepare a written response. The lead agency shall respond to comments raising significant environmental issues received during the noticed comment period and any extensions and may respond to late comments.

(b) The lead agency shall provide a written proposed response, either in a printed copy or in an electronic format, to a public agency on comments made by that public agency at least 10 days prior to certifying an environmental impact report.

(c) The written response shall describe the disposition of significant environmental issues raised (e.g., revisions to the proposed project to mitigate anticipated impacts or objections). In particular, the major environmental issues raised when the lead agency's position is at variance with recommendations and objections raised in the comments must be addressed in detail giving reasons why specific comments and suggestions were not accepted. There must be good faith, reasoned analysis in response. Conclusory statements unsupported by factual information will not suffice. The level of detail contained in the response, however, may correspond to the level of detail provided in the comment (i.e., responses to general comments may be general). A general response may be appropriate when a comment does not contain or specifically refer to readily available information, or does not explain the relevance of evidence submitted with the comment.

(d) The response to comments may take the form of a revision to the draft EIR or may be a separate section in the final EIR. Where the response to comments makes important changes in the information contained in the text of the draft EIR, the lead agency should either:

(1) Revise the text in the body of the EIR, or

(2) Include marginal notes showing that the information is revised in the response to comments.

[Amended effective December 28, 2018]

15088.5.   Recirculation of an EIR Prior to Certification.

(a) A lead agency is required to recirculate an EIR when significant new information is added to the EIR after public notice is given of the availability of the draft EIR for public review under Section 15087 but before certification. As used in this section, the term "information" can include changes in the project or environmental setting as well as additional data or other information. New information added to an EIR is not "significant" unless the EIR is changed in a way that deprives the public of a meaningful opportunity to comment upon a substantial adverse environmental effect of the project or a feasible way to mitigate or avoid such an effect (including a feasible project alternative) that the project's proponents have declined to implement. "Significant new information" requiring recirculation include, for example, a disclosure showing that:

(1) A new significant environmental impact would result from the project or from a new mitigation measure proposed to be implemented.

(2) A substantial increase in the severity of an environmental impact would result unless mitigation measures are adopted that reduce the impact to a level of insignificance.

(3) A feasible project alternative or mitigation measure considerably different from others previously analyzed would clearly lessen the significant environmental impacts of the project, but the project's proponents decline to adopt it.

(4) The draft EIR was so fundamentally and basically inadequate and conclusory in nature that meaningful public review and comment were precluded.

(b) Recirculation is not required where the new information added to the EIR merely clarifies or amplifies or makes insignificant modifications in an adequate EIR.

(c) If the revision is limited to a few chapters or portions of the EIR, the lead agency need only recirculate the chapters or portions that have been modified.

(d) Recirculation of an EIR requires notice pursuant to Section 15087, and consultation pursuant to Section 15086.

(e) A decision not to recirculate an EIR must be supported by substantial evidence in the administrative record.

(f) The lead agency shall evaluate and respond to comments as provided in Section 15088. Recirculating an EIR can result in the lead agency receiving more than one set of comments from reviewers. The following are two ways in which the lead agency may identify the set of comments to which it will respond. This dual approach avoids confusion over whether the lead agency must respond to comments which are duplicates or which are no longer pertinent due to revisions to the EIR. In no case shall the lead agency fail to respond to pertinent comments on significant environmental issues.

(1) When an EIR is substantially revised and the entire document is recirculated, the lead agency may require reviewers to submit new comments and, in such cases, need not respond to those comments received during the earlier circulation period. The lead agency shall advise reviewers, either in the text of the revised EIR or by an attachment to the revised EIR, that although part of the administrative record, the previous comments do not require a written response in the final EIR, and that new comments must be submitted for the revised EIR. The lead agency need only respond to those comments submitted in response to the recirculated revised EIR.

(2) When the EIR is revised only in part and the lead agency is recirculating only the revised chapters or portions of the EIR, the lead agency may request that reviewers limit their comments to the revised chapters or portions of the recirculated EIR. The lead agency need only respond to (i) comments received during the initial circulation period that relate to chapters or portions of the document that were not revised and recirculated, and (ii) comments received during the recirculation period that relate to the chapters or portions of the earlier EIR that were revised and recirculated. The lead agency's request that reviewers limit the scope of their comments shall be included either within the text of the revised EIR or by an attachment to the revised EIR.

(3) As part of providing notice of recirculation as required by Public Resources Code Section 21092.1, the lead agency shall send a notice of recirculation to every agency, person, or organization that commented on the prior EIR. The notice shall indicate, at a minimum, whether new comments may be submitted only on the recirculated portions of the EIR or on the entire EIR in order to be considered by the agency.

(g) When recirculating a revised EIR, either in whole or in part, the lead agency shall, in the revised EIR or by an attachment to the revised EIR, summarize the revisions made to the previously circulated draft EIR.

[Amended effective September 7, 2004]

15089.   Preparation of Final EIR.

(a) The lead agency shall prepare a final EIR before approving the project. The contents of a final EIR are specified in Section 15132 of these guidelines.

(b) Lead agencies may provide an opportunity for review of the final EIR by the public or by commenting agencies before approving the project. The review of a final EIR should focus on the responses to comments on the draft EIR.

15090.   Certification of the Final EIR.

(a) Prior to approving a project the lead agency shall certify that:

(1) The final EIR has been completed in compliance with CEQA;

(2) The final EIR was presented to the decisionmaking body of the lead agency and that the decisionmaking body reviewed and considered the information contained in the final EIR prior to approving the project; and

(3) The final EIR reflects the lead agency's independent judgment and analysis.

(b) When an EIR is certified by a non-elected decision-making body within a local lead agency, that certification may be appealed to the local lead agency's elected decision-making body, if one exists. For example, certification of an EIR for a tentative subdivision map by a city's planning commission may be appealed to the city council. Each local lead agency shall provide for such appeals.

15091.   Findings.

(a) No public agency shall approve or carry out a project for which an EIR has been certified which identifies one or more significant environmental effects of the project unless the public agency makes one or more written findings for each of those significant effects, accompanied by a brief explanation of the rationale for each finding. The possible findings are:

(1) Changes or alterations have been required in, or incorporated into, the project which avoid or substantially lessen the significant environmental effect as identified in the final EIR.

(2) Such changes or alterations are within the responsibility and jurisdiction of another public agency and not the agency making the finding. Such changes have been adopted by such other agency or can and should be adopted by such other agency.

(3) Specific economic, legal, social, technological, or other considerations, including provision of employment opportunities for highly trained workers, make infeasible the mitigation measures or project alternatives identified in the final EIR.

(b) The findings required by subdivision (a) shall be supported by substantial evidence in the record.

(c) The finding in subdivision (a) (2) shall not be made if the agency making the finding has concurrent jurisdiction with another agency to deal with identified feasible mitigation measures or alternatives. The finding in subdivision (a) (3) shall describe the specific reasons for rejecting identified mitigation measures and project alternatives.

(d) When making the findings required in subdivision (a)(1), the agency shall also adopt a program for reporting on or monitoring the changes which it has either required in the project or made a condition of approval to avoid or substantially lessen significant environmental effects. These measures must be fully enforceable through permit conditions, agreements, or other measures.

(e) The public agency shall specify the location and custodian of the documents or other materials which constitute the record of the proceedings upon which its decision is based.

(f) A statement made pursuant to Section 15093 does not substitute for the findings required by this section.

[Amended effective November 1, 2005]

219

15092.   Approval.

(a) After considering the final EIR and in conjunction with making findings under Section 15091, the lead agency may decide whether or how to approve or carry out the project.

(b) A public agency shall not decide to approve or carry out a project for which an EIR was prepared unless either:

(1) The project as approved will not have a significant effect on the environment, or

(2) The agency has:

(A) Eliminated or substantially lessened all significant effects on the environment where feasible as shown in findings under Section 15091, and

(B) Determined that any remaining significant effects on the environment found to be unavoidable under Section 15091 are acceptable due to overriding concerns as described in Section 15093.

(c) With respect to a project which includes housing development, the public agency shall not reduce the proposed number of housing units as a mitigation measure if it determines that there is another feasible specific mitigation measure available that will provide a comparable level of mitigation.

15093.   Statement of Overriding Considerations.

(a) CEQA requires the decision-making agency to balance, as applicable, the economic, legal, social, technological, or other benefits, including region-wide or statewide environmental benefits, of a proposed project against its unavoidable environmental risks when determining whether to approve the project. If the specific economic, legal, social, technological, or other benefits, including region-wide or statewide environmental benefits, of a proposal project outweigh the unavoidable adverse environmental effects, the adverse environmental effects may be considered "acceptable."

(b) When the lead agency approves a project which will result in the occurrence of significant effects which are identified in the final EIR but are not avoided or substantially lessened, the agency shall state in writing the specific reasons to support its action based on the final EIR and/or other information in the record. The statement of overriding considerations shall be supported by substantial evidence in the record.

(c) If an agency makes a statement of overriding considerations, the statement should be included in the record of the project approval and should be mentioned in the notice of determination. This statement does not substitute for, and shall be in addition to, findings required pursuant to Section 15091.

[Amended effective March 18, 2010]

15094.   Notice of Determination.

(a) The lead agency shall file a Notice of Determination within five working days after deciding to carry out or approve the project.

(b) The notice of determination shall include:

(1) An identification of the project including the project title as identified on the draft EIR, and the location of the project (either by street address and cross street for a project in an urbanized area or by attaching a specific map, preferably a copy of a U.S.G.S. 15' or 7-1/2' topographical map identified by quadrangle name). If the notice of determination is filed with the State Clearinghouse, the State Clearinghouse identification number for the draft EIR shall be provided.

(2) A brief description of the project.

(3) The lead agency's name, the applicant's name, if any, and the date on which the agency approved the project. If a responsible agency files the notice of determination pursuant to Section 15096(i), the responsible agency's name, the applicant's name, if any, and date of approval shall also be identified.

(4) The determination of the agency whether the project in its approved form will have a significant effect on the environment.

(5) A statement that an EIR was prepared and certified pursuant to the provisions of CEQA.

(6) Whether mitigation measures were made a condition of the approval of the project, and whether a mitigation monitoring plan/program was adopted.

(7) Whether findings were made pursuant to Section 15091.

(8) Whether a statement of overriding considerations was adopted for the project.

(9) The address where a copy of the final EIR and the record of project approval may be examined.

(10) If different from the applicant, the identity of the person undertaking the project which is supported, in whole or in part, through contracts, grants, subsidies, loans, or other forms of assistance from one or more public agencies or the identity of the person receiving a lease, permit, license, certificate, or other entitlement for use from one or more public agencies.

(c) If the lead agency is a state agency, the lead agency shall file the notice of determination with the Office of Planning and Research within five working days after approval of the project by the lead agency.

(d) If the lead agency is a local agency, the local lead agency shall file the notice of determination with the county clerk of the county or counties in which the project will be located, within five working days after approval of the project by the lead agency. If the project requires discretionary approval from any state agency, the local lead agency shall also, within five working days of this approval, file a copy of the notice of determination with the Office of Planning and Research.

(e) A notice of determination filed with the county clerk shall be available for public inspection and shall be posted within 24 hours of receipt for a period of at least 30 days. Thereafter, the clerk shall return the notice to the local lead agency with a notation of the period during which it was posted. The local lead agency shall retain the notice for not less than 12 months.

(f) A notice of determination filed with the Office of Planning and Research shall be available for public inspection and shall be posted for a period of at least 30 days. The Office of Planning and Research shall retain each notice for not less than 12 months.

(g) The filing of the notice of determination pursuant to subdivision (c) above for state agencies and the filing and posting of the notice of determination pursuant to subdivisions (d) and (e) above for local agencies, start a 30-day statute of limitations on court challenges to the approval under CEQA.

(h) A sample notice of determination is provided in Appendix D. Each public agency may devise its own form, but any such form shall include, at a minimum, the information required by subdivision (b). Public agencies are encouraged to make copies of all notices filed pursuant to this section available in electronic format on the Internet. Such electronic notices are in addition to the posting requirements of the Guidelines and the Public Resources Code.

[Amended effective December 28, 2018]

15095.   Disposition of a Final EIR.

The lead agency shall:

(a) File a copy of the final EIR with the appropriate planning agency of any city, county, or city and county where significant effects on the environment may occur.

(b) Include the final EIR as part of the regular project report which is used in the existing project review and budgetary process if such a report is used.

(c) Retain one or more copies of the final EIR as public records for a reasonable period of time.

(d) Require the applicant to provide a copy of the certified, final EIR to each responsible agency.

15096.   Process for a Responsible Agency.

(a) General. A responsible agency complies with CEQA by considering the EIR or negative declaration prepared by the lead agency and by reaching its own conclusions on whether and how to approve the project involved. This section identifies the special duties a public agency will have when acting as a responsible agency.

(b) Response to Consultation. A responsible agency shall respond to consultation by the lead agency in order to assist the lead agency in preparing adequate environmental documents for the project. By this means, the responsible agency will ensure that the documents it will use will comply with CEQA.

(1) In response to consultation, a responsible agency shall explain its reasons for recommending whether the lead agency should prepare an EIR or negative declaration for a project. Where the responsible agency disagrees with the lead agency's proposal to prepare a negative declaration for a project, the responsible agency should identify the significant environmental effects which it believes could result from the project and recommend either that an EIR be prepared or that the project be modified to eliminate the significant effects.

(2) As soon as possible, but not longer than 30 days after receiving a notice of preparation from the lead agency, the responsible agency shall send a

written reply by certified mail or any other method which provides the agency with a record showing that the notice was received. The reply shall specify the scope and content of the environmental information which would be germane to the responsible agency's statutory responsibilities in connection with the proposed project. The lead agency shall include this information in the EIR.

(c) Meetings. The responsible agency shall designate employees or representatives to attend meetings requested by the lead agency to discuss the scope and content of the EIR.

(d) Comments on Draft EIRs and Negative Declarations. A responsible agency should review and comment on draft EIRs and negative declarations for projects which the responsible agency would later be asked to approve. Comments should focus on any shortcomings in the EIR, the appropriateness of using a negative declaration, or on additional alternatives or mitigation measures which the EIR should include. The comments shall be limited to those project activities which are within the agency's area of expertise or which are required to be carried out or approved by the agency or which will be subject to the exercise of powers by the agency. Comments shall be as specific as possible and supported by either oral or written documentation.

(e) Decision on Adequacy of EIR or Negative Declaration. If a responsible agency believes that the final EIR or negative declaration prepared by the lead agency is not adequate for use by the responsible agency, the responsible agency must either:

    (1) Take the issue to court within 30 days after the lead agency files a notice of determination;

    (2) Be deemed to have waived any objection to the adequacy of the EIR or negative declaration;

    (3) Prepare a subsequent EIR if permissible under Section 15162; or

    (4) Assume the lead agency role as provided in Section 15052 (a) (3).

(f) Consider the EIR or Negative Declaration. Prior to reaching a decision on the project, the responsible agency must consider the environmental effects of the project as shown in the EIR or negative declaration. A subsequent or supplemental EIR can be prepared only as provided in Sections 15162 or 15163.

(g) Adoption of Alternatives or Mitigation Measures.

    (1) When considering alternatives and mitigation measures, a responsible agency is more limited than a lead agency. A responsible agency has responsibility for mitigating or avoiding only the direct or indirect environmental effects of those parts of the project which it decides to carry out, finance, or approve.

    (2) When an EIR has been prepared for a project, the Responsible Agency shall not approve the project as proposed if the agency finds any feasible alternative or feasible mitigation measures within its powers that would substantially lessen or avoid any significant effect the project would have on the environment. With respect to a project which includes housing development, the responsible agency shall not reduce the proposed number of housing units as a mitigation measure if it determines that there is

another feasible specific mitigation measure available that will provide a comparable level of mitigation.

(h) Findings. The responsible agency shall make the findings required by Section 15091 for each significant effect of the project and shall make the findings in Section 15093 if necessary.

(i) Notice of Determination. The responsible agency should file a notice of determination in the same manner as a lead agency under Section 15075 or 15094 except that the responsible agency does not need to state that the EIR or negative declaration complies with CEQA. The responsible agency should state that it considered the EIR or negative declaration as prepared by a lead agency.

15097.   Mitigation Monitoring or Reporting.

(a) This section applies when a public agency has made the findings required under paragraph (1) of subdivision (a) of Section 15091 relative to an EIR or adopted a mitigated negative declaration in conjunction with approving a project. In order to ensure that the mitigation measures and project revisions identified in the EIR or negative declaration are implemented, the public agency shall adopt a program for monitoring or reporting on the revisions which it has required in the project and the measures it has imposed to mitigate or avoid significant environmental effects. A public agency may delegate reporting or monitoring responsibilities to another public agency or to a private entity which accepts the delegation; however, until mitigation measures have been completed the lead agency remains responsible for ensuring that implementation of the mitigation measures occurs in accordance with the program.

(b) Where the project at issue is the adoption of a general plan, specific plan, community plan or other plan-level document (zoning, ordinance, regulation, policy), the monitoring plan shall apply to policies and any other portion of the plan that is a mitigation measure or adopted alternative. The monitoring plan may consist of policies included in plan-level documents. The annual report on general plan status required pursuant to the Government Code is one example of a reporting program for adoption of a city or county general plan.

(c) The public agency may choose whether its program will monitor mitigation, report on mitigation, or both. "Reporting" generally consists of a written compliance review that is presented to the decision making body or authorized staff person. A report may be required at various stages during project implementation or upon completion of the mitigation measure. "Monitoring" is generally an ongoing or periodic process of project oversight. There is often no clear distinction between monitoring and reporting and the program best suited to ensuring compliance in any given instance will usually involve elements of both. The choice of program may be guided by the following:

(1) Reporting is suited to projects which have readily measurable or quantitative mitigation measures or which already involve regular review. For example, a report may be required upon issuance of final occupancy to a project whose mitigation measures were confirmed by building inspection.

(2) Monitoring is suited to projects with complex mitigation measures, such as wetlands restoration or archeological protection, which may exceed the

expertise of the local agency to oversee, are expected to be implemented over a period of time, or require careful implementation to assure compliance.

(3) Reporting and monitoring are suited to all but the most simple projects. Monitoring ensures that project compliance is checked on a regular basis during and, if necessary after, implementation. Reporting ensures that the approving agency is informed of compliance with mitigation requirements.

(d) Lead and responsible agencies should coordinate their mitigation monitoring or reporting programs where possible. Generally, lead and responsible agencies for a given project will adopt separate and different monitoring or reporting programs. This occurs because of any of the following reasons: the agencies have adopted and are responsible for reporting on or monitoring different mitigation measures; the agencies are deciding on the project at different times; each agency has the discretion to choose its own approach to monitoring or reporting; and each agency has its own special expertise.

(e) At its discretion, an agency may adopt standardized policies and requirements to guide individually adopted monitoring or reporting programs. Standardized policies and requirements may describe, but are not limited to:

(1) The relative responsibilities of various departments within the agency for various aspects of monitoring or reporting, including lead responsibility for administering typical programs and support responsibilities.

(2) The responsibilities of the project proponent.

(3) Agency guidelines for preparing monitoring or reporting programs.

(4) General standards for determining project compliance with the mitigation measures or revisions and related conditions of approval.

(5) Enforcement procedures for noncompliance, including provisions for administrative appeal.

(6) Process for informing staff and decision makers of the relative success of mitigation measures and using those results to improve future mitigation measures.

(f) Where a trustee agency, in timely commenting upon a draft EIR or a proposed mitigated negative declaration, proposes mitigation measures or project revisions for incorporation into a project, that agency, at the same time, shall prepare and submit to the lead or responsible agency a draft monitoring or reporting program for those measures or revisions. The lead or responsible agency may use this information in preparing its monitoring or reporting program.

(g) When a project is of statewide, regional, or areawide importance, any transportation information generated by a required monitoring or reporting program shall be submitted to the transportation planning agency in the region where the project is located and to the California Department of Transportation. Each transportation planning agency and the California Department of Transportation shall adopt guidelines for the submittal of such information.

[Amended effective September 7, 2004]

Article 8. Time Limits

15100.　　　General.

(a) Public agencies shall adopt time limits to govern their implementation of CEQA consistent with this article.

(b) Public agencies should carry out their responsibilities for preparing and reviewing EIRs within a reasonable period of time. The requirement for the preparation of an EIR should not cause undue delays in the processing of applications for permits or other entitlements to use.

15101.　　　Review of Application for Completeness.

A Lead Agency or Responsible Agency shall determine whether an application for a permit or other entitlement for use is complete within 30 days from the receipt of the application except as provided in Section 15111. If no written determination of the completeness of the application is made within that period, the application will be deemed complete on the 30th day.

15102.　　　Initial Study.

The Lead Agency shall determine within 30 days after accepting an application as complete whether it intends to prepare an EIR or a negative declaration or use a previously prepared EIR or negative declaration except as provided in Section 15111. The 30 day period may be extended 15 days upon the consent of the lead agency and the project applicant.

15103.　　　Response to Notice of Preparation.

Responsible and Trustee Agencies, and the Office of Planning and Research shall provide a response to a Notice of Preparation to the Lead Agency within 30 days after receipt of the notice. If they fail to reply within the 30 days with either a response or a well justified request for additional time, the Lead Agency may assume that none of those entities have a response to make and may ignore a late response.

[Amended effective November 1, 2005]

15104.　　　Convening of Meetings.

The Lead Agency shall convene a meeting with agency representatives to discuss the scope and content of the environmental information a Responsible Agency will need in the EIR as soon as possible but no later than 30 days after receiving a request for the meeting. The meeting may be requested by the Lead Agency, a Responsible Agency, a Trustee Agency, the Office of Planning and Research, or by the project applicant.

[Amended effective November 1, 2005]

15105.　　　Public Review Period for a Draft EIR or a Proposed Negative Declaration or Mitigated Negative Declaration.

(a) The public review period for a draft EIR should not be less than 30 days nor longer than 60 days except in unusual circumstances. When a draft EIR is submitted to the State Clearinghouse for review by state agencies, the public review period shall not be less than 45 days, unless a shorter period, not less than 30 days, is approved by the State Clearinghouse.

(b) The public review period for a proposed negative declaration or mitigated negative declaration shall be not less than 20 days. When a proposed negative declaration or mitigated negative declaration is submitted to the State Clearinghouse for review by state agencies, the public review period shall not be less than 30 days, unless a shorter period, not less than 20 days, is approved by the State Clearinghouse.

(c) If a draft EIR or proposed negative declaration or mitigated negative declaration has been submitted to the State Clearinghouse for review by state agencies, the public review period shall be at least as long as the review period established by the State Clearinghouse. The public review period and the state agency review period may, but are not required to, begin and end at the same time. Day one of the state review period shall be the date that the State Clearinghouse distributes the document to state agencies.

(d) A shortened Clearinghouse review period may be granted in accordance with the provisions of Appendix K and the following principles:

(1) A shortened review shall not be granted for any proposed project of statewide, areawide, or regional environmental significance.

(2) Requests for shortened review periods shall be submitted to the Clearinghouse in writing by the decision-making body of the lead agency, or a representative authorized by ordinance, resolution, or delegation of the decision-making body.

(3) The lead agency has contacted responsible and trustee agencies and they have agreed to the shortened review period.

(e) The State Clearinghouse shall distribute a draft EIR or proposed negative declaration or mitigated negative declaration within three working days after the date of receipt if the submittal is determined by the State Clearinghouse to be complete.

[Amended effective July 27, 2007]

15107. **Completion of Negative Declaration for Certain Private Projects.**

With private projects involving the issuance of a lease, permit, license, certificate, or other entitlement for use by one or more public agencies, the negative declaration must be completed and approved within 180 days from the date when the lead agency accepted the application as complete. Lead agency procedures may provide that the 180-day time limit may be extended once for a period of not more than 90 days upon consent of the lead agency and the applicant.

[Amended effective December 28, 2018]

15108. **Completion and Certification of EIR.**

With a private project, the Lead Agency shall complete and certify the final EIR as provided in Section 15090 within one year after the date when the Lead Agency accepted the application as complete. Lead agency procedures may provide that the one-year time limit may be extended once for a period of not more than 90 days upon consent of the Lead Agency and the applicant.

15109. Suspension of Time Periods.

An unreasonable delay by an applicant in meeting requests by the Lead Agency necessary for the preparation of a negative declaration or an EIR shall suspend the running of the time periods described in Sections 15107 and 15108 for the period of the unreasonable delay. Alternatively, an agency may disapprove a project application where there is unreasonable delay in meeting requests. The agency may allow a renewed application to start at the same point in the process where the application was when it was disapproved.

15110. Projects with Federal Involvement.

(a) At the request of an applicant, the Lead Agency may waive the one year time limit for completing and certifying a final EIR or the 105-day period for completing a negative declaration if:

    (1) The project will be subject to CEQA and to the National Environmental Policy Act,

    (2) Additional time will be required to prepare a combined EIR-EIS or combined negative declaration-finding of no significant impact as provided in Section 15221, and

    (3) The time required to prepare the combined document will be shorter than the time required to prepare the documents separately.

(b) The time limits for taking final action on a permit for a development project may also be waived where a combined EIR-EIS will be prepared.

(c) The time limits for processing permits for development projects under Government Code Sections 65950-65960 shall not apply if federal statutes or regulations require time schedules which exceed the state time limits. In this event, any state agencies involved shall make a final decision on the project within the federal time limits.

15111. Projects with Short Time Periods for Approval.

(a) A few statues or ordinances require agencies to make decisions on permits within time limits that are so short that review of the project under CEQA would be difficult. To enable the Lead Agency to comply with both the permit statute and CEQA, the Lead Agency shall deem an application for a project not received for filing under the permit statute or ordinance until such time as progress toward completing the environmental documentation required by CEQA is sufficient to enable the Lead Agency to finish the CEQA process within the short permit time limit. This section will apply where all of the following conditions are met:

    (1) The enabling legislation for a program, other than Chapter 4.5 (commencing with Section 65920) of Division 1 of Title 7 of the Government Code, requires the Lead Agency to take action on an application within a specified period of time that is six months or less, and

228

(2) The enabling legislation provides that the project will become approved by operation of law if the Lead Agency fails to take any action within such specified time period, and

(3) The project involves the issuance of a lease, permit, license, certificate, or other entitlement for use.

(b) Examples of time periods subject to this section include but are not limited to:

(1) Action on a timber harvesting plan by the Director of Forestry within 15 days pursuant to Section 4582.7 of the Public Resources Code,

(2) Action on a permit by the San Francisco Bay Conservation and Development Commission within 90 days pursuant to Section 66632(f) of the Government Code, and

(3) Action on an oil and gas permit by the Division of Oil and Gas within 10 days pursuant to Sections 3203 or 3724 of the Public Resources Code.

(c) In any case described in this section, the environmental document shall be completed or certified and the decision on the project shall be made within the period established under the Permit Streamlining Act (Government Code Section 65920, et seq.).

15112.   Statutes of Limitations.

(a) CEQA provides unusually short statutes of limitations on filing court challenges to the approval of projects under the act.

(b) The statute of limitations periods are not public review periods or waiting periods for the person whose project has been approved. The project sponsor may proceed to carry out the project as soon as the necessary permits have been granted. The statute of limitations cuts off the right of another person to file a court action challenging approval of the project after the specified time period has expired.

(c) The statute of limitations periods under CEQA are as follows:

(1) Where the public agency filed a notice of determination in compliance with Sections 15075 or 15094, 30 days after the filing of the notice and the posting on a list of such notices.

(2) Where the public agency filed a notice of exemption in compliance with Section 15062, 35 days after the filing of the notice and the posting on a list of such notices.

(3) Where a certified state regulatory agency files a notice of decision in compliance with Public Resources Code Section 21080.5(d)(2)(E), 30 days after the filing of the notice.

(4) Where the Secretary for Resources certifies a state environmental regulatory agency under Public Resources Code Section 21080.5, the certification may be challenged only during the 30 days following the certification decision.

(5) Where none of the other statute of limitations periods in this section apply, 180 days after either:

(A) The public agency's decision to carry out or approve the project, or

(B) Commencement of the project if the project is undertaken without a formal decision by the public agency.

[Amended effective July 22, 2003]

Article 9. Contents of Environmental Impact Reports

15120.   General.

(a) Environmental Impact Reports shall contain the information outlined in this article, but the format of the document may be varied. Each element must be covered, and when these elements are not separated into distinct sections, the document shall state where in the document each element is discussed.

(b) The EIR may be prepared as a separate document, as part of a general plan, or as part of a project report. If prepared as a part of the project report, it must still contain one separate and distinguishable section providing either analysis of all the subjects required in an EIR or as a minimum, a table showing where each of the subjects is discussed. When the Lead Agency is a state agency, the EIR shall be included as part of the regular project report if such a report is used in the agency's existing review and budgetary process.

(c) Draft EIRs shall contain the information required by Sections 15122 through 15131. Final EIRs shall contain the same information and the subjects described in Section 15132.

(d) No document prepared pursuant to this article that is available for public examination shall include a "trade secret" as defined in Section 6254.7 of the Government Code, information about the location of archaeological sites and sacred lands, or any other information that is subject to the disclosure restrictions of Section 6254 of the Government Code.

15121.   Informational Document.

(a) An EIR is an informational document which will inform public agency decisionmakers and the public generally of the significant environmental effect of a project, identify possible ways to minimize the significant effects, and describe reasonable alternatives to the project. The public agency shall consider the information in the EIR along with other information which may be presented to the agency.

(b) While the information in the EIR does not control the agency's ultimate discretion on the project, the agency must respond to each significant effect identified in the EIR by making findings under Section 15091 and if necessary by making a statement of overriding considerations under Section 15093.

(c) The information in an EIR may constitute substantial evidence in the record to support the agency's action on the project if its decision is later challenged in court.

15122.   Table of Contents or Index.

An EIR shall contain at least a table of contents or an index to assist readers in finding the analysis of different subjects and issues.

15123. Summary.

(a) An EIR shall contain a brief summary of the proposed actions and its consequences. The language of the summary should be as clear and simple as reasonably practical.

(b) The summary shall identify:

    (1) Each significant effect with proposed mitigation measures and alternatives that would reduce or avoid that effect;

    (2) Areas of controversy known to the Lead Agency including issues raised by agencies and the public; and

    (3) Issues to be resolved including the choice among alternatives and whether or how to mitigate the significant effects.

(c) The summary should normally not exceed 15 pages.

15124. Project Description.

The description of the project shall contain the following information but should not supply extensive detail beyond that needed for evaluation and review of the environmental impact.

(a) The precise location and boundaries of the proposed project shall be shown on a detailed map, preferably topographic. The location of the project shall also appear on a regional map.

(b) A statement of the objectives sought by the proposed project. A clearly written statement of objectives will help the Lead Agency develop a reasonable range of alternatives to evaluate in the EIR and will aid the decision makers in preparing findings or a statement of overriding considerations, if necessary. The statement of objectives should include the underlying purpose of the project and may discuss the project benefits.

(c) A general description of the project's technical, economic, and environmental characteristics, considering the principal engineering proposals if any and supporting public service facilities.

(d) A statement briefly describing the intended uses of the EIR.

    (1) This statement shall include, to the extent that the information is known to the Lead Agency,

        (A) A list of the agencies that are expected to use the EIR in their decision-making, and

        (B) A list of permits and other approvals required to implement the project.

        (C) A list of related environmental review and consultation requirements required by federal, state, or local laws, regulations, or policies. To the fullest extent possible, the Lead Agency should integrate CEQA review with these related environmental review and consultation requirements.

    (2) If a public agency must make more than one decision on a project, all its decisions subject to CEQA should be listed, preferably in the order in

which they will occur. On request, the Office of Planning and Research will provide assistance in identifying state permits for a project.

[Amended effective December 28, 2018]

15125.   Environmental Setting.

(a) An EIR must include a description of the physical environmental conditions in the vicinity of the project. This environmental setting will normally constitute the baseline physical conditions by which a Lead Agency determines whether an impact is significant. The description of the environmental setting shall be no longer than is necessary to provide an understanding of the significant effects of the proposed project and its alternatives. The purpose of this requirement is to give the public and decision makers the most accurate and understandable picture practically possible of the project's likely near-term and long-term impacts.

(1) Generally, the lead agency should describe physical environmental conditions as they exist at the time the notice of preparation is published, or if no notice of preparation is published, at the time environmental analysis is commenced, from both a local and regional perspective. Where existing conditions change or fluctuate over time, and where necessary to provide the most accurate picture practically possible of the project's impacts, a lead agency may define existing conditions by referencing historic conditions, or conditions expected when the project becomes operational, or both, that are supported with substantial evidence. In addition, a lead agency may also use baselines consisting of both existing conditions and projected future conditions that are supported by reliable projections based on substantial evidence in the record.

(2) A lead agency may use projected future conditions (beyond the date of project operations) as the sole baseline for analysis only if it demonstrates with substantial evidence that use of existing conditions would be either misleading or without informative value to decision-makers and the public. Use of projected future conditions as the only baseline must be supported by reliable projections based on substantial evidence in the record.

(3) An existing conditions baseline shall not include hypothetical conditions, such as those that might be allowed, but have never actually occurred, under existing permits or plans, as the baseline.

(b) When preparing an EIR for a plan for the reuse of a military base, lead agencies should refer to the special application of the principle of baseline conditions for determining significant impacts contained in Section 15229.

(c) Knowledge of the regional setting is critical to the assessment of environmental impacts. Special emphasis should be placed on environmental resources that are rare or unique to that region and would be affected by the project. The EIR must demonstrate that the significant environmental impacts of the proposed project were adequately investigated and discussed and it must permit the significant effects of the project to be considered in the full environmental context.

(d) The EIR shall discuss any inconsistencies between the proposed project and applicable general plans, specific plans and regional plans. Such regional plans include, but are not limited to, the applicable air quality attainment or maintenance plan (or State Implementation Plan), area-wide waste treatment and water quality control plans, regional transportation plans, regional housing allocation plans, regional blueprint plans, plans for the reduction of greenhouse gas emissions, habitat conservation plans, natural community conservation plans and regional land use plans for the protection of the coastal zone, Lake Tahoe Basin, San Francisco Bay, and Santa Monica Mountains.

(e) Where a proposed project is compared with an adopted plan, the analysis shall examine the existing physical conditions at the time the notice of preparation is published, or if no notice of preparation is published, at the time environmental analysis is commenced as well as the potential future conditions discussed in the plan.

[Amended effective December 28, 2018]

15126.   Consideration and Discussion of Environmental Impacts.

All phases of a project must be considered when evaluating its impact on the environment: planning, acquisition, development, and operation. The subjects listed below shall be discussed as directed in Sections 15126.2, 15126.4 and 15126.6, preferably in separate sections or paragraphs of the EIR. If they are not discussed separately, the EIR shall include a table showing where each of the subjects is discussed.

(a) Significant Environmental Effects of the Proposed Project.

(b) Significant Environmental Effects Which Cannot be Avoided if the Proposed Project is Implemented.

(c) Significant Irreversible Environmental Changes Which Would be Involved in the Proposed Project Should it be Implemented.

(d) Growth-Inducing Impact of the Proposed Project.

(e) The Mitigation Measures Proposed to Minimize the Significant Effects.

(f) Alternatives to the Proposed Project.

15126.2   Consideration and Discussion of Significant Environmental Impacts.

(a) The Significant Environmental Effects of the Proposed Project. An EIR shall identify and focus on the significant effects of the proposed project on the environment. In assessing the impact of a proposed project on the environment, the Lead Agency should normally limit its examination to changes in the existing physical conditions in the affected area as they exist at the time the notice of preparation is published, or where no notice of preparation is published, at the time environmental analysis is commenced. Direct and indirect significant effects of the project on the environment shall be clearly identified and described, giving due consideration to both the short-term and long-term effects. The discussion should include relevant specifics of the area, the resources involved, physical changes, alterations to ecological systems, and changes induced in population distribution, population concentration, the human use of the land (including commercial and residential development), health and safety problems caused by the physical changes, and other aspects of the resource base such as water, historical resources, scenic quality, and public services. The EIR shall also analyze any significant environmental effects the project might cause or risk exacerbating by bringing development and people into the area affected. For example, the EIR should evaluate any potentially significant direct, indirect, or cumulative environmental impacts of locating development in areas susceptible to hazardous conditions (e.g., floodplains, coastlines, wildfire risk areas), including both short-term and long-term conditions, as identified in authoritative hazard maps, risk assessments or in land use plans addressing such hazards areas.

(b) Energy Impacts. If analysis of the project's energy use reveals that the project may result in significant environmental effects due to wasteful, inefficient, or unnecessary use of energy, or wasteful use of energy resources, the EIR shall mitigate that energy use. This analysis should include the project's energy use for all project phases and components, including transportation-related energy, during construction and operation. In addition to building code compliance, other relevant considerations may include, among others, the project's size, location, orientation, equipment use and any renewable energy features that could be incorporated into the project. (Guidance on information that may be included in such an analysis is presented in Appendix F.) This analysis is subject to the rule of reason and shall focus on energy use that is caused by the project. This analysis may be included in related analyses of air quality, greenhouse gas emissions, transportation or utilities in the discretion of the lead agency.

(c) Significant Environmental Effects Which Cannot be Avoided if the Proposed Project is Implemented. Describe any significant impacts, including those which can be mitigated but not reduced to a level of insignificance. Where there are impacts that cannot be alleviated without imposing an alternative design, their implications and the reasons why the project is being proposed, notwithstanding their effect, should be described.

(d) Significant Irreversible Environmental Changes Which Would be Caused by the Proposed Project Should it be Implemented. Uses of nonrenewable resources during the initial and continued phases of the project may be irreversible since a large commitment of such resources makes removal or nonuse thereafter unlikely. Primary impacts and, particularly, secondary impacts (such as highway improvement which provides access to a previously inaccessible area) generally commit future generations to similar uses. Also irreversible damage can result from environmental accidents associated with the project. Irretrievable commitments of resources should be evaluated to assure that such current consumption is justified. (See Public Resources Code section 21100.1 and Title 14, California Code of Regulations, section 15127 for limitations to applicability of this requirement.)

(e) Growth-Inducing Impact of the Proposed Project. Discuss the ways in which the proposed project could foster economic or population growth, or the construction of additional housing, either directly or indirectly, in the surrounding environment. Included in this are projects which would remove obstacles to population growth (a major expansion of a waste water treatment plant might, for example, allow for more construction in service areas). Increases in the population may tax existing community service facilities, requiring construction of new facilities that could cause significant environmental effects. Also discuss the characteristic of some projects which may encourage and facilitate other activities that could significantly affect the environment, either individually or cumulatively. It must not be assumed that growth in any area is necessarily beneficial, detrimental, or of little significance to the environment.

[Amended effective December 28, 2018]

15126.4 Consideration and Discussion of Mitigation Measures Proposed to Minimize Significant Effects.

(a) Mitigation Measures in General.

(1) An EIR shall describe feasible measures which could minimize significant adverse impacts, including where relevant, inefficient and unnecessary consumption of energy.

(A) The discussion of mitigation measures shall distinguish between the measures which are proposed by project proponents to be included in the project and other measures proposed by the lead, responsible or trustee agency or other persons which are not included but the Lead Agency determines could reasonably be expected to reduce adverse impacts if required as conditions of approving the project. This discussion shall identify mitigation measures for each significant environmental effect identified in the EIR.

(B) Where several measures are available to mitigate an impact, each should be discussed and the basis for selecting a particular measure should be identified. Formulation of mitigation measures shall not be deferred until some future time. The specific details of a mitigation measure, however, may be developed after project approval when it is impractical or infeasible to include those details during the project's environmental review, provided that the agency (1) commits itself to the mitigation, (2) adopts specific performance standards the mitigation will achieve, and (3) identifies the type(s) of potential action(s) that can feasibly achieve that performance standard that will be considered, analyzed, and potentially incorporated in the mitigation measure. Compliance with a regulatory permit or other similar process may be identified as mitigation if compliance would result in implementation of measures that would be reasonably expected, based on substantial evidence in the record, to reduce the significant impact to the specified performance standards.

(C) Energy conservation measures, as well as other appropriate mitigation measures, shall be discussed when relevant. Examples of energy conservation measures are provided in Appendix F.

(D) If a mitigation measure would cause one or more significant effects in addition to those that would be caused by the project as proposed, the effects of the mitigation measure shall be discussed but in less detail than the significant effects of the project as proposed. (Stevens v. City of Glendale (1981) 125 Cal.App.3d 986.)

(2) Mitigation measures must be fully enforceable through permit conditions, agreements, or other legally-binding instruments. In the case of the

adoption of a plan, policy, regulation, or other public project, mitigation measures can be incorporated into the plan, policy, regulation, or project design.

(3) Mitigation measures are not required for effects which are not found to be significant.

(4) Mitigation measures must be consistent with all applicable constitutional requirements, including the following:

(A) There must be an essential nexus (i.e. connection) between the mitigation measure and a legitimate governmental interest. Nollan v. California Coastal Commission, 483 U.S. 825 (1987); and

(B) The mitigation measure must be "roughly proportional" to the impacts of the project. Dolan v. City of Tigard, 512 U.S. 374 (1994). Where the mitigation measure is an ad hoc exaction, it must be "roughly proportional" to the impacts of the project. Ehrlich v. City of Culver City (1996) 12 Cal.4th 854.

(5) If the Lead Agency determines that a mitigation measure cannot be legally imposed, the measure need not be proposed or analyzed. Instead, the EIR may simply reference that fact and briefly explain the reasons underlying the Lead Agency's determination.

(b) Mitigation Measures Related to Impacts on Historical Resources.

(1) Where maintenance, repair, stabilization, rehabilitation, restoration, preservation, conservation or reconstruction of the historical resource will be conducted in a manner consistent with the Secretary of the Interior's Standards for the Treatment of Historic Properties with Guidelines for Preserving, Rehabilitating, Restoring, and Reconstructing Historic Buildings (1995), Weeks and Grimmer, the project's impact on the historical resource shall generally be considered mitigated below a level of significance and thus is not significant.

(2) In some circumstances, documentation of an historical resource, by way of historic narrative, photographs or architectural drawings, as mitigation for the effects of demolition of the resource will not mitigate the effects to a point where clearly no significant effect on the environment would occur.

(3) Public agencies should, whenever feasible, seek to avoid damaging effects on any historical resource of an archaeological nature. The following factors shall be considered and discussed in an EIR for a project involving such an archaeological site:

(A) Preservation in place is the preferred manner of mitigating impacts to archaeological sites. Preservation in place maintains the relationship between artifacts and the archaeological context. Preservation may also avoid conflict with religious or cultural values of groups associated with the site.

(B) Preservation in place may be accomplished by, but is not limited to, the following:

1. Planning construction to avoid archaeological sites;

2. Incorporation of sites within parks, greenspace, or other open space;

3. Covering the archaeological sites with a layer of chemically stable soil before building tennis courts, parking lots, or similar facilities on the site.

4. Deeding the site into a permanent conservation easement.

(C) When data recovery through excavation is the only feasible mitigation, a data recovery plan, which makes provision for adequately recovering the scientifically consequential information from and about the historical resource, shall be prepared and adopted prior to any excavation being undertaken. Such studies shall be deposited with the California Historical Resources Regional Information Center. Archaeological sites known to contain human remains shall be treated in accordance with the provisions of Section 7050.5 Health and Safety Code. If an artifact must be removed during project excavation or testing, curation may be an appropriate mitigation.

(D) Data recovery shall not be required for an historical resource if the Lead Agency determines that testing or studies already completed have adequately recovered the scientifically consequential information from and about the archaeological or historical resource, provided that the determination is documented in the EIR and that the studies are deposited with the California Historical Resources Regional Information Center.

(c) Mitigation Measures Related to Greenhouse Gas Emissions.

Consistent with section 15126.4(a), lead agencies shall consider feasible means, supported by substantial evidence and subject to monitoring or reporting, of mitigating the significant effects of greenhouse gas emissions. Measures to mitigate the significant effects of greenhouse gas emissions may include, among others:

(1) Measures in an existing plan or mitigation program for the reduction of emissions that are required as part of the lead agency's decision;

(2) Reductions in emissions resulting from a project through implementation of project features, project design, or other measures, such as those described in Appendix F;

(3) Off-site measures, including offsets that are not otherwise required, to mitigate a project's emissions;

(4) Measures that sequester greenhouse gases;

(5) In the case of the adoption of a plan, such as a general plan, long range development plan, or plans for the reduction of greenhouse gas emissions, mitigation may include the identification of specific measures that may be implemented on a project-by-project basis. Mitigation may also include the incorporation of specific measures or policies found in an adopted ordinance or regulation that reduces the cumulative effect of emissions.

[Amended effective December 28, 2018]

15126.6   Consideration and Discussion of Alternatives to the Proposed Project.

(a) Alternatives to the Proposed Project. An EIR shall describe a range of reasonable alternatives to the project, or to the location of the project, which would feasibly attain most of the basic objectives of the project but would avoid or substantially lessen any of the significant effects of the project, and evaluate the comparative merits of the alternatives. An EIR need not consider every conceivable alternative to a project. Rather it must consider a reasonable range of potentially feasible alternatives that will foster informed decisionmaking and public participation. An EIR is not required to consider alternatives which are infeasible. The Lead Agency is responsible for selecting a range of project alternatives for examination and must publicly disclose its reasoning for selecting those alternatives. There is no ironclad rule governing the nature or scope of the alternatives to be discussed other than the rule of reason. (Citizens of Goleta Valley v. Board of Supervisors (1990) 52 Cal.3d 553 and Laurel Heights Improvement Association v. Regents of the University of California (1988) 47 Cal.3d 376).

(b) Purpose. Because an EIR must identify ways to mitigate or avoid the significant effects that a project may have on the environment (Public Resources Code Section 21002.1), the discussion of alternatives shall focus on alternatives to the project or its location which are capable of avoiding or substantially lessening any significant effects of the project, even if these alternatives would impede to some degree the attainment of the project objectives, or would be more costly.

(c) Selection of a range of reasonable alternatives. The range of potential alternatives to the proposed project shall include those that could feasibly accomplish most of the basic objectives of the project and could avoid or substantially lessen one or more of the significant effects. The EIR should briefly describe the rationale for selecting the alternatives to be discussed. The EIR should also identify any alternatives that were considered by the Lead Agency but were rejected as infeasible during the scoping process and briefly explain the reasons underlying the Lead Agency's determination. Additional information explaining the choice of alternatives may be included in the administrative record. Among the factors that may be used to eliminate alternatives from detailed consideration in an EIR are:(i) failure to meet most of the basic project objectives, (ii) infeasibility, or (iii) inability to avoid significant environmental impacts.

(d) Evaluation of alternatives. The EIR shall include sufficient information about each alternative to allow meaningful evaluation, analysis, and comparison with the proposed project. A matrix displaying the major characteristics and significant environmental effects of each alternative may be used to summarize the comparison. If an alternative would cause one or more significant effects in addition to those that would be caused by the project as proposed, the significant effects of the alternative shall be discussed, but in less detail than the significant effects of the project as proposed. (County of Inyo v. City of Los Angeles (1981) 124 Cal.App.3d 1).

(e) "No project" alternative.

238

(1) The specific alternative of "no project" shall also be evaluated along with its impact. The purpose of describing and analyzing a no project alternative is to allow decisionmakers to compare the impacts of approving the proposed project with the impacts of not approving the proposed project. The no project alternative analysis is not the baseline for determining whether the proposed project's environmental impacts may be significant, unless it is identical to the existing environmental setting analysis which does establish that baseline (see Section 15125).

(2) The "no project" analysis shall discuss the existing conditions at the time the notice of preparation is published, or if no notice of preparation is published, at the time environmental analysis is commenced, as well as what would be reasonably expected to occur in the foreseeable future if the project were not approved, based on current plans and consistent with available infrastructure and community services. If the environmentally superior alternative is the "no project" alternative, the EIR shall also identify an environmentally superior alternative among the other alternatives.

(3) A discussion of the "no project" alternative will usually proceed along one of two lines:

(A) When the project is the revision of an existing land use or regulatory plan, policy or ongoing operation, the "no project" alternative will be the continuation of the existing plan, policy or operation into the future. Typically this is a situation where other projects initiated under the existing plan will continue while the new plan is developed. Thus, the projected impacts of the proposed plan or alternative plans would be compared to the impacts that would occur under the existing plan.

(B) If the project is other than a land use or regulatory plan, for example a development project on identifiable property, the "no project" alternative is the circumstance under which the project does not proceed. Here the discussion would compare the environmental effects of the property remaining in its existing state against environmental effects which would occur if the project is approved. If disapproval of the project under consideration would result in predictable actions by others, such as the proposal of some other project, this "no project" consequence should be discussed. In certain instances, the no project alternative means "no build" wherein the existing environmental setting is maintained. However, where failure to proceed with the project will not result in preservation of existing environmental conditions, the analysis should identify the practical result of the project's non-approval and not create and analyze a set of artificial assumptions that would be required to preserve the existing physical environment.

(C) After defining the no project alternative using one of these approaches, the Lead Agency should proceed to analyze the impacts of the no project alternative by projecting what would reasonably be expected to occur in the foreseeable future if the project were not approved, based on current plans and consistent with available infrastructure and community services.

(f) Rule of reason. The range of alternatives required in an EIR is governed by a "rule of reason" that requires the EIR to set forth only those alternatives necessary to permit a reasoned choice. The alternatives shall be limited to ones that would avoid or substantially lessen any of the significant effects of the project. Of those alternatives, the EIR need examine in detail only the ones that the Lead Agency determines could feasibly attain most of the basic objectives of the project. The range of feasible alternatives shall be selected and discussed in a manner to foster meaningful public participation and informed decision making.

(1) Feasibility. Among the factors that may be taken into account when addressing the feasibility of alternatives are site suitability, economic viability, availability of infrastructure, general plan consistency, other plans or regulatory limitations, jurisdictional boundaries (projects with a regionally significant impact should consider the regional context), and whether the proponent can reasonably acquire, control or otherwise have access to the alternative site (or the site is already owned by the proponent). No one of these factors establishes a fixed limit on the scope of reasonable alternatives. (Citizens of Goleta Valley v. Board of Supervisors (1990) 52 Cal.3d 553; see Save Our Residential Environment v. City of West Hollywood (1992) 9 Cal.App.4th 1745, 1753, fn. 1).

(2) Alternative locations.

(A) Key question. The key question and first step in analysis is whether any of the significant effects of the project would be avoided or substantially lessened by putting the project in another location. Only locations that would avoid or substantially lessen any of the significant effects of the project need be considered for inclusion in the EIR.

(B) None feasible. If the Lead Agency concludes that no feasible alternative locations exist, it must disclose the reasons for this conclusion, and should include the reasons in the EIR. For example, in some cases there may be no feasible alternative locations for a geothermal plant or mining project which must be in close proximity to natural resources at a given location.

(C) Limited new analysis required. Where a previous document has sufficiently analyzed a range of reasonable alternative locations and environmental impacts for projects with the same basic purpose, the Lead Agency should review the previous document. The EIR may rely on the previous document to help it assess the feasibility of potential project alternatives to the extent the circumstances remain substantially the same as they relate to the alternative. (Citizens of Goleta Valley v. Board of Supervisors (1990) 52 Cal.3d 553, 573).

(3) An EIR need not consider an alternative whose effect cannot be reasonably ascertained and whose implementation is remote and speculative. (Residents Ad Hoc Stadium Committee v. Board of Trustees (1979) 89 Cal. App.3d 274).

15127.　Limitations on Discussion of Environmental Impact.

The information required by Section 15126.2 (c) concerning irreversible changes, need be included only in EIRs prepared in connection with any of the following activities:

(a) The adoption, amendment, or enactment of a plan, policy, or ordinance of a public agency;

(b) The adoption by a local agency formation commission of a resolution making determinations; or

(c) A project which will be subject to the requirement for preparing an environmental impact statement pursuant to the requirements of the National Environmental Policy Act of 1969, 42 U.S.C. 4321-4347.

15128.　Effects Not Found to be Significant.

An EIR shall contain a statement briefly indicating the reasons that various possible significant effects of a project were determined not to be significant and were therefore not discussed in detail in the EIR. Such a statement may be contained in an attached copy of an initial study.

15129.　Organizations and Persons Consulted.

The EIR shall identify all federal, state, or local agencies, other organizations, and private individuals consulted in preparing the draft EIR, and the persons, firm, or agency preparing the draft EIR, by contract or other authorization.

15130.　Discussion of Cumulative Impacts.

(a) An EIR shall discuss cumulative impacts of a project when the project's incremental effect is cumulatively considerable, as defined in section 15065(a)(3). Where a Lead Agency is examining a project with an incremental effect that is not "cumulatively considerable", a Lead Agency need not consider that effect significant, but shall briefly describe its basis for concluding that the incremental effect is not cumulatively considerable.

(1) As defined in Section 15355, a cumulative impact consists of an impact which is created as a result of the combination of the project evaluated in the EIR together with other projects causing related impacts. An EIR should not discuss impacts which do not result in part from the project evaluated in the EIR.

(2) When the combined cumulative impact associated with the project's incremental effect and the effects of other projects is not significant, the EIR shall briefly indicate why the cumulative impact is not significant and is not discussed in further detail in the EIR. A Lead Agency shall identify facts and analysis supporting the Lead Agency's conclusion that the cumulative impact is less than significant.

(3) An EIR may determine that a project's contribution to a significant cumulative impact will be rendered less than cumulatively considerable and thus is not significant. A project's contribution is less than cumulatively considerable if the project is required to implement or fund its fair share of a mitigation measure or measures designed to alleviate the cumulative impact. The Lead Agency shall identify facts and analysis supporting its

241

conclusion that the contribution will be rendered less than cumulatively considerable.

(b) The discussion of cumulative impacts shall reflect the severity of the impacts and their likelihood of occurrence, but the discussion need not provide as great detail as is provided for the effects attributable to the project alone. The discussion should be guided by the standards of practicality and reasonableness, and should focus on the cumulative impact to which the identified other projects contribute rather than the attributes of other projects which do not contribute to the cumulative impact. The following elements are necessary to an adequate discussion of significant cumulative impacts:

(1) Either:

(A) A list of past, present, and probable future projects producing related or cumulative impacts, including, if necessary, those projects outside the control of the agency, or

(B) A summary of projections contained in an adopted local, regional or statewide plan, or related planning document, that describes or evaluates conditions contributing to the cumulative effect. Such plans may include: a general plan, regional transportation plan, or plans for the reduction of greenhouse gas emissions. A summary of projections may also be contained in an adopted or certified prior environmental document for such a plan. Such projections may be supplemented with additional information such as a regional modeling program. Any such document shall be referenced and made available to the public at a location specified by the lead agency.

(2) When utilizing a list, as suggested in paragraph (1) of subdivision (b), factors to consider when determining whether to include a related project should include the nature of each environmental resource being examined, the location of the project and its type. Location may be important, for example, when water quality impacts are at issue since projects outside the watershed would probably not contribute to a cumulative effect. Project type may be important, for example, when the impact is specialized, such as a particular air pollutant or mode of traffic.

(3) Lead agencies should define the geographic scope of the area affected by the cumulative effect and provide a reasonable explanation for the geographic limitation used.

(4) A summary of the expected environmental effects to be produced by those projects with specific reference to additional information stating where that information is available, and

(5) A reasonable analysis of the cumulative impacts of the relevant projects. An EIR shall examine reasonable, feasible options for mitigating or avoiding the project's contribution to any significant cumulative effects.

(c) With some projects, the only feasible mitigation for cumulative impacts may involve the adoption of ordinances or regulations rather than the imposition of conditions on a project-by-project basis.

(d) Previously approved land use documents, including, but not limited to, general plans, specific plans, regional transportation plans, plans for the reduction of greenhouse gas emissions, and local coastal plans may be used in cumulative impact analysis. A pertinent discussion of cumulative impacts contained in one or more previously certified EIRs may be incorporated by reference pursuant to the provisions for tiering and program EIRs. No further cumulative impacts analysis is required when a project is consistent with a general, specific, master or comparable programmatic plan where the Lead Agency determines that the regional or areawide cumulative impacts of the proposed project have already been adequately addressed, as defined in section 15152(f), in a certified EIR for that plan.

(e) If a cumulative impact was adequately addressed in a prior EIR for a community plan, zoning action, or general plan, and the project is consistent with that plan or action, then an EIR for such a project should not further analyze that cumulative impact, as provided in Section 15183(j).

[Amended effective March 18, 2010]

15131. Economic and Social Effects.

Economic or social information may be included in an EIR or may be presented in whatever form the agency desires.

(a) Economic or social effects of a project shall not be treated as significant effects on the environment. An EIR may trace a chain of cause and effect from a proposed decision on a project through anticipated economic or social changes resulting from the project to physical changes caused in turn by the economic or social changes. The intermediate economic or social changes need not be analyzed in any detail greater than necessary to trace the chain of cause and effect. The focus of the analysis shall be on the physical changes.

(b) Economic or social effects of a project may be used to determine the significance of physical changes caused by the project. For example, if the construction of a new freeway or rail line divides an existing community, the construction would be the physical change, but the social effect on the community would be the basis for determining that the effect would be significant. As an additional example, if the construction of a road and the resulting increase in noise in an area disturbed existing religious practices in the area, the disturbance of the religious practices could be used to determine that the construction and use of the road and the resulting noise would be significant effects on the environment. The religious practices would need to be analyzed only to the extent to show that the increase in traffic and noise would conflict with the religious practices. Where an EIR uses economic or social effects to determine that a physical change is significant, the EIR shall explain the reason for determining that the effect is significant.

(c) Economic, social, and particularly housing factors shall be considered by public agencies together with technological and environmental factors in deciding whether changes in a project are feasible to reduce or avoid the significant effects on the environment identified in the EIR. If information on these factors is not contained in the EIR, the information must be added to the record in some other manner to allow the agency to consider the factors in reaching a decision on the project.

15132.   Contents of Final Environmental Impact Report.

The final EIR shall consist of:

(a) The Draft EIR or a revision of the draft.

(b) Comments and recommendations received on the Draft EIR either verbatim or in summary.

(c) A list of persons, organizations, and public agencies commenting on the Draft EIR.

(d) The responses of the Lead Agency to significant environmental points raised in the review and consultation process.

(e) Any other information added by the lead agency.

Article 10. Considerations in Preparing EIRs and Negative Declarations

15140.   Writing.

EIRs shall be written in plain language and may use appropriate graphics so that decisionmakers and the public can rapidly understand the documents.

15141.   Page Limits.

The text of draft EIRs should normally be less than 150 pages and for proposals of unusual scope or complexity should normally be less than 300 pages.

15142.   Interdisciplinary Approach.

An EIR shall be prepared using an interdisciplinary approach which will ensure the integrated use of the natural and social sciences and the consideration of qualitative as well as quantitative factors. The interdisciplinary analysis shall be conducted by competent individuals, but no single discipline shall be designated or required to undertake this evaluation.

15143.   Emphasis.

The EIR shall focus on the significant effects on the environment. The significant effects should be discussed with emphasis in proportion to their severity and probability of occurrence. Effects dismissed in an Initial Study as clearly insignificant and unlikely to occur need not be discussed further in the EIR unless the Lead Agency subsequently receives information inconsistent with the finding in the Initial Study. A copy of the Initial Study may be attached to the EIR to provide the basis for limiting the impacts discussed.

15144.   Forecasting.

Drafting an EIR or preparing a negative declaration necessarily involves some degree of forecasting. While foreseeing the unforeseeable is not possible, an agency must use its best efforts to find out and disclose all that it reasonably can.

15145.   Speculation.

If, after thorough investigation, a lead agency finds that a particular impact is too speculative for evaluation, the agency should note its conclusion and terminate discussion of the impact.

15146.   Degree of Specificity.

The degree of specificity required in an EIR will correspond to the degree of specificity involved in the underlying activity which is described in the EIR.

(a) An EIR on a construction project will necessarily be more detailed in the specific effects of the project than will be an EIR on the adoption of a local general plan or comprehensive zoning ordinance because the effects of the construction can be predicted with greater accuracy.

(b) An EIR on a project such as the adoption or amendment of a comprehensive zoning ordinance or a local general plan should focus on the secondary effects that can be expected to follow from the adoption, or amendment, but the EIR need not be as detailed as an EIR on the specific construction projects that might follow.

15147.   Technical Detail.

The information contained in an EIR shall include summarized technical data, maps, plot plans, diagrams, and similar relevant information sufficient to permit full assessment of significant environmental impacts by reviewing agencies and members of the public. Placement of highly technical and specialized analysis and data in the body of an EIR should be avoided through inclusion of supporting information and analyses as appendices to the main body of the EIR. Appendices to the EIR may be prepared in volumes separate from the basic EIR document, but shall be readily available for public examination and shall be submitted to all clearinghouses which assist in public review.

15148.   Citation.

Preparation of EIRs is dependent upon information from many sources, including engineering project reports and many scientific documents relating to environmental features. These documents should be cited but not included in the EIR. The EIR shall cite all documents used in its preparation including, where possible, the page and section number of any technical reports which were used as the basis for any statements in the EIR.

15149.   Use of Registered Professionals in Preparing EIRs.

(a) A number of statutes provide that certain professional services can be provided to the public only by individuals who have been registered by a registration board established under California law. Such statutory restrictions apply to a number of professions including but not limited to engineering, land surveying, forestry, geology, and geophysics.

(b) In its intended usage, an EIR is not a technical document that can be prepared only by a registered professional. The EIR serves as a public disclosure document explaining the effects of the proposed project on the environment, alternatives to the project, and ways to minimize adverse effects and to increase beneficial effects. As a result of information in the EIR, the lead agency should establish requirements or conditions on project design, construction, or operation in order to protect or enhance the environment. State statutes may provide that only registered professionals can prepare technical studies which will be used in or which will control the detailed design, construction, or

245

operation of the proposed project and which will be prepared in support of an EIR.

15150.   Incorporation by Reference.

(a) An EIR or negative declaration may incorporate by reference all or portions of another document which is a matter of public record or is generally available to the public. Where all or part of another document is incorporated by reference, the incorporated language shall be considered to be set forth in full as part of the text of the EIR or negative declaration.

(b) Where part of another document is incorporated by reference, such other document shall be made available to the public for inspection at a public place or public building. The EIR or negative declaration shall state where the incorporated documents will be available for inspection. At a minimum, the incorporated documents shall be made available to the public in an office of the lead agency in the county where the project would be carried out or in one or more public buildings such as county offices or public libraries if the lead agency does not have an office in the county.

(c) Where an EIR or negative declaration uses incorporation by reference, the incorporated part of the referenced document shall be briefly summarized where possible or briefly described if the data or information cannot be summarized. The relationship between the incorporated part of the referenced document and the EIR shall be described.

(d) Where an agency incorporates information from an EIR that has previously been reviewed through the state review system, the state identification number of the incorporated document should be included in the summary or designation described in subdivision (c).

(e) Examples of materials that may be incorporated by reference include but are not limited to:

  (1) A description of the environmental setting from another EIR.

  (2) A description of the air pollution problems prepared by an air pollution control agency concerning a process involved in the project.

  (3) A description of the city or county general plan that applies to the location of the project.

  (4) A description of the effects of greenhouse gas emissions on the environment.

(f) Incorporation by reference is most appropriate for including long, descriptive, or technical materials that provide general background but do not contribute directly to the analysis of the problem at hand.

[Amended effective March 18, 2010]

15151.   Standards for Adequacy of an EIR.

An EIR should be prepared with a sufficient degree of analysis to provide decisionmakers with information which enables them to make a decision which intelligently takes account of environmental consequences. An evaluation of the environmental effects of a proposed project need not be exhaustive, but the sufficiency of an EIR is to be reviewed in the light of what is reasonably feasible.

Disagreement among experts does not make an EIR inadequate, but the EIR should summarize the main points of disagreement among the experts. The courts have looked not for perfection but for adequacy, completeness, and a good faith effort at full disclosure.

15152. Tiering.

(a) "Tiering" refers to using the analysis of general matters contained in a broader EIR (such as one prepared for a general plan or policy statement) with later EIRs and negative declarations on narrower projects; incorporating by reference the general discussions from the broader EIR; and concentrating the later EIR or negative declaration solely on the issues specific to the later project.

(b) Agencies are encouraged to tier the environmental analyses which they prepare for separate but related projects including general plans, zoning changes, and development projects. This approach can eliminate repetitive discussions of the same issues and focus the later EIR or negative declaration on the actual issues ripe for decision at each level of environment review. Tiering is appropriate when the sequence of analysis is from an EIR prepared for a general plan, policy, or program to an EIR or negative declaration for another plan, policy, or program of lesser scope, or to a site-specific EIR or negative declaration. Tiering does not excuse the lead agency from adequately analyzing reasonably foreseeable significant environmental effects of the project and does not justify deferring such analysis to a later tier EIR or negative declaration. However, the level of detail contained in a first tier EIR need not be greater than that of the program, plan, policy, or ordinance being analyzed.

(c) Where a lead agency is using the tiering process in connection with an EIR for a large-scale planning approval, such as a general plan or component thereof (e.g., an area plan or community plan), the development of detailed, site-specific information may not be feasible but can be deferred, in many instances, until such time as the lead agency prepares a future environmental document in connection with a project of a more limited geographical scale, as long as deferral does not prevent adequate identification of significant effects of the planning approval at hand.

(d) Where an EIR has been prepared and certified for a program, plan, policy, or ordinance consistent with the requirements of this section, any lead agency for a later project pursuant to or consistent with the program, plan, policy, or ordinance should limit the EIR or negative declaration on the later project to effects which:

(1) Were not examined as significant effects on the environment in the prior EIR; or

(2) Are susceptible to substantial reduction or avoidance by the choice of specific revisions in the project, by the imposition of conditions, or other means.

(e) Tiering under this section shall be limited to situations where the project is consistent with the general plan and zoning of the city or county in which the project is located, except that a project requiring a rezone to achieve or maintain conformity with a general plan may be subject to tiering.

(f) A later EIR shall be required when the initial study or other analysis finds that the later project may cause significant effects on the environment that were not adequately addressed in the prior EIR. A negative declaration shall be required when the provisions of Section 15070 are met.

    (1) Where a lead agency determines that a cumulative effect has been adequately addressed in the prior EIR, that effect is not treated as significant for purposes of the later EIR or negative declaration, and need not be discussed in detail.

    (2) When assessing whether there is a new significant cumulative effect, the lead agency shall consider whether the incremental effects of the project would be considerable when viewed in the context of past, present, and probable future projects. At this point, the question is not whether there is a significant cumulative impact, but whether the effects of the project are cumulatively considerable. For a discussion on how to assess whether project impacts are cumulatively considerable, see Section 15064(i).

    (3) Significant environmental effects have been "adequately addressed" if the lead agency determines that:

        (A) they have been mitigated or avoided as a result of the prior environmental impact report and findings adopted in connection with that prior environmental report; or

        (B) they have been examined at a sufficient level of detail in the prior environmental impact report to enable those effects to be mitigated or avoided by site specific revisions, the imposition of conditions, or by other means in connection with the approval of the later project.

(g) When tiering is used, the later EIRs or negative declarations shall refer to the prior EIR and state where a copy of the prior EIR may be examined. The later EIR or negative declaration should state that the lead agency is using the tiering concept and that it is being tiered with the earlier EIR.

(h) The rules in this section govern tiering generally. Several other methods to streamline the environmental review process exist, which are governed by the more specific rules of those provisions. Where multiple methods may apply, lead agencies have discretion regarding which to use. These other methods include, but are not limited to, the following:

    (1) General plan EIR (Section 15166).

    (2) Staged EIR (Section 15167).

    (3) Program EIR (Section 15168).

    (4) Master EIR (Section 15175).

    (5) Multiple-family residential development / residential and commercial or retail mixed-use development (Section 15179.5).

    (6) Redevelopment project (Section 15180).

    (7) Projects consistent with community plan, general plan, or zoning (Section 15183).

    (8) Infill projects (Section 15183.3).

[Amended effective December 28, 2018]

15153.   Use of an EIR From an Earlier Project.

(a) The Lead Agency may employ a single EIR to describe more than one project, if such projects are essentially the same in terms of environmental impact. Further, the Lead Agency may use an earlier EIR prepared in connection with an earlier project to apply to a later project, if the circumstances of the projects are essentially the same.

(b) When a Lead Agency proposes to use an EIR from an earlier project as the EIR for a separate, later project, the Lead Agency shall use the following procedures:

(1) The Lead Agency shall review the proposed project with an initial study, using incorporation by reference if necessary, to determine whether the EIR would adequately describe:

(A) The general environmental setting of the project,

(B) The significant environmental impacts of the project, and

(C) Alternatives and mitigation measures related to each significant effect.

(2) If the Lead Agency believes that the EIR would meet the requirements of subdivision (1), it shall provide public review as provided in Section 15087 stating that it plans to use the previously prepared EIR as the draft EIR for this project. The notice shall include as a minimum:

(A) An identification of the project with a brief description;

(B) A statement that the agency plans to use a certain EIR prepared for a previous project as the EIR for this project;

(C) A listing of places where copies of the EIR may be examined; and

(D) A statement that the key issues involving the EIR are whether the EIR should be used for this project and whether there are any additional, reasonable alternatives or mitigation measures that should be considered as ways of avoiding or reducing the significant effects of the project.

(3) The Lead Agency shall prepare responses to comments received during the review period.

(4) Before approving the project, the decisionmaker in the Lead Agency shall:

(A) Consider the information in the EIR including comments received during the review period and responses to those comments,

(B) Decide either on its own or on a staff recommendation whether the EIR is adequate for the project at hand, and

(C) Make or require certification to be made as described in Section 15090.

(D) Make findings as provided in Sections 15091 and 15093 as necessary.

(5) After making a decision on the project, the Lead Agency shall file a notice of determination.

(c) An EIR prepared for an earlier project may also be used as part of an initial study to document a finding that a later project will not have a significant effect. In this situation a negative declaration will be prepared.

(d) An EIR prepared for an earlier project shall not be used as the EIR for a later project if any of the conditions described in Section 15162 would require preparation of a subsequent or supplemental EIR.

[Amended effective November 1, 2005]

15154.   Projects Near Airports.

(a) When a lead agency prepares an EIR for a project within the boundaries of a comprehensive airport land use plan or, if a comprehensive airport land use plan has not been adopted for a project within two nautical miles of a public airport or public use airport, the agency shall utilize the Airport Land Use Planning Handbook published by Caltrans' Division of Aeronautics to assist in the preparation of the EIR relative to potential airport or related safety hazards and noise problems.

(b) A lead agency shall not adopt a negative declaration or mitigated negative declaration for a project described in subdivision (a) unless the lead agency considers whether the project will result in a safety hazard or noise problem for persons using the airport or for persons residing or working in the project area.

[Amended effective November 1, 2005]

15155.   Water Supply Analysis; City or County Consultation with Water Agencies.

(a) The following definitions are applicable to this section.

   (1) A "water-demand project" means:

      (A) A residential development of more than 500 dwelling units.

      (B) A shopping center or business establishment employing more than 1,000 persons or having more than 500,000 square feet of floor space.

      (C) A commercial office building employing more than 1,000 persons or having more than 250,000 square feet of floor space.

      (D) A hotel or motel, or both, having more than 500 rooms.

      (E) An industrial, manufacturing, or processing plant, or industrial park planned to house more than 1,000 persons, occupying more than 40 acres of land, or having more than 650,000 square feet of floor area.

      (F) A mixed-use project that includes one or more of the projects specified in subdivisions (a)(1)(A), (a)(1)(B), (a)(1)(C), (a)(1)(D), (a)(1)(E), and (a)(1)(G) of this section.

      (G) A project that would demand an amount of water equivalent to, or greater than, the amount of water required by a 500 dwelling unit project.

      (H) For public water systems with fewer than 5,000 service connections, a project that meets the following criteria:

         1. A proposed residential, business, commercial, hotel or motel, or industrial development that would account for an increase of 10 percent or more in the number of a public water system's existing service connections; or

2. A mixed-use project that would demand an amount of water equivalent to, or greater than, the amount of water required by residential development that would represent an increase of 10 percent or more in the number of the public water system's existing service connections.

(2) "Public water system" means a system for the provision of piped water to the public for human consumption that has 3000 or more service connections. A public water system includes all of the following:

(A) Any collection, treatment, storage, and distribution facility under control of the operator of the system which is used primarily in connection with the system.

(B) Any collection or pretreatment storage facility not under the control of the operator that is used primarily in connection with the system.

(C) Any person who treats water on behalf of one or more public water systems for the purpose of rendering it safe for human consumption.

(3) "Water acquisition plans" means any plans for acquiring additional water supplies prepared by the public water system or a city or county lead agency pursuant to subdivision (a) of section 10911 of the Water Code.

(4) "Water assessment" means the water supply assessment that must be prepared by the governing body of a public water system, or the city or county lead agency, pursuant to and in compliance with sections 10910 to 10915 of the Water Code, and that includes, without limitation, the elements of the assessment required to comply with subdivisions (d), (e), (f), and (g) of section 10910 of the Water Code.

(5) "City or county lead agency" means a city or county, acting as lead agency, for the purposes of certifying or approving an environmental impact report, a negative declaration, or a mitigated negative declaration for a water-demand project.

(b) Subject to section 15155, subdivision (d) below, at the time a city or county lead agency determines whether an environmental impact report, a negative declaration, or a mitigated negative declaration, or any supplement thereto, is required for the water-demand project, the city or county lead agency shall take the following steps:

(1) The city or county lead agency shall identify any water system that either: (A) is a public water system that may supply water to the water-demand project, or (B) that may become such a public water system as a result of supplying water to the water-demand project. The city or county lead agency shall request the governing body of each such public water system to determine whether the projected water demand associated with a water-demand project was included in the most recently adopted urban water management plan adopted pursuant to Part 2.6 (commencing with section 10610) of the Water Code, and to prepare a water assessment approved at a regular or special meeting of that governing body.

(2) If the city or county lead agency is not able to identify any public water system that may supply water for the water-demand project, the city or county lead agency shall prepare a water assessment after consulting with

any entity serving domestic water supplies whose service area includes the site of the water-demand project, the local agency formation commission, and the governing body of any public water system adjacent to the site of the water-demand project. The governing body of the city or county lead agency must approve the water assessment prepared pursuant to this section at a regular or special meeting.

(c) The city or county lead agency shall grant any reasonable request for an extension of time that is made by the governing body of a public water system preparing the water assessment, provided that the request for an extension of time is made within 90 days after the date on which the governing body of the public water system received the request to prepare a water assessment. If the governing body of the public water system fails to request and receive an extension of time, or fails to submit the water assessment notwithstanding the 30-day extension, the city or county lead agency may seek a writ of mandamus to compel the governing body of the public water system to comply with the requirements of Part 2.10 of Division 6 (commencing with section 10910) of the Water Code relating to the submission of the water assessment.

(d) If a water-demand project has been the subject of a water assessment, no additional water assessment shall be required for subsequent water-demand projects that were included in such larger water-demand project if all of the following criteria are met:

(1) The entity completing the water assessment had concluded that its water supplies are sufficient to meet the projected water demand associated with the larger water-demand project, in addition to the existing and planned future uses, including, but not limited to, agricultural and industrial uses; and

(2) None of the following changes has occurred since the completion of the water assessment for the larger water-demand project:

(A) Changes in the larger water-demand project that result in a substantial increase in water demand for the water-demand project.

(B) Changes in the circumstances or conditions substantially affecting the ability of the public water system or the water supplying city or county identified in the water assessment to provide a sufficient supply of water for the water demand project.

(C) Significant new information becomes available which was not known and could not have been known at the time when the entity had reached the conclusion in subdivision (d)(1).

(e) The city or county lead agency shall include the water assessment, and any water acquisition plan in the EIR, negative declaration, or mitigated negative declaration, or any supplement thereto, prepared for the water-demand project, and may include an evaluation of the water assessment and water acquisition plan information within such environmental document. The city or county lead agency shall determine, based on the entire record, whether projected water supplies will be sufficient to satisfy the demands of the project, in addition to existing and planned future uses. If a city or county lead agency determines that

252

water supplies will not be sufficient, the city or county lead agency shall include that determination in its findings for the water-demand project.

(f) The degree of certainty regarding the availability of water supplies will vary depending on the stage of project approval. A lead agency should have greater confidence in the availability of water supplies for a specific project than might be required for a conceptual plan (i.e. general plan, specific plan). An analysis of water supply in an environmental document may incorporate by reference information in a water supply assessment, urban water management plan, or other publicly available sources. The analysis shall include the following:

(1) Sufficient information regarding the project's proposed water demand and proposed water supplies to permit the lead agency to evaluate the pros and cons of supplying the amount of water that the project will need.

(2) An analysis of the reasonably foreseeable environmental impacts of supplying water throughout all phases of the project.

(3) An analysis of circumstances affecting the likelihood of the water's availability, as well as the degree of uncertainty involved. Relevant factors may include but are not limited to, drought, salt-water intrusion, regulatory or contractual curtailments, and other reasonably foreseeable demands on the water supply.

(4) If the lead agency cannot determine that a particular water supply will be available, it shall conduct an analysis of alternative sources, including at least in general terms the environmental consequences of using those alternative sources, or alternatives to the project that could be served with available water.

[Amended effective December 28, 2018]

Article 11. Types of EIRs

15160.   General.

This article describes a number of examples of variations in EIRs as the documents are tailored to different situations and intended uses. These variations are not exclusive. Lead agencies may use other variations consistent with the guidelines to meet the needs of other circumstances. All EIRs must meet the content requirements discussed in Article 9 beginning with Section 15120.

15161.   Project EIR.

The most common type of EIR examines the environmental impacts of a specific development project. This type of EIR should focus primarily on the changes in the environment that would result from the development project. The EIR shall examine all phases of the project including planning, construction, and operation.

15162.   Subsequent EIRs and Negative Declarations.

(a) When an EIR has been certified or negative declaration adopted for a project, no subsequent EIR shall be prepared for that project unless the lead agency determines, on the basis of substantial evidence in the light of the whole record, one or more of the following:

(1) Substantial changes are proposed in the project which will require major revisions of the previous EIR or negative declaration due to the involvement of new significant environmental effects or a substantial increase in the severity of previously identified significant effects;

(2) Substantial changes occur with respect to the circumstances under which the project is undertaken which will require major revisions of the previous EIR or negative declaration due to the involvement of new significant environmental effects or a substantial increase in the severity of previously identified significant effects; or

(3) New information of substantial importance, which was not known and could not have been known with the exercise of reasonable diligence at the time the previous EIR was certified as complete or the negative declaration was adopted, shows any of the following:

(A) The project will have one or more significant effects not discussed in the previous EIR or negative declaration;

(B) Significant effects previously examined will be substantially more severe than shown in the previous EIR;

(C) Mitigation measures or alternatives previously found not to be feasible would in fact be feasible and would substantially reduce one or more significant effects of the project, but the project proponents decline to adopt the mitigation measure or alternative; or

(D) Mitigation measures or alternatives which are considerably different from those analyzed in the previous EIR would substantially reduce one or more significant effects on the environment, but the project proponents decline to adopt the mitigation measure or alternative.

(b) If changes to a project or its circumstances occur or new information becomes available after adoption of a negative declaration, the lead agency shall prepare a subsequent EIR if required under subdivision (a). Otherwise the lead agency shall determine whether to prepare a subsequent negative declaration, and addendum, or no further documentation.

(c) Once a project has been approved, the lead agency's role in project approval is completed, unless further discretionary approval on that project is required. Information appearing after an approval does not require reopening of that approval. If after the project is approved, any of the conditions described in subdivision (a) occurs, a subsequent EIR or negative declaration shall only be prepared by the public agency which grants the next discretionary approval for the project, if any. In this situation no other responsible agency shall grant an approval for the project until the subsequent EIR has been certified or subsequent negative declaration adopted.

(d) A subsequent EIR or subsequent negative declaration shall be given the same notice and public review as required under Section 15087 or Section 15072. A subsequent EIR or negative declaration shall state where the previous document is available and can be reviewed.

[Amended effective November 1, 2005]

15163.   Supplement to an EIR.

(a) The lead or responsible agency may choose to prepare a supplement to an EIR rather than a subsequent EIR if:

(1) Any of the conditions described in Section 15162 would require the preparation of a subsequent EIR, and

(2) Only minor additions or changes would be necessary to make the previous EIR adequately apply to the project in the changed situation.

(b) The supplement to the EIR need contain only the information necessary to make the previous EIR adequate for the project as revised.

(c) A supplement to an EIR shall be given the same kind of notice and public review as is given to a draft EIR under Section 15087.

(d) A supplement to an EIR may be circulated by itself without recirculating the previous draft or final EIR.

(e) When the agency decides whether to approve the project, the decision-making body shall consider the previous EIR as revised by the supplemental EIR. A finding under Section 15091 shall be made for each significant effect shown in the previous EIR as revised.

15164.   Addendum to an EIR or Negative Declaration.

(a) The lead agency or a responsible agency shall prepare an addendum to a previously certified EIR if some changes or additions are necessary but none of the conditions described in Section 15162 calling for preparation of a subsequent EIR have occurred.

(b) An addendum to an adopted negative declaration may be prepared if only minor technical changes or additions are necessary or none of the conditions described in Section 15162 calling for the preparation of a subsequent EIR or negative declaration have occurred.

(c) An addendum need not be circulated for public review but can be included in or attached to the final EIR or adopted negative declaration.

(d) The decision-making body shall consider the addendum with the final EIR or adopted negative declaration prior to making a decision on the project.

(e) A brief explanation of the decision not to prepare a subsequent EIR pursuant to Section 15162 should be included in an addendum to an EIR, the lead agency's required findings on the project, or elsewhere in the record. The explanation must be supported by substantial evidence.

15165.   Multiple and Phased Projects.

Where individual projects are, or a phased project is, to be undertaken and where the total undertaking comprises a project with significant environmental effect, the lead agency shall prepare a single program EIR for the ultimate project as described in Section 15168. Where an individual project is a necessary precedent for action on a larger project, or commits the lead agency to a larger project, with significant environmental effect, an EIR must address itself to the scope of the larger project. Where one project is one of several similar projects of a public agency, but is not deemed a part of a larger undertaking or a larger project, the agency may prepare one EIR for all projects, or one for each project, but shall in either case comment upon the cumulative effect.

15166. **EIR as Part of a General Plan.**

(a) The requirements for preparing an EIR on a local general plan, element, or amendment thereof will be satisfied by using the general plan, or element document, as the EIR and no separate EIR will be required, if:

(1) The general plan addresses all the points required to be in an EIR by Article 9 of these guidelines and

(2) The document contains a special section or a cover sheet identifying where the general plan document addresses each of the points required.

(b) Where an EIR rather than a negative declaration has been prepared for a general plan, element, or amendment thereto, the EIR shall be forwarded to the State Clearinghouse for review. The requirement shall apply regardless of whether the EIR is prepared as a separate document or as a part of the general plan or element document.

15167. **Staged EIR.**

(a) Where a large capital project will require a number of discretionary approvals from government agencies and one of the approvals will occur more than two years before construction will begin, a staged EIR may be prepared covering the entire project in a general form. The staged EIR shall evaluate the proposal in light of current and contemplated plans and produce an informed estimate of the environmental consequences of the entire project. The aspect of the project before the public agency for approval shall be discussed with a greater degree of specificity.

(b) When a staged EIR has been prepared, a supplement to the EIR shall be prepared when a later approval is required for the project, and the information available at the time of the later approval would permit consideration of additional environmental impacts, mitigation measures, or reasonable alternatives to the project.

(c) Where a statute such as the Warren-Alquist Energy Resources Conservation and Development Act provides that a specific agency shall be the lead agency for a project and requires the lead agency to prepare an EIR, a responsible agency which must grant an approval for the project before the lead agency has completed the EIR may prepare and consider a staged EIR.

(d) An agency requested to prepare a staged EIR may decline to act as the lead agency if it determines, among other factors, that:

(1) Another agency would be the appropriate lead agency; and

(2) There is no compelling need to prepare a staged EIR and grant an approval for the project before the appropriate lead agency will take its action on the project.

15168. **Program EIR.**

(a) General. A program EIR is an EIR which may be prepared on a series of actions that can be characterized as one large project and are related either:

256

(1) Geographically,

(2) As logical parts in the chain of contemplated actions,

(3) In connection with issuance of rules, regulations, plans, or other general criteria to govern the conduct of a continuing program, or

(4) As individual activities carried out under the same authorizing statutory or regulatory authority and having generally similar environmental effects which can be mitigated in similar ways.

(b) Advantages. Use of a program EIR can provide the following advantages. The program EIR can:

(1) Provide an occasion for a more exhaustive consideration of effects and alternatives than would be practical in an EIR on an individual action,

(2) Ensure consideration of cumulative impacts that might be slighted in a case-by-case analysis,

(3) Avoid duplicative reconsideration of basic policy considerations,

(4) Allow the lead agency to consider broad policy alternatives and program wide mitigation measures at an early time when the agency has greater flexibility to deal with basic problems or cumulative impacts,

(5) Allow reduction in paperwork.

(c) Use With Later Activities. Later activities in the program must be examined in the light of the program EIR to determine whether an additional environmental document must be prepared.

(1) If a later activity would have effects that were not examined in the program EIR, a new initial study would need to be prepared leading to either an EIR or a negative declaration. That later analysis may tier from the program EIR as provided in Section 15152.

(2) If the agency finds that pursuant to Section 15162, no subsequent EIR would be required, the agency can approve the activity as being within the scope of the project covered by the program EIR, and no new environmental document would be required. Whether a later activity is within the scope of a program EIR is a factual question that the lead agency determines based on substantial evidence in the record. Factors that an agency may consider in making that determination include, but are not limited to, consistency of the later activity with the type of allowable land use, overall planned density and building intensity, geographic area analyzed for environmental impacts, and covered infrastructure as described in the program EIR.

(3) An agency shall incorporate feasible mitigation measures and alternatives developed in the program EIR into later activities in the program.

(4) Where the later activities involve site specific operations, the agency should use a written checklist or similar device to document the evaluation of the site and the activity to determine whether the environmental effects of the operation were within the scope of the program EIR.

(5) A program EIR will be most helpful in dealing with later activities if it provides a description of planned activities that would implement the program and deals with the effects of the program as specifically and

comprehensively as possible. With a good and detailed project description and analysis of the program, many later activities could be found to be within the scope of the project described in the program EIR, and no further environmental documents would be required.

(d) Use With Subsequent EIRS and Negative Declarations. A program EIR can be used to simplify the task of preparing environmental documents on later activities in the program. The program EIR can:

(1) Provide the basis in an initial study for determining whether the later activity may have any significant effects.

(2) Be incorporated by reference to deal with regional influences, secondary effects, cumulative impacts, broad alternatives, and other factors that apply to the program as a whole.

(3) Focus an EIR on a later activity to permit discussion solely of new effects which had not been considered before.

(e) Notice With Later Activities. When a law other than CEQA requires public notice when the agency later proposes to carry out or approve an activity within the program and to rely on the program EIR for CEQA compliance, the notice for the activity shall include a statement that:

(1) This activity is within the scope of the program approved earlier, and

(2) The program EIR adequately describes the activity for the purposes of CEQA.

[Amended effective December 28, 2018]

15169.   Master Environmental Assessment.

(a) General. A public agency may prepare a master environmental assessment, inventory, or data base for all, or a portion of, the territory subject to its control in order to provide information which may be used or referenced in EIRs or negative declarations. Neither the content, the format, nor the procedures to be used to develop a master environmental assessment are prescribed by these guidelines. The descriptions contained in this section are advisory. A master environmental assessment is suggested solely as an approach to identify and organize environmental information for a region or area of the state.

(b) Contents. A master environmental assessment may contain an inventory of the physical and biological characteristics of the area for which it is prepared and may contain such additional data and information as a public agency determines is useful or necessary to describe environmental characteristics of the area. It may include identification of existing levels of quality and supply of air and water, capacities and levels of use of existing services and facilities, and generalized incremental effects of different categories of development projects by type, scale, and location.

(c) Preparation.

(1) A master environmental assessment or inventory may be prepared in many possible ways. For example, a master environmental assessment may be prepared as a special, comprehensive study of the area involved, as part of the EIR on a general plan, or as a data base accumulated by indexing EIRs prepared for individual projects or programs in the area involved.

258

(2) The information contained in a master environmental assessment should be reviewed periodically and revised as needed so that it is accurate and current.

(3) When advantageous to do so, master environmental assessments may be prepared through a joint exercise of powers agreement with neighboring local agencies or with the assistance of the appropriate Council of Governments.

(d) Uses.

(1) A master environmental assessment can identify the environmental characteristics and constraints of an area. This information can be used to influence the design and location of individual projects.

(2) A master environmental assessment may provide information agencies can use in initial studies to decide whether certain environmental effects are likely to occur and whether certain effects will be significant.

(3) A master environmental assessment can provide a central source of current information for use in preparing individual EIRs and negative declarations.

(4) Relevant portions of a master environmental assessment can be referenced and summarized in EIRs and negative declarations.

(5) A master environmental assessment can assist in identifying long range, areawide, and cumulative impacts of individual projects proposed in the area covered by the assessment.

(6) A master environmental assessment can assist a city or county in formulating a general plan or any element of such a plan by identifying environmental characteristics and constraints that need to be addressed in the general plan.

(7) A master environmental assessment can serve as a reference document to assist public agencies which review other environmental documents dealing with activities in the area covered by the assessment. The public agency preparing the assessment should forward a completed copy to each agency which will review projects in the area.

15170.   Joint EIR-EIS.

A lead agency under CEQA may work with a federal agency to prepare a joint document which will meet the requirements of both CEQA and NEPA. Use of such a joint document is described in Article 14, beginning with Section 15220.

Article 11.5. Master Environmental Impact Report

15175.   Master EIR.

(a) The Master EIR procedure is an alternative to preparing a project EIR, staged EIR, or program EIR for certain projects which will form the basis for later decision making. It is intended to streamline the later environmental view of projects or approval included within the project, plan or program analyzed in the Master EIR. Accordingly, a Master EIR shall, to the greatest extent feasible, evaluate the cumulative impacts, growth inducing impacts, and irreversible significant effects on the environment of subsequent projects.

(b) A lead agency may prepare a Master EIR for any of the following classes of projects:

(1) A general plan, general plan update, general plan element, general plan amendment, or specific plan.

(2) Public or private projects that will be carried out or approved pursuant to, or in furtherance of, a redevelopment plan.

(3) A project that consists of smaller individual projects which will be carried out in phases.

(4) A rule or regulation which will be implemented by later projects.

(5) Projects that will be carried out or approved pursuant to a development agreement.

(6) A state highway project or mass transit project which will be subject to multiple stages of review or approval.

(7) A plan proposed by a local agency, including a joint powers authority, for the reuse of a federal military base or reservation that has been closed or is proposed for closure by the federal government.

(8) A regional transportation plan or congestion management plan.

(9) Regulations adopted by the California Department of Fish and Game for the regulation of hunting and fishing.

(c) A lead agency may develop and implement a fee program in accordance with applicable provisions of law to generate the revenue necessary to prepare a Master EIR.

15176.   Contents of a Master EIR.

A lead agency shall include in a Master EIR all of the following:

(a) A detailed discussion as required by Section 15126.

(b) A description of anticipated subsequent projects that are within the scope of the Master EIR, including information with regard to the kind, size, intensity, and location of the subsequent projects, including, but not limited to all of the following:

(1) The specific type of project anticipated to be undertaken such as a single family development, office-commercial development, sewer line installation or other activities.

(2) The maximum and minimum intensity of any anticipated subsequent project, such as the number of residences in a residential development, and with regard to a public works facility, its anticipated capacity and service area.

(3) The anticipated location for any subsequent development projects, and, consistent with the rule of reason set forth in Section 15126.6(f), alternative locations for any such projects.

(4) A capital outlay or capital improvement program, or other scheduling or implementing device that governs the submission and approval of subsequent projects, or an explanation as to why practical planning

considerations render it impractical to identify any such program or scheduling or other device at the time of preparing the Master EIR.

(c) A description of potential impacts of anticipated projects for which there is not sufficient information reasonably available to support a full assessment of potential impacts in the Master EIR. This description shall not be construed as a limitation on the impacts which may be considered in a focused EIR.

(d) Where a Master EIR is prepared in connection with a project identified in subdivision (b)(1) of section 15175, the anticipated subsequent projects included within a Master EIR may consist of later planning approvals, including parcel-specific approvals, consistent with the overall planning decision (e.g., general plan, or specific plan, or redevelopment plan) for which the Master EIR has been prepared. Such subsequent projects shall be adequately described for purposes of subdivision (b) or of this section (15176) if the Master EIR and any other documents embodying or relating to the overall planning decision identify the land use designations and the permissible densities and intensities of use for the affected parcel(s). The proponents of such subsequent projects shall not be precluded from relying on the Master EIR solely because that document did not specifically identify or list, by name, the subsequent project as ultimately proposed for approval.

15177.   Subsequent Projects Within the Scope of the MEIR.

(a) After a Master EIR has been prepared and certified, subsequent projects which the lead agency determines as being within the scope of the Master EIR will be subject to only limited environmental review.

(b) Except as provided in subdivision (2) of this subdivision, neither a new environmental document nor the preparation of findings pursuant to section 15091 shall be required of a subsequent project when all of the following requirements are met:

(1) The lead agency for the subsequent project is the lead agency or any responsible agency identified in the Master EIR.

(2) The lead agency for the subsequent project prepares an initial study on the proposal. The initial study shall analyze whether the subsequent project was described in the Master EIR and whether the subsequent project may cause any additional significant effect on the environment which was not previously examined in the Master EIR.

(3) The lead agency for the subsequent project determines, on the basis of written findings, that no additional significant environmental effect will result from the proposal, no new additional mitigation measures or alternatives may be required, and that the project is within the scope of the Master EIR. "Additional significant environmental effect" means any project-specific effect which was not addressed as a significant effect in the Master EIR.

(c) Whether a subsequent project is within the scope of the Master EIR is a question of fact to be determined by the lead agency based upon a review of the initial study to determine whether there are additional significant effects or new additional mitigation measures or alternatives required for the subsequent project that are not already discussed in the Master EIR.

(d) Prior to approval of the proposed subsequent project, the lead agency shall incorporate all feasible mitigation measures or feasible alternatives appropriate to the project as set forth in the Master EIR and provide notice in the manner required by Section 15087.

(e) When the lead agency approves a project pursuant to this section, the lead agency shall file a notice in the manner required by Section 15075.

[Amended effective November 1, 2005]

15178.   Subsequent Projects Identified in the MEIR.

(a) When a proposed subsequent project is identified in the Master EIR, but the lead agency cannot make a determination pursuant to section 15177 that the subsequent project is within the scope of the Master EIR, and the lead agency determines that the cumulative impacts, growth inducing impacts and irreversible significant effects analysis in the Master EIR is adequate for the subsequent project, the lead agency shall prepare a mitigated negative declaration or a focused EIR if, after preparing an initial study, the lead agency determines that the project may result in new or additional significant effects. Whether the cumulative impacts, growth inducing impacts and irreversible significant effects analyses are adequate is a question of fact to be determined by the lead agency based upon a review of the proposed subsequent project in light of the Master EIR.

(b) A lead agency shall prepare a mitigated negative declaration for any proposed subsequent project if both of the following occur:

(1) The initial study prepared pursuant to Section 15177 has identified potentially new or additional significant environmental effects that were not analyzed in the Master EIR; and

(2) Feasible mitigation measures or alternatives will be incorporated to revise the subsequent project before the negative declaration is released for public review pursuant to Section 15073 in order to avoid or mitigate the identified effects to a level of insignificance.

(c) A lead agency shall prepare a focused EIR if the subsequent project may have a significant effect on the environment and mitigated negative declaration pursuant to subdivision (b) of this section cannot be prepared.

(1) The focused EIR shall incorporate by reference the Master EIR and analyze only the subsequent project's additional significant environmental effects and any new or additional mitigation measures or alternatives that were not identified and analyzed by the Master EIR. "Additional significant environmental effects" are those project-specific effects on the environment which were not addressed as significant in the Master EIR.

(2) A focused EIR need not examine those effects which the lead agency, prior to public release of the focused EIR, finds, on the basis of the initial study, related documents, and commitments from the proponent of a subsequent project, have been mitigated in one of the following manners:

(A) Mitigated or avoided as a result of mitigation measures identified in the Master EIR which the lead agency will require as part of the approval of the subsequent project;

(B) Examined at a sufficient level of detail in the Master EIR to enable those significant effects to be mitigated or avoided by specific revisions to the project, the imposition of conditions of approval, or by other means in connection with approval of the subsequent project; or

(C) The mitigation or avoidance of which is the responsibility of and within the jurisdiction of another public agency and is, or can and should be, undertaken by that agency.

(3) The lead agency's findings pursuant to subdivision (2) shall be included in the focused EIR prior to public release pursuant to Section 15087.

(4) A focused EIR prepared pursuant to this section shall analyze any significant environmental effects when:

(A) Substantial new or additional information shows that the adverse environmental effect may be more significant that was described in the Master EIR; or

(B) Substantial new or additional information shows that mitigation measures or alternatives which were previously determined to be infeasible are feasible and will avoid or reduce the significant effects of the subsequent project to a level of insignificance.

(d) A lead agency shall file a notice of determination shall be filed pursuant to Section 15075 if a project has been approved for which a mitigated negative declaration has been prepared pursuant to this section and a notice of determination shall be filed pursuant to Section 15094 if a project has been approved for which a focused EIR has been prepared pursuant to this section.

(e) When a lead agency determines that the cumulative impacts, growth inducing impacts and irreversible significant effects analysis in the Master EIR is inadequate for the subsequent project, the subsequent project is no longer eligible for the limited environmental review available under the Master EIR process and shall be reviewed according to Article 7 (commencing with Section 15080) of these guidelines. The lead agency shall tier the project specific EIR upon the Master EIR to the extent feasible under Section 15152.

15179.   Limitations on the Use of the Master EIR.

(a) The certified Master EIR shall not be used for a subsequent project described in the Master EIR in accordance with this article if either;

(1) The Master EIR was certified more than five years prior to the filing of an application for a subsequent project except as set forth in subsection (b) below, or

(2) After the certification of the Master EIR, a project not described in the certified Master EIR as an anticipated subsequent project is approved and the approved project may affect the adequacy of the Master EIR for any subsequent project that was described in the Master EIR.

(b) A Master EIR that was certified more than five years prior to the filing of an application for a subsequent project described in the Master EIR may be used in accordance with this article to review such a subsequent project if the least agency reviews the adequacy of the Master EIR and takes either of the following steps:

(1) Finds that no substantial changes have occurred with respect to the circumstances under which the Master EIR was certified, or that there is no new available information which was not known and could not have been known at the time the Master EIR was certified; or

(2) Prepares an initial study and, pursuant to the findings of the initial study, does either (A) or (B) below:

(A) certifies a subsequent or supplemental EIR that updates or revises the Master EIR and which either

1.   is incorporated into the previously certified Master EIR, or

2.   references any deletions, additions or other modifications to the previously certified Master EIR;

(B) approves a mitigated negative declaration that addresses substantial changes that have occurred with respect to the circumstances under which the Master EIR was certified or the new information that was not known and could not have been known at the time the Master EIR was certified.

[Amended effective July 27, 2007]

15179.5.   Focused EIRs and Small Projects.

(a) When a project is a multiple family residential development of 100 units or less or is a residential and commercial or retail mixed-use commercial development of not more then 100.000 square feet, whether or not the project is identified in the Master EIR, a focused EIR shall be prepared pursuant to this section when the following conditions are met:

(1) The project is consistent with a general plan, specific plan, community plan, or zoning ordinance for which an EIR was prepared within five years of certification of the focused EIR; and

(2) The parcel on which the project is to be developed is either:

(A) Surrounded by immediately contiguous urban development;

(B) Previously developed with urban uses; or

(C) Within one-half mile of an existing rail transit station.

(b) A focused environmental impact report prepared pursuant to this section shall be limited to a discussion of potentially significant effects on the environment specific to the project, or which substantial new information shows will be more significant than described in the prior environmental impact report. No discussion shall be required of alternatives to the project, cumulative impacts of the project, or the growth inducing impacts of the project.

(c) This section does not apply where the lead agency can make a finding pursuant to Section 15177 that the subsequent project is within the scope of the Master EIR, where the lead agency can prepare a mitigated negative declaration or focused EIR pursuant to Section 15178, or where, pursuant to Section 15162 or Section 15163, the environmental impact report referenced in subdivision (a)(1) of this section must be updated through the preparation of a subsequent environmental impact report or a supplemental environmental impact report.

Article 12. Special Situations

15180. **Redevelopment Projects.**

(a) An EIR for a redevelopment plan may be a Master EIR, a program EIR, or a project EIR. An EIR for a redevelopment plan must specify whether it is a Master EIR, a program EIR, or a project EIR.

(b) If the EIR for a redevelopment plan is a project EIR, all public and private activities or undertakings pursuant to or in furtherance of the redevelopment plan shall constitute a single project, which shall be deemed approved at the time of adoption of the redevelopment plan by the legislative body. The EIR in connection with the redevelopment plan shall be submitted in accordance with Section 33352 of the Health and Safety Code.

If a project EIR has been certified for the redevelopment plan, no subsequent EIRs are required for individual components of the redevelopment plan unless a subsequent EIR or a supplement to an EIR would be required by Section 15162 or 15163.

(c) If the EIR for a redevelopment plan is a Master EIR subsequent projects which the lead agency determines as being within the scope of the Master EIR will be subject to the review required by Section 15177. If the EIR for a redevelopment plan is a program EIR, subsequent activities in the program will be subject to the review required by Section 15168.

[Amended effective July 27, 2007]

15182. **Projects Pursuant to a Specific Plan.**

(a) General. Certain residential, commercial and mixed-use projects that are consistent with a specific plan adopted pursuant to Article 8, Chapter 3 of the Government Code are exempt from CEQA, as described in subdivisions (b) and (c) of this section.

(b) Projects Proximate to Transit.

(1) Eligibility. A residential or mixed-use project, or a project with a floor area ratio of at least 0.75 on commercially-zoned property, including any required subdivision or zoning approvals, is exempt if the project satisfies the following criteria:

(A) It is located within a transit priority area as defined in Public Resources Code section 21099(a)(7);

(B) It is consistent with a specific plan for which an environmental impact report was certified; and

(C) It is consistent with the general use designation, density, building intensity, and applicable policies specified for the project area in either a sustainable communities strategy or an alternative planning strategy for which the State Air Resources Board has accepted the determination that the sustainable communities strategy or the alternative planning strategy would achieve the applicable greenhouse gas emissions reduction targets.

(2) Limitation. Additional environmental review shall not be required for a project described in this subdivision unless one of the events in section 15162 occurs with respect to that project.

(3) Statute of Limitations. A challenge to a project described in this subdivision is subject to the statute of limitations periods described in section 15112.

(c) Residential Projects Implementing Specific Plans.

(1) Eligibility. Where a public agency has prepared an EIR on a specific plan after January 1, 1980, a residential project undertaken pursuant to and in conformity to that specific plan is exempt from CEQA if the project meets the requirements of this section.

Residential projects covered by this section include but are not limited to land subdivisions, zoning changes, and residential planned unit developments.

(2) Limitation. If after the adoption of the specific plan, an event described in Section 15162 occurs, the exemption in this subdivision shall not apply until the city or county which adopted the specific plan completes a subsequent EIR or a supplement to an EIR on the specific plan. The exemption provided by this section shall again be available to residential projects after the lead agency has filed a Notice of Determination on the specific plan as reconsidered by the subsequent EIR or supplement to the EIR.

(3) Statute of Limitations. A court action challenging the approval of a project under this subdivision for failure to prepare a supplemental EIR shall be commenced within 30 days after the lead agency's decision to carry out or approve the project in accordance with the specific plan.

(d) Fees. The lead agency has authority to charge fees to applicants for projects which benefit from this section. The fees shall be calculated in the aggregate to defray but not to exceed the cost of developing and adopting the specific plan including the cost of preparing the EIR.

[Amended effective December 28, 2018]

15183. Projects Consistent with a Community Plan, General Plan, or Zoning.

(a) CEQA mandates that projects which are consistent with the development density established by existing zoning, community plan, or general plan policies for which an EIR was certified shall not require additional environmental review, except as might be necessary to examine whether there are project-specific significant effects which are peculiar to the project or its site. This streamlines the review of such projects and reduces the need to prepare repetitive environmental studies.

(b) In approving a project meeting the requirements of this section, a public agency shall limit its examination of environmental effects to those which the agency determines, in an initial study or other analysis:

(1) Are peculiar to the project or the parcel on which the project would be located.

266

(2) Were not analyzed as significant effects in a prior EIR on the zoning action, general plan or community plan with which the project is consistent.

(3) Are potentially significant off-site impacts and cumulative impacts which were not discussed in the prior EIR prepared for the general plan, community plan or zoning action, or

(4) Are previously identified significant effects which, as a result of substantial new information which was not known at the time the EIR was certified, are determined to have a more severe adverse impact than discussed in the prior EIR.

(c) If an impact is not peculiar to the parcel or to the project, has been addressed as a significant effect in the prior EIR, or can be substantially mitigated by the imposition of uniformly applied development policies or standards, as contemplated by subdivision (e) below, then an additional EIR need not be prepared for the project solely on the basis of that impact.

(d) This section shall apply only to projects which meet the following conditions:

(1) The project is consistent with:

(A) A community plan adopted as part of a general plan,

(B) A zoning action which zoned or designated the parcel on which the project would be located to accommodate a particular density of development, or

(C) A general plan of a local agency, and

(2) An EIR was certified by the lead agency for the zoning action, the community plan, or the general plan.

(e) This section shall limit the analysis of only those significant environmental effects for which:

(1) Each public agency with authority to mitigate any of the significant effects on the environment identified in the EIR on the planning or zoning action undertakes or requires others to undertake mitigation measures specified in the EIR which the lead agency found to be feasible, and

(2) The lead agency makes a finding at a public hearing as to whether the feasible mitigation measures will be undertaken.

(f) An effect of a project on the environment shall not be considered peculiar to the project or the parcel for the purposes of this section if uniformly applied development policies or standards have been previously adopted by the city or county with a finding that the development policies or standards will substantially mitigate that environmental effect when applied to future projects, unless substantial new information shows that the policies or standards will not substantially mitigate the environmental effect. The finding shall be based on substantial evidence which need not include an EIR. Such development policies or standards need not apply throughout the entire city or county, but can apply only within the zoning district in which the project is located, or within the area subject to the community plan on which the lead agency is relying. Moreover, such policies or standards need not be part of the general plan or any community plan, but can be found within another pertinent planning document such as a zoning ordinance. Where a city or county, in previously adopting uniformly applied development policies or standards for imposition on future projects, failed to make a finding as to whether such policies or standards would substantially mitigate the effects of future projects, the decisionmaking body of the city or county, prior to approving such a future project pursuant to this section, may hold a public hearing for the purpose of considering whether, as applied to the project, such standards or policies would substantially mitigate the effects of the project. Such a public hearing need only be held if the city or county decides to apply the standards or policies as permitted in this section.

(g) Examples of uniformly applied development policies or standards include, but are not limited to:

(1) Parking ordinances,

(2) Public access requirements,

(3) Grading ordinances.

(4) Hillside development ordinances.

(5) Flood plain ordinances.

(6) Habitat protection or conservation ordinances.

(7) View protection ordinances.

(8) Requirements for reducing greenhouse gas emissions, as set forth in adopted land use plans, policies, or regulations.

(h) An environmental effect shall not be considered peculiar to the project or parcel solely because no uniformly applied development policy or standard is applicable to it.

(i) Where the prior EIR relied upon by the lead agency was prepared for a general plan or community plan that meets the requirements of this section, any rezoning action consistent with the general plan or community plan shall be treated as a project subject to this section.

(1) "Community plan" is defined as a part of the general plan of a city or county which applies to a defined geographic portion of the total area included in the general plan, includes or references each of the mandatory elements specified in Section 65302 of the Government Code, and contains specific development policies and implementation measures which will apply those policies to each involved parcel.

(2) For purposes of this section, "consistent" means that the density of the proposed project is the same or less than the standard expressed for the involved parcel in the general plan, community plan or zoning action for which an EIR has been certified, and that the project complies with the density-related standards contained in that plan or zoning. Where the zoning ordinance refers to the general plan or community plan for its density standard, the project shall be consistent with the applicable plan.

(j) This section does not affect any requirement to analyze potentially significant offsite or cumulative impacts if those impacts were not adequately discussed in the prior EIR. If a significant offsite or cumulative impact was adequately discussed in the prior EIR, then this section may be used as a basis for excluding further analysis of that offsite or cumulative impact.

[Amended effective March 18, 2010]

15183.3.   Streamlining for Infill Projects.

(a) Purpose. The purpose of this section is to streamline the environmental review process for eligible infill projects by limiting the topics subject to review at the project level where the effects of infill development have been addressed in a planning level decision or by uniformly applicable development policies.

(b) Eligibility. To be eligible for the streamlining procedures prescribed in this section, an infill project must:

(1) Be located in an urban area on a site that either has been previously developed or that adjoins existing qualified urban uses on at least seventy-five percent of the site's perimeter. For the purpose of this subdivision "adjoin" means the infill project is immediately adjacent to qualified urban uses, or is only separated from such uses by an improved public right-of-way;

(2) Satisfy the performance standards provided in Appendix M; and

(3) Be consistent with the general use designation, density, building intensity, and applicable policies specified for the project area in either a sustainable communities strategy or an alternative planning strategy, except as provided in subdivisions (b)(3)(A) or (b)(3)(B) below.

(A) Only where an infill project is proposed within the boundaries of a metropolitan planning organization for which a sustainable communities strategy or an alternative planning strategy will be, but is not yet, in effect, a residential infill project must have a density of at least 20 units per acre, and a retail or commercial infill project must have a floor area ratio of at least 0.75.

(B) Where an infill project is proposed outside of the boundaries of a metropolitan planning organization, the infill project must meet the definition of a small walkable community project in subdivision (f)(5), below.

(c) Streamlined Review. CEQA does not apply to the effects of an eligible infill project under two circumstances. First, if an effect was addressed as a significant effect in a prior EIR for a planning level decision, then, with some exceptions, that effect need not be analyzed again for an individual infill project even when that effect was not reduced to a less than significant level in the prior EIR. Second, an effect need not be analyzed, even if it was not analyzed in a prior EIR or is more significant than previously analyzed, if the lead agency makes a finding that uniformly applicable development policies or standards, adopted by the lead agency or a city or county, apply to the infill project and would substantially mitigate that effect. Depending on the effects addressed in the prior EIR and the availability of uniformly applicable development policies or standards that apply to the eligible infill project, streamlining under this section will range from a complete exemption to an obligation to prepare a narrowed, project-specific environmental document. A prior EIR will be most helpful in dealing with later infill projects if it deals with the effects of infill development as specifically and comprehensively as possible. With a good and detailed analysis of such development, the effects of many infill projects could be found to have been addressed in the prior EIR, and no further environmental documents would be required.

(d) Procedure. Following preliminary review of an infill project pursuant to Section 15060, the lead agency must examine an eligible infill project in light of the prior EIR to determine whether the infill project will cause any effects that require additional review under CEQA. Determinations pursuant to this section are questions of fact to be resolved by the lead agency. Such determinations must be supported with enough relevant information and reasonable inferences from this information to support a conclusion, even though other conclusions might also be reached. (See Section 15384.)

(1) Evaluation of the Infill Project. A lead agency should prepare a written checklist or similar device to document the infill project's eligibility for streamlining and to assist in making the determinations required by this section. The sample written checklist provided in Appendix N may be used for this purpose. A written checklist prepared pursuant to this section should do all of the following:

(A) Document whether the infill project satisfies the applicable performance standards in Appendix M.

(B) Explain whether the effects of the infill project were analyzed in a prior EIR. The written checklist should cite the specific portions of the prior EIR, including page and section references, containing the analysis of the infill project's significant effects. The written checklist should also indicate whether the infill project incorporates all applicable mitigation measures from the prior EIR.

(C) Explain whether the infill project will cause new specific effects. For the purposes of this section, a new specific effect is an effect that was not addressed in the prior EIR and that is specific to the infill project or the infill project site. A new specific effect may result if, for example, the prior EIR stated that sufficient site-specific information was not available to analyze the significance of that effect. Substantial changes in circumstances following certification of a prior EIR may also result in a new specific effect.

(D) Explain whether substantial new information shows that the adverse environmental effects of the infill project are more significant than described in the prior EIR. For the purpose of this section, "more significant" means an effect will be substantially more severe than described in the prior EIR. More significant effects include those that result from changes in circumstances or changes in the development assumptions underlying the prior EIR's analysis. An effect is also more significant if substantial new information shows that: (1) mitigation measures that were previously rejected as infeasible are in fact feasible, and such measures are not included in the project; (2) feasible mitigation measures considerably different than those previously analyzed could substantially reduce a significant effect described in the prior EIR, but such measures are not included in the project; or (3) an applicable mitigation measure was adopted in connection with a

270

planning level decision, but the lead agency determines that it is not feasible for the infill project to implement that measure.

(E) If the infill project will cause new specific effects or more significant effects, the written checklist should indicate whether uniformly applicable development policies or standards will substantially mitigate those effects. For the purpose of this section, "substantially mitigate" means that the policy or standard will substantially lessen the effect, but not necessarily below the level of significance. The written checklist should specifically identify the uniformly applicable development policy or standard and explain how it will substantially mitigate the effects of the infill project. The explanation in the written checklist may be used to support the finding required in subdivision (d)(2)(D) below.

(2) Environmental Document. After examining the effects of the infill project in light of the analysis in any prior EIR and uniformly applicable development policies or standards, the lead agency shall determine what type of environmental document shall be prepared for the infill project.

(A) No Further Review. No additional environmental review is required if the infill project would not cause any new specific effects or more significant effects, or if uniformly applicable development policies or standards would substantially mitigate such effects. Where the lead agency determines that no additional environmental review of the effects of the infill project is required, the lead agency shall file a Notice of Determination as provided in Section 15094. Where the lead agency finds that uniformly applicable development policies substantially mitigate a significant effect of an infill project, the lead agency shall make the finding described in subdivision (d)(2)(D).

(B) Negative Declaration, Mitigated Negative Declaration or Sustainable Communities Environmental Assessment. If the infill project would result in new specific effects or more significant effects, and uniformly applicable development policies or standards would not substantially mitigate such effects, those effects shall be subject to CEQA. If a new specific effect is less than significant, the lead agency may prepare a negative declaration. If new specific effects or more significant effects can be mitigated to a less than significant level through project changes agreed to prior to circulation of the written checklist, the lead agency may prepare a mitigated negative declaration. In these circumstances, the lead agency shall follow the procedure set forth in Sections 15072 to 15075. Alternatively, if the infill project is a transit priority project, the lead agency may follow the procedures in Section 21155.2 of the Public Resources Code. In either instance, the written checklist should clearly state which effects are new or more significant, and are subject to CEQA, and which effects have been previously analyzed and are not subject to further environmental review. Where the lead agency finds that uniformly applicable development policies or standards substantially mitigate a significant effect of an infill project, the lead agency shall make the finding described in subdivision (d)(2)(D).

(C) Infill EIR. If the infill project would result in new specific effects or more significant effects, and uniformly applicable development policies or standards would not substantially mitigate such effects, those effects are subject to CEQA. With respect to those effects that are subject to CEQA, the lead agency shall prepare an infill EIR if the written checklist shows that the effects of the infill project would be potentially significant. In this circumstance, the lead agency shall prepare an infill EIR as provided in subdivision (e) and, except as otherwise provided in this section, shall follow the procedures in Article 7. Where the lead agency finds that uniformly applicable development policies or standards substantially mitigate a significant effect of an infill project, the lead agency shall make the finding described in subdivision (d)(2)(D).

(D) Findings. Any findings or statement of overriding considerations required by Sections 15091 or 15093 shall be limited to those effects analyzed in an infill EIR. Findings for such effects should incorporate by reference any such findings made in connection with a planning level decision. Where uniformly applicable development policies or standards substantially mitigate the significant effects of an infill project, the lead agency shall also make a written finding, supported with substantial evidence, providing a brief explanation of the rationale for the finding.

(e) Infill EIR Contents. An infill EIR shall analyze only those significant effects that uniformly applicable development policies or standards do not substantially mitigate, and that are either new specific effects or are more significant than a prior EIR analyzed. All other effects of the infill project should be described in the written checklist as provided in subdivision (d)(1), and that written checklist should be circulated for public review along with the infill EIR. The written checklist should clearly set forth those effects that are new specific effects, and are subject to CEQA, and those effects which have been previously analyzed and are not subject to further environmental review. The analysis of alternatives in an infill EIR need not address alternative locations, densities, or building intensities. An infill EIR need not analyze growth inducing impacts. Except as provided in this subdivision, an infill EIR shall contain all elements described in Article 9.

(f) Terminology. The following definitions apply to this section:

(1) "Infill project" includes the whole of an action consisting of residential, commercial, retail, transit station, school, or public office building uses, or any combination of such uses that meet the eligibility requirements set forth in subdivision (b). For retail and commercial projects, no more than one half of the project area may be used for parking. "Transit station" means a rail or light-rail station, ferry terminal, bus hub, bus transfer station, or bus stop, and includes all streetscape improvements constructed in the public right-of-way within one-quarter mile of such facility to improve multi-modal access to the facility, such as pedestrian and bicycle safety improvements and traffic-calming design changes that support pedestrian and bicycle access.

(2) "Planning level decision" means the enactment or amendment of a general plan or any general plan element, community plan, specific plan, or zoning code.

(3) "Prior EIR" means the environmental impact report certified for a planning level decision, as supplemented by any subsequent or supplemental environmental impact reports, negative declarations, or addenda to those documents.

(4) "Qualified urban use" is defined in Public Resources Code Section 21072.

(5) "Small walkable community project" means a project that is all of the following:

(A) In an incorporated city that is not within the boundary of metropolitan planning organization;

(B) Within an area of approximately one-quarter mile diameter of contiguous land that includes a residential area adjacent to a retail downtown area and that is designated by the city for infill development consisting of residential and commercial uses. A city may designate such an area within its general plan, zoning code, or by any legislative act creating such a designation, and may make such designation concurrently with project approval; and

(C) Either a residential project that has a density of at least eight units to the acre or a commercial project with a floor area ratio of at least 0.5, or both.

(6) The terms "sustainable communities strategy" and "alternative planning strategy" refer to a strategy for which the State Air Resources Board, pursuant to subparagraph (H) of paragraph (2) of subdivision (b) of Section 65080 of the Government Code, has accepted a metropolitan planning organization's determination that the sustainable communities strategy or the alternative planning strategy would, if implemented, achieve its greenhouse gas emission reduction targets.

(7) "Uniformly applicable development policies or standards" are policies or standards adopted or enacted by a city or county, or by a lead agency, that reduce one or more adverse environmental effects. Examples of uniformly applicable development policies or standards include, but are not limited to:

(A) Regulations governing construction activities, including noise regulations, dust control, provisions for discovery of archeological and paleontological resources, stormwater runoff treatment and containment, protection against the release of hazardous materials, recycling of construction and demolition waste, temporary street closure and traffic rerouting, and similar regulations.

(B) Requirements in locally adopted building, grading and stormwater codes.

(C) Design guidelines.

(D) Requirements for protecting residents from sources of air pollution including high volume roadways and stationary sources.

(E) Impact fee programs to provide public improvements, police, fire, parks and other open space, libraries and other public services and infrastructure, including transit, bicycle and pedestrian infrastructure and traffic calming devices.

(F) Traffic impact fees.

(G) Requirements for reducing greenhouse gas emissions, as set forth in adopted land use plans, policies, or regulations.

(H) Ordinances addressing protection of urban trees and historic resources.

(8) "Urban area" is defined in Public Resources Code Section 21094.5(e)(5).

[Added effective February 14, 2013]

15183.5.   Tiering and Streamlining the Analysis of Greenhouse Gas Emissions.

(a) Lead agencies may analyze and mitigate the significant effects of greenhouse gas emissions at a programmatic level, such as in a general plan, a long range development plan, or a separate plan to reduce greenhouse gas emissions. Later project-specific environmental documents may tier from and/or incorporate by reference that existing programmatic review. Project-specific environmental documents may rely on an EIR containing a programmatic analysis of greenhouse gas emissions as provided in section 15152 (tiering), 15167 (staged EIRs), 15168 (program EIRs), 15175-15179.5 (Master EIRs), 15182 (EIRs Prepared for Specific Plans), and 15183 (EIRs Prepared for General Plans, Community Plans, or Zoning).

(b) Plans for the Reduction of Greenhouse Gas Emissions. Public agencies may choose to analyze and mitigate significant greenhouse gas emissions in a plan for the reduction of greenhouse gas emissions or similar document. A plan to reduce greenhouse gas emissions may be used in a cumulative impacts analysis as set forth below. Pursuant to sections 15064(h)(3) and 15130(d), a lead agency may determine that a project's incremental contribution to a cumulative effect is not cumulatively considerable if the project complies with the requirements in a previously adopted plan or mitigation program under specified circumstances.

(1) Plan Elements. A plan for the reduction of greenhouse gas emissions should:

(A) Quantify greenhouse gas emissions, both existing and projected over a specified time period, resulting from activities within a defined geographic area;

(B) Establish a level, based on substantial evidence, below which the contribution to greenhouse gas emissions from activities covered by the plan would not be cumulatively considerable;

(C) Identify and analyze the greenhouse gas emissions resulting from specific actions or categories of actions anticipated within the geographic area;

(D) Specify measures or a group of measures, including performance standards, that substantial evidence demonstrates, if implemented on a

274

project-by-project basis, would collectively achieve the specified emissions level;

(E) Establish a mechanism to monitor the plan's progress toward achieving the level and to require amendment if the plan is not achieving specified levels;

(F) Be adopted in a public process following environmental review.

(2) Use with Later Activities. A plan for the reduction of greenhouse gas emissions, once adopted following certification of an EIR or adoption of an environmental document, may be used in the cumulative impacts analysis of later projects. An environmental document that relies on a greenhouse gas reduction plan for a cumulative impacts analysis must identify those requirements specified in the plan that apply to the project, and, if those requirements are not otherwise binding and enforceable, incorporate those requirements as mitigation measures applicable to the project. If there is substantial evidence that the effects of a particular project may be cumulatively considerable notwithstanding the project's compliance with the specified requirements in the plan for the reduction of greenhouse gas emissions, an EIR must be prepared for the project.

(c) Special Situations. As provided in Public Resources Code sections 21155.2 and 21159.28, environmental documents for certain residential and mixed use projects, and transit priority projects, as defined in section 21155, that are consistent with the general use designation, density, building intensity, and applicable policies specified for the project area in an applicable sustainable communities strategy or alternative planning strategy need not analyze global warming impacts resulting from cars and light duty trucks. A lead agency should consider whether such projects may result in greenhouse gas emissions resulting from other sources, however, consistent with these Guidelines.

[Added effective March 18, 2010]

15184.　　State Mandated Local Projects.

Whenever a state agency issues an order which requires a local agency to carry out a project subject to CEQA, the following rules apply:

(a) If an EIR is prepared for the project, the local agency shall limit the EIR to considering those factors and alternatives which will not conflict with the order.

(b) If a local agency undertakes a project to implement a rule or regulation imposed by a certified state environmental regulatory program listed in Section 15251, the project shall be exempt from CEQA with regard to the significant effects analyzed in the document prepared by the state agency as a substitute for an EIR. The local agency shall comply with CEQA with regard to any site-specific effect of the project which was not analyzed by the certified state agency as a significant effect on the environment. The local agency need not re-examine the general environmental effects of the state rule or regulation.

15185.　　Administrative Appeals.

(a) Where an agency allows administrative appeals upon the adequacy of an environmental document, an appeal shall be handled according to the procedures of that agency. Public notice shall be handled in accordance with individual agency requirements and Section 15202(e).

(b) The decisionmaking body to which an appeal has been made shall consider the environmental document and make findings under Sections 15091 and 15093 if appropriate.

15186.   School Facilities.

(a) CEQA establishes a special requirement for certain school projects, as well as certain projects near schools, to ensure that potential health impacts resulting from exposure to hazardous materials, wastes, and substances will be carefully examined and disclosed in a negative declaration or EIR, and that the lead agency will consult with other agencies in this regard.

(b) Before certifying an EIR or adopting a negative declaration for a project located within one-fourth mile of a school involves the construction or alteration of a facility that might reasonably be anticipated to emit hazardous air emissions, or that would handle an extremely hazardous substance or a mixture containing extremely hazardous substances in a quantity equal to or greater than the state threshold quantity specified in subdivision (j) of Section 25532 of the Health and Safety Code, that may impose a health or safety hazard to persons who would attend or would be employed at the school, the lead agency must do both of the following:

(1) Consult with the affected school district or districts regarding the potential impact of the project on the school; and

(2) Notify the affected school district or districts of the project, in writing, not less than 30 days prior to approval or certification of the negative declaration or EIR.

(c) When the project involves the purchase of a school site or the construction of a secondary or elementary school by a school district, the negative declaration or EIR prepared for the project shall not be adopted or certified unless:

(1) The negative declaration, mitigated declaration, or EIR contains sufficient information to determine whether the property is:

(A) The site of a current or former hazardous waste or solid waste disposal facility and, if so, whether wastes have been removed.

(B) A hazardous substance release site identified by the Department of Toxic Substances Control in a current list adopted pursuant to Section 25356 of the Health and Safety Code for removal or remedial action pursuant to Chapter 6.8 (commencing with Section 25300) of Division 20 of the Health and Safety Code.

(C) The site of one or more buried or above ground pipelines which carry hazardous substances, acutely hazardous materials, or hazardous wastes, as defined in Division 20 of the Health and Safety Code. This does not include a natural gas pipeline used only to supply the school or neighborhood.

(D) Within 500 feet of the edge of the closest traffic lane of a freeway or other busy traffic corridor.

(2) The lead agency has notified in writing and consulted with the county or city administering agency (as designated pursuant to Section 25502 of the Health and Safety Code) and with any air pollution control district or air quality management district having jurisdiction, to identify facilities within one-fourth mile of the proposed school site which might reasonably be anticipated to emit hazardous emissions or handle hazardous or acutely hazardous material, substances, or waste. The notice shall include a list of the school sites for which information is sought. Each agency or district receiving notice shall provide the requested information and provide a written response to the lead agency within 30 days of receiving the notification. If any such agency or district fails to respond within that time, the negative declaration or EIR shall be conclusively presumed to comply with this section as to the area of responsibility of that agency.

(3) The school district makes, on the basis of substantial evidence, one of the following written findings:

(A) Consultation identified none of the facilities specified in paragraph (2).

(B) The facilities specified in paragraph (2) exist, but one of the following conditions applies:

1. The health risks from the facilities do not and will not constitute an actual or potential endangerment of public health to persons who would attend or be employed at the proposed school.

2. Corrective measures required under an existing order by another agency having jurisdiction over the facilities will, before the school is occupied, mitigate all chronic or accidental hazardous air emissions to levels that do not constitute any actual or potential public health danger to persons who would attend or be employed at the proposed school. When the school district board makes such a finding, it shall also make a subsequent finding, prior to occupancy of the school, that the emissions have been so mitigated.

3. For a school site with boundary that is within 500 feet of the edge of the closest traffic lane of a freeway or other busy traffic corridor, the school district determines, through a health risk assessment pursuant to subdivision (b)(2) of Section 44360 of the Health and Safety Code, based on appropriate air dispersion modeling, and after considering any potential mitigation measures, that the air quality at the proposed site is such that neither short-term nor long-term exposure poses significant health risks to pupils.

(C) The facilities or other pollution sources specified in subsection (c)(2) exist, but conditions in subdivisions (c)(3)(B)(1), (2) or (3) cannot be met, and the school district is unable to locate an alternative site that is suitable due to a severe shortage of sites that meet the requirements in subdivision (a) of Section 17213 of the Education Code. If the school district makes this finding, the school board shall prepare an EIR and adopt a statement of overriding considerations.

This finding shall be in addition to any findings which may be required pursuant to Sections 15074, 15091 or 15093.

(d) When the lead agency has carried out the consultation required by paragraph (2) of subdivision (b), the negative declaration or EIR shall be conclusively presumed to comply with this section, notwithstanding any failure of the consultation to identify an existing facility.

(e) The following definitions shall apply for the purposes of this section:

(1) "Acutely hazardous material," is as defined in 22 C.C.R. SS66260.10.

(2) "Administering agency," is as defined in Section 25501 of the Health and Safety Code.

(3) "Extremely hazardous substance," is as defined in subdivision (g)(2)(B) of Section 25532 of the Health and Safety Code and listed in Section 2770.5, Table 3, of Title 19 of the California Code of Regulations.

(4) "Facilities" means any source with a potential to use, generate, emit or discharge hazardous air pollutants, including, but not limited to, pollutants that meet the definition of a hazardous substance, and whose process or operation is identified as an emission source pursuant to the most recent list of source categories published by the California Air Resources Board.

(5) "Freeway or other busy traffic corridors" means those roadways that, on an average day, have traffic in excess of 50,000 vehicles in a rural area, as defined in Section 50101 of the Health and Safety Code, and 100,000 vehicles in an urban area, as defined in Section 50104.7 of the Health and Safety Code.

(6) "Handle" means to use, generate, process, produce, package, treat, store, emit, discharge, or dispose of a hazardous material in any fashion.

(7) "Hazardous air emissions," is as defined in subdivisions (a) to (f), inclusive, of Section 44321 of the Health and Safety Code.

(8) "Hazardous substance," is as defined in Section 25316 of the Health and Safety Code.

(9) "Hazardous waste," is as defined in Section 25117 of the Health and Safety Code.

(10) "Hazardous waste disposal site," is as defined in Section 25114 of the Health and Safety Code.

[Amended effective July 27, 2007]

15187.   Environmental Review of New Rules and Regulations.

(a) At the time of the adoption of a rule or regulation requiring the installation of pollution control equipment, establishing a performance standard, or establishing a treatment requirement, the California Air Resources Board, Department of Toxic Substances Control, Integrated Waste Management Board, State Water Resources Control Board, all regional water quality control boards, and all air pollution control districts and air quality management districts, as defined in Section 39025 of the Health and Safety Code, must perform an environmental analysis of the reasonably foreseeable methods by which compliance with that rule or regulation will be achieved.

(b) If an EIR is prepared by the agency at the time of adoption of a rule or regulation, it satisfies the requirements of this section provided that the document contains the information specified in subdivision (c) below. Similarly, for those State agencies whose regulatory programs have been certified by the Resources Agency pursuant to Section 21080.5 of the Public Resources Code, an environmental document prepared pursuant to such programs satisfies the requirements of this section, provided that the document contains the information specified in subdivision (c) below.

(c) The environmental analysis shall include at least the following:

(1) An analysis of reasonably foreseeable environmental impacts of the methods of compliance;

(2) An analysis of reasonably foreseeable feasible mitigation measures relating to those impacts; and

(3) An analysis of reasonably foreseeable alternative means of compliance with the rule or regulation, which would avoid or eliminate the identified impacts.

(d) The environmental analysis shall take into account a reasonable range of environmental, economic, and technical factors, population and geographic areas, and specific sites. The agency may utilize numerical ranges and averages where specific data is not available, but is not required to, nor should it, engage in speculation or conjecture.

(e) Nothing in this section shall require the agency to conduct a project level analysis.

(f) Nothing in this section is intended, or may be used, to delay the adoption of any rule or regulation for which this section requires an environmental analysis.

15188.   Focused EIR for Pollution Control Equipment.

This section applies to projects consisting solely of the installation of pollution control equipment and other components necessary to the installation of that equipment which are undertaken for the purpose of complying with a rule or regulation which was the subject of an environmental analysis as described in Section 15187.

(a) The lead agency for the compliance project may prepare a focused EIR to analyze the effects of that project when the following occur:

(1) the agency which promulgated the rule or regulation certified an EIR on that rule or regulation, or reviewed it pursuant to an environmental analysis prepared under a certified regulatory program and, in either case, the review included an assessment of growth inducing impacts and cumulative impacts of, and alternatives to, the project;

(2) the focused EIR for the compliance project is certified within five years of the certified EIR or environmental analysis required by subdivision (a) (1); and

(3) the EIR prepared in connection with the adoption of the rule or regulation need not be updated through the preparation of a subsequent EIR or supplemental EIR pursuant to section 15162 or section 15163.

279

(b) The discussion of significant environmental effects in the focused EIR shall be limited to project-specific, potentially significant effects which were not discussed in the environmental analysis required under Section 15187. No discussion of growth-inducing or cumulative impacts is required. Discussion of alternatives shall be limited to alternative means of compliance, if any, with the rule or regulation.

15189.   Compliance with Performance Standard or Treatment Requirement Rule or Regulation.

This section applies to projects consisting solely of compliance with a performance standard or treatment requirement which was the subject of an environmental analysis as described in Section 15187.

(a) If preparing a negative declaration, mitigated negative declaration or EIR on the compliance project the lead agency for the compliance project shall, to the greatest extent feasible, use the environmental analysis prepared pursuant to Section 15187. The use of numerical averages or ranges in the environmental analysis prepared under Section 15187 does not relieve the lead agency on the compliance project from its obligation to identify and evaluate the environmental effects of the project.

(b) Where the lead agency determines that an EIR is required for the compliance project, the EIR need address only the project-specific issues or other issues that were not discussed in sufficient detail in the environmental analysis prepared under Section 15187. The mitigation measures imposed by the lead agency shall be limited to addressing the significant effects on the environment of the compliance project. The discussion of alternatives shall be limited to a discussion of alternative means of compliance, if any, with the rule or regulation.

15190.   Deadlines for Compliance with Sections 15188 and 15189.

(a) The lead agency for a compliance project under either Section 15188 or Section 15189 shall determine whether an EIR or negative declaration should be prepared within 30 days of its determination that the application for the project is complete.

(b) Where the EIR will be prepared under contract to the lead agency for the compliance project, the agency shall issue a request for proposal for preparation of the EIR not later than 30 days after the deadline for response to the notice of preparation has expired. The contract shall be awarded within 30 days of the response date on the request for proposals.

15190.5.   Department of Defense Notification Requirement.

(a) For purposes of this section, the following definitions are applicable.

(1) "Low-level flight path" means any flight path for any aircraft owned, maintained, or that is under the jurisdiction of the United States Department of Defense that flies lower than 1,500 feet above ground level, as indicated in the United States Department of Defense Flight Information Publication, "Area Planning Military Training Routes: North and South America (AP/1B)" published by the United States National Imagery and Mapping

Agency, or its successor, as of the date the military service gives written notification to a lead agency pursuant to subdivision (b).

(2) "Military impact zone" means any area, including airspace, that meets both of the following criteria:

(A) Is within two miles of a military installation, including, but not limited to, any base, military airport, camp, post, station, yard, center, homeport facility for a ship, or any other military activity center that is under the jurisdiction of the United States Department of Defense; and

(B) Covers greater than 500 acres of unincorporated land, or greater than 100 acres of city incorporated land.

(3) "Military service" means the United States Department of Defense or any branch of the United States Armed Forces.

(4) "Special use airspace" means the land area underlying the airspace that is designated for training, research, development, or evaluation for a military service, as that land area is established by the United States Department of Defense Flight Information Publication, "Area Planning: Special Use Airspace: North and South America (AP/1A)" published by the United States National Imagery and Mapping Agency, or its successor, as of the date the military service gives written notification to a lead agency pursuant to subdivision (b).

(b) A military service may give written notification to a lead agency of the specific boundaries of a low-level flight path, military impact zone, or special use airspace, and provide the lead agency, in writing, the military contact office and address for the military service. If the notice references the specific boundaries of a low-level flight path, such notification must include a copy of the applicable United Stated Department of Defense Flight Information Publication, " Area Planning Military Training Routes: North and South America (AP/1B)." If the notice references the specific boundaries of a special use airspace, such notification must include a copy of the applicable United States Department of Defense Flight Information Publication, "Area Planning: Special Use Airspace: North and South America (AP/1A)."

(c) If a military service provides the written notification specified in subdivision (b) of this section, a lead agency must include the specified military contact office in the list of organizations and individuals receiving a notice of intent to adopt a negative declaration or a mitigated negative declaration pursuant to Section 15072, in the list of organizations and individuals receiving a notice of preparation of an EIR pursuant to Section 15082, and in the list of organizations and individuals receiving a notice of availability of a draft EIR pursuant to Section 15087 for any project that meets all of the criteria specified below:

(1) The project to be carried out or approved by the lead agency is within the boundaries specified in subdivision (b).

(2) The project is one of the following:

(A) a project that includes a general plan amendment; or

(B) a project that is of statewide, regional, or areawide significance; or

(C) a project that relates to a public use airport and the area surrounding such airport which is required to be referred to the airport land use commission, or appropriately designated body, pursuant to Sections 21670-21679.5 of the Public Utilities Code.

(3) The project is not one of the actions described below. A lead agency does not need to send to the specified military contact office a notice of intent to adopt a negative declaration or a mitigated negative declaration, a notice of preparation of an EIR, or a notice of availability of a draft EIR for such actions.

(A) a response action taken pursuant to Chapter 6.8 (commencing with Section 25300) of Division 20 of the Health and Safety Code.

(B) a response action taken pursuant to Chapter 6.85 (commencing with Section 25396) of Division 20 of the Health and Safety Code.

(C) a project undertaken at a site in response to a corrective action order issued pursuant to Section 25187 of the Health and Safety Code.

The lead agency shall send the specified military contact office a notice of intent or a notice of availability sufficiently prior to adoption or certification of the environmental documents by the lead agency to allow the military service the review period provided under Section 15105.

(d) The effect or potential effect that a project may have on military activities does not itself constitute an adverse effect on the environment for the purposes of CEQA.

[Added effective July 27, 2007]

Article 12.5 Exemptions for Agricultural Housing, Affordable Housing, and Residential Infill Projects

15191   Definitions.

For purposes of this Article 12.5 only, the following words shall have the following meanings:

(a) "Agricultural employee" means a person engaged in agriculture, including: farming in all its branches, and, among other things, includes: (1) the cultivation and tillage of the soil, (2) dairying, (3) the production, cultivation, growing, and harvesting of any agricultural or horticultural commodities (including commodities defined as agricultural commodities in Section 1141j(g) of Title 12 of the United States Code), (4) the raising of livestock, bees, furbearing animals, or poultry, and (5) any practices (including any forestry or lumbering operations) performed by a farmer or on a farm as an incident to or in conjunction with such farming operations, including preparation for market and delivery to storage or to market or to carriers for transportation to market. This definition is subject to the following limitations:

This definition shall not be construed to include any person other than those employees excluded from the coverage of the National Labor Relations Act, as amended, as agricultural employees, pursuant to Section 2(3) of the Labor Management Relations Act (Section 152(3), Title 29, United States Code), and

Section 3(f) of the Fair Labor Standards Act (Section 203(f), Title 29, United States Code). This definition shall not apply, or be construed to apply, to any employee who performs work to be done at the site of the construction, alteration, painting, or repair of a building, structure, or other work (as these terms have been construed under Section 8 (e) of the Labor Management Relations Act, 29 U.S.C. Sec. 158(e)) or logging or timber-clearing operations in initial preparation of land for farming, or who does land leveling or only land surveying for any of the above. As used in this definition, "land leveling" shall include only major land moving operations changing the contour of the land, but shall not include annual or seasonal tillage or preparation of land for cultivation.

(b) "Census-defined place" means a specific unincorporated land area within boundaries determined by the United States Census Bureau in the most recent decennial census.

(c) "Community-level environmental review" means either of the following:

(1) An EIR certified on any of the following:

(A) A general plan.

(B) A revision or update to the general plan that includes at least the land use and circulation elements.

(C) An applicable community plan.

(D) An applicable specific plan.

(E) A housing element of the general plan, if the environmental impact report analyzed the environmental effects of the density of the proposed project.

(2) A negative declaration or mitigated negative declaration adopted as a subsequent environmental review document, following and based upon an EIR on a general plan, an applicable community plan, or an applicable specific plan, provided that the subsequent environmental review document is allowed by CEQA following a master EIR or a program EIR, or is required pursuant to Section 21166.

(d) "Developed open space" means land that meets all of the following criteria:

(1) land that is publicly owned, or financed in whole or in part by public funds,

(2) is generally open to, and available for use by, the public, and

(3) is predominantly lacking in structural development other than structures associated with open spaces, including, but not limited to, playgrounds, swimming pools, ball fields, enclosed child play areas, and picnic facilities.

Developed open space may include land that has been designated for acquisition by a public agency for developed open space but does not include lands acquired by public funds dedicated to the acquisition of land for housing purposes.

(e) "Infill site" means a site in an urbanized area that meets one of the following criteria:

(1) The site has been previously developed for qualified urban uses; or

(2) The site has not been developed for qualified urban uses but all immediately adjacent parcels are developed with existing qualified urban uses; or

(3) The site has not been developed for qualified urban uses, no parcel within the site has been created within the past 10 years, and the site is situated so that:

(A) at least 75 percent of the perimeter of the site is adjacent to parcels that are developed with existing qualified urban uses at the time the lead agency receives an application for an approval; and

(B) the remaining 25 percent of the perimeter of the site adjoins parcels that had been previously developed for qualified urban uses.

(f) "Low- and moderate-income households" means "persons and families of low or moderate income" as defined in Section 50093 of the Health and Safety Code to mean persons and families whose income does not exceed 120 percent of area median income, adjusted for family size by the Department of Housing and Community Development, in accordance with adjustment factors adopted and amended from time to time by the United States Department of Housing and Urban Development pursuant to Section 8 of the United States Housing Act of 1937.

(g) "Low-income households" means households of persons and families of very low and low income, which are defined in Sections 50093 and 50105 of the Health and Safety Code as follows:

(1) "Persons and families of low income" or "persons of low income" is defined in Section 50093 of the Health & Safety Code to mean persons or families who are eligible for financial assistance specifically provided by a governmental agency for the benefit of occupants of housing financed pursuant to this division.

(2) "Very low income households" is defined in Section 50105 of the Health & Safety Code to mean persons and families whose incomes do not exceed the qualifying limits for very low income families as established and amended from time to time pursuant to Section 8 of the United States Housing Act of 1937. "Very low income households" includes extremely low income households, as defined in Section 50106 of the Health & Safety Code.

(h) "Lower income households" is defined in Section 50079.5 of the Health and Safety Code to mean any of the following:

(1) "Lower income households," which means persons and families whose income does not exceed the qualifying limits for lower income families as established and amended from time to time pursuant to Section 8 of the United States Housing Act of 1937.

(2) "Very low income households," which means persons and families whose incomes do not exceed the qualifying limits for very low income families as established and amended from time to time pursuant to Section 8 of the United States Housing Act of 1937.

(3) "Extremely low income households," which means persons and families whose incomes do not exceed the qualifying limits for extremely low

income families as established and amended from time to time by the Secretary of Housing and Urban Development and defined in Section 5.603(b) of Title 24 of the Code of Federal Regulations.

(i) "Major transit stop" means a site containing an existing rail transit station, a ferry terminal served by either a bus or rail transit service, or the intersection of two or more major bus routes with a frequency of service interval of 15 minutes or less during the morning and afternoon peak commute periods.

(j) "Project-specific effect" means all the direct or indirect environmental effects of a project other than cumulative effects and growth-inducing effects.

(k) "Qualified urban use" means any residential, commercial, public institutional, transit or transportation passenger facility, or retail use, or any combination of those uses.

(l) "Residential" means a use consisting of either of the following:

(1) Residential units only.

(2) Residential units and primarily neighborhood-serving goods, services, or retail uses that do not exceed 15 percent of the total floor area of the project.

(m) "Urbanized area" means either of the following:

(1) An incorporated city that either by itself or in combination with two contiguous incorporated cities has a population of at least 100,000 persons; or

(2) An unincorporated area that meets the requirements set forth in subdivision (m)(2)(A) and subdivision (m)(2)(B) below.

(A) The unincorporated area must meet one of the following location or density requirements:

1. The unincorporated area must be: (i) completely surrounded by one or more incorporated cities, (ii) have a population of at least 100,000 persons either by itself or in combination with the surrounding incorporated city or cities, and (iii) have a population density that at least equals the population density of the surrounding city or cities; or

2. The unincorporated area must be located within an urban growth boundary and have an existing residential population of at least 5,000 persons per square mile. For purposes of this subparagraph, an "urban growth boundary" means a provision of a locally adopted general plan that allows urban uses on one side of the boundary and prohibits urban uses on the other side.

(B) The board of supervisors with jurisdiction over the unincorporated area must have taken the following steps:

1. The board has prepared a draft document by which the board would find that the general plan, zoning ordinance, and related policies and programs applicable to the unincorporated area are consistent with principles that: (i) encourage compact development in a manner that promotes efficient transportation systems, economic growth, affordable housing, energy efficiency,

285

and an appropriate balance of jobs and housing, and (ii) protects the environment, open space, and agricultural areas.

2. The board has submitted the draft document to OPR and allowed OPR thirty days to submit comments on the draft findings to the board.

3. No earlier than thirty days after submitting the draft document to OPR, the board has adopted a final finding in substantial conformity with the draft finding described in the draft document referenced in subdivision (m)(2)(B)(1) above.

[Added effective July 27, 2007]

15192. Threshold Requirements for Exemptions for Agricultural Housing, Affordable Housing, and Residential Infill Projects.

In order to qualify for an exemption set forth in sections 15193, 15194 or 15195, a housing project must meet all of the threshold criteria set forth below.

(a) The project must be consistent with:

(1) Any applicable general plan, specific plan, or local coastal program, including any mitigation measures required by such plan or program, as that plan or program existed on the date that the application for the project pursuant to Section 65943 of the Government Code was deemed complete; and

(2) Any applicable zoning ordinance, as that zoning ordinance existed on the date that the application for the project pursuant to Section 65943 of the Government Code was deemed complete, unless the zoning of project property is inconsistent with the general plan because the project property has not been rezoned to conform to the general plan.

(b) Community-level environmental review has been adopted or certified.

(c) The project and other projects approved prior to the approval of the project can be adequately served by existing utilities, and the project applicant has paid, or has committed to pay, all applicable in-lieu or development fees.

(d) The site of the project:

(1) Does not contain wetlands, as defined in Section 328.3 of Title 33 of the Code of Federal Regulations.

(2) Does not have any value as an ecological community upon which wild animals, birds, plants, fish, amphibians, and invertebrates depend for their conservation and protection.

(3) Does not hard any species protected by the federal Endangered Species Act of 1973 (16 U.S.C. Sec. 1531 et seq.) or by the Native Plant Protection Act (Chapter 10 (commencing with Section 1900) of Division 2 of the Fish and Game Code), the California Endangered Species Act (Chapter 1.5 (commencing with Section 2050) of Division 3 of the Fish and Game Code.

(4) Does not cause the destruction or removal of any species protected by a local ordinance in effect at the time the application for the project was deemed complete.

(e) The site of the project is not included on any list of facilities and sites compiled pursuant to Section 65962.5 of the Government Code.

(f) The site of the project is subject to a preliminary endangerment assessment prepared by a registered environmental assessor to determine the existence of any release of a hazardous substance on the site and to determine the potential for exposure of future occupants to significant health hazards from any nearby property or activity. In addition, the following steps have been taken in response to the results of this assessment:

(1) If a release of a hazardous substance is found to exist on the site, the release shall be removed, or any significant effects of the release shall be mitigated to a level of insignificance in compliance with state and federal requirements.

(2) If a potential for exposure to significant hazards from surrounding properties or activities is found to exist, the effects of the potential exposure shall be mitigated to a level of insignificance in compliance with state and federal requirements.

(g) The project does not have a significant effect on historical resources pursuant to Section 21084.1 of the Public Resources Code.

(h) The project site is not subject to wildland fire hazard, as determined by the Department of Forestry and Fire Protection, unless the applicable general plan or zoning ordinance contains provisions to mitigate the risk of a wildland fire hazard.

(i) The project site does not have an unusually high risk of fire or explosion from materials stored or used on nearby properties.

(j) The project site does not present a risk of a public health exposure at a level that would exceed the standards established by any state or federal agency.

(k) Either the project site is not within a delineated earthquake fault zone or a seismic hazard zone, as determined pursuant to Section 2622 and 2696 of the Public Resources Code respectively, or the applicable general plan or zoning ordinance contains provisions to mitigate the risk of an earthquake or seismic hazard.

(l) Either the project site does not present a landslide hazard, flood plain, flood way, or restriction zone, or the applicable general plan or zoning ordinance contains provisions to mitigate the risk of a landslide or flood.

(m) The project site is not located on developed open space.

(n) The project site is not located within the boundaries of a state conservancy.

(o) The project has not been divided into smaller projects to qualify for one or more of the exemptions set forth in section 15193 to 15195.

[Added effective July 27, 2007]

15193.   Agricultural Housing Exemption.

CEQA does not apply to any development project that meets the following criteria.

(a) The project meets the threshold criteria set forth in section 15192.

(b) The project site meets the following size criteria:

(1) The project site is located in an area with a population density of at least 1,000 persons per square mile and is two acres or less in area; or

(2) The project site is located in an area with a population density of less than 1,000 persons per square mile and is five acres or less in area.

(c) The project meets the following requirements regarding location and number of units.

(1) If the proposed development project is located on a project site within city limits or in a census-defined place, it must meet the following requirements:

(A) The proposed project location must be within one of the following:

1. Incorporated city limits; or

2. A census defined place with a minimum population density of at least 5,000 persons per square mile; or

3. A census-defined place with a minimum population density of at least 1,000 persons per square mile, unless a public agency that is carrying out or approving the project determines that there is a reasonable possibility that the project, if completed, would have a significant effect on the environment due to unusual circumstances or that the cumulative impacts of successive projects of the same type in the same area, over time, would be significant.

(B) The proposed development project must be located on a project site that is adjacent, on at least two sides, to land that has been developed.

(C) The proposed development project must meet either of the following requirements:

1. Consist of not more than 45 units, or

2. Consist of housing for a total of 45 or fewer agricultural employees if the housing consists of dormitories, barracks, or other group living facilities.

(2) If the proposed development project is located on a project site zoned for general agricultural use, it must meet either of the following requirements:

(A) Consist of not more than 20 units, or

(B) Consist of housing for a total of 20 or fewer agricultural employees if the housing consists of dormitories, barracks, or other group living facilities.

(d) The project meets the following requirements regarding provision of housing for agricultural employees:

(1) The project must consist of the construction, conversion, or use of residential housing for agricultural employees.

(2) If the project lacks public financial assistance, then:

(A) The project must be affordable to lower income households; and

(B) The developer of the development project must provide sufficient legal commitments to the appropriate local agency to ensure the continued availability and use of the housing units for lower income households for a period of at least 15 years.

(3) If public financial assistance exists for the project, then:

    (A) The project must be housing for very low, low-, or moderate-income households; and

    (B) The developer of the development project must provide sufficient legal commitments to the appropriate local agency to ensure the continued availability and use of the housing units for low- and moderate-income households for a period of at least 15 years.

[Added effective July 27, 2007]

15194.   Affordable Housing Exemption.

CEQA does not apply to any development project that meets the following criteria:

(a) The project meets the threshold criteria set forth in section 15192.

(b) The project meets the following size criteria: the project site is not more than five acres in area.

(c) The project meets both of the following requirements regarding location:

    (1) The project meets one of the following location requirements relating to population density:

        (A) The project site is located within an urbanized area or within a census-defined place with a population density of at least 5,000 persons per square mile.

        (B) If the project consists of 50 or fewer units, the project site is located within an incorporated city with a population density of at least 2,500 persons per square mile and a total population of at least 25,000 persons.

        (C) The project is located within either an incorporated city or a census defined place with a population density of at least 1,000 persons per square mile and there is no reasonable possibility that the project would have a significant effect on the environment or the residents of the project due to unusual circumstances or due to the related or cumulative impacts of reasonably foreseeable projects in the vicinity of the project.

    (2) The project meets one of the following site-specific location requirements:

        (A) The project site has been previously developed for qualified urban uses; or

        (B) The parcels immediately adjacent to the project site are developed with qualified urban uses.

        (C) The project site has not been developed for urban uses and all of the following conditions are met:

            1. No parcel within the site has been created within 10 years prior to the proposed development of the site.

            2. At least 75 percent of the perimeter of the site adjoins parcels that are developed with qualified urban uses.

3. The existing remaining 25 percent of the perimeter of the site adjoins parcels that have previously been developed for qualified urban uses.

(d) The project meets both of the following requirements regarding provision of affordable housing.

(1) The project consists of the construction, conversion, or use of residential housing consisting of 100 or fewer units that are affordable to low-income households.

(2) The developer of the project provides sufficient legal commitments to the appropriate local agency to ensure the continued availability and use of the housing units for lower income households for a period of at least 30 years, at monthly housing costs deemed to be "affordable rent" for lower income, very low income, and extremely low income households, as determined pursuant to Section 50053 of the Health and Safety Code.

[Added effective July 27, 2007]

15195.   Residential Infill Exemption.

(a) Except as set forth in subdivision (b), CEQA does not apply to any development project that meets the following criteria:

(1) The project meets the threshold criteria set forth in section 15192; provided that with respect to the requirement in section 15192(b) regarding community-level environmental review, such review must be certified or adopted within five years of the date that the lead agency deems the application for the project to be complete pursuant to Section 65943 of the Government Code.

(2) The project meets both of the following size criteria:

(A) The site of the project is not more than four acres in total area.

(B) The project does not include any single level building that exceeds 100,000 square feet.

(3) The project meets both of the following requirements regarding location:

(A) The project is a residential project on an infill site.

(B) The project is within one-half mile of a major transit stop.

(4) The project meets both of the following requirements regarding number of units:

(A) The project does not contain more than 100 residential units.

(B) The project promotes higher density infill housing. The lead agency may establish its own criteria for determining whether the project promotes higher density infill housing except in either of the following two circumstances:

1. A project with a density of at least 20 units per acre is conclusively presumed to promote higher density infill housing.

2. A project with a density of at least 10 units per acre and a density greater than the average density of the residential properties within 1,500 feet shall be presumed to promote higher density

infill housing unless the preponderance of the evidence demonstrates otherwise.

(5) The project meets the following requirements regarding availability of affordable housing: The project would result in housing units being made available to moderate, low or very low income families as set forth in either A or B below:

(A) The project meets one of the following criteria, and the project developer provides sufficient legal commitments to the appropriate local agency to ensure the continued availability and use of the housing units as set forth below at monthly housing costs determined pursuant to paragraph (3) of subdivision (h) of Section 65589.5 of the Government Code.

1. At least 10 percent of the housing is sold to families of moderate income, or

2. Not less than 10 percent of the housing is rented to families of low income, or

3. Not less than 5 percent of the housing is rented to families of very low income.

(B) If the project does not result in housing units being available as set forth in subdivision (A) above, then the project developer has paid or will pay in-lieu fees pursuant to a local ordinance in an amount sufficient to result in the development of an equivalent number of units that would otherwise be required pursuant to subparagraph (A).

(b) A project that otherwise meets the criteria set forth in subdivision (a) is not exempt from CEQA if any of the following occur:

(1) There is a reasonable possibility that the project will have a project-specific, significant effect on the environment due to unusual circumstances.

(2) Substantial changes with respect to the circumstances under which the project is being undertaken that are related to the project have occurred since community-level environmental review was certified or adopted.

(3) New information becomes available regarding the circumstances under which the project is being undertaken and that is related to the project that was not known, and could not have been known at the time that community-level environmental review was certified or adopted.

If a project is not exempt from CEQA due to subdivision (b), the analysis of the environmental effects of the project covered in the EIR or the negative declaration shall be limited to an analysis of the project-specific effect of the projects and any effects identified pursuant to subdivisions (b)(2) and (3).

[Added effective July 27, 2007]

15196.   Notice of Exemption for Agricultural Housing, Affordable Housing, and Residential Infill Projects.

(a) When a local agency determines that a project is not subject to CEQA under Section 15193, 15194, or 15195, and it approves or determines to carry out that project, the lead agency or person seeking project approval shall file the notice required by Section 21152.1 of the Public Resources Code, pursuant to Section 15062.

(b) Failure to file the notice required by this section does not affect the validity of a project.

(c) Nothing in this section affects the time limitations contained in Section 21167.

[Added effective July 27, 2007]

Article 13. Review and Evaluation of EIRs and Negative Declarations

15200.   Purposes of Review.

The purposes of review of EIRs and negative declarations include:

(a) Sharing expertise,

(b) Disclosing agency analyses,

(c) Checking for accuracy,

(d) Detecting omissions,

(e) Discovering public concerns, and

(f) Soliciting counter proposals.

15201.   Public Participation.

Public participation is an essential part of the CEQA process. Each public agency should include provisions in its CEQA procedures for wide public involvement, formal and informal, consistent with its existing activities and procedures, in order to receive and evaluate public reactions to environmental issues related to the agency's activities. Such procedures should include, whenever possible, making environmental information available in electronic format on the Internet, on a web site maintained or utilized by the public agency.

15202.   Public Hearings.

(a) CEQA does not require formal hearings at any stage of the environmental review process. Public comments may be restricted to written communications.

(b) If an agency provides a public hearing on its decision to carry out or approve a project, the agency should include environmental review as one of the subjects for the hearing.

(c) A public hearing on the environmental impact of a project should usually be held when the lead agency determines it would facilitate the purposes and goals of CEQA to do so. The hearing may be held in conjunction with and as a part of normal planning activities.

(d) A draft EIR or negative declaration should be used as a basis for discussion at a public hearing. The hearing may be held at a place where public hearings are regularly conducted by the lead agency or at another location expected to be convenient to the public.

(e) Notice of all public hearings shall be given in a timely manner. This notice may be given in the same form and time as notice for other regularly conducted public hearings of the public agency. To the extent that the public agency maintains an Internet web site, notice of all public hearings should be made available in electronic format on that site.

(f) A public agency may include, in its implementing procedures, procedures for the conducting of public hearings pursuant to this section. The procedures may adopt existing notice and hearing requirements of the public agency for regularly conducted legislative, planning, and other activities.

(g) There is no requirement for a public agency to conduct a public hearing in connection with its review of an EIR prepared by another public agency.

15203.   Adequate Time for Review and Comment.

The lead agency shall provide adequate time for other public agencies and members of the public to review and comment on a draft EIR or negative declaration that it has prepared.

(a) Public agencies may establish time periods for review in their implementing procedures and shall notify the public and reviewing agencies of the time for receipt of comments on EIRs. These time periods shall be consistent with applicable statutes, the State CEQA Guidelines, and applicable clearinghouse review periods.

(b) A review period for an EIR does not require a halt in other planning or evaluation activities related to a project. Planning should continue in conjunction with environmental evaluation.

15204.   Focus of Review.

(a) In reviewing draft EIRs, persons and public agencies should focus on the sufficiency of the document in identifying and analyzing the possible impacts on the environment and ways in which the significant effects of the project might be avoided or mitigated. Comments are most helpful when they suggest additional specific alternatives or mitigation measures that would provide better ways to avoid or mitigate the significant environmental effects. At the same time, reviewers should be aware that the adequacy of an EIR is determined in terms of what is reasonably feasible, in light of factors such as the magnitude of the project at issue, the severity of its likely environmental impacts, and the geographic scope of the project. CEQA does not require a lead agency to conduct every test or perform all research, study, and experimentation recommended or demanded by commentors. When responding to comments, lead agencies need only respond to significant environmental issues and do not need to provide all information requested by reviewers, as long as a good faith effort at full disclosure is made in the EIR.

(b) In reviewing negative declarations, persons and public agencies should focus on the proposed finding that the project will not have a significant effect on the environment. If persons and public agencies believe that the project may have a significant effect, they should:

(1) Identify the specific effect,

(2) Explain why they believe the effect would occur, and

(3) Explain why they believe the effect would be significant.

(c) Reviewers should explain the basis for their comments, and should submit data or references offering facts, reasonable assumptions based on facts, or expert opinion supported by facts in support of the comments. Pursuant to Section 15064, an effect shall not be considered significant in the absence of substantial evidence.

(d) Reviewing agencies or organizations should include with their comments the name of a contact person who would be available for later consultation if necessary. Each responsible agency and trustee agency shall focus its comments on environmental information germane to that agency's statutory responsibility.

(e) This section shall not be used to restrict the ability of reviewers to comment on the general adequacy of a document or of the lead agency to reject comments not focused as recommended by this section.

(f) Prior to the close of the public review period for an EIR or mitigated negative declaration, a responsible or trustee agency which has identified significant effects on the environment may submit to the lead agency proposed mitigation measures which would address those significant effects. Any such measures shall be limited to impacts affecting those resources which are subject to the statutory authority of that agency. If mitigation measures are submitted, the responsible or trustee agency shall either submit to the lead agency complete and detailed performance objectives for the mitigation measures, or shall refer the lead agency to appropriate, readily available guidelines or reference documents which meet the same purpose.

15205.   Review by State Agencies.

(a) Draft EIRs and negative declarations to be reviewed by state agencies shall be submitted to the State Clearinghouse, 1400 Tenth Street, Sacramento, California 95814. For U.S. Mail, submit to P.O. Box 3044, Sacramento, California 95812-3044. When submitting such documents to the State Clearinghouse, the public agency shall include, in addition to the printed copy, a copy of the document in electronic form on a diskette or by electronic mail transmission, if available.

(b) The following environmental documents shall be submitted to the State Clearinghouse for review by state agencies:

   (1) Draft EIRs and negative declarations prepared by a state agency where such agency is a lead agency.

   (2) Draft EIRs and negative declarations prepared by a public agency where a state agency is a responsible agency, trustee agency, or otherwise has jurisdiction by law with respect to the project.

   (3) Draft EIRs and negative declarations on projects identified in Section 15206 as being of statewide, regional, or areawide significance.

   (4) Draft EIRs, environmental assessments, and findings of no significant impact prepared pursuant to NEPA, the Federal Guidelines (Title 40 CFR, Part 1500, commencing with Section 1500.1).

(c) Public agencies may send environmental documents to the State Clearinghouse for review where a state agency has special expertise with regard to the environmental impacts involved. The areas of statutory authorities of state agencies are identified in Appendix B. Any such environmental documents submitted to the State Clearinghouse shall include, in addition to the printed copy, a copy of the document in electronic format, on a diskette or by electronic mail transmission, if available.

(d) When an EIR or negative declaration is submitted to the State Clearinghouse for review, the review period set by the lead agency shall be at least as long as the period provided in the state review system operated by the State Clearinghouse. In the state review system, the normal review period is 45 days for EIRs and 30 days for negative declarations. In exceptional circumstances, the State Clearinghouse may set shorter review periods when requested by the lead agency.

(e) A sufficient number of copies of an EIR, negative declaration, or mitigated negative declaration, shall be submitted to the State Clearinghouse for review and comment by state agencies. The notice of completion form required by the State Clearinghouse must be submitted together with the copies of the EIR and may be submitted together with the copies of the negative declaration or mitigated negative declaration. The notice of completion form required by the State Clearinghouse is included in Appendix C. If the lead agency uses the on-line process for submittal of the notice of completion form to the State Clearinghouse, the form generated from the Internet shall satisfy this requirement (refer to www.ceganet.ca.gov).

(f) While the lead agency is encouraged to contact the regional and district offices of state responsible agencies, the lead agency must, in all cases, submit documents to the State Clearinghouse for distribution in order to comply with the review requirements of this section.

[Amended effective September 7, 2004]

15206.   Projects of Statewide, Regional, or Areawide Significance.

(a) Projects meeting the criteria in this section shall be deemed to be of statewide, regional, or area wide significance.

(1) A draft EIR or negative declaration prepared by any public agency on a project described in this section shall be submitted to the State Clearinghouse and should be submitted also to the appropriate metropolitan area council of governments for review and comment. The notice of completion form required by the State Clearinghouse must be submitted together with the copies of the EIR and may be submitted together with the copies of the negative declaration. The notice of completion form required by the State Clearinghouse is included in Appendix C. If the lead agency uses the on-line process for submittal of the notice of completion form to the State Clearinghouse, the form generated from the Internet shall satisfy this requirement (refer to www.ceqanet.ca.gov).

(2) When such documents are submitted to the State Clearinghouse, the public agency shall include, in addition to the printed copy, a copy of the document in electronic format on a diskette or by electronic mail transmission, if available.

(b) The lead agency shall determine that a proposed project is of statewide, regional, or areawide significance if the project meets any of the following criteria:

(1) A proposed local general plan, element, or amendment thereof for which an EIR was prepared. If a negative declaration was prepared for the plan, element, or amendment, the document need not be submitted for review.

(2) A project has the potential for causing significant effects on the environment extending beyond the city or county in which the project would be located. Examples of the effects include generating significant amounts of traffic or interfering with the attainment or maintenance of state or national air quality standards. Projects subject to this subdivision include:

   (A) A proposed residential development of more than 500 dwelling units.

   (B) A proposed shopping center or business establishment employing more than 1,000 persons or encompassing more than 500,000 square feet of floor space.

   (C) A proposed commercial office building employing more than 1,000 persons or encompassing more than 250,000 square feet of floor space.

   (D) A proposed hotel/motel development of more than 500 rooms.

   (E) A proposed industrial, manufacturing, or processing plant, or industrial park planned to house more than 1,000 persons, occupying more than 40 acres of land, or encompassing more than 650,000 square feet of floor area.

(3) A project which would result in the cancellation of an open space contract made pursuant to the California Land Conservation Act of 1965 (Williamson Act) for any parcel of 100 or more acres.

(4) A project for which an EIR and not a negative declaration was prepared which would be located in and would substantially impact the following areas of critical environmental sensitivity:

   (A) The Lake Tahoe Basin.

   (B) The Santa Monica Mountains Zone as defined by Section 33105 of the Public Resources Code.

   (C) The California Coastal Zone as defined in, and mapped pursuant to, Section 30103 of the Public Resources Code.

   (D) An area within 1/4 mile of a wild and scenic river as defined by Section 5093.5 of the Public Resources Code.

   (E) The Sacramento-San Joaquin Delta, as defined in Water Code Section 12220.

   (F) The Suisun Marsh as defined in Public Resources Code Section 29101.

   (G) The jurisdiction of the San Francisco Bay Conservation and Development Commission as defined in Government Code Section 66610.

(5) A project which would substantially affect sensitive wildlife habitats including but not limited to riparian lands, wet lands, bays, estuaries,

296

marshes, and habitats for endangered, rare and threatened species as defined by Section 15380 of this Chapter.

(6) A project which would interfere with attainment of regional water quality standards as stated in the approved areawide waste treatment management plan.

(7) A project which would provide housing, jobs, or occupancy for 500 or more people within 10 miles of a nuclear power plant.

[Amended effective November 1, 2005]

15207. Failure to Comment.

If any public agency or person who is consulted with regard to an EIR or negative declaration fails to comment within a reasonable time as specified by the lead agency, it shall be assumed, absent a request for a specific extension of time, that such agency or person has no comment to make. Although the lead agency need not respond to late comments, the lead agency may choose to respond to them.

15208. Retention and Availability of Comments.

Comments received through the consultation process shall be retained for a reasonable period and available for public inspection at an address given in the final EIR. Comments which may be received on a draft EIR or negative declaration under preparation shall also be considered and kept on file.

15209. Comments on Initiative of Public Agencies.

Every public agency may comment on environmental documents dealing with projects which affect resources with which the agency has special expertise regardless of whether its comments were solicited or whether the effects fall within the legal jurisdiction of the agency.

Article 14. Projects Also Subject to the National Environmental Policy Act (NEPA)

15220. General.

This article applies to projects that are subject to both CEQA and NEPA. NEPA applies to projects which are carried out, financed, or approved in whole or in part by federal agencies. Accordingly, this article applies to projects which involve one or more state or local agencies and one or more federal agencies.

15221. NEPA Document Ready Before CEQA Document.

(a) When a project will require compliance with both CEQA and NEPA, state or local agencies should use the EIS or finding of no significant impact rather than preparing an EIR or negative declaration if the following two conditions occur:

(1) An EIS or finding of no significant impact will be prepared before an EIR or negative declaration would otherwise be completed for the project; and

(2) The EIS or finding of no significant impact complies with the provisions of these guidelines.

(b) Because NEPA does not require separate discussion of mitigation measures or growth inducing impacts, these points of analysis will need to be added, supplemented, or identified before the EIS can be used as an EIR.

15222.   Preparation of Joint Documents.

If a lead agency finds that an EIS or finding of no significant impact for a project would not be prepared by the federal agency by the time when the lead agency will need to consider an EIR or negative declaration, the lead agency should try to prepare a combined EIR-EIS or negative declaration-finding of no significant impact. To avoid the need for the federal agency to prepare a separate document for the same project, the lead agency must involve the federal agency in the preparation of the joint document. The lead agency may also enter into a Memorandum of Understanding with the federal agency to ensure that both federal and state requirements are met. This involvement is necessary because federal law generally prohibits a federal agency from using an EIR prepared by a state agency unless the federal agency was involved in the preparation of the document.

[Amended effective December 28, 2018]

15223.   Consultation with Federal Agencies.

When it plans to use an EIS or finding of no significant impact or to prepare such a document jointly with a federal agency, the lead agency shall consult as soon as possible with the federal agency.

15224.   Time Limits.

Where a project will be subject to both CEQA and the National Environmental Policy Act, the one year time limit and the 105 day time limit may be waived pursuant to Section 15110.

15225.   Circulation of Documents.

(a) Where the federal agency circulated the EIS or finding of no significant impact for public review as broadly as state or local law may require and gave notice meeting the standards in Section 15072(a) or 15087(a), the lead agency under CEQA may use the federal document in the place of an EIR or negative declaration without recirculating the federal document for public review. One review and comment period is enough. Prior to using the federal document in this situation, the lead agency shall give notice that it will use the federal document in the place of an EIR or negative declaration and that it believes that the federal document meets the requirements of CEQA. The notice shall be given in the same manner as a notice of the public availability of a draft EIR under Section 15087.

(b) If an EIS has been prepared and filed pursuant to NEPA on the closure and reuse of a military base and the Lead Agency decides that the EIS does not fully meet the requirements of CEQA or has not been circulated for public review as state and local law may require, the Lead Agency responsible for preparation of an EIR for a reuse plan for the same base may proceed in the following manner:

(1) Prepare and circulate a notice of preparation pursuant to Section 15082. The notice shall include a description of the reuse plan, a copy of the EIS, an address to which to send comments, and the deadline for submitting

298

comments. The notice shall state that the lead agency intends to utilize the EIS as a draft EIR and requests comments on whether the EIS provides adequate information to serve as a draft EIR and what specific additional information, if any, is necessary.

(2) Upon the close of the comment period, the lead agency may proceed with preparation and circulation for comment of the draft EIR for the reuse plan. To the greatest extent feasible, the lead agency shall avoid duplication and utilize the EIS or information in the EIS as all or part of the draft EIR. The EIR shall be completed in compliance with the provisions of CEQA.

15226.   Joint Activities.

State and local agencies should cooperate with federal agencies to the fullest extent possible to reduce duplication between the California Environmental Quality Act and the National Environmental Policy Act. Such cooperation should, to the fullest extent possible, include:

(a) Joint planning processes,

(b) Joint environmental research and studies,

(c) Joint public hearings,

(d) Joint environmental documents.

15227.   State Comments on a Federal Project.

When a state agency officially comments on a proposed federal project which may have a significant effect on the environment, the comments shall include or reference a discussion of the material specified in Section 15126. An EIS on the federal project may be referenced to meet the requirements of this section.

15228.   Where Federal Agency Will Not Cooperate.

Where a federal agency will not cooperate in the preparation of joint document and will require separate NEPA compliance for the project at a later time, the state or local agency should persist in efforts to cooperate with the federal agency. Because NEPA expressly allows federal agencies to use environmental documents prepared by an agency of statewide jurisdiction, a local agency should try to involve a state agency in helping prepare an EIR or negative declaration for the project. In this way there will be a greater chance that the federal agency may later use the CEQA document and not require the applicant to pay for preparation of a second document to meet NEPA requirements at a later time.

15229.   Baseline Analysis for Military Base Reuse Plan EIRs.

When preparing and certifying an EIR for a plan for the reuse of a military base, including when utilizing an Environmental Impact Statement pursuant to Section 21083.5 of the Public Resources Code, the determination of whether the reuse plan may have a significant effect on the environment may, at the discretion of the lead agency, be based upon the physical conditions which were present at the time that the federal decision for the closure or realignment of the base or reservation became final. These conditions shall be referred to as the "baseline physical conditions." Impacts which do not exceed the baseline physical conditions shall not be considered significant.

(a) Prior to circulating a draft EIR pursuant to the provisions of this Section, the lead agency shall do all of the following, in order:

(1) Prepare proposed baseline physical conditions, identify pertinent responsible and trustee agencies and consult with those agencies prior to the public hearing required by subdivision (a) (2) as to the application of their regulatory authority and permitting standards to the proposed baseline physical conditions, the proposed reuse plan, and specific, planned future nonmilitary land uses of the base or reservation. The affected agencies shall have not less than 30 days prior to the public hearing to review the proposed baseline physical conditions and the proposed reuse plan and to submit their comments to the lead agency.

(2) Hold a public hearing at which is discussed the federal EIS prepared for, or being prepared for, the closure or realignment of the military base or reservation. The discussion shall include the significant effects on the environment, if any, examined in the EIS, potential methods of mitigating those effects, including feasible alternatives, and the mitigative effects of federal, state, and local laws applicable to future nonmilitary activities. Prior to the close of the hearing, the lead agency shall specify whether it will adopt any of the baseline physical conditions for the reuse plan EIR and identify those conditions. The lead agency shall specify particular baseline physical conditions, if any, which it will examine in greater detail than they were examined in the EIS. Notice of the hearing shall be given pursuant to Section 15087. The hearing may be continued from time to time.

(3) Prior to the close of the hearing, the lead agency shall do all of the following:

(A) Specify the baseline physical conditions which it intends to adopt for the reuse plan EIR, and specify particular physical conditions, if any, which it will examine in greater detail than were examined in the EIS.

(B) State specifically how it intends to integrate its discussion of the baseline physical conditions in the EIR with the reuse planning process, taking into account the adopted environmental standards of the community, including but not limited to, the adopted general plan, specific plan or redevelopment plan, and including other applicable provisions of adopted congestion management plans, habitat conservation or natural communities conservation plans, air quality management plans, integrated waste management plans, and county hazardous waste management plans.

(C) State the specific economic or social reasons, including but not limited to, new job creation, opportunities for employment of skilled workers, availability of low and moderate-income housing, and economic continuity which support selection of the baseline physical conditions.

(b) An EIR prepared under this section should identify any adopted baseline physical conditions in the environmental setting section. The baseline physical conditions should be cited in discussions of effects. The no-project alternative analyzed in an EIR prepared under this section shall discuss the conditions on the base as they exist at the time of preparation, as well as what could be reasonably expected to occur in the foreseeable future if the reuse plan were not approved, based on current plans and consistent with available infrastructure and services.

(c) All public and private activities taken pursuant to or in furtherance of a reuse plan for which an EIR was prepared and certified pursuant to this section shall be deemed to be a single project. A subsequent or supplemental EIR shall be required only if the lead agency determines that any of the circumstances described in Section 15162 or 15163 exist.

(d) Limitations:

(1) Nothing in this section shall in any way limit the scope of review or determination of significance of the presence of hazardous or toxic wastes, substances, and materials, including but not limited to, contaminated soils and ground water. The regulation of hazardous or toxic wastes, substances, and materials shall not be constrained by this section.

(2) This section does not apply to hazardous waste regulation and remediation projects undertaken pursuant to Chapter 6.5 (commencing with Section 25100) or Chapter 6.8 (commencing with Section 25300) of Division 20 of the Health and Safety Code or pursuant to the Porter-Cologne Water Quality Control Act (Water Code Section 13000, et seq.)

(3) All subsequent development at the military base or reservation shall be subject to all applicable federal, state, or local laws, including but not limited to, those relating to air quality, water quality, traffic, threatened and endangered species, noise, and hazardous or toxic wastes, substances, or materials.

(e) "Reuse plan" means the initial plan for the reuse of military base adopted by a local government, including a redevelopment agency or joint powers authority, in the form of a general plan, general plan amendment, specific plan, redevelopment plan, or other planning document. For purposes of this section, a reuse plan also shall include a statement of development policies, a diagram or diagrams illustrating its provisions, including a designation of the proposed general distribution, location, and development intensity for housing, business, industry, open space, recreation, natural resources, public buildings and grounds, roads, and other transportation facilities, infrastructure, and other categories of proposed uses, whether public or private.

(f) This section may be applied to any reuse plan EIR for which a notice of preparation is issued within one year from the date that the federal record of decision was rendered for the military base or reservation closure or realignment and reuse, or prior to January 1, 1997, whichever is later, but only if the EIR is completed and certified within five years from the date that the federal record of decision was rendered.

[Amended effective November 1, 2005]

Article 15. Litigation

15230.   **Time Limits and Criteria.**

Litigation under CEQA must be handled under the time limits and criteria described in Sections 21167 et seq. of the Public Resources Code and Section 15112 of these guidelines in addition to provisions in this article.

15231.   **Adequacy of EIR or Negative Declaration for Use by Lead and Responsible Agencies.**

A final EIR prepared by a lead agency or a negative declaration adopted by a lead agency shall be conclusively presumed to comply with CEQA for purposes of use by responsible agencies which were consulted pursuant to Sections 15072 or 15082 unless one of the following conditions occurs:

(a) The EIR or negative declaration is finally adjudged in a legal proceeding not to comply with the requirements of CEQA, or

(b) A subsequent EIR is made necessary by Section 15162 of these guidelines.

15232.   **Request for Hearing.**

In a writ of mandate proceeding challenging approval of a project under CEQA, the petitioner shall, within 90 days of filing the petition, request a hearing or otherwise be subject to dismissal on the court's own motion or on the motion of any party to the suit.

15233.   **Conditional Permits.**

If a lawsuit is filed challenging an EIR or negative declaration for noncompliance with CEQA, responsible agencies shall act as if the EIR or negative declaration complies with CEQA and continue to process the application for the project according to the time limits for responsible agency action contained in Government Code Section 65952.

(a) If an injunction or a stay has been granted in the lawsuit prohibiting the project from being carried out, the responsible agency shall have authority only to disapprove the project or to grant a conditional approval of the project. A conditional approval shall constitute permission to proceed with a project only when the court action results in a final determination that the EIR or negative declaration does comply with the provisions of CEQA (Public Resources Code Section 21167.3a).

(b) If no injunction or stay is granted in the lawsuit, the responsible agency shall assume that the EIR or negative declaration fully meets the requirements of CEQA. The responsible agency shall approve or disapprove the project within the time limits described in Article 8, commencing with Section 15100, of these guidelines and described in Government Code Section 65952. An approval granted by a responsible agency in this situation provides only permission to proceed with the project at the applicant's risk prior to a final decision in the lawsuit (Public Resources Code Section 21167.3b).

15234.   Remand.

(a) Courts may fashion equitable remedies in CEQA litigation. If a court determines that a public agency has not complied with CEQA, and that noncompliance was a prejudicial abuse of discretion, the court shall issue a peremptory writ of mandate requiring the agency to do one or more of the following:

   (1) void the project approval, in whole or in part;

   (2) suspend any project activities that preclude consideration and implementation of mitigation measures and alternatives necessary to comply with CEQA; or

   (3) take specific action necessary to bring the agency's consideration of the project into compliance with CEQA.

(b) Following a determination described in subdivision (a), an agency or project proponent may only proceed with those portions of the challenged determinations, findings, or decisions for the project or those project activities that the court finds:

   (1) are severable;

   (2) will not prejudice the agency's compliance with CEQA as described in the court's peremptory writ of mandate; and

   (3) complied with CEQA.

(c) An agency may also proceed with a project, or individual project activities, during the remand period where the court has exercised its equitable discretion to permit project activities to proceed during that period.

(d) As to those portions of an environmental document that a court finds to comply with CEQA, additional environmental review shall only be required by the court consistent with principles of res judicata. In general, the agency need not expand the scope of analysis on remand beyond that specified by the court.

[Added effective December 28, 2018]

Article 16. EIR Monitor

15240.   EIR Monitor.

The Secretary for Resources may provide for publication of a bulletin entitled "California EIR Monitor" on a subscription basis to provide public notice of amendments to the guidelines, the completion of draft EIRs, and other matters as deemed appropriate. Inquiries and subscription request should be sent to the following address:

   Secretary for Resources
   Attention: California EIR Monitor
   1416 Ninth Street, Room 1311
   Sacramento, California 95814

Article 17. Exemption for Certified State Regulatory Programs

15250.   General.

Section 21080.5 of the Public Resources Code provides that a regulatory program of a state agency shall be certified by the Secretary for Resources as being exempt from the requirements for preparing EIRs, negative declaration, and initial studies if the Secretary finds that the program meets the criteria contained in that code section. A certified program remains subject to other provisions in CEQA such as the policy of avoiding significant adverse effects on the environment where feasible. This article provides information concerning certified programs.

15251.   List of Certified Programs.

The following programs of state regulatory agencies have been certified by the Secretary for Resources as meeting the requirements of Section 21080.5:

(a) The regulation of timber harvesting operations by the California Department of Forestry and the State Board of Forestry pursuant to Chapter 8, commencing with Section 4511 of Part 2 of Division 4 of the Public Resources Code.

(b) The regulatory program of the Fish and Game Commission pursuant to the Fish and Game Code.

(c) The regulatory program of the California Coastal Commission and the regional coastal commissions dealing with the consideration and granting of coastal development permits under the California Coastal Act of 1976, Division 20 (commencing with Section 30000) of the Public Resources Code.

(d) That portion of the regulatory program of the Air Resources Board which involves the adoption, approval, amendment, or repeal of standards, rules, regulations, or plans to be used in the regulatory program for the protection and enhancement of ambient air quality in California.

(e) The regulatory program of the State Board of Forestry in adopting, amending, or repealing standards, rules, regulations, or plans under the Z'berg-Nejedly Forest Practice Act, Chapter 8 (commencing with Section 4511) of Part 2 of Division 4 of the Public Resources Code.

(f) The program of the California Coastal Commission involving the preparation, approval, and certification of local coastal programs as provided in Sections 30500 through 30522 of the Public Resources Code.

(g) The Water Quality Control (Basin)/208 Planning Program of the State Water Resources Control Board and the Regional Water Quality Control Boards.

(h) The permit and planning programs of the San Francisco Bay Conservation and Development Commission under the McAteer-Petris Act, Title 7.2 (commencing with Section 66600) of the Government Code; and the planning program of the San Francisco Bay Conservation and Development Commission under the Suisun Marsh Preservation Act, Division 19 (commencing with Section 29000) of the Public Resources Code.

(i) The pesticide regulatory program administered by the Department of Pesticide Regulation and the county agricultural commissioners insofar as the program consists of:

(1) The registration, evaluation, and classification of pesticides.

(2) The adoption, amendment, or repeal of regulations and standards for the licensing and regulation of pesticide dealers and pest control operators and advisors.

(3) The adoption, amendment, or repeal of regulations for standards dealing with the monitoring of pesticides and of the human health and environmental effects of pesticides.

(4) The regulation of the use of pesticides in agricultural and urban areas of the state through the permit system administered by the county agricultural commissioners.

(j) The power plant site certification program of the State Energy Resources Conservation and Development Commission under Chapter 6 of the Warren-Alquist Act, commencing with Public Resources Code Section 25500.

(k) The regulatory program of the State Water Resources Control Board to establish instream beneficial use protection programs.

(l) That portion of the regulatory program of the South Coast Air Quality Management District which involves the adoption, amendment, and repeal of regulations pursuant to the provisions of the Health and Safety Code.

(m) The program of the Delta Protection Commission involving the preparation and adoption of a Resource Management Plan for the Sacramento-San Joaquin Delta (Pub. Resources Code §29760 ff.), and the Commission's review and action on general plan amendments proposed by local governments to make their plans consistent with the provisions of the Commission's Resource Management Plan (Pub. Resources Code §29763.5).

(n) The program of the Department of Fish and Game for the adoption of regulations under the Fish and Game Code.

(o) The program of the Department of Fish and Game implementing the incidental take permit application process under the California Endangered Species Act ("CESA"). Fish and Game Code sections 2080 and 2081, and specifically the regulation governing the Department of Fish and Game's role as a "lead agency" when issuing incidental take permits, found at California Code of Regulations, Title 14, section 783.5(d).

(p) The regulatory program of the Department of Fish and Game for review and approval of voluntary local programs for routine and ongoing agricultural activities, as authorized by the California Endangered Species Act, Fish and Game Code section 2086.

[Amended effective July 11, 2006]

15252.   Substitute Document.

(a) The document used as a substitute for an EIR or negative declaration in a certified program shall include at least the following items:

(1) A description of the proposed activity, and

(2) Either:

(A) Alternatives to the activity and mitigation measures to avoid or reduce any significant or potentially significant effects that the project might have on the environment, or

(B) A statement that the agency's review of the project showed that the project would not have any significant or potentially significant effects on the environment and therefore no alternatives or mitigation measures are proposed to avoid or reduce any significant effects on the environment. This statement shall be supported by a checklist or other documentation to show the possible effects that the agency examined in reaching this conclusion.

(b) The notice of the decision on the proposed activity shall be filed with the Secretary for Resources.

[Amended effective September 7, 2004]

15253.   Use of an EIR Substitute by a Responsible Agency.

(a) An environmental analysis document prepared for a project under a certified program listed in Section 15251 shall be used by another agency granting an approval for the same project where the conditions in subdivision (b) have been met. In this situation, the certified agency shall act as lead agency, and the other permitting agencies shall act as responsible agencies using the certified agency's document.

(b) The conditions under which a public agency shall act as a responsible agency when approving a project using an environmental analysis document prepared under a certified program in the place of an EIR or negative declaration are as follows:

(1) The certified agency is the first agency to grant a discretionary approval for the project.

(2) The certified agency consults with the responsible agencies, but the consultation need not include the exchange of written notices.

(3) The environmental analysis document identifies:

(A) The significant environmental effects within the jurisdiction or special expertise of the responsible agency.

(B) Alternatives or mitigation measures that could avoid or reduce the severity of the significant environmental effects.

(4) Where written notices were not exchanged in the consultation process, the responsible agency was afforded the opportunity to participate in the review of the property by the certified agency in a regular manner designed to inform the certified agency of the concerns of the responsible agency before release of the EIR substitute for public review.

(5) The certified agency established a consultation period between the certified agency and the responsible agency that was at least as long as the period allowed for public review of the EIR substitute document.

(6) The certified agency exercised the powers of a lead agency by considering all the significant environmental effects of the project and making a finding under Section 15091 for each significant effect.

(c) Certified agencies are not required to adjust their activities to meet the criteria in subdivision (b). Where a certified agency does not meet the criteria in subdivision (b):

(1) The substitute document prepared by the agency shall not be used by other permitting agencies in the place of an EIR or negative declaration, and

(2) Any other agencies granting approvals for the project shall comply with CEQA in the normal manner. A permitting agency shall act as a lead agency and prepare an EIR or a negative declaration. Other permitting agencies, if any, shall act as responsible agencies and use the EIR or negative declaration prepared by the lead agency.

[Amended effective November 1, 2005]

Article 18. Statutory Exemptions

15260. General.

This article describes the exemptions from CEQA granted by the legislature. The exemptions take several forms. Some exemptions are complete exemptions from CEQA. Other exemptions apply to only part of the requirements of CEQA, and still other exemptions apply only to the timing of CEQA compliance.

15261. Ongoing Project.

(a) If a project being carried out by a public agency was approved prior to November 23, 1970, the project shall be exempt from CEQA unless either of the following conditions exists:

(1) A substantial portion of public funds allocated for the project have not been spent, and it is still feasible to modify the project to mitigate potentially adverse environmental effects, or to choose feasible alternatives to the project, including the alternative of "no project" or halting the project; provided that a project subject to the National Environmental Policy Act (NEPA) shall be exempt from CEQA as an on-going project if, under regulations promulgated under NEPA, the project would be too far advanced as of January 1, 1970, to require preparation of an EIS.

(2) A public agency proposes to modify the project in such a way that the project might have a new significant effect on the environment.

(b) A private project shall be exempt from CEQA if the project received approval of a lease, license, certificate, permit, or other entitlement for use from a public agency prior to April 5, 1973, subject to the following provisions:

(1) CEQA does not prohibit a public agency from considering environmental factors in connection with the approval or disapproval of a project, or from imposing reasonable fees on the appropriate private person or entity for preparing an environmental report under authority other than CEQA. Local agencies may require environmental reports for projects covered by this paragraph pursuant to local ordinances during this interim period.

(2) Where a project was approved prior to December 5, 1972, and prior to the date the project was legally challenged for noncompliance with CEQA, the project shall be bound by special rules set forth in Section 21170 of CEQA.

(3) Where a private project has been granted a discretionary governmental approval for part of the project before April 5, 1973, and another or additional discretionary governmental approvals after April 5, 1973, the project shall be subject to CEQA only if the approval or approvals after April 5, 1973, involve a greater degree of responsibility or control over the project as a whole than did the approval or approvals prior to that date.

15262.   Feasibility and Planning Studies.

A project involving only feasibility or planning studies for possible future actions which the agency, board, or commission has not approved, adopted, or funded does not require the preparation of an EIR or negative declaration but does require consideration of environmental factors. This section does not apply to the adoption of a plan that will have a legally binding effect on later activities.

15263.   Discharge Requirements.

The State Water Resources Control Board and the regional boards are exempt from the requirement to prepare an EIR or a negative declaration prior to the adoption of waste discharge requirements, except requirements for new sources as defined in the Federal Water Pollution Control Act or in other acts which amend or supplement the Federal Water Pollution Control Act. The term "waste discharge requirements" as used in this section is the equivalent of the term "permits" as used in the Federal Water Pollution Control Act.

15264.   Timberland Preserves.

Local agencies are exempt from the requirement to prepare an EIR or negative declaration on the adoption of timberland preserve zones under Government Code Sections 51100 et seq. (Gov. Code, Sec 51119).

15265.   Adoption of Coastal Plans and Programs.

(a) CEQA does not apply to activities and approvals pursuant to the California Coastal Act (commencing with Section 30000 of the Public Resources Code) by:

(1) Any local government, as defined in Section 30109 of the Public Resources Code, necessary for the preparation and adoption of a local coastal program, or

(2) Any state university or college, as defined in Section 30119, as necessary for the preparation and adoption of a long-range land use development plan.

(b) CEQA shall apply to the certification of a local coastal program or long-range land use development plan by the California Coastal Commission.

(c) This section shifts the burden of CEQA compliance from the local agency or the state university or college to the California Coastal Commission. The Coastal Commission's program of certifying local coastal programs and long-range land use development plans has been certified under Section 21080.5, Public Resources Code. See Section 15192.

15266.   General Plan Time Extension.

CEQA shall not apply to the granting of an extension of time by the Office of Planning and Research to a city or county for the preparation and adoption of one or more elements of a city or county general plan.

15267.   Financial Assistance to Low or Moderate Income Housing.

CEQA does not apply to actions taken by the Department of Housing and Community Development to provide financial assistance for the development and construction of residential housing for persons and families of low or moderate income, as defined in Section 50093 of the Health and Safety Code. The residential project which is the subject of the application for financial assistance will be subject to CEQA when approvals are granted by another agency.

15268.   Ministerial Projects.

(a) Ministerial projects are exempt from the requirements of CEQA. The determination of what is "ministerial" can most appropriately be made by the particular public agency involved based upon its analysis of its own laws, and each public agency should make such determination either as a part of its implementing regulations or on a case-by-case basis.

(b) In the absence of any discretionary provision contained in the local ordinance or other law establishing the requirements for the permit, license, or other entitlement for use, the following actions shall be presumed to be ministerial:

(1) Issuance of building permits.

(2) Issuance of business licenses.

(3) Approval of final subdivision maps.

(4) Approval on individual utility service connections and disconnections.

(c) Each public agency should, in its implementing regulations or ordinances, provide an identification or itemization of its projects and actions which are deemed ministerial under the applicable laws and ordinances.

(d) Where a project involves an approval that contains elements of both a ministerial action and a discretionary action, the project will be deemed to be discretionary and will be subject to the requirements of CEQA.

15269.   Emergency Projects.

The following emergency projects are exempt from the requirements of CEQA.

(a) Projects to maintain, repair, restore, demolish, or replace property or facilities damaged or destroyed as a result of a disaster in a disaster stricken area in which a state of emergency has been proclaimed by the Governor pursuant to the California Emergency Services Act, commencing with Section 8550 of the Government Code. This includes projects that will remove, destroy, or significantly alter an historical resource when that resource represents an imminent threat to the public of bodily harm or of damage to adjacent property or when the project has received a determination by the State Office of Historic Preservation pursuant to Section 5028(b) of Public Resources Code.

(b) Emergency repairs to publicly or privately owned serviced facilities necessary to maintain service essential to the public health, safety or welfare. Emergency repairs include those that require a reasonable amount of planning to address an anticipated emergency.

(c) Specific actions necessary to prevent or mitigate an emergency. This does not include long-term projects undertaken for the purpose of preventing or mitigating a situation that has a low probability of occurrence in the short-term, but this exclusion does not apply (i) if the anticipated period of time to conduct an environmental review of such a long-term project would create a risk to public health, safety or welfare, or (ii) if activities (such as fire or catastrophic risk mitigation or modifications to improve facility integrity) are proposed for existing facilities in response to an emergency at a similar existing facility.

(d) Projects undertaken, carried out, or approved by a public agency to maintain, repair, or restore an existing highway damaged by fire, flood, storm, earthquake, land subsidence, gradual earth movement, or landslide, provided that the project is within the existing right of way of that highway and is initiated within one year of the damage occurring. This exemption does not apply to highways designated as official state scenic highways, nor any project undertaken, carried out, or approved by a public agency to expand or widen a highway damaged by fire, flood, storm, earthquake, land subsidence, gradual earth movement, or landslide.

(e) Seismic work on highways and bridges pursuant to Section 180.2 of the Streets and Highways Code, Section 180 et seq.

[Amended effective December 28, 2018]

15270.   Projects Which Are Disapproved.

(a) CEQA does not apply to projects which a public agency rejects or disapproves.

(b) This section is intended to allow an initial screening of projects on the merits for quick disapprovals prior to the initiation of the CEQA process where the agency can determine that the project cannot be approved.

(c) This section shall not relieve an applicant from paying the costs for an EIR or negative declaration prepared for his project prior to the lead agency's disapproval of the project after normal evaluation and processing.

15271.   Early Activities Related to Thermal Power Plants.

(a) CEQA does not apply to actions undertaken by a public agency relating to any thermal power plant site or facility, including the expenditure, obligation, or encumbrance of funds by a public agency for planning, engineering, or design purposes, or for the conditional sale or purchase of equipment, fuel, water (except groundwater), steam, or power for such a thermal power plant, if the thermal power plant site and related facility will be the subject of an EIR or negative declaration or other document or documents prepared pursuant to a regulatory program certified pursuant to Public Resources Code Section 21080.5, which will be prepared by:

(1) The State Energy Resources Conservation and Development Commission,

(2) The Public Utilities Commission, or

(3) The city or county in which the power plant and related facility would be located.

(b) The EIR, negative declaration, or other document prepared for the thermal power plant site or facility, shall include the environmental impact, if any, of the early activities described in this section.

(c) This section acts to delay the timing of CEQA compliance from the early activities of a utility to the time when a regulatory agency is requested to approve the thermal power plant and shifts the responsibility for preparing the document to the regulatory agency.

15272.   Olympic Games.

CEQA does not apply to activities or approvals necessary to the bidding for, hosting or staging of, and funding or carrying out of, Olympic Games under the authority of the International Olympic Committee, except for the construction of facilities necessary for such Olympic Games. If the facilities are required by the International Olympic Committee as a condition of being awarded the Olympic Games, the lead agency need not discuss the "no project" alternative in an EIR with respect to those facilities.

15273.   Rates, Tolls, Fares, and Charges.

(a) CEQA does not apply to the establishment, modification, structuring, restructuring, or approval of rates, tolls, fares, and other charges by public agencies which the public agency finds are for the purpose of:

(1) Meeting operating expenses, including employee wage rates and fringe benefits,

(2) Purchasing or leasing supplies, equipment, or materials,

(3) Meeting financial reserve needs and requirements,

(4) Obtaining funds for capital projects, necessary to maintain service within existing service areas, or

(5) Obtaining funds necessary to maintain such intra-city transfers as are authorized by city charter.

(b) Rate increases to fund capital projects for the expansion of a system remain subject to CEQA. The agency granting the rate increase shall act either as the lead agency if no other agency has prepared environmental documents for the capital project or as a responsible agency if another agency has already complied with CEQA as the lead agency.

(c) The public agency shall incorporate written findings in the record of any proceeding in which an exemption under this section is claimed setting forth with specificity the basis for the claim of exemption.

15274.   Family Day Care Homes.

(a) CEQA does not apply to establishment or operation of a large family day care home, which provides in-home care for up to fourteen children, as defined in Section 1596.78 of the Health and Safety Code.

(b) Under the Health and Safety Code, local agencies cannot require use permits for the establishment or operation of a small family day care home, which provides in-home care for up to eight children, and the establishment or operation of a small family day care home is a ministerial action which is not subject to CEQA.

15275. Specified Mass Transit Projects.

CEQA does not apply to the following mass transit projects:

(a) The institution or increase of passenger or commuter service on rail lines or high-occupancy vehicle lanes already in use, including the modernization of existing stations and parking facilities;

(b) Facility extensions not to exceed four miles in length which are required for transfer of passengers from or to exclusive public mass transit guideway or busway public transit services.

15276. Transportation Improvement and Congestion Management Programs.

(a) CEQA does not apply to the development or adoption of a regional transportation improvement program or the state transportation improvement program. Individual projects developed pursuant to these programs shall remain subject to CEQA.

(b) CEQA does not apply to preparation and adoption of a congestion management program by a county congestion management agency pursuant to Government Code Section 65089, et seq.

15277. Projects Located Outside California.

CEQA does not apply to any project or portion thereof located outside of California which will be subject to environmental impact review pursuant to the National Environmental Policy Act of 1969 or pursuant to a law of that state requiring preparation of a document containing essentially the same points of analysis as in an environmental impact statement prepared under the National Environmental Policy Act of 1969. Any emissions or discharges that would have a significant effect on the environment in the State of California are subject to CEQA where a California public agency has authority over the emissions or discharges.

15278. Application of Coatings.

(a) CEQA does not apply to a discretionary decision by an air quality management district for a project consisting of the application of coatings within an existing facility at an automotive manufacturing plant if the district finds all of the following:

(1) The project will not cause a net increase in any emissions of any pollutant for which a national or state ambient air quality standard has been established after the internal emission accounting for previous emission reductions achieved at the facility and recognized by the district.

(2) The project will not cause a net increase in adverse impacts of toxic air contaminants as determined by a health risk assessment. The term "net increase in adverse impacts of toxic air contaminants as determined by a health risk assessment" shall be determined in accordance with the rules and regulations of the district.

312

(3) The project will not cause any other adverse effect on the environment.

(b) The district shall provide a 10-day notice, at the time of the issuance of the permit, of any such exemption. Notice shall be published in two newspapers of general circulation in the area of the project and shall be mailed to any person who makes a written request for such a notice. The notice shall state that the complete file on the project and the basis for the district's findings of exemption are available for inspection and copying at the office of the district.

(c) Any person may appeal the issuance of a permit based on an exemption under subdivision (a) to the hearing board as provided in Section 42302.1 of the Health and Safety Code. The permit shall be revoked by the hearing board if there is substantial evidence in light of the whole record before the board that the project may not satisfy one or more of the criteria established pursuant to subdivision (a). If there is no such substantial evidence, the exemption shall be upheld. Any appeal under this subdivision shall be scheduled for hearing on the calendar of the hearing board within 10 working days of the appeal being filed. The hearing board shall give the appeal priority on its calendar and shall render a decision on the appeal within 21 working days of the appeal being filed. The hearing board may delegate the authority to hear and decide such an appeal to a subcommittee of its body.

15281.   Air Quality Permits.

CEQA does not apply to the issuance, modification, amendment, or renewal of any permit by an air pollution control district or air quality management district pursuant to Title V, as defined in Section 39053.3 of the Health and Safety Code, or pursuant to an air district Title V program established under Sections 42301.10, 42301.11, and 42301.12 of the Health and Safety Code, unless the issuance, modification, amendment, or renewal authorizes a physical or operational change to a source or facility.

15282.   Other Statutory Exemptions.

The following is a list of existing statutory exemptions. Each subdivision summarizes statutory exemptions found in the California Code. Lead agencies are not to rely on the language contained in the summaries below but must rely on the actual statutory language that creates the exemption. This list is intended to assist lead agencies in finding them, but not as a substitute for them. This section is merely a reference tool.

(a) The notification of discovery of Native American burial sites as set forth in Section 5097.98(c) of the Public Resources Code.

(b) Specified prison facilities as set forth in Sections 21080.01, 21080.02 and 21080.03 of the Public Resources Code.

(c) The lease or purchase of the rail right-of-way used for the San Francisco Peninsula commute service between San Francisco and San Jose as set forth in Section 21080.05 of the Public Resources Code.

(d) Any activity or approval necessary for or incidental to project funding or authorization for the expenditure of funds for the project, by the Rural Economic Development Infrastructure Panel as set forth in Section 21080.08 of the Public Resources Code.

(e) The conversion of an existing rental mobile home park to a resident initiated subdivision, cooperative, or condominium for mobile homes as set forth in Section 21080.8 of the Public Resources Code.

(f) Settlements of title and boundary problems by the State Lands Commission and to exchanges or leases in connection with those settlements as set forth in Section 21080.11 of the Public Resources Code.

(g) Any railroad grade separation project which eliminates an existing grade crossing or which reconstructs an existing grade separation as set forth in Section 21080.13 of the Public Resources Code.

(h) The adoption of an ordinance regarding second units in a single-family or multifamily residential zone by a city or county to implement the provisions of Sections 65852.1 and 65852.2 of the Government Code as set forth in Section 21080.17 of the Public Resources Code.

(i) The closing of any public school or the transfer of students from that public school to another school in which kindergarten or any grades 1 through 12 is maintained as set forth in 21080.18 of the Public Resources Code.

(j) A project for restriping streets or highways to relieve traffic congestion as set forth in Section 21080.19 of the Public Resources Code.

(k) The installation of new pipeline or maintenance, repair, restoration, removal, or demolition of an existing pipeline as set forth in Section 21080.21 of the Public Resources Code, as long as the project does not exceed one mile in length.

(l) The activities and approvals by a local government necessary for the preparation of general plan amendments pursuant to Public Resources Code 29763 as set forth in Section 21080.22 of the Public Resources Code. Section 29763 of the Public Resources Code refers to local government amendments made for consistency with the Delta Protection Commission's regional plan.

(m) Minor alterations to utilities made for the purposes of complying with Sections 116410 and 116415 of the Health and Safety Code as set forth in Section 21080.26 of the Public Resources Code.

(n) The adoption of an ordinance exempting a city or county from the provisions of the Solar Shade Control Act as set forth in Section 25985 of the Public Resources Code.

(o) The acquisition of land by the Department of Transportation if received or acquired within a statewide or regional priority corridor designated pursuant to Section 65081.3 of the Government Code as set forth in Section 33911 of the Public Resources Code.

(p) The adoption or amendment of a non disposal facility element as set forth in Section 41735 of the Public Resources Code.

(q) Cooperative agreements for the development of Solid Waste Management Facilities on Indian country as set forth in Section 44203(g) of the Public Resources Code.

(r) Determinations made regarding a city or county's regional housing needs as set forth in Section 65584 of the Government Code.

314

(s) Any action necessary to bring a general plan or relevant mandatory element of the general plan into compliance pursuant to a court order as set forth in Section 65759 of the Government Code.

(t) Industrial Development Authority activities as set forth in Section 91543 of the Government Code.

(u) Temporary changes in the point of diversion, place of use, of purpose of use due to a transfer or exchange of water or water rights as set forth in Section 1729 of the Water Code.

(v) The preparation and adoption of Urban Water Management Plans pursuant to the provisions of Section 10652 of the Water Code.

[Amended effective November 1, 2005]

15283.   Housing Needs Allocation.

CEQA does not apply to regional housing needs determinations made by the Department of Housing and Community Development, a council of governments, or a city or county pursuant to Section 65584 of the Government Code.

15284.   Pipelines.

(a) CEQA does not apply to any project consisting of the inspection, maintenance, repair, restoration, reconditioning, relocation, replacement, or removal of an existing hazardous or volatile liquid pipeline or any valve, flange, meter, or other piece of equipment that is directly attached to the pipeline.

(b) To qualify for this exemption, the diameter of the affected pipeline must not be increased and the project must be located outside the boundaries of an oil refinery. The project must also meet all of the following criteria:

(1) The affected section of pipeline is less than eight miles in length and actual construction and excavation activities are not undertaken over a length of more than one-half mile at a time.

(2) The affected section of pipeline is not less than eight miles distance from any section of pipeline that had been subject to this exemption in the previous 12 months.

(3) The project is not solely for the purpose of excavating soil that is contaminated by hazardous materials.

(4) To the extent not otherwise required by law, the person undertaking the project has, in advance of undertaking the project, prepared a plan that will result in notification of the appropriate agencies so that they may take action, if necessary, to provide for the emergency evacuation of members of the public who may be located in close proximity to the project, and those agencies, including but not limited to the local fire department, police, sheriff, and California Highway Patrol as appropriate, have reviewed and agreed to that plan.

(5) Project activities take place within an existing right-of-way and that right-of-way will be restored to its pre-project condition upon completion of the project.

(6) The project applicant will comply with all conditions otherwise authorized by law, imposed by the city or county as part of any local agency permit

process, and to comply with the Keene-Nejedly California Wetlands Preservation Act (Public Resources Code Section 5810, et seq.), the California Endangered Species Act (Fish and Game Code Section 2050, et seq.), other applicable state laws, and all applicable federal laws.

(c) When the lead agency determines that a project meets all of the criteria of subdivisions (a) and (b), the party undertaking the project shall do all of the following:

    (1) Notify in writing all responsible and trustee agencies, as well as any public agency with environmental, public health protection, or emergency response authority, of the lead agency's invocation of this exemption.

    (2) Mail notice of the project to the last known name and address of all organizations and individuals who have previously requested such notice and notify the public in the affected area by at least one of the following procedures:

        (A) Publication at least one time in a newspaper of general circulation in the area affected by the proposed project. If more than one area is affected, the notice shall be published in the newspaper of largest circulation from among the newspapers of general circulation in those areas.

        (B) Posting of notice on and off site in the area where the project is to be located.

        (C) Direct mailing to the owners and occupants of contiguous property shown on the latest equalized assessment roll.

    The notice shall include a brief description of the proposed project and its location, and the date, time, and place of any public meetings or hearings on the proposed project. This notice may be combined with the public notice required under other law, as applicable, but shall meet the preceding minimum requirements.

    (3) In the case of private rights-of-way over private property, receive from the underlying property owner permission for access to the property.

    (4) Immediately inform the lead agency if any soil contaminated with hazardous materials is discovered.

    (5) Comply with all conditions otherwise authorized by law, imposed by the city or county as part of any local agency permit process, and to comply with the Keene-Nejedly California Wetlands Preservation Act (Public Resources Code Section 5810, et seq.), the California Endangered Species Act (Fish and Game Code Section 2050, et seq.), other applicable state laws, and all applicable federal laws.

(d) For purposes of this section, "pipeline" is used as defined in subdivision (a) of Government Code Section 51010.5. This definition includes every intrastate pipeline used for the transportation of hazardous liquid substances or highly volatile liquid substances, including a common carrier pipeline, and all piping containing those substances located within a refined products bulk loading facility which is owned by a common carrier and is served by a pipeline of that common carrier, and the common carrier owns and serves by pipeline at least five such facilities in California.

15285. Transit Agency Responses to Revenue Shortfalls.

(a) CEQA does not apply to actions taken on or after July 1, 1995 to implement budget reductions made by a publicly owned transit agency as a result of a fiscal emergency caused by the failure of agency revenues to adequately fund agency programs and facilities. Actions shall be limited to those directly undertaken by or financially supported in whole or in part by the transit agency pursuant to Section 15378(a)(1) or (2), including actions which reduce or eliminate the availability of an existing publicly owned transit service, facility, program, or activity.

(b) When invoking this exemption, the transit agency shall make a specific finding that there is a fiscal emergency. Before taking its proposed budgetary actions and making the finding of fiscal emergency, the transit agency shall hold a public hearing. After this public hearing, the transit agency shall respond within 30 days at a regular public meeting to suggestions made by the public at that initial hearing. The transit agency may make the finding of fiscal emergency only after it has responded to public suggestions.

(c) For purposes of this subdivision, "fiscal emergency" means that the transit agency is projected to have negative working capital within one year from the date that the agency finds that a fiscal emergency exists. "Working capital" is defined as the sum of all unrestricted cash, unrestricted short-term investments, and unrestricted short-term accounts receivable, minus unrestricted accounts payable. Employee retirement funds, including deferred compensation plans and Section 401(k) plans, health insurance reserves, bond payment reserves, workers' compensation reserves, and insurance reserves shall not be included as working capital.

(d) This exemption does not apply to the action of any publicly owned transit agency to reduce or eliminate a transit service, facility, program, or activity that was approved or adopted as a mitigation measure in any environmental document certified or adopted by any public agency under either CEQA or NEPA. Further, it does not apply to actions of the Los Angeles County Metropolitan Transportation Authority.

Article 19. Categorical Exemptions

15300. Categorical Exemptions.

Section 21084 of the Public Resources Code requires these guidelines to include a list of classes of projects which have been determined not to have a significant effect on the environment and which shall, therefore, be exempt from the provisions of CEQA.

In response to that mandate, the Secretary for Resources has found that the following classes of projects listed in this article do not have a significant effect on the environment, and they are declared to be categorically exempt from the requirement for the preparation of environmental documents.

15300.1. Relation to Ministerial Projects.

Section 21080 of the Public Resources Code exempts from the application of CEQA those projects over which public agencies exercise only ministerial authority. Since ministerial projects are already exempt, Categorical Exemptions should be applied only where a project is not ministerial under a public agency's statutes and ordinances. The inclusion of activities which may be ministerial within the classes and examples contained in this article shall not be construed as a finding by the Secretary for Resources that such activity is discretionary.

15300.2. Exceptions.

(a) Location. Classes 3, 4, 5, 6, and 11 are qualified by consideration of where the project is to be located—a project that is ordinarily insignificant in its impact on the environment may in a particularly sensitive environment be significant. Therefore, these classes are considered to apply in all instances, except where the project may impact on an environmental resource of hazardous or critical concern where designated, precisely mapped, and officially adopted pursuant to law by federal, state, or local agencies.

(b) Cumulative Impact. All exemptions for these classes are inapplicable when the cumulative impact of successive projects of the same type in the same place, over time is significant.

(c) Significant Effect. A categorical exemption shall not be used for an activity where there is a reasonable possibility that the activity will have a significant effect on the environment due to unusual circumstances.

(d) Scenic Highways. A categorical exemption shall not be used for a project which may result in damage to scenic resources, including but not limited to, trees, historic buildings, rock outcroppings, or similar resources, within a highway officially designated as a state scenic highway. This does not apply to improvements which are required as mitigation by an adopted negative declaration or certified EIR.

(e) Hazardous Waste Sites. A categorical exemption shall not be used for a project located on a site which is included on any list compiled pursuant to Section 65962.5 of the Government Code.

(f) Historical Resources. A categorical exemption shall not be used for a project which may cause a substantial adverse change in the significance of a historical resource.

15300.3. Revisions to List of Categorical Exemptions.

Any public agency may, at any time, request that a new class of Categorical Exemptions be added, or an existing one amended or deleted. This request must be made in writing to the Office of Planning and Research and shall contain detailed information to support the request. The granting of such request shall be by amendment to these guidelines.

15300.4. Application by Public Agencies.

Each public agency shall, in the course of establishing its own procedures, list those specific activities which fall within each of the exempt classes, subject to the qualification that these lists must be consistent with both the letter and the intent expressed in the classes. Public agencies may omit from their implementing procedures classes and examples that do not apply to their activities, but they may not require EIRs for projects described in the classes and examples in this article except under the provisions of Section 15300.2.

## 15301.	Existing Facilities.

Class 1 consists of the operation, repair, maintenance, permitting, leasing, licensing, or minor alteration of existing public or private structures, facilities, mechanical equipment, or topographical features, involving negligible or no expansion of existing or former use. The types of "existing facilities" itemized below are not intended to be all-inclusive of the types of projects which might fall within Class 1. The key consideration is whether the project involves negligible or no expansion of use.

Examples include but are not limited to:

(a) Interior or exterior alterations involving such things as interior partitions, plumbing, and electrical conveyances;

(b) Existing facilities of both investor and publicly-owned utilities used to provide electric power, natural gas, sewerage, or other public utility services;

(c) Existing highways and streets, sidewalks, gutters, bicycle and pedestrian trails, and similar facilities (this includes road grading for the purpose of public safety, and other alterations such as the addition of bicycle facilities, including but not limited to bicycle parking, bicycle-share facilities and bicycle lanes, transit improvements such as bus lanes, pedestrian crossings, street trees, and other similar alterations that do not create additional automobile lanes).

(d) Restoration or rehabilitation of deteriorated or damaged structures, facilities, or mechanical equipment to meet current standards of public health and safety, unless it is determined that the damage was substantial and resulted from an environmental hazard such as earthquake, landslide, or flood;

(e) Additions to existing structures provided that the addition will not result in an increase of more than:

  (1) 50 percent of the floor area of the structures before the addition, or 2,500 square feet, whichever is less; or

  (2) 10,000 square feet if:

   (A) The project is in an area where all public services and facilities are available to allow for maximum development permissible in the General Plan and

   (B) The area in which the project is located is not environmentally sensitive.

(f) Addition of safety or health protection devices for use during construction of or in conjunction with existing structures, facilities, or mechanical equipment, or topographical features including navigational devices;

(g) New copy on existing on and off-premise signs;

(h) Maintenance of existing landscaping, native growth, and water supply reservoirs (excluding the use of pesticides, as defined in Section 12753 Division 7, Chapter 2, Food and Agricultural Code);

319

(i) Maintenance of fish screens, fish ladders, wildlife habitat areas, artificial wildlife waterway devices, streamflows, springs and waterholes, and stream channels (clearing of debris) to protect fish and wildlife resources;

(j) Fish stocking by the California Department of Fish and Game;

(k) Division of existing multiple family or single-family residences into common-interest ownership and subdivision of existing commercial or industrial buildings, where no physical changes occur which are not otherwise exempt;

(l) Demolition and removal of individual small structures listed in this subdivision;

(1) One single-family residence. In urbanized areas, up to three single-family residences may be demolished under this exemption.

(2) A duplex or similar multifamily residential structure. In urbanized areas, this exemption applies to duplexes and similar structures where not more than six dwelling units will be demolished.

(3) A store, motel, office, restaurant, and similar small commercial structure if designed for an occupant load of 30 persons or less. In urbanized areas, the exemption also applies to the demolition of up to three such commercial buildings on sites zoned for such use.

(4) Accessory (appurtenant) structures including garages, carports, patios, swimming pools, and fences.

(m) Minor repairs and alterations to existing dams and appurtenant structures under the supervision of the Department of Water Resources.

(n) Conversion of a single family residence to office use.

(o) Installation, in an existing facility occupied by a medical waste generator, of a steam sterilization unit for the treatment of medical waste generated by that facility provided that the unit is installed and operated in accordance with the Medical Waste Management Act (Section 117600, et seq., of the Health and Safety Code) and accepts no offsite waste.

(p) Use of a single-family residence as a small family day care home, as defined in Section 1596.78 of the Health and Safety Code.

[Amended effective December 28, 2018]

15302.   Replacement or Reconstruction.

Class 2 consists of replacement or reconstruction of existing structures and facilities where the new structure will be located on the same site as the structure replaced and will have substantially the same purpose and capacity as the structure replaced, including but not limited to:

(a) Replacement or reconstruction of existing schools and hospitals to provide earthquake resistant structures which do not increase capacity more than 50 percent;

(b) Replacement of a commercial structure with a new structure of substantially the same size, purpose, and capacity.

(c) Replacement or reconstruction of existing utility systems and/or facilities involving negligible or no expansion of capacity.

(d) Conversion of overhead electric utility distribution system facilities to underground including connection to existing overhead electric utility distribution lines where the surface is restored to the condition existing prior to the undergrounding.

15303. New Construction or Conversion of Small Structures.

Class 3 consists of construction and location of limited numbers of new, small facilities or structures; installation of small new equipment and facilities in small structures; and the conversion of existing small structures from one use to another where only minor modifications are made in the exterior of the structure. The numbers of structures described in this section are the maximum allowable on any legal parcel. Examples of this exemption include but are not limited to:

(a) One single-family residence, or a second dwelling unit in a residential zone. In urbanized areas, up to three single-family residences may be constructed or converted under this exemption.

(b) A duplex or similar multi-family residential structure totaling no more than four dwelling units. In urbanized areas, this exemption applies to apartments, duplexes, and similar structures designed for not more than six dwelling units.

(c) A store, motel, office, restaurant or similar structure not involving the use of significant amounts of hazardous substances, and not exceeding 2500 square feet in floor area. In urbanized areas, the exemption also applies to up to four such commercial buildings not exceeding 10,000 square feet in floor area on sites zoned for such use, if not involving the use of significant amounts of hazardous substances where all necessary public services and facilities are available and the surrounding area is not environmentally sensitive.

(d) Water main, sewage, electrical, gas, and other utility extensions, including street improvements, of reasonable length to serve such construction.

(e) Accessory (appurtenant) structures including garages, carports, patios, swimming pools, and fences.

(f) An accessory steam sterilization unit for the treatment of medical waste at a facility occupied by a medical waste generator, provided that the unit is installed and operated in accordance with the Medical Waste Management Act (Section 117600, et seq., of the Health and Safety Code) and accepts no offsite waste.

15304. Minor Alterations to Land.

Class 4 consists of minor public or private alterations in the condition of land, water, and/or vegetation which do not involve removal of healthy, mature, scenic trees except for forestry and agricultural purposes. Examples include but are not limited to:

(a) Grading on land with a slope of less than 10 percent, except that grading shall not be exempt in a waterway, in any wetland, in an officially designated (by federal, state, or local government action) scenic area, or in officially mapped areas of severe geologic hazard such as an Alquist-Priolo Earthquake Fault Zone or within an official Seismic Hazard Zone, as delineated by the State Geologist.

(b) New gardening or landscaping, including the replacement of existing conventional landscaping with water efficient or fire resistant landscaping.

(c) Filling of earth into previously excavated land with material compatible with the natural features of the site.

(d) Minor alterations in land, water, and vegetation on existing officially designated wildlife management areas or fish production facilities which result in improvement of habitat for fish and wildlife resources or greater fish production.

(e) Minor temporary use of land having negligible or no permanent effects on the environment, including carnivals, sales of Christmas trees, etc.

(f) Minor trenching and backfilling where the surface is restored.

(g) Maintenance dredging where the spoil is deposited in a spoil area authorized by all applicable state and federal regulatory agencies.

(h) The creation of bicycle lanes on existing rights-of-way.

(i) Fuel management activities within 30 feet of structures to reduce the volume of flammable vegetation, provided that the activities will not result in the taking of endangered, rare, or threatened plant or animal species or significant erosion and sedimentation of surface waters. This exemption shall apply to fuel management activities within 100 feet of a structure if the public agency having fire protection responsibility for the area has determined that 100 feet of fuel clearance is required due to extra hazardous fire conditions.

15305.   Minor Alterations in Land Use Limitations.

Class 5 consists of minor alterations in land use limitations in areas with an average slope of less than 20%, which do not result in any changes in land use or density, including but not limited to:

(a) Minor lot line adjustments, side yard, and set back variances not resulting in the creation of any new parcel;

(b) Issuance of minor encroachment permits;

(c) Reversion to acreage in accordance with the Subdivision Map Act.

15306.   Information Collection.

Class 6 consists of basic data collection, research, experimental management, and resource evaluation activities which do not result in a serious or major disturbance to an environmental resource. These may be strictly for information gathering purposes, or as part of a study leading to an action which a public agency has not yet approved, adopted, or funded.

15307.   Actions by Regulatory Agencies for Protection of Natural Resources.

Class 7 consists of actions taken by regulatory agencies as authorized by state law or local ordinance to assure the maintenance, restoration, or enhancement of a natural resource where the regulatory process involves procedures for protection of the environment. Examples include but are not limited to wildlife preservation activities of the State Department of Fish and Game. Construction activities are not included in this exemption.

15308. Actions by Regulatory Agencies for Protection of the Environment.

Class 8 consists of actions taken by regulatory agencies, as authorized by state or local ordinance, to assure the maintenance, restoration, enhancement, or protection of the environment where the regulatory process involves procedures for protection of the environment. Construction activities and relaxation of standards allowing environmental degradation are not included in this exemption.

15309. Inspections.

Class 9 consists of activities limited entirely to inspections, to check for performance of an operation, or quality, health, or safety of a project, including related activities such as inspection for possible mislabeling, misrepresentation, or adulteration of products.

15310. Loans.

Class 10 consists of loans made by the Department of Veterans Affairs under the Veterans Farm and Home Purchase Act of 1943, mortgages for the purchase of existing structures where the loan will not be used for new construction and the purchase of such mortgages by financial institutions. Class 10 includes but is not limited to the following examples:

(a) Loans made by the Department of Veterans Affairs under the Veterans Farm and Home Purchase Act of 1943.

(b) Purchases of mortgages from banks and mortgage companies by the Public Employees Retirement System and by the State Teachers Retirement System.

15311. Accessory Structures.

Class 11 consists of construction, or replacement of minor structures accessory to (appurtenant to) existing commercial, industrial, or institutional facilities, including but not limited to:

(a) On-premise signs;

(b) Small parking lots;

(c) Placement of seasonal or temporary use items such as lifeguard towers, mobile food units, portable restrooms, or similar items in generally the same locations from time to time in publicly owned parks, stadiums, or other facilities designed for public use.

15312. Surplus Government Property Sales.

Class 12 consists of sales of surplus government property except for parcels of land located in an area of statewide, regional, or areawide concern identified in Section 15206(b)(4). However, even if the surplus property to be sold is located in any of those areas, its sale is exempt if:

(a) The property does not have significant values for wildlife habitat or other environmental purposes, and

(b) Any of the following conditions exist:

    (1) The property is of such size, shape, or inaccessibility that it is incapable of independent development or use; or

(2) The property to be sold would qualify for an exemption under any other class of categorical exemption in these guidelines; or

(3) The use of the property and adjacent property has not changed since the time of purchase by the public agency.

15313. Acquisition of Lands for Wildlife Conservation Purposes.

Class 13 consists of the acquisition of lands for fish and wildlife conservation purposes including (a) preservation of fish and wildlife habitat, (b) establishing ecological reserves under Fish and Game Code Section 1580, and (c) preserving access to public lands and waters where the purpose of the acquisition is to preserve the land in its natural condition.

[Amended effective September 7, 2004]

15314. Minor Additions to Schools.

Class 14 consists of minor additions to existing schools within existing school grounds where the addition does not increase original student capacity by more than 25% or ten classrooms, whichever is less. The addition of portable classrooms is included in this exemption.

15315. Minor Land Divisions.

Class 15 consists of the division of property in urbanized areas zoned for residential, commercial, or industrial use into four or fewer parcels when the division is in conformance with the General Plan and zoning, no variances or exceptions are required, all services and access to the proposed parcels to local standards are available, the parcel was not involved in a division of a larger parcel within the previous 2 years, and the parcel does not have an average slope greater than 20 percent.

15316. Transfer of Ownership of Land in Order to Create Parks.

Class 16 consists of the acquisition, sale, or other transfer of land in order to establish a park where the land is in a natural condition or contains historical or archaeological resources and either:

(a) The management plan for the park has not been prepared, or

(b) The management plan proposes to keep the area in a natural condition or preserve the historical or archaeological resources. CEQA will apply when a management plan is proposed that will change the area from its natural condition or cause substantial adverse change in the significance of the historic or archaeological resource.

15317. Open Space Contracts or Easements.

Class 17 consists of the establishment of agricultural preserves, the making and renewing of open space contracts under the Williamson Act, or the acceptance of easements or fee interests in order to maintain the open space character of the area. The cancellation of such preserves, contracts, interests, or easements is not included and will normally be an action subject to the CEQA process.

15318.   Designation of Wilderness Areas.

Class 18 consists of the designation wilderness areas under the California Wilderness System.

15319.   Annexations of Existing Facilities and Lots for Exempt Facilities.

Class 19 consists of only the following annexations:

(a) Annexations to a city or special district of areas containing existing public or private structures developed to the density allowed by the current zoning or pre-zoning of either the gaining or losing governmental agency whichever is more restrictive, provided, however, that the extension of utility services to the existing facilities would have a capacity to serve only the existing facilities.

(b) Annexations of individual small parcels of the minimum size for facilities exempted by Section 15303, New Construction or Conversion of Small Structures.

15320.   Changes in Organization of Local Agencies.

Class 20 consists of changes in the organization or reorganization of local governmental agencies where the changes do not change the geographical area in which previously existing powers are exercised. Examples include but are not limited to:

(a) Establishment of a subsidiary district.

(b) Consolidation of two or more districts having identical powers.

(c) Merger with a city of a district lying entirely within the boundaries of the city.

15321.   Enforcement Actions by Regulatory Agencies.

Class 21 consists of:

(a) Actions by regulatory agencies to enforce or revoke a lease, permit, license, certificate, or other entitlement for use issued, adopted, or prescribed by the regulatory agency or enforcement of a law, general rule, standard, or objective, administered or adopted by the regulatory agency. Such actions include, but are not limited to, the following:

  (1) The direct referral of a violation of lease, permit, license, certificate, or entitlement for use or of a general rule, standard, or objective to the Attorney General, District Attorney, or City Attorney as appropriate, for judicial enforcement.

  (2) The adoption of an administrative decision or order enforcing or revoking the lease, permit, license, certificate, or entitlement for use or enforcing the general rule, standard, or objective.

(b) Law enforcement activities by peace officers acting under any law that provides a criminal sanction.

(c) Construction activities undertaken by the public agency taking the enforcement or revocation action are not included in this exemption.

15322. **Educational or Training Programs Involving No Physical Changes.**

Class 22 consists of the adoption, alteration, or termination of educational or training programs which involve no physical alteration in the area affected or which involve physical changes only in the interior of existing school or training structures. Examples include but are not limited to:

(a) Development of or changes in curriculum or training methods.

(b) Changes in the grade structure in a school which do not result in changes in student transportation.

15323. **Normal Operations of Facilities for Public Gatherings.**

Class 23 consists of the normal operations of existing facilities for public gatherings for which the facilities were designed, where there is a past history of the facility being used for the same or similar kind of purpose. For the purposes of this section, "past history" shall mean that the same or similar kind of activity has been occurring for at least three years and that there is a reasonable expectation that the future occurrence of the activity would not represent a change in the operation of the facility. Facilities included within this exemption include, but are not limited to, racetracks, stadiums, convention centers, auditoriums, amphitheaters, planetariums, swimming pools, and amusement parks.

15324. **Regulations of Working Conditions.**

Class 24 consists of actions taken by regulatory agencies, including the Industrial Welfare Commission as authorized by statute, to regulate any of the following:

(a) Employee wages,

(b) Hours of work, or

(c) Working conditions where there will be no demonstrable physical changes outside the place of work.

15325. **Transfers of Ownership in Land to Preserve Existing Natural Conditions and Historical Resources.**

Class 25 consists of the transfers of ownership of interests in land in order to preserve open space, habitat, or historical resources. Examples include but are not limited to:

(a) Acquisition, sale, or other transfer of areas to preserve the existing natural conditions, including plant or animal habitats.

(b) Acquisition, sale, or other transfer of areas to allow continued agricultural use of the areas.

(c) Acquisition, sale, or other transfer to allow restoration of natural conditions, including plant or animal habitats.

(d) Acquisition, sale, or other transfer to prevent encroachment of development into flood plains.

(e) Acquisition, sale, or other transfer to preserve historical resources.

(f) Acquisition, sale, or other transfer to preserve open space or lands for park purposes.

[Amended effective September 7, 2004]

15326.   Acquisition of Housing for Housing Assistance Programs.

Class 26 consists of actions by a redevelopment agency, housing authority, or other public agency to implement an adopted Housing Assistance Plan by acquiring an interest in housing units. The housing units may be either in existence or possessing all required permits for construction when the agency makes its final decision to acquire the units.

15327.   Leasing New Facilities.

(a) Class 27 consists of the leasing of a newly constructed or previously unoccupied privately owned facility by a local or state agency where the local governing authority determined that the building was exempt from CEQA. To be exempt under this section, the proposed use of the facility:

(1) Shall be in conformance with existing state plans and policies and with general, community, and specific plans for which an EIR or negative declaration has been prepared,

(2) Shall be substantially the same as that originally proposed at the time the building permit was issued,

(3) Shall not result in a traffic increase of greater than 10% of front access road capacity, and

(4) Shall include the provision of adequate employee and visitor parking facilities.

(b) Examples of Class 27 include, but are not limited to:

(1) Leasing of administrative offices in newly constructed office space.

(2) Leasing of client service offices in newly constructed retail space.

(3) Leasing of administrative and/or client service offices in newly constructed industrial parks.

15328.   Small Hydroelectric Projects at Existing Facilities.

Class 28 consists of the installation of hydroelectric generating facilities in connection with existing dams, canals, and pipelines where:

(a) The capacity of the generating facilities is 5 megawatts or less,

(b) Operation of the generating facilities will not change the flow regime in the affected stream, canal, or pipeline including but not limited to:

(1) Rate and volume of flow,

(2) Temperature,

(3) Amounts of dissolved oxygen to a degree that could adversely affect aquatic life, and

(4) Timing of release.

(c) New power lines to connect the generating facilities to existing power lines will not exceed one mile in length if located on a new right of way and will not be located adjacent to a wild or scenic river.

(d) Repair or reconstruction of the diversion structure will not raise the normal maximum surface elevation of the impoundment.

(e) There will be no significant upstream or downstream passage of fish affected by the project.

(f) The discharge from the power house will not be located more than 300 feet from the toe of the diversion structure.

(g) The project will not cause violations of applicable state or federal water quality standards.

(h) The project will not entail any construction on or alteration of a site included in or eligible for inclusion in the National Register of Historic Places, and

(i) Construction will not occur in the vicinity of any endangered, rare, or threatened species.

15329.   Cogeneration Projects at Existing Facilities.

Class 29 consists of the installation of cogeneration equipment with a capacity of 50 megawatts or less at existing facilities meeting the conditions described in this section.

(a) At existing industrial facilities, the installation of cogeneration facilities will be exempt where it will:

    (1) Result in no net increases in air emissions from the industrial facility, or will produce emissions lower than the amount that would require review under the new source review rules applicable in the county, and

    (2) Comply with all applicable state, federal, and local air quality laws.

(b) At commercial and industrial facilities, the installation of cogeneration facilities will be exempt if the installation will:

    (1) Meet all the criteria described in subdivision (a),

    (2) Result in no noticeable increase in noise to nearby residential structures,

    (3) Be contiguous to other commercial or institutional structures.

[Amended effective November 1, 2005]

15330.   Minor Actions to Prevent, Minimize, Stabilize, Mitigate or Eliminate the Release or Threat of Release of Hazardous Waste or Hazardous Substances.

Class 30 consists of any minor cleanup actions taken to prevent, minimize, stabilize, mitigate, or eliminate the release or threat of release of a hazardous waste or substance which are small or medium removal actions costing $1 million or less.

(a) No cleanup action shall be subject to this Class 30 exemption if the action requires the onsite use of a hazardous waste incinerator or thermal treatment unit, or the relocation of residences or businesses, or the action involves the potential release into the air of volatile organic compounds as defined in Health and Safety Code Section 25123.6, except for small scale in situ soil vapor extraction and treatment systems which have been permitted by the local Air

Pollution Control District or Air Quality Management District. All actions must be consistent with applicable state and local environmental permitting requirements including, but not limited to, off-site disposal, air quality rules such as those governing volatile organic compounds and water quality standards, and approved by the regulatory body with jurisdiction over the site.

(b) Examples of such minor cleanup actions include but are not limited to:

(1) Removal of sealed, non-leaking drums or barrels of hazardous waste or substances that have been stabilized, containerized and are designated for a lawfully permitted destination;

(2) Maintenance or stabilization of berms, dikes, or surface impoundments;

(3) Construction or maintenance of interim or temporary surface caps;

(4) Onsite treatment of contaminated soils or sludges provided treatment system meets Title 22 requirements and local air district requirements;

(5) Excavation and/or offsite disposal of contaminated soils or sludges in regulated units;

(6) Application of dust suppressants or dust binders to surface soils;

(7) Controls for surface water run-on and run-off that meets seismic safety standards;

(8) Pumping of leaking ponds into an enclosed container;

(9) Construction of interim or emergency ground water treatment systems;

(10) Posting of warning signs and fencing for a hazardous waste or substance site that meets legal requirements for protection of wildlife.

[Amended effective September 7, 2004]

15331   Historical Resource Restoration/Rehabilitation.

Class 31 consists of projects limited to maintenance, repair, stabilization, rehabilitation, restoration, preservation, conservation or reconstruction of historical resources in a manner consistent with the Secretary of the Interior's Standards for the Treatment of Historic Properties with Guidelines for Preserving, Rehabilitating, Restoring, and Reconstructing Historic Buildings (1995), Weeks and Grimmer.

15332.   In-Fill Development Projects.

Class 32 consists of projects characterized as in-fill development meeting the conditions described in this section.

(a) The project is consistent with the applicable general plan designation and all applicable general plan policies as well as with applicable zoning designation and regulations.

(b) The proposed development occurs within city limits on a project site of no more than five acres substantially surrounded by urban uses.

(c) The project site has no value as habitat for endangered, rare or threatened species.

(d) Approval of the project would not result in any significant effects relating to traffic, noise, air quality, or water quality.

(d) The site can be adequately served by all required utilities and public services.

15333.   Small Habitat Restoration Projects.

Class 33 consists of projects not to exceed five acres in size to assure the maintenance, restoration, enhancement, or protection of habitat for fish, plants, or wildlife provided that:

(a) There would be no significant adverse impact on endangered, rare or threatened species or their habitat pursuant to section 15065,

(b) There are no hazardous materials at or around the project site that may be disturbed or removed, and

(c) The project will not result in impacts that are significant when viewed in connection with the effects of past projects, the effects of other current projects, and the effects of probable future projects.

(d) Examples of small restoration projects may include, but are not limited to:

(1) revegetation of disturbed areas with native plant species;

(2) wetland restoration, the primary purpose of which is to improve conditions for waterfowl or other species that rely on wetland habitat;

(3) stream or river bank revegetation, the primary purpose of which is to improve habitat for amphibians or native fish;

(4) projects to restore or enhance habitat that are carried out principally with hand labor and not mechanized equipment.

(5) stream or river bank stabilization with native vegetation or other bioengineering techniques, the primary purpose of which is to reduce or eliminate erosion and sedimentation; and

(6) culvert replacement conducted in accordance with published guidelines of the Department of Fish and Game or NOAA Fisheries, the primary purpose of which is to improve habitat or reduce sedimentation.

[Added effective September 7, 2004]

Article 20. Definitions

15350.   General.

The definitions contained in this article apply to terms used throughout the guidelines unless a term is otherwise defined in a particular section.

15351.   Applicant.

"Applicant" means a person who proposes to carry out a project which needs a lease, permit, license, certificate, or other entitlement for use or financial assistance from one or more public agencies when that person applies for the governmental approval or assistance.

15352.   Approval.

(a) "Approval" means the decision by a public agency which commits the agency to a definite course of action in regard to a project intended to be carried out by any person. The exact date of approval of any project is a matter determined by each public agency according to its rules, regulations, and ordinances. Legislative action in regard to a project often constitutes approval.

(b) With private projects, approval occurs upon the earliest commitment to issue or the issuance by the public agency of a discretionary contract, grant, subsidy, loan, or other form of financial assistance, lease, permit, license, certificate, or other entitlement for use of the project.

15353.   CEQA.

"CEQA" means the California Environmental Quality Act, California Public Resources Code Sections 21000 et seq.

15354.   Categorical Exemption.

"Categorical exemption" means an exemption from CEQA for a class of projects based on a finding by the Secretary for Resources that the class of projects does not have a significant effect on the environment.

15355.   Cumulative Impacts.

"Cumulative impacts" refer to two or more individual effects which, when considered together, are considerable or which compound or increase other environmental impacts.

(a) The individual effects may be changes resulting from a single project or a number of separate projects.

(b) The cumulative impact from several projects is the change in the environment which results from the incremental impact of the project when added to other closely related past, present, and reasonable foreseeable probable future projects. Cumulative impacts can result from individually minor but collectively significant projects taking place over a period of time.

15356.   Decision-Making Body.

"Decision-making body" means any person or group of people within a public agency permitted by law to approve or disapprove the project at issue.

15357.   Discretionary Project.

"Discretionary project" means a project which requires the exercise of judgment or deliberation when the public agency or body decides to approve or disapprove a particular activity, as distinguished from situations where the public agency or body merely has to determine whether there has been conformity with applicable statutes, ordinances, regulations, or other fixed standards. The key question is whether the public agency can use its subjective judgment to decide whether and how to carry out or approve a project. A timber harvesting plan submitted to the State Forester for approval under the requirements of the Z'berg-Nejedly Forest Practice Act of 1973 (Pub. Res. Code Sections 4511 et seq.) constitutes a discretionary project within the meaning of the California Environmental Quality Act. Section 21065(c).

[Amended effective December 28, 2018]

15358.   Effects.

"Effects" and "impacts" as used in these guidelines are synonymous.

(a) Effects include:

(1) Direct or primary effects which are caused by the project and occur at the same time and place.

(2) Indirect or secondary effects which are caused by the project and are later in time or farther removed in distance, but are still reasonably foreseeable. Indirect or secondary effects may include growth-inducing effects and other effects related to induced changed in the pattern of land use, population density, or growth rate, and related effects on air and water and other natural systems, including ecosystems.

(b) Effects analyzed under CEQA must be related to a physical change.

15359.   Emergency.

"Emergency" means a sudden, unexpected occurrence, involving a clear and imminent danger, demanding immediate action to prevent or mitigate loss of, or damage to life, health, property, or essential public services. Emergency includes such occurrences as fire, flood, earthquake, or other soil or geologic movements, as well as such occurrences as riot, accident, or sabotage.

15360.   Environment.

"Environment" means the physical conditions which exist within the area which will be affected by a proposed project including land, air, water, minerals, flora, fauna, ambient noise, and objects of historic or aesthetic significance. The area involved shall be the area in which significant effects would occur either directly or indirectly as a result of the project. The "environment" includes both natural and man-made conditions.

15361.   Environmental Documents.

"Environmental documents" means initial studies, negative declaration, draft and final EIRs, documents prepared as substitutes for EIRs and negative declarations under a program certified pursuant to Public Resources Code Section 21080.5, and documents prepared under NEPA and used by a state or local agency in the place on an initial study, negative declaration, or an EIR.

15362.   EIR—Environmental Impact Report.

"EIR" or "environmental impact report" means a detailed statement prepared under CEQA describing and analyzing the significant environmental effects of a project and discussing ways to mitigate or avoid the effects. The contents of an EIR are discussed in Article 9, commencing with section 15120 of these guidelines. The term "EIR" may mean either a draft or a final EIR depending on the context.

(a) Draft EIR means an EIR containing the information specified in Sections 15122 through 15131.

(b) Final EIR means an EIR containing the information contained in the draft EIR, comments either verbatim or in summary received in the review process, a list of persons commenting, and the response of the lead agency to the comments received. The final EIR is discussed in detail in Section 15132.

15363.   EIS—Environmental Impact Statement.

"EIS" or "Environmental Impact Statement" means an environmental impact document prepared pursuant to the National Environmental Policy Act (NEPA). NEPA uses the term EIS in the place of the term EIR which is used in CEQA.

15364.   Feasible.

"Feasible" means capable of being accomplished in a successful manner within a reasonable period of time, taking into account economic, environmental, legal, social, and technological factors.

15364.5.   Greenhouse Gas.

"Greenhouse gas" or "greenhouse gases" includes but is not limited to: carbon dioxide, methane, nitrous oxide, hydrofluorocarbons, perfluorocarbons and sulfur hexafluoride.

[Added effective March 18, 2010]

15365.   Initial Study.

"Initial Study" means a preliminary analysis prepared by the lead agency to determine whether an EIR or a negative declaration must be prepared or to identify the significant environmental effects to be analyzed in an EIR. Use of the initial study is discussed in Article 5, commencing with Section 15060.

15366.   Jurisdiction by Law.

(a) "Jurisdiction by law" means the authority of any public agency:

   (1) To grant a permit or other entitlement for use,

   (2) To provide funding for the project in question, or

   (3) To exercise authority over resources which may be affected by the project.

(b) A city or county will have jurisdiction by law with respect to a project when the city or county having primary jurisdiction over the area involved is:

   (1) The site of the project;

   (2) The area in which the major environmental effects will occur; and/or

   (3) The area in which reside those citizens most directly concerned by any such environmental effects.

(c) Where an agency having jurisdiction by law must exercise discretionary authority over a project in order for the project to proceed, it is also a responsible agency, see Section 15381, or the lead agency, see Section 15367.

15367.   Lead Agency.

"Lead agency" means the public agency which has the principal responsibility for carrying out or approving a project. The lead agency will decide whether an EIR or negative declaration will be required for the project and will cause the document to be prepared. Criteria for determining which agency will be the lead agency for a project are contained in Section 15051.

15368.   Local Agency.

"Local agency" means any public agency other than a state agency, board, or commission. Local agency includes but is not limited to cities, counties, charter cities and counties, districts, school districts, special districts, redevelopment agencies, local agency formation commissions, and any board, commission, or organizational subdivision of a local agency when so designated by order or resolution of the governing legislative body of the local agency.

15369.   Ministerial.

"Ministerial" describes a governmental decision involving little or no personal judgment by the public official as to the wisdom or manner of carrying out the project. The public official merely applies the law to the facts as presented but uses no special discretion or judgment in reaching a decision. A ministerial decision involves only the use of fixed standards or objective measurements, and the public official cannot use personal, subjective judgment in deciding whether or how the project should be carried out. Common examples of ministerial permits include automobile registrations, dog licenses, and marriage licenses. A building permit is ministerial if the ordinance requiring the permit limits the public official to determining whether the zoning allows the structure to be built in the requested location, the structure would meet the strength requirements in the Uniform Building Code, and the applicant has paid his fee.

15369.5.   Mitigated Negative Declaration.

Mitigated negative declaration" means a negative declaration prepared for a project when the initial study has identified potentially significant effects on the environment, but (1) revisions in the project plans or proposals made by, or agreed to by, the applicant before the proposed negative declaration and initial study are released for public review would avoid the effects or mitigate the effects to a point where clearly no significant effect on the environment would occur, and (2) there is no substantial evidence in light of the whole record before the public agency that the project, as revised, may have a significant effect on the environment.

15370.   Mitigation.

"Mitigation" includes:

(a) Avoiding the impact altogether by not taking a certain action or parts of an action.

(b) Minimizing impacts by limiting the degree or magnitude of the action and its implementation.

(c) Rectifying the impact by repairing, rehabilitating, or restoring the impacted environment.

(d) Reducing or eliminating the impact over time by preservation and maintenance operations during the life of the action.

(e) Compensating for the impact by replacing or providing substitute resources or environments, including through permanent protection of such resources in the form of conservation easements.

[Amended effective December 28, 2018]

15371. Negative Declaration.

"Negative Declaration" means a written statement by the lead agency briefly describing the reasons that a proposed project, not exempt from CEQA, will not have a significant effect on the environment and therefore does not require the preparation of an EIR. The contents of a negative declaration are described in Section 15071.

15372. Notice of Completion.

"Notice of Completion" means a brief notice filed with the Office of Planning and Research by a Lead Agency as soon as it has completed a draft EIR and is prepared to send out copies for review. The contents of this notice are explained in Section 15085.

[Amended effective November 1, 2005]

15373. Notice of Determination.

"Notice of Determination" means a brief notice to be filed by a public agency after it approves or determines to carry out a project which is subject to the requirements of CEQA. The contents of this notice are explained in Sections 15075 and 15094.

15374. Notice of Exemption.

"Notice of Exemption" means a brief notice which may be filed by a public agency after it has decided to carry out or approve a project and has determined that the project is exempt from CEQA as being ministerial, categorically exempt, an emergency, or subject to another exemption from CEQA. Such a notice may also be filed by an applicant where such a determination has been made by a public agency which must approve the project. The contents of this notice are explained in Section 15062.

15375. Notice of Preparation.

"Notice of Preparation" means a brief notice sent by a Lead Agency to notify the Responsible Agencies, Trustee Agencies, the Office of Planning and Research, and involved federal agencies that the Lead Agency plans to prepare an EIR for the project. The purpose of the notice is to solicit guidance from those agencies as to the scope and content of the environmental information to be included in the EIR. Public agencies are free to develop their own formats for this notice. The contents of this notice are described in Section 15082.

[Amended effective November 1, 2005]

15376. Person.

"Person" includes any person, firm, association, organization, partnership, business, trust, corporation, limited liability company, company, district, city, county, city and county, town, the state, and any of the agencies or political subdivisions of such entities, and, to the extent permitted by federal law, the United States, or any of its agencies or political subdivisions.

[Amended effective November 1, 2005]

15377.   Private Project.

A "private project" means a project which will be carried out by a person other than a governmental agency, but the project will need a discretionary approval from one or more governmental agencies for:

(a) A contract or financial assistance, or

(b) A lease, permit, license, certificate, or other entitlement for use.

15378.   Project.

(a) "Project" means the whole of an action, which has a potential for resulting in either a direct physical change in the environment, or a reasonably foreseeable indirect physical change in the environment, and that is any of the following:

(1) An activity directly undertaken by any public agency including but not limited to public works construction and related activities clearing or grading of land, improvements to existing public structures, enactment and amendment of zoning ordinances, and the adoption and amendment of local General Plans or elements thereof pursuant to Government Code Sections 65100-65700.

(2) An activity undertaken by a person which is supported in whole or in part through public agency contracts, grants, subsidies, loans, or other forms of assistance from one or more public agencies.

(3) An activity involving the issuance to a person of a lease, permit, license, certificate, or other entitlement for use by one or more public agencies.

(b) Project does not include:

(1) Proposals for legislation to be enacted by the State Legislature;

(2) Continuing administrative or maintenance activities, such as purchases for supplies, personnel-related actions, general policy and procedure making (except as they are applied to specific instances covered above);

(3) The submittal of proposals to a vote of the people of the state or of a particular community that does not involve a public agency sponsored initiative. (Stein v. City of Santa Monica (1980), 110 Cal. App. 3d 458; Friends of Sierra Madre v. City of Sierra Madre (2001) 25 Cal.4th 165);

(4) The creation of government funding mechanisms or other government fiscal activities which do not involve any commitment to any specific project which may result in a potentially significant physical impact on the environment.

(5) Organizational or administrative activities of governments that will not result in direct or indirect physical changes in the environment.

(c) The term "project" refers to the activity which is being approved and which may be subject to several discretionary approvals by governmental agencies. The term "project" does not mean each separate governmental approval.

(d) Where the Lead Agency could describe the project as either the adoption of a particular regulation under subdivision (a)(1) or as a development proposal which will be subject to several governmental approvals under subdivisions (a)(2) or (a)(3), the lead agency shall describe the project as the development

336

proposal for the purpose of environmental analysis. This approach will implement the lead agency principle as described in Article 4.

[Amended effective November 1, 2005]

15379.   Public Agency.

"Public agency" includes any state agency, board, or commission and any local or regional agency, as defined in these guidelines. It does not include the courts of the state. This term does not include agencies of the federal government.

15380.   Endangered, Rare or Threatened Species.

(a) "Species" as used in this section means a species or subspecies of animal or plant or a variety of plant.

(b) A species of animal or plant is:

    (1) "Endangered" when its survival and reproduction in the wild are in immediate jeopardy from one or more causes, including loss of habitat, change in habitat, overexploitation, predation, competition, disease, or other factors; or

    (2) "Rare" when either:

        (A) Although not presently threatened with extinction, the species is existing in such small numbers throughout all or a significant portion of its range that it may become endangered if its environment worsens; or

        (B) The species is likely to become endangered within the foreseeable future throughout all or significant portion of its range and may be considered "threatened" as that term is used in the Federal Endangered Species Act.

(c) A species of animal or plant shall be presumed to be endangered, rare or threatened as it is listed in:

    (1) Sections 670.2 or 670.5, Title 14, California Code of Regulations; or

    (2) Title 50, Code of Federal Regulations Sections 17.11 or 17.12 pursuant to the Federal Endangered Species Act as rare, threatened, or endangered.

(d) A species not included in any listing identified in subdivision (c) shall nevertheless be considered to be endangered, rare or threatened, if the species can be shown to meet the criteria in subdivision (b).

(e) This definition shall not include any species of the Class Insecta which is a pest whose protection under the provisions of CEQA would present an overwhelming and overriding risk to man as determined by:

    (1) The Director of food and Agriculture with regard to economic pests; or

    (2) The Director of Health Services with regard to health risks.

[Amended effective November 1, 2005]

15381.   Responsible Agency.

"Responsible Agency" means a public agency which proposes to carry out or approve a project, for which lead agency is preparing or has prepared an EIR or negative declaration. For the purposes of CEQA, the term "responsible agency" includes all public agencies other than the lead agency which have discretionary approval power over the project.

15382.   Significant Effect on the Environment.

"Significant effect on the environment" means a substantial, or potentially substantial, adverse change in any of the physical conditions within the area affected by the project including land, air, water, minerals, flora, fauna, ambient noise, and objects of historic or aesthetic significance. An economic or social change by itself shall not be considered a significant effect on the environment. A social or economic change related to a physical change may be considered in determining whether the physical change is significant.

15383.   State Agency.

"State agency" means a governmental agency in the executive branch of the State Government or an entity which operates under the direction and control of an agency in the executive branch of State Government and is funded primarily by the State Treasury.

15384.   Substantial Evidence.

(a) "Substantial evidence" as used in these guidelines means enough relevant information and reasonable inferences from this information that a fair argument can be made to support a conclusion, even though other conclusions might also be reached. Whether a fair argument can be made that the project may have a significant effect on the environment is to be determined by examining the whole record before the lead agency. Argument, speculation, unsubstantiated opinion or narrative, evidence which is clearly erroneous or inaccurate, or evidence of social or economic impacts which do not contribute to or are not caused by physical impacts on the environment does not constitute substantial evidence.

(b) Substantial evidence shall include facts, reasonable assumptions predicated upon facts, and expert opinion supported by facts.

15385.   Tiering.

"Tiering" refers to the coverage of general matters in broader EIRs (such as on general plans or policy statements) with subsequent narrower EIRs or ultimately site-specific EIRs incorporating by reference the general discussions and concentrating solely on the issues specific to the EIR subsequently prepared. Tiering is appropriate when the sequence of EIRs is:

(a) From a general plan, policy, or program EIR to a program, plan, or policy EIR of lesser scope or to a site-specific EIR.

(b) From an EIR on specific action at an early stage to a subsequent EIR or a supplement to an EIR at a later stage. Tiering in such cases is appropriate when it helps the lead agency to focus on the issues which are ripe for decision and exclude from consideration issues already decided or not yet ripe.

15386.   Trustee Agency.

"Trustee agency" means a state agency having jurisdiction by law over natural resources affected by a project which are held in trust for the people of the State of California. Trustee agencies include:

(a) The California Department of Fish and Game with regard to the fish and wildlife of the state, to designated rare of endangered native plants, and to game refuges, ecological reserves, and other areas administered by the department.

(b) The State Lands Commission with regard to state owned "sovereign" land such as the beds of navigable waters and state school lands.

(c) The State Department of Parks and Recreation with regard to units of State Park System.

(d) The University of California with regard to sites within the Natural Land and Water Reserves System.

15387.   Urbanized Area.

"Urbanized area" means a central city or a group of contiguous cities with a population of 50,000 or more, together with adjacent densely populated areas having a population density of a least 1,000 persons per square mile. A lead agency shall determine whether a particular area meets the criteria in this section either by examining the area or by referring to a map prepared by the U.S. Bureau of the Census which designates the area as urbanized. Maps of the designated urbanized areas can be found in the California EIR Monitor of February 7, 1979. The maps are also for sale by the Superintendent of Documents, U.S. Government Printing Office, Washington, D.C. 20402. The maps are sold in sets only as Stock Number 0301-3466. Use of the term "urbanized area" in Section 15182 is limited to areas mapped and designated as urbanized by the U.S. Bureau of the Census.

Appendices

Reprinted with the permission of the California Resources Agency

---

Notice

All Notices and Forms sent to the State Clearinghouse should be sent to their PO Box instead of the street address. Mail sent to the street address should be forwarded to the PO Box, however, it may be returned to the sender.
The PO Box address is:
State Clearinghouse, PO Box 3044, Sacramento, CA 95812-3044

Appendix A
CEQA PROCESS FLOW CHART

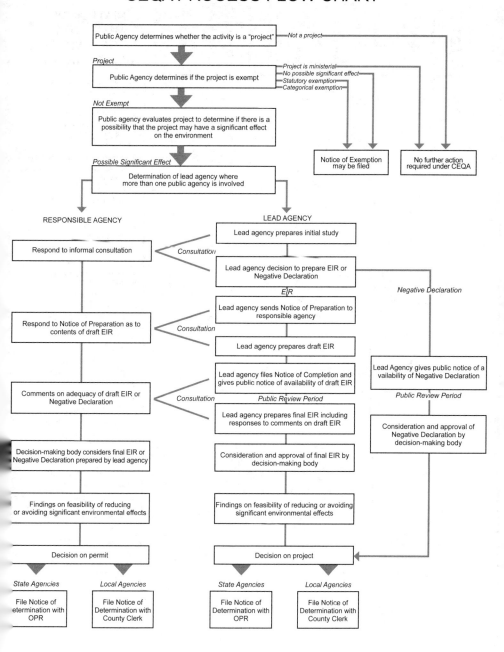

Public Agency determines whether the activity is a "project" — Not a project

Project

Public Agency determines if the project is exempt — Project is ministerial — No possible significant effect — Statutory exemption — Categorical exemption

Not Exempt

Public agency evaluates project to determine if there is a possibility that the project may have a significant effect on the environment

Possible Significant Effect

Determination of lead agency where more than one public agency is involved

Notice of Exemption may be filed

No further action required under CEQA

RESPONSIBLE AGENCY

LEAD AGENCY

Lead agency prepares initial study

Respond to informal consultation — Consultation

Lead agency decision to prepare EIR or Negative Declaration

EIR   *Negative Declaration*

Lead agency sends Notice of Preparation to responsible agency

Respond to Notice of Preparation as to contents of draft EIR — Consultation

Lead agency prepares draft EIR

Lead agency files Notice of Completion and gives public notice of availability of draft EIR

Lead Agency gives public notice of availability of Negative Declaration

Comments on adequacy of draft EIR or Negative Declaration — Consultation — *Public Review Period*

Public Review Period

Lead agency prepares final EIR including responses to comments on draft EIR

Consideration and approval of Negative Declaration by decision-making body

Decision-making body considers final EIR or Negative Declaration prepared by lead agency

Consideration and approval of final EIR by decision-making body

Findings on feasibility of reducing or avoiding significant environmental effects

Findings on feasibility of reducing or avoiding significant environmental effects

Decision on permit

Decision on project

| *State Agencies* | *Local Agencies* | *State Agencies* | *Local Agencies* |

File Notice of Determination with OPR

File Notice of Determination with County Clerk

File Notice of Determination with OPR

File Notice of Determination with County Clerk

341

Appendix B

STATUTORY AUTHORITY OF STATE DEPARTMENTS

Bay Conservation and Development Commission	Air Resources Board	Resources Agency		Health Services	Savings and Loan	Real Estate	Caltrans	Dept of Housing and Community Development	Dept of Motor Vehicles	Corporations	California Highway Patrol	Aeronautics		Food and Agriculture	
	✖			✖					✖		16	✖		1	1. Air quality and air pollution control
				✖										✖	2. Chemical contamination and food products
26				7											3. Coastal areas, wetlands, estuaries, waterfowl refuges, and beaches
	24			8		✖		✖							4. Congestion in urban areas, housing, and building displacement
				✖										✖	5. Disease control
	✖			✖											6. Electric energy generation and supply
				9		✖	✖	✖							7. Environmental effects with special impact in low-income neighborhoods
						✖								✖	8. Flood plains and watersheds
				✖										✖	9. Food additives and food sanitation
		✖		✖										✖	10. Herbicides
							✖								11. Historic and archaeological sites
	✖			✖										2	12. Human ecology
				✖										✖	13. Microbiological contamination
															14. Mineral land reclamation
															15. Natural gas energy development generation and supply
	16			10								✖			16. Navigable airways
25															17. Navigable waterways
				✖							✖	✖			18. Noise control and abatement
25														✖	19. Parks, forests, trees and outdoor recreation areas
		✖		✖										✖	20. Pesticides
		✖		✖											21. Radiation and radiological health
	24			11	✖	✖	✖	✖				✖			22. Regional comprehensive planning
				✖										✖	23. Rodent control
				✖										3	24. Sanitation and waste systems
				✖											25. Shellfish sanitation
														✖	26. Soil and plant life, sedimentation, erosion, and hydrologic conditions
				✖										✖	27. Toxic Materials
				✖						✖	✖			4	28. Transportation and handling of hazardous materials
				✖										✖	29. Water quality and water pollution control
				12										5	30. Fish and wildlife
25				13											31. Activities with special impact on regional jurisdictions
	24														32. Water project formulation
	24														33. Geothermal energy
															34. Oil and petroleum development, generation and supply
															35. Statewide land use patterns
	24														36. Open space policy
						✖									37. Statewide overview — cumulative impact of separate projects
								✖							38. Seismic hazards

342

Appendix B
continued

Office of Planning & Research	Native American Heritage Commission	Water Resources	State Water Resources Control Board	State Reclamation Board	State Lands Commission	Solid Waste Mgmt Board	Parks and Recreation	Forestry	Fish and Game	Energy Commission	Conservation	Colorado River Board	CTRPA	Coastal Commission	Boating and Waterways	Topic
		X									X		27			1. Air quality and air pollution control
		X							X							2. Chemical contamination and food products
	X	X			X		X		X		14		27	26	X	3. Coastal areas, wetlands, estuaries, waterfowl refuges, and beaches
		21											27	26		4. Congestion in urban areas, housing, and building displacement
							X	22	X		14					5. Disease control
	X						X	23	X	X	14			26	X	6. Electric energy generation and supply
									19							7. Environmental effects with special impact in low-income neighborhoods
	X	20		X	X		X		X		14		27	26		8. Flood plains and watersheds
																9. Food additives and food sanitation
							X	22	X		14					10. Herbicides
	X				X		X						27	26		11. Historic and archaeological sites
X							X		X				27	26		12. Human ecology
		X							X		14					13. Microbiological contamination
					X		X		X		X		27	26		14. Mineral land reclamation
					X				15	X	X			26		15. Natural gas energy development generation and supply
									16							16. Navigable airways
		20	X						X		14		27	26	X	17. Navigable waterways
									17							18. Noise control and abatement
	X						X	X	X		14		27	26	X	19. Parks, forests, trees and outdoor recreation areas
		X	X				X	22	X							20. Pesticides
									X	X	14					21. Radiation and radiological health
X	X	X			X		X		X	X	14		27	26	X	22. Regional comprehensive planning
							X	22	X							23. Rodent control
		X	X			X			18	X	14			26		24. Sanitation and waste systems
		X							X							25. Shellfish sanitation
	X	X			X		X		X		14		27	26		26. Soil and plant life, sedimentation, erosion, and hydrologic conditions
		X				X	X		X		14					27. Toxic Materials
		X							X	X						28. Transportation and handling of hazardous materials
		X	X						X		14		27	26	X	29. Water quality and water pollution control
		21							X	X	14		27	26		30. Fish and wildlife
	X	20							X		14		27	26		31. Activities with special impact on regional jurisdictions
X	X	20		X				23	X		14				X	32. Water project formulation
	X	21			X				X	X	14					33. Geothermal energy
		21			X				X	X	X			26		34. Oil and petroleum development, generation and supply
X		X							X	X			27	26		35. Statewide land use patterns
X	X	X							X	X			27	26		36. Open space policy
X									X	X						37. Statewide overview — cumulative impact of separate projects
	X								X	X			27	26		38. Seismic hazards

Appendix B Footnotes

1. **Food and Agriculture** - Effects on plants and animals.
2. **Food and Agriculture** - Protection of food and fiber.
3. **Food and Agriculture** - Agricultural, dairy and feed lot Systems.
4. **Food and Agriculture** - As pertains to transportation, handling, storage and decontamination of pesticides.
5. **Food and Agriculture** - Pesticide effects, predatory animal control, bird control.
6. **California Highway Patrol** - Enforcement of motor vehicle regulations.
7. **Health Services - Beach sanitation,** water pollution, solid waste and mosquito control.
8. **Health Services** - Pertains to health component.
9. **Health Services** - Most if these are strongly related to health.
10. **Health Services -** Pertains to noise.
11. **Health Services** - Pertains to personal and environmental health components.
12. **Health Services** - As it may pertain to human health hazards.
13. **Health Services** - Pertains to comprehensive health planning.
14. **Colorado River Board** - As pertains to the Colorado, New and Alamo Rivers.
15. **Fish and Game** - As field development and distribution systems may affect fish and wildlife.
16. **Fish and Game** - As may affect migrating and resident wildlife.
17. **Fish and Game -** As excessive noise may affect wildlife.
18. Fish and Game - As water quality may affect fish and wildlife.
19. **Parks and Recreation - In impacted** areas only.
20. **Reclamation Board** - In areas of Board's jurisdiction only — the Sacramento-San Joaquin Valley.
21. **State Water Resources Control Board** - As may pertain to water quality.
22. **Forestry** - With respect to forest land.
23. **Forestry** - (6) and (32) - As related to fire protection or State (fire protection) responsibility land.
24. **Air Resources Board** - (4), (22), (32), (33), and (36) - As may pertain to residential, commercial, industrial or transportation growth.
25. **San Francisco Bay Conservation and Development Commission** - (3), (17), (19), and (30) - With respect to San Francisco Bay, Suisun Bay and adjacent shore areas.
26. **California Coastal Commission -** (3), (4), (6), (8), (11), (12), (14), (15), (17), (19), (22), (23), (26), (29), (30), (31), (34), (35), and (36) - With respect to effects within the California Coastal Zone.
27. **California Tahoe Regional Planning Agency** - With respect to effects in theTahoe Basin.
28. **Native American Heritage Commission** - With respect to places of special religious or social significance to Native Americans including archaeological sites, cemeteries, and places of worship.

NOTE: Authority cited: Section 21083, Public Resources Code; Reference: Sections 21080.3, 21080.4, 21104, and 21153, Public Resources Code.

344

Notice of Completion & Environmental Document Transmittal

Mail to: State Clearinghouse, P.O. Box 3044, Sacramento, CA 95812-3044   (916) 445-0613
For Hand Delivery/Street Address: 1400 Tenth Street, Sacramento, CA 95814

SCH # _____

Project Title: _____

Lead Agency: _____   Contact Person: _____

Mailing Address: _____   Phone: _____

City: _____ Zip: _____   County: _____

- -

Project Location: County: _____ City/Nearest Community: _____

Cross Streets: _____ Zip Code: _____

Longitude/Latitude (degrees, minutes and seconds): ____° ____' ____" N / ____° ____' ____" W Total Acres: _____

Assessor's Parcel No.: _____ Section: _____ Twp.: _____ Range: _____ Base: _____

Within 2 Miles: State Hwy #: _____ Waterways: _____

Airports: _____ Railways: _____ Schools: _____

- -

Document Type:

CEQA: ☐ NOP   ☐ Draft EIR   NEPA: ☐ NOI   Other: ☐ Joint Document
☐ Early Cons   ☐ Supplement/Subsequent EIR   ☐ EA   ☐ Final Document
☐ Neg Dec   (Prior SCH No.) _____   ☐ Draft EIS   ☐ Other: _____
☐ Mit Neg Dec   Other: _____   ☐ FONSI

- -

Local Action Type:

☐ General Plan Update   ☐ Specific Plan   ☐ Rezone   ☐ Annexation
☐ General Plan Amendment   ☐ Master Plan   ☐ Prezone   ☐ Redevelopment
☐ General Plan Element   ☐ Planned Unit Development   ☐ Use Permit   ☐ Coastal Permit
☐ Community Plan   ☐ Site Plan   ☐ Land Division (Subdivision, etc.) ☐ Other: _____

- -

Development Type:

☐ Residential: Units _____ Acres _____
☐ Office: Sq.ft. _____ Acres _____ Employees _____   ☐ Transportation: Type _____
☐ Commercial:Sq.ft. _____ Acres _____ Employees _____   ☐ Mining: Mineral _____
☐ Industrial: Sq.ft. _____ Acres _____ Employees _____   ☐ Power: Type _____ MW _____
☐ Educational: _____   ☐ Waste Treatment:Type _____ MGD _____
☐ Recreational: _____   ☐ Hazardous Waste:Type _____
☐ Water Facilities:Type _____ MGD _____   ☐ Other: _____

- -

Project Issues Discussed in Document:

☐ Aesthetic/Visual   ☐ Fiscal   ☐ Recreation/Parks   ☐ Vegetation
☐ Agricultural Land   ☐ Flood Plain/Flooding   ☐ Schools/Universities   ☐ Water Quality
☐ Air Quality   ☐ Forest Land/Fire Hazard   ☐ Septic Systems   ☐ Water Supply/Groundwater
☐ Archeological/Historical ☐ Geologic/Seismic   ☐ Sewer Capacity   ☐ Wetland/Riparian
☐ Biological Resources   ☐ Minerals   ☐ Soil Erosion/Compaction/Grading ☐ Growth Inducement
☐ Coastal Zone   ☐ Noise   ☐ Solid Waste   ☐ Land Use
☐ Drainage/Absorption   ☐ Population/Housing Balance ☐ Toxic/Hazardous   ☐ Cumulative Effects
☐ Economic/Jobs   ☐ Public Services/Facilities ☐ Traffic/Circulation   ☐ Other: _____

- -

Present Land Use/Zoning/General Plan Designation:

- -

Project Description: *(please use a separate page if necessary)*

Note: The State Clearinghouse will assign identification numbers for all new projects. If a SCH number already exists for a project (e.g. Notice of Preparation or previous draft document) please fill in.

Revised 2008

Reviewing Agencies Checklist

Lead Agencies may recommend State Clearinghouse distribution by marking agencies below with and "**X**".
If you have already sent your document to the agency please denote that with an "**S**".

_____ Air Resources Board	_____ Office of Emergency Services
_____ Boating & Waterways, Department of	_____ Office of Historic Preservation
_____ California Highway Patrol	_____ Office of Public School Construction
_____ Caltrans District # _____	_____ Parks & Recreation, Department of
_____ Caltrans Division of Aeronautics	_____ Pesticide Regulation, Department of
_____ Caltrans Planning	_____ Public Utilities Commission
_____ Central Valley Flood Protection Board	_____ Regional WQCB # _____
_____ Coachella Valley Mtns. Conservancy	_____ Resources Agency
_____ Coastal Commission	_____ S.F. Bay Conservation & Development Comm.
_____ Colorado River Board	_____ San Gabriel & Lower L.A. Rivers & Mtns. Conservancy
_____ Conservation, Department of	_____ San Joaquin River Conservancy
_____ Corrections, Department of	_____ Santa Monica Mtns. Conservancy
_____ Delta Protection Commission	_____ State Lands Commission
_____ Education, Department of	_____ SWRCB: Clean Water Grants
_____ Energy Commission	_____ SWRCB: Water Quality
_____ Fish & Game Region # _____	_____ SWRCB: Water Rights
_____ Food & Agriculture, Department of	_____ Tahoe Regional Planning Agency
_____ Forestry and Fire Protection, Department of	_____ Toxic Substances Control, Department of
_____ General Services, Department of	_____ Water Resources, Department of
_____ Health Services, Department of	
_____ Housing & Community Development	_____ Other: _____
_____ Integrated Waste Management Board	_____ Other: _____
_____ Native American Heritage Commission	

- -

Local Public Review Period (to be filled in by lead agency)

Starting Date _____   Ending Date _____

- -

Lead Agency (Complete if applicable):

Consulting Firm: _____   Applicant: _____
Address: _____   Address: _____
City/State/Zip: _____   City/State/Zip: _____
Contact: _____   Phone: _____
Phone: _____

- -

Signature of Lead Agency Representative: _____   **Date:** _____

Authority cited: Section 21083, Public Resources Code. Reference: Section 21161, Public Resources Code.

Revised 2008

346

TO:		FROM:
☐ Office of Planning and Research		Public Agency:_____
For U.S. Mail:	*Street Address:*	
P.O. Box Box 3044	1400 Tenth Street	Address:_____
Sacramento, CA 95812-3044	Sacramento, CA 95814	
		Contact:_____
☐ County Clerk		Phone:_____
County of:_____		Lead Agency (if different from above):
Address:_____		
_____		Address:_____
		Contact:_____
		Phone:_____

SUBJECT: **Filing of Notice of Determination in compliance with Section 21108 or 21152 of the Public Resources Code.**

State Clearinghouse Number (if submitted to State Clearinghouse): _____

Project Title:_____

Project Applicant:_____

Project Location (include county):_____

Project Description:_____
_____
_____
_____
_____

1. The project [☐ will ☐ will not] have a significant effect on the environment.
2. ☐ An Environmental Impact Report was prepared for this project pursuant to the provisions of CEQA.
   ☐ A Negative Declaration was prepared for this project pursuant to the provisions of CEQA.
3. Mitigation measures [☐ were ☐ were not] made a condition of the approval of the project.
4. A mitigation reporting or monitoring plan [☐ was ☐ was not] adopted for this project.
5. A statement of Overriding Considerations [☐ was ☐ was not] adopted for this project.
6. Findings [☐ were ☐ were not] made pursuant to the provisions of CEQA.

This is to certify that the final EIR with comments and responses and record of project approval, or the Negative Declaration, is available to the General Public at:

_____

Signature (Public Agency)_____ Title:_____
Date:_____ Date Received for filing at OPR:_____

Authority cited: Section 21083, Public Resources Code.
Reference: Sections 21000-21174, Public Resources Code. **Revised 2011**

Notice of Exemption

To: ❏   Office of Planning and Research
         P.O. Box 3044, Room 212
         Sacramento, CA 95812-3044

    ❏   County Clerk
         County of_____

From: (Public Agency)_____

Project Title:_____

Project Applicant:_____

Project Location – Specific:_____

Project Location – City:_____ **Project Location – County:**_____

Description of Nature, Purpose, and Beneficiaries of Project:

_____

_____

_____

Name of Public Agency Approving Project:_____

Name of Person or Agency Carrying Out Project:_____

Exempt Status: *(check one)*
    ❏ Ministerial (Sec. 15268);
    ❏ Declared Emergency (Sec. 15269(a));
    ❏ Emergency Project (Sec. 15269(b)(c));
    ❏ Categorical Exemption. State type and section number:

Reasons why project is exempt:_____

_____

_____

Contact Person:_____ Area Code/Telephone Extension:_____

If filed by applicant:
    1. Attach certified document of exemption finding.
    2. Has a Notice of Exemption been filed by the public agency approving the project? ❏ Yes   ❏ No

Signature:_____ Title:_____

Date received for filing at OPR:_____

Revised 2011

Note: *Authority cited: Sections 21083 and 21110, Public Resources Code.*
      Reference: Sections 21108, 21152, and 21152.1, Public Resources Code.

Appendix F
ENERGY CONSERVATION

I. Introduction

The goal of conserving energy implies the wise and efficient use of energy. The means of achieving this goal include:

    (1) decreasing overall per capita energy consumption,
    (2) decreasing reliance on fossil fuels such as coal, natural gas and oil, and
    (3) increasing reliance on renewable energy sources.

In order to assure that energy implications are considered in project decisions, the California Environmental Quality Act requires that EIRs include a discussion of the potential energy impacts of proposed projects, with particular emphasis on avoiding or reducing inefficient, wasteful and unnecessary consumption of energy (see Public Resources Code section 21100(b)(3)). Energy conservation implies that a project's cost effectiveness be reviewed not only in dollars, but also in terms of energy requirements. For many projects, cost effectiveness may be determined more by energy efficiency than by initial dollar costs. A lead agency may consider the extent to which an energy source serving the project has already undergone environmental review that adequately analyzed and mitigated the effects of energy production.

II. EIR Contents

Potentially significant energy implications of a project shall be considered in an EIR to the extent relevant and applicable to the project. The following list of energy impact possibilities and potential conservation measures is designed to assist in the preparation of an EIR. In many instances specific items may not apply or additional items may be needed. Where items listed below are applicable or relevant to the project, they should be considered in the EIR.

A. Project Description may include the following items:
    1. Energy consuming equipment and processes which will be used during construction, operation and/or removal of the project. If appropriate, this discussion should consider the energy intensiveness of materials and equipment required for the project.
    2. Total energy requirements of the project by fuel type and end use.
    3. Energy conservation equipment and design features.
    4. Identification of energy supplies that would serve the project.
    5. Total estimated daily vehicle trips to be generated by the project and the additional energy consumed per trip by mode.

B. Environmental Settings may include existing energy supplies and energy use patterns in the region and locality.

C. Environmental Impacts may include:
    1. The project's energy requirements and its energy use efficiencies by amount and fuel type for each stage of the project including construction, operation, maintenance and/or removal. If appropriate, the energy intensiveness of materials may be discussed.
    2. The effects of the project on local and regional energy supplies and on requirements for additional capacity.
    3. The effects of the project on peak and base period demands for electricity and other forms of energy.
    4. The degree to which the project complies with existing energy standards.
    5. The effects of the project on energy resources.
    6. The project's projected transportation energy use requirements and its overall use of efficient transportation alternatives.

D. Mitigation Measures may include:
    1. Potential measures to reduce wasteful, inefficient and unnecessary consumption of energy during construction, operation, maintenance and/or removal. The discussion should explain why certain measures were incorporated in the project and why other measures were dismissed.
    2. The potential of siting, orientation, and design to minimize energy consumption, including transportation energy, increase water conservation and reduce solid-waste.
    3. The potential for reducing peak energy demand.
    4. Alternate fuels (particularly renewable ones) or energy systems.
    5. Energy conservation which could result from recycling efforts.

E. Alternatives should be compared in terms of overall energy consumption and in terms of reducing wasteful, inefficient and unnecessary consumption of energy.

F. Unavoidable Adverse Effects may include wasteful, inefficient and unnecessary consumption of energy during the project construction, operation, maintenance and/or removal that cannot be feasibly mitigated.

G. Irreversible Commitment of Resources may include a discussion of how the project preempts future energy development or future energy conservation.

H. Short-Term Gains versus Long-Term Impacts can be compared by calculating the project's energy costs over the project's lifetime.

I. Growth Inducing Effects may include the estimated energy consumption of growth induced by the project.

CEQA APPENDIX G:
ENVIRONMENTAL CHECKLIST FORM

NOTE: The following is a sample form that may be tailored to satisfy individual agencies' needs and project circumstances. It may be used to meet the requirements for an initial study when the criteria set forth in CEQA Guidelines have been met. Substantial evidence of potential impacts that are not listed on this form must also be considered. The sample questions in this form are intended to encourage thoughtful assessment of impacts, and do not necessarily represent thresholds of significance.

1. Project title: _____

2. Lead agency name and address:

_____

_____

3. Contact person and phone number:_____

4. Project location: _____

5. Project sponsor's name and address:

_____

_____

6. General plan designation: _____ 7. Zoning: _____

8. Description of project: (Describe the whole action involved, including but not limited to later phases of the project, and any secondary, support, or off-site features necessary for its implementation. Attach additional sheets if necessary.)

_____

_____

_____

9. Surrounding land uses and setting: Briefly describe the project's surroundings:

_____

_____

_____

10. Other public agencies whose approval is required (e.g., permits, financing approval, or participation agreement.)

_____

_____

11. Have California Native American tribes traditionally and culturally affiliated with the project area requested consultation pursuant to Public Resources Code section 21080.3.1? If so, is there a plan for consultation that includes, for example, the determination of significance of impacts to tribal cultural resources, procedures regarding confidentiality, etc.? _____

Note: Conducting consultation early in the CEQA process allows tribal governments, lead agencies, and project proponents to discuss the level of environmental review, identify and address potential adverse impacts to tribal cultural resources, and reduce the potential for delay and conflict in the environmental review process. (See Public Resources Code section 21083.3.2.) Information may also be available from the California Native American Heritage Commission's Sacred Lands File per Public Resources Code section 5097.96 and the California Historical Resources Information System administered by the California Office of Historic Preservation. Please also note that Public Resources Code section 21082.3(c) contains provisions specific to confidentiality.

ENVIRONMENTAL FACTORS POTENTIALLY AFFECTED:

The environmental factors checked below would be potentially affected by this project, involving at least one impact that is a "Potentially Significant Impact" as indicated by the checklist on the following pages.

☐ Aesthetics

☐ Agriculture & Forestry Resources

☐ Air Quality

☐ Biological Resources

☐ Cultural Resources

☐ Energy

☐ Geology/Soils

☐ Greenhouse Gas Emissions

☐ Hazards & Hazardous Materials

☐ Hydrology/Water Quality

☐ Land Use/Planning

☐ Mineral Resources

☐ Noise

☐ Population/Housing

☐ Public Services

☐ Recreation

☐ Transportation

☐ Tribal Cultural Resources

☐ Utilities/Service Systems

☐ Wildfire

☐ Mandatory Findings of Significance

DETERMINATION: (To be completed by the Lead Agency)

On the basis of this initial evaluation:

☐ I find that the proposed project COULD NOT have a significant effect on the environment, and a NEGATIVE DECLARATION will be prepared.

☐ I find that although the proposed project could have a significant effect on the environment, there will not be a significant effect in this case because revisions in the project have been made by or agreed to by the project proponent. A MITIGATED NEGATIVE DECLARATION will be prepared.

☐ I find that the proposed project MAY have a significant effect on the environment, and an ENVIRONMENTAL IMPACT REPORT is required.

☐ I find that the proposed project MAY have a "potentially significant impact" or "potentially significant unless mitigated" impact on the environment, but at least one effect 1) has been adequately analyzed in an earlier document pursuant to applicable legal standards, and 2) has been addressed by mitigation measures based on the earlier analysis as described on attached sheets. An ENVIRONMENTAL IMPACT REPORT is required, but it must analyze only the effects that remain to be addressed.

☐ I find that although the proposed project could have a significant effect on the environment, because all potentially significant effects (a) have been analyzed adequately in an earlier EIR or NEGATIVE DECLARATION pursuant to applicable standards, and (b) have been avoided or mitigated pursuant to that earlier EIR or NEGATIVE DECLARATION, including revisions or mitigation measures that are imposed upon the proposed project, nothing further is required.

_____   _____
Signature   Date

EVALUATION OF ENVIRONMENTAL IMPACTS:

1) A brief explanation is required for all answers except "No Impact" answers that are adequately supported by the information sources a lead agency cites in the parentheses following each question. A "No Impact" answer is adequately supported if the referenced information sources show that the impact simply does not apply to projects like the one involved (e.g., the project falls outside a fault rupture zone). A "No Impact" answer should be explained where it is based on project-specific factors as well as general standards (e.g., the project will not expose sensitive receptors to pollutants, based on a project-specific screening analysis).

2) All answers must take account of the whole action involved, including off-site as well as on-site, cumulative as well as project-level, indirect as well as direct, and construction as well as operational impacts.

3) Once the lead agency has determined that a particular physical impact may occur, then the checklist answers must indicate whether the impact is potentially significant, less than significant with mitigation, or less than significant. "Potentially Significant Impact" is appropriate if there is substantial evidence that an effect may be significant. If there are one or more "Potentially Significant Impact" entries when the determination is made, an EIR is required.

4) "Negative Declaration: Less Than Significant With Mitigation Incorporated" applies where the incorporation of mitigation measures has reduced an effect from "Potentially Significant Impact" to a "Less Than Significant Impact." The lead agency must describe the mitigation measures, and briefly explain how they reduce the effect to a less than significant level (mitigation measures from "Earlier Analyses," as described in (5) below, may be cross-referenced).

5) Earlier analyses may be used where, pursuant to the tiering, program EIR, or other CEQA process, an effect has been adequately analyzed in an earlier EIR or negative declaration. Section 15063(c)(3)(D). In this case, a brief discussion should identify the following:

    a) Earlier Analysis Used. Identify and state where they are available for review.

    b) Impacts Adequately Addressed. Identify which effects from the above checklist were within the scope of and adequately analyzed in an earlier document pursuant to applicable legal standards, and state whether such effects were addressed by mitigation measures based on the earlier analysis.

    c) Mitigation Measures. For effects that are "Less than Significant with Mitigation Measures Incorporated," describe the mitigation measures which were incorporated or refined from the earlier document and the extent to which they address site-specific conditions for the project.

6) Lead agencies are encouraged to incorporate into the checklist references to information sources for potential impacts (e.g., general plans, zoning ordinances). Reference to a previously prepared or outside document should, where appropriate, include a reference to the page or pages where the statement is substantiated.

7) Supporting Information Sources: A source list should be attached, and other sources used or individuals contacted should be cited in the discussion.

8) This is only a suggested form, and lead agencies are free to use different formats; however, lead agencies should normally address the questions from this checklist that are relevant to a project's environmental effects in whatever format is selected.

9) The explanation of each issue should identify:
   a) the significance criteria or threshold, if any, used to evaluate each question; and
   b) the mitigation measure identified, if any, to reduce the impact to less than significance

SAMPLE QUESTIONS

Issues:

	Potentially Significant Impact	Less Than Significant with Mitigation Incorporated	Less Than Significant Impact	No Impact
I. AESTHETICS. Except as provided in Public Resources Code Section 21099, would the project;				
a) Have a substantial adverse effect on a scenic vista?	☐	☐	☐	☐
b) Substantially damage scenic resources, including, but not limited to, trees, rock outcroppings, and historic buildings within a state scenic highway?	☐	☐	☐	☐
c) In non-urbanized areas, substantially degrade the existing visual character or quality of public views of the site and its surroundings? (Public views are those that are experienced from publicly accessible vantage point.) If the project is in an urbanized area, would the project conflict with applicable zoning and other regulations governing scenic quality?	☐	☐	☐	☐
d) Create a new source of substantial light or glare which would adversely affect day or nighttime views in the area?	☐	☐	☐	☐

II. AGRICULTURE AND FORESTRY RESOURCES. In determining whether impacts to agricultural resources are significant environmental effects, lead agencies may refer to the California Agricultural Land Evaluation and Site Assessment Model (1997) prepared by the California Dept. of Conservation as an optional model to use in assessing impacts on agriculture and farmland. In determining whether impacts to forest resources, including timberland, are significant environmental effects, lead agencies may refer to information compiled by the California Dept. of Forestry and Fire Protection regarding the state's inventory of forest land, including the Forest and Range Assessment Project and the Forest Legacy Assessment project; and forest carbon measurement methodology provided in Forest Protocols adopted by the California Air Resources Board. Would the project:

	Potentially Significant Impact	Less Than Significant with Mitigation Incorporated	Less Than Significant Impact	No Impact
a) Convert Prime Farmland, Unique Farmland, or Farmland of Statewide Importance (Farmland), as shown on the maps prepared pursuant to the Farmland Mapping and Monitoring Program of the California Resources Agency, to non-agricultural use?	☐	☐	☐	☐
b) Conflict with existing zoning for agricultural use, or a Williamson Act contract?	☐	☐	☐	☐
c) Conflict with existing zoning for, or cause rezoning of, forest land (as defined in Public Resources Code section 12220(g)), timberland (as defined by Public Resources Code section 4526), or timberland zoned Timberland Production (as defined by Government Code section 51104(g))?	☐	☐	☐	☐
d) Result in the loss of forest land or conversion of forest land to non-forest use?	☐	☐	☐	☐
e) Involve other changes in the existing environment which, due to their location or nature, could result in conversion of Farmland, to non-agricultural use or conversion of forest land to non-forest use?	☐	☐	☐	☐

III. AIR QUALITY. Where available, the significance criteria established by the applicable air quality management district or air pollution control district may be relied upon to make the following determinations. Would the project:

a) Conflict with or obstruct implementation of the applicable air quality plan?	☐	☐	☐	☐
b) Result in a cumulatively considerable net increase of any criteria pollutant for which the project region is non-attainment under an applicable federal or state ambient air quality standard?	☐	☐	☐	☐
c) Expose sensitive receptors to substantial pollutant concentrations?	☐	☐	☐	☐
d) Result in other emissions (such as those leading to odors) adversely affecting a substantial number of people?	☐	☐	☐	☐

354

	Potentially Significant Impact	Less Than Significant with Mitigation Incorporated	Less Than Significant Impact	No Impact

IV. BIOLOGICAL RESOURCES.
Would the project:

a) Have a substantial adverse effect, either directly or through habitat modifications, on any species identified as a candidate, sensitive, or special status species in local or regional plans, policies, or regulations, or by the California Department of Fish and Game or U.S. Fish and Wildlife Service? ☐ ☐ ☐ ☐

b) Have a substantial adverse effect on any riparian habitat or other sensitive natural community identified in local or regional plans, policies, regulations or by the California Department of Fish and Game or US Fish and Wildlife Service? ☐ ☐ ☐ ☐

c) Have a substantial adverse effect on state or federally protected wetlands (including, but not limited to, marsh, vernal pool, coastal, etc.) through direct removal, filling, hydrological interruption, or other means? ☐ ☐ ☐ ☐

d) Interfere substantially with the movement of any native resident or migratory fish or wildlife species or with established native resident or migratory wildlife corridors, or impede the use of native wildlife nursery sites? ☐ ☐ ☐ ☐

e) Conflict with any local policies or ordinances protecting biological resources, such as a tree preservation policy or ordinance? ☐ ☐ ☐ ☐

f) Conflict with the provisions of an adopted Habitat Conservation Plan, Natural Community Conservation Plan, or other approved local, regional, or state habitat conservation plan? ☐ ☐ ☐ ☐

V. CULTURAL RESOURCES. Would the project:

a) Cause a substantial adverse change in the significance of a historical resource pursuant to § 15064.5? ☐ ☐ ☐ ☐

	Potentially Significant Impact	Less Than Significant with Mitigation Incorporated	Less Than Significant Impact	No Impact
b) Cause a substantial adverse change in the significance of an archaeological resource pursuant to § 15064.5?	☐	☐	☐	☐
c) Disturb any human remains, including those interred outside of dedicated cemeteries?	☐	☐	☐	☐

VI. Energy. Would the project:

a) Result in potentially significant environmental impact due to wasteful, inefficient, or unnecessary consumption of energy resources, during project construction or operation?	☐	☐	☐	☐
b) Conflict with or obstruct a state or local plan for renewable energy or energy efficiency?	☐	☐	☐	☐

VII. GEOLOGY AND SOILS. Would the project:

a) Directly or indirectly cause potential substantial adverse effects, including the risk of loss, injury, or death involving:	☐	☐	☐	☐
i) Rupture of a known earthquake fault, as delineated on the most recent Alquist-Priolo Earthquake Fault Zoning Map issued by the State Geologist for the area or based on other substantial evidence of a known fault? Refer to Division of Mines and Geology Special Publication 42.	☐	☐	☐	☐
ii) Strong seismic ground shaking?	☐	☐	☐	☐
iii) Seismic-related ground failure, including liquefaction?	☐	☐	☐	☐
iv) Landslides?	☐	☐	☐	☐
b) Result in substantial soil erosion or the loss of topsoil?	☐	☐	☐	☐
c) Be located on a geologic unit or soil that is unstable, or that would become unstable as a result of the project, and potentially result in on- or off-site landslide, lateral spreading, subsidence, liquefaction or collapse?	☐	☐	☐	☐

	Potentially Significant Impact	Less Than Significant with Mitigation Incorporated	Less Than Significant Impact	No Impact
d) Be located on expansive soil, as defined in Table 18-1-B of the Uniform Building Code (1994), creating substantial direct or indirect risks to life or property?	☐	☐	☐	☐
e) Have soils incapable of adequately supporting the use of septic tanks or alternative waste water disposal systems where sewers are not available for the disposal of waste water?	☐	☐	☐	☐
f) Directly or indirectly destroy a unique paleontological resource or site or unique geologic feature?	☐	☐	☐	☐

VIII. GREENHOUSE GAS EMISSIONS.
Would the project:

a) Generate greenhouse gas emissions, either directly or indirectly, that may have a significant impact on the environment?	☐	☐	☐	☐
b) Conflict with an applicable plan, policy or regulation adopted for the purpose of reducing the emissions of greenhouse gases?	☐	☐	☐	☐

IX. HAZARDS AND HAZARDOUS MATERIALS.
Would the project:

a) Create a significant hazard to the public or the environment through the routine transport, use, or disposal of hazardous materials?	☐	☐	☐	☐
b) Create a significant hazard to the public or the environment through reasonably foreseeable upset and accident conditions involving the release of hazardous materials into the environment?	☐	☐	☐	☐
c) Emit hazardous emissions or handle hazardous or acutely hazardous materials, substances, or waste within one-quarter mile of an existing or proposed school?	☐	☐	☐	☐

	Potentially Significant Impact	Less Than Significant with Mitigation Incorporated	Less Than Significant Impact	No Impact
d) Be located on a site which is included on a list of hazardous materials sites compiled pursuant to Government Code Section 65962.5 and, as a result, would it create a significant hazard to the public or the environment?	☐	☐	☐	☐
e) For a project located within an airport land use plan or, where such a plan has not been adopted, within two miles of a public airport or public use airport, would the project result in a safety hazard or excessive noise for people residing or working in the project area?	☐	☐	☐	☐
f) Impair implementation of or physically interfere with an adopted emergency response plan or emergency evacuation plan?	☐	☐	☐	☐
g) Expose people or structures, either directly or indirectly, to a significant risk of loss, injury or death involving wildland fires?	☐	☐	☐	☐

X. HYDROLOGY AND WATER QUALITY. Would the project:

	Potentially Significant Impact	Less Than Significant with Mitigation Incorporated	Less Than Significant Impact	No Impact
a) Violate any water quality standards or waste discharge requirements or otherwise substantially degrade surface or ground water quality?	☐	☐	☐	☐
b) Substantially decrease groundwater supplies or interfere substantially with groundwater recharge such that the project may impede sustainable groundwater management of the basin?	☐	☐	☐	☐
c) Substantially alter the existing drainage pattern of the site or area, including through the alteration of the course of a stream or river or through the addition of impervious surfaces, in a manner which would:	☐	☐	☐	☐
i) Result in substantial erosion or siltation on- or off-site;	☐	☐	☐	☐

	Potentially Significant Impact	Less Than Significant with Mitigation Incorporated	Less Than Significant Impact	No Impact
ii) substantially increase the rate or amount of surface runoff in a manner which would result in flooding on- or off-site;	☐	☐	☐	☐
iii) create or contribute runoff water which would exceed the capacity of existing or planned stormwater drainage systems or provide substantial additional sources of polluted runoff; or	☐	☐	☐	☐
iv) impede or redirect flood flows?	☐	☐	☐	☐
d) In flood hazard, tsunami, or seiche zones, risk release of pollutants due to project inundation?	☐	☐	☐	☐
e) Conflict with or obstruct implementation of a water quality control plan or sustainable groundwater management plan?	☐	☐	☐	☐

XI. <u>LAND USE AND PLANNING.</u> Would the project:

a) Physically divide an established community?	☐	☐	☐	☐
b) Cause a significant environmental impact due to a conflict with any land use plan, policy, or regulation adopted for the purpose of avoiding or mitigating an environmental effect?	☐	☐	☐	☐

XII. <u>MINERAL RESOURCES.</u> Would the project:

a) Result in the loss of availability of a known mineral resource that would be of value to the region and the residents of the state?	☐	☐	☐	☐
b) Result in the loss of availability of a locally-important mineral resource recovery site delineated on a local general plan, specific plan or other land use plan?	☐	☐	☐	☐

	Potentially Significant Impact	Less Than Significant with Mitigation Incorporated	Less Than Significant Impact	No Impact

XIII. <u>NOISE.</u> Would the project result in:

a) Generation of a substantial temporary or permanent increase in ambient noise levels in the vicinity of the project in excess of standards established in the local general plan or noise ordinance, or applicable standards of other agencies? ☐ ☐ ☐ ☐

b) Generation of excessive groundborne vibration or groundborne noise levels? ☐ ☐ ☐ ☐

c) For a project located within the vicinity of a private airstrip or an airport land use plan or, where such a plan has not been adopted, within two miles of a public airport or public use airport, would the project expose people residing or working in the project area to excessive noise levels? ☐ ☐ ☐ ☐

XIV. POPULATION AND HOUSING.
Would the project:

a) Induce substantial unplanned population growth in an area, either directly (for example, by proposing new homes and businesses) or indirectly (for example, through extension of roads or other infrastructure)? ☐ ☐ ☐ ☐

b) Displace substantial numbers of existing people or housing, necessitating the construction of replacement housing elsewhere? ☐ ☐ ☐ ☐

360

	Potentially Significant Impact	Less Than Significant with Mitigation Incorporated	Less Than Significant Impact	No Impact

XV. PUBLIC SERVICES.

a) Would the project result in substantial adverse physical impacts associated with the provision of new or physically altered governmental facilities, need for new or physically altered governmental facilities, the construction of which could cause significant environmental impacts, in order to maintain acceptable service ratios, response times or other performance objectives for any of the public services:

	☐	☐	☐	☐

Fire protection?	☐	☐	☐	☐
Police protection?	☐	☐	☐	☐
Schools?	☐	☐	☐	☐
Parks?	☐	☐	☐	☐
Other public facilities?	☐	☐	☐	☐

XVI. RECREATION.

a) Would the project increase the use of existing neighborhood and regional parks or other recreational facilities such that substantial physical deterioration of the facility would occur or be accelerated?

	☐	☐	☐	☐

b) Does the project include recreational facilities or require the construction or expansion of recreational facilities which might have an adverse physical effect on the environment?

	☐	☐	☐	☐

361

	Potentially Significant Impact	Less Than Significant with Mitigation Incorporated	Less Than Significant Impact	No Impact

XVII. <u>TRANSPORTATION.</u>

Would the project:

a) Conflict with a program, plan, ordinance or policy addressing the circulation system, including transit, roadway, bicycle and pedestrian facilities?

☐ ☐ ☐ ☐

b) Conflict or be inconsistent with CEQA Guidelines section 15064.3, subdivision (b)?

☐ ☐ ☐ ☐

c) Substantially increase hazards due to a geometric design feature (e.g., sharp curves or dangerous intersections) or incompatible uses (e.g., farm equipment)?

☐ ☐ ☐ ☐

d) Result in inadequate emergency access?

☐ ☐ ☐ ☐

XVIII. <u>TRIBAL CULTURAL RESOURCES.</u>

a) Would the project cause a substantial adverse change in the significance of a tribal cultural resource, defined in Public Resources Code section 21074 as either a site, feature, place, cultural landscape that is geographically defined in terms of the size and scope of the landscape, sacred place, or object with cultural value to a California Native American tribe, and that is:

☐ ☐ ☐ ☐

i) Listed or eligible for listing in the California Register of Historical Resources, or in a local register of historical resources as defined in Public Resources Code section 5020.1(k), or

☐ ☐ ☐ ☐

ii) A resource determined by the lead agency, in its discretion and supported by substantial evidence, to be significant pursuant to criteria set forth in subdivision (c) of Public Resources Code Section 5024.1. In applying the criteria set forth in subdivision (c) of Public Resources Code Section 5024.1, the lead agency shall consider the significance of the resource to a California Native American tribe.

☐ ☐ ☐ ☐

	Potentially Significant Impact	Less Than Significant with Mitigation Incorporated	Less Than Significant Impact	No Impact

XIX. <u>UTILITIES AND SERVICE SYSTEMS.</u>

Would the project:

a) Require or result in the relocation or construction of new or expanded water, wastewater treatment or storm water drainage, electric power, natural gas, or telecommunications facilities, the construction or relocation of which could cause significant environmental effects? ☐ ☐ ☐ ☐

b) Have sufficient water supplies available to serve the project and reasonably foreseeable future development during normal, dry and multiple dry years? ☐ ☐ ☐ ☐

c) Result in a determination by the wastewater treatment provider which serves or may serve the project that it has adequate capacity to serve the project's projected demand in addition to the provider's existing commitments? ☐ ☐ ☐ ☐

d) Generate solid waste in excess of State or local standards, or in excess of the capacity of local infrastructure, or otherwise impair the attainment of solid waste reduction goals? ☐ ☐ ☐ ☐

e) Comply with federal, state, and local management and reduction statutes and regulations related to solid waste? ☐ ☐ ☐ ☐

XX. <u>WILDFIRE.</u> If located in or near state responsibility areas or lands classified as very high fire hazard severity zones, would the project:

a) Substantially impair an adopted emergency response plan or emergency evacuation plan? ☐ ☐ ☐ ☐

	Potentially Significant Impact	Less Than Significant with Mitigation Incorporated	Less Than Significant Impact	No Impact

b) Due to slope, prevailing winds, and other factors, exacerbate wildfire risks, and thereby expose project occupants to, pollutant concentrations from a wildfire or the uncontrolled spread of a wildfire? ☐ ☐ ☐ ☐

c) Require the installation or maintenance of associated infrastructure (such as roads, fuel breaks, emergency water sources, power lines or other utilities) that may exacerbate fire risk or that may result in temporary or ongoing impacts to the environment? ☐ ☐ ☐ ☐

d) Expose people or structure to significant risks, including downslope or downstream flooding or landslides, as a result of runoff, post-fire slope instability, or drainage changes? ☐ ☐ ☐ ☐

XXI MANDATORY FINDINGS OF SIGNIFICANCE.

a) Does the project have the potential to substantially degrade the quality of the environment, substantially reduce the habitat of a fish or wildlife species, cause a fish or wildlife population to drop below self-sustaining levels, threaten to eliminate a plant or animal community, substantially reduce the number or restrict the range of a rare or endangered plant or animal or eliminate important examples of the major periods of California history or prehistory? ☐ ☐ ☐ ☐

b) Does the project have impacts that are individually limited, but cumulatively considerable? ("Cumulatively considerable" means that the incremental effects of a project are considerable when viewed in connection with the effects of past projects, the effects of other current projects, and the effects of probable future projects)? ☐ ☐ ☐ ☐

	Potentially Significant Impact	Less Than Significant with Mitigation Incorporated	Less Than Significant Impact	No Impact
c) Does the project have environmental effects which will cause substantial adverse effects on human beings, either directly or indirectly?	☐	☐	☐	☐

Note: Authority cited: Sections 21083 and 21083.05, Public Resources Code. Reference: Section 65088.4, Gov. Code; Sections 21080(c), 21080.1, 21080.3, 21083, 21083.05, 21083.3, 21093, 21094, 21095, and 21151, Public Resources Code; *Sundstrom v. County of Mendocino,* (1988) 202 Cal.App.3d 296; *Leonoff v. Monterey Board of Supervisors,* (1990) 222

Cal.App.3d 1337; *Eureka Citizens for Responsible Govt. v. City of Eureka* (2007) 147 Cal.App.4th 357; *Protect the Historic Amador Waterways v. Amador Water Agency* (2004) 116 Cal.App.4th at 1109; *San Franciscans Upholding the Downtown Plan v. City and County of San Francisco* (2002) 102 Cal.App.4th 656.

Authority: Public Resources Code sections 21083 and 21083.09
Reference: Public Resources Code sections 21073, 21074, 21080.3.1, 21080.3.2,
21082.3/ 21084.2 and 21084.3

Revised December 28, 2018

Appendix H

ENVIRONMENTAL INFORMATION FORM

(To be Completed by Applicant)

Date Filed _____

General Information

1. Name and address of developer or project sponsor: _____

2. Address of project: _____

   Assessor's Block and Lot Number: _____

3. Name, address, and telephone number of person to be contacted concerning this project:

   _____

   _____

4. Indicate number of the permit application for the project to which this form pertains: _____

5. List and describe any other related permits and other public approvals required for this project, including those required by city, regional, state and federal agencies:

   _____

6. Existing zoning district:: _____

7. Proposed use of site (Project for which this form is filed): _____

   _____

Project Description

8. Site size.
9. Square footage.
10. Number of floors of construction.
11. Amount of off-street parking provided.
12. Attach plans.
13. Proposed scheduling.
14. Associated projects.
15. Anticipated incremental development.
16. If residential, include the number of units, schedule of unit sizes, range of sale prices or rents, and type of household size expected.
17. If commercial, indicate the type, whether neighborhood, city or regionally oriented, square footage of sales area, and loading facilities.
18. If industrial, indicate type, estimated employment per shift, and loading facilities.

19. If institutional, indicate the major function, estimated employment per shift, estimated occupancy, loading facilities, and community benefits to be derived from the project.

20. If the project involves a variance, conditional use or rezoning application, state this and indicate clearly why the application is required.

Are the following items applicable to the project or its effects? Discuss below all items checked yes (attach additional sheets as necessary).

	Yes	No
21. Change in existing features of any bays, tidelands, beaches, or hills, or substantial alteration of ground contours.	☐	☐
22. Change in scenic views or vistas from existing residential areas or public lands or roads.	☐	☐
23. Change in pattern, scale or character of general area of project.	☐	☐
24. Significant amounts of solid waste or litter.	☐	☐
25. Change in dust, ash, smoke, fumes or odors in vicinity.	☐	☐
26. Change in ocean, bay, lake, stream or ground water quality or quantity, or alteration of existing drainage patterns.	☐	☐
27. Substantial change in existing noise or vibration levels in the vicinity.	☐	☐
28. Site on filled land or on slope of 10 percent or more.	☐	☐
29. Use of disposal of potentially hazardous materials, such as toxic substances, flammables or explosives.	☐	☐
30. Substantial change in demand for municipal services (police, fire, water, sewage, etc.).	☐	☐
31. Substantially increase fossil fuel consumption (electricity, oil, natural gas, etc.).	☐	☐
32. Relationship to a larger project or series of projects.	☐	☐

Environmental Setting

33. Describe the project site as it exists before the project, including information on topography, soil stability, plants and animals, and any cultural, historical or scenic aspects. Describe any existing structures on the site, and the use of the structures. Attach photographs of the site. Snapshots or polaroid photos will be accepted.

34. Describe the surrounding properties, including information on plant~ and animals and any cultural, historical or scenic aspects. Indicate the type of land use (residential, commercial, etc.), intensity of land use (one-family, apartment houses, shops, department stores, etc.), and scale of development (height, frontage, set-back, rear yard, etc.). Attach photographs of the vicinity. Snapshots or polaroid photos will be accepted.

Certification

I hereby certify that the statements furnished above and in the attached exhibits present the data and information required for this initial evaluation to the best of my ability, and that the facts, statements, and in formation presented are true and correct to the best of my knowledge and belief.

Date _____   Signature _____

For   _____

Appendix I
NOTICE OF PREPARATION

To: _____   From: _____

_____   _____
(Address)   (Address)

_____   _____

Subject: **Notice of Preparation of a Draft Environmental Impact Report**

_____ will be the Lead Agency and will prepare an environmental impact report for the project identified below. We need to know the views of your agency as to the scope and content of the environmental information which is germane to your agency's statutory responsibilities in connection with the proposed project. Your agency will need to use the EIR prepared by our agency when considering your permit or other approval for the project.

The project description, location, and the potential environmental effects are contained in the attached materials. A copy of the Initial Study (☐ is ☐ is not) attached.

Due to the time limits mandated by State law, your response must be sent at the earliest possible date but not later than 30 days after receipt of this notice.

Please send your response to _____ at the address shown above. We will need the name for a contact person in your **agency**.

Project Title: _____

Project Applicant, if any: _____

Date _____   Signature _____

Title _____

Telephone _____

.

Reference: California Code of Regulations, Title 14, (CEQA Guidelines) Sections 15082(a), 15103, 15375.

APPENDIX J
Examples of Tiering EIR's

| FIRST TIER EIR (15152) | • project encompasses separate but related projects such as general plan, zoning, development |
| | • later tiers move from general to specific analysis of projects |

Later Project EIR	• later project is consistent with general plan or zoning
	• initial study must examine significant effects not covered in prior EIR
	• later EIR must state lead agency is using tiering concept and must comply with section 15152

| STAGED EIR (15167) | • one large project will require a number of discretionary approvals from govt. agencies and one of those approvals will occur more than two years before construction commences |

| Supplement to the Staged EIR | • supplements to the staged EIR are prepared for later government agency approvals on the same overall project if information available at the time of that later approval would permit consideration of additional environmental impacts, mitigation measures or reasonable alternatives |

PROGRAM EIR (15168)	• series of actions or activities that can be characterized as one large project and are related either:
	• geographically
	• as logical parts of a chain of activities
	• in connection with rules, regulations, plans or other general criteria governing a continuing program
	• as individual activities carried out under common authority (statutory or regulatory) and having similar environmental effects which can be mitigated in similar ways

Revised 1998

369

| Subsequent Project EIR | • | only if subsequent activity has effects not examined in the previously certified program EIR will additional environmental documentation be required (if subsequent activity has no new effects, that activity is covered by the program EIR) |

| MASTER EIR (15175) | • | alternative to project, staged, or program EIR |

- • can be used for:
  - general plan (or gen. plan element, amendment, or update)
  - redevelopment plan projects (public or private)
  - project consisting of phases of smaller individual projects
  - other activities described in 15175
- • after five years from initial certification, adopting authority must review the Master EIR and prepare subsequent or supplemental EIR if substantial changes have occurred with respect to circumstances under which the original Master EIR was adopted
- • no new EIR is required for subsequent projects within the scope of the Master EIR which cause no additional significant effect

| Focused EIR (15177) | • | a subsequent, Focused EIR is required only where: |

- substantial new/additional information shows adverse environmental effects not examined in Master EIR or more significant than described in EIR, or
- substantial new/additional information shows mitigation measures previously determined to be infeasible are now feasible and will avoid/reduce the significant effects to a level of insignificance

---

SPECIAL SITUATIONS / EIRs

Multiple-family residential development / residential and commercial or retail mixed-use development (PRC 21158.5 and Guideline §15179.5)
- project is multiple-family residential development up to 100 units or is a residential and commercial or retail mixed-use development of not more than 100,000 square feet
- if project complies with procedures in section 21158.5, only a focused EIR need be prepared, notwithstanding the fact that the project wasn't identified in the Master EIR

Redevelopment Project (15180)
- all public and private activities or undertakings in furtherance of a redevelopment plan (public or private) constitute a single project
- the redevelopment plan EIR is treated as a program EIR

Revised 1998

- no subsequent EIR is required for individual components of the redevelopment plan unless substantial changes or substantial new information triggers a subsequent EIR or supplement to an EIR pursuant to (sections 15162 or 15163)

Housing/neighborhood commercial facilities (15181)
- a project involving construction of housing or neighborhood commercial facilities in an urbanized area
- a prior EIR for a specific plan, local coastal program, or port master plan may be used as the EIR for such a project (no new EIR need be prepared) provided section 15181 procedures are complied with

Projects Consistent with Community Plan, General Plan, or Zoning (15183)
- a project which is consistent with a community plan adopted as part of a general plan or zoning ordinance or a general plan of a local agency <u>and</u> where there was an EIR certified for the zoning action or master plan
- the EIR for the residential project need only examine certain significant environmental effects, as outlined in section 15183

Regulations on Pollution Control Equipment (PRC section 21159)
- section 21159 requires environmental analysis of reasonably foreseeable methods of compliance at the time of adoption of rule or regulation requiring the installation of pollution control equipment
- an EIR prepared at the time of adoption of the rule or regulation is deemed to satisfy the requirement of section 21159

Installation of Pollution Control Equipment (PRC section 21159.1)
- a focused EIR is permitted where project 1) consists solely of installation of pollution control equipment; 2) is required by rule or regulation adopted by the State Air Resources Board, an air pollution control district or air quality management district, the State Water Resources Control Board, a California regional water quality control board, the Dept. of Toxic Substances Control, or the California Integrated Waste Management Board; and 3) meets the procedural requirements outlined in section 21159.1

Revised 1998

Appendix K

Criteria for Shortened Clearinghouse Review

Under exceptional circumstances, and when requested in writing by the lead agency, the State Clearinghouse in the Office of Planning and Research (OPR) may shorten the usual review periods for proposed negative declarations, mitigated negative declarations and draft EIRs submitted to the Clearinghouse. A request must be made by the decision-making body of the lead agency, or by a properly authorized representative of the decision-making body.

A shortened review period may be granted when any of the following circumstances exist:

(1) The lead agency is operating under an extension of the one-year period for completion of an EIR and would not otherwise be able to complete the EIR within the extended period.

(2) The public project applicant is under severe time constraints with regard to obtaining financing or exercising options which cannot be met without shortening the review period.

(3) The document is a supplement to a draft EIR or proposed negative declaration or mitigated negative declaration previously submitted to the State Clearinghouse.

(4) The health and safety of the community would be at risk unless the project is approved expeditiously.

(5) The document is a revised draft EIR, or proposed negative declaration or mitigated negative declaration, where changes in the document are primarily the result of comments from agencies and the public.

Shortened review cannot be provided to a draft EIR or proposed negative declaration or mitigated negative declaration which has already begun the usual review process. Prior to requesting shortened review, the lead agency should have already issued a notice of preparation and received comments from applicable State agencies, in the case of an EIR, or consulted with applicable State agencies, in the case of a proposed negative declaration or mitigated negative declaration.

No shortened review period shall be granted unless the lead agency has contacted and obtained prior approval for a shortened review from the applicable state responsible and trustee agencies. No shortened review shall be granted for any project which is of statewide, regional, or area wide significance, as defined in Section 15206 of the guidelines.

Notice of Completion of Draft EIR   *Appendix L*

Project Title

Project Location – Specific

Project Location – City   Project
Location – County

Description of Nature, Purpose, and Beneficiaries of Project

Lead Agency   Division

Address Where Copy of EIR is Available

Review Period

Contact Person   Area Code   Phone
Extension

Authority cited: Section 21083, Public Resources Code. Reference: Sections 21092, 21152, and 21153, Public Resources Code.
Revised 2005

Appendix M: Performance Standards for Infill Projects Eligible for Streamlined Review

I. Introduction

Section 15183.3 provides a streamlined review process for infill projects that satisfy specified performance standards. This appendix contains those performance standards. The lead agency's determination that the project satisfies the performance standards shall be supported with substantial evidence, which should be documented on the Infill Checklist in Appendix N. Section II defines terms used in this Appendix. Performance standards that apply to all project types are set forth in Section III. Section IV contains performance standards that apply to particular project types (i.e., residential, commercial/retail, office building, transit stations, and schools).

II. Definitions

The following definitions apply to the terms used in this Appendix.

"High-quality transit corridor" means an existing corridor with fixed route bus service with service intervals no longer than 15 minutes during peak commute hours. For the purposes of this Appendix, an "existing stop along a high-quality transit corridor" may include a planned and funded stop that is included in an adopted regional transportation improvement program.

Unless more specifically defined by an air district, city or county, "high-volume roadway" means freeways, highways, urban roads with 100,000 vehicles per day, or rural roads with 50,000 vehicles per day.

"Low vehicle travel area" means a traffic analysis zone that exhibits a below average existing level of travel as determined using a regional travel demand model. For residential projects, travel refers to either home-based or household vehicle miles traveled per capita. For commercial and retail projects, travel refers to non-work attraction trip length; however, where such data are not available, commercial projects reference either home-based or household vehicle miles traveled per capita. For office projects, travel refers to commute attraction vehicle miles traveled per employee; however, where such data are not available, office projects reference either home-based or household vehicle miles traveled per capita.

"Major Transit Stop" means a site containing an existing rail transit station, a ferry terminal served by either a bus or rail transit service, or the intersection of two or more major bus routes with frequencies of service intervals of 15 minutes or less during the morning and afternoon peak commute periods. For the purposes of this Appendix, an "existing major transit stop" may include a planned and funded stop that is included in an adopted regional transportation improvement program.

"Office building" generally refers to centers for governmental or professional services; however, the lead agency shall have discretion in determining whether a project is "commercial" or "office building" for the purposes of this Appendix based on local zoning codes.

"Significant sources of air pollution" include airports, marine ports, rail yards and dist ibution centers that receive more than 100 heavy-duty truck visits per day, as well as stationary sources that are designated major by the Clean Air Act.

A "Traffic Analysis Zone" is an analytical unit used by a travel demand model to estimate vehicle travel within a region.

III. Performance Standards Related to Project Design

To be eligible for streamlining pursuant to Section 15183.3, a project must implement all of the following:

Renewable Energy. All non-residential projects shall include on-site renewable power generation, such as solar photovoltaic, solar thermal and wind power generation, or clean back- up power supplies, where feasible. Residential projects are also encouraged to include such on-site renewable power generation.

Soil and Water Remediation. If the project site is included on any list compiled pursuant to Section 65962.5 of the Government Code, the project shall document how it has remediated the site, if remediation is completed. Alternatively, the project shall implement the recommendations provided in a preliminary endangerment assessment or comparable document that identifies remediation appropriate for the site.

Residential Units Near High-Volume Roadways and Stationary Sources. If a project includes residential units located within 500 feet, or other distance determined to be appropriate by the local agency or air district based on local conditions, of a high volume roadway or other significant sources of air pollution, the project shall comply with any policies and standards identified in the local general plan, specific plan, zoning code or community risk reduction plan for the protection of public health from such sources of air pollution. If the local government has not adopted such plans or policies, the project shall include measures, such as enhanced air filtration and project design, that the lead agency finds, based on substantial evidence, will promote the protection of public health from sources of air pollution. Those measure may include, among others, the recommendations of the California Air Resources Board, air districts, and the California Air Pollution Control Officers Association.

IV. Additional Performance Standards by Project Type

In addition to the project features described above in Section III, specific eligibility requirements are provided below by project type.

Several of the performance standards below refer to "low vehicle travel areas". Such areas can be illustrated on maps based on data developed by the regional Metropolitan Planning Organization (MPO) using its regional travel demand model.

Several of the performance standards below refer to distance to transit. Distance should be calculated so that at least 75 percent of the surface area of the project site is within the specified distance.

A. Residential

To be eligible for streamlining pursuant to Section 15183.3, a project must satisfy one of the following:

Projects achieving below average regional per capita vehicle miles traveled (VMT). A residential project is eligible if it is located in a "low vehicle travel area" within the region. ·

Projects located within 1/2 mile of an Existing Major Transit Stop or High Quality Transit Corridor. A residential project is eligible if it is located within 1/2 mile of an existing major transit stop or an existing stop along a high quality transit corridor.

Low-Income Housing. A residential or mixed-use project consisting of 300 or fewer residential units all of which are affordable to low income households is eligible if the developer of the development project provides sufficient legal commitments to the lead agency to ensure the continued availability and use of the housing units for lower income households, as defined in Section 50079.5 of the Health and Safety Code, for a period of at least 30 years, at monthly housing costs, as determined pursuant to Section 50053 of the Health and Safety Code.

B. Commercial/Retail

To be eligible for streamlining pursuant to Section 15183.3, a project must satisfy one of the following:

Regional Location. A commercial project with no single-building floor-plate greater than 50,000 square feet is eligible if it locates in a "low vehicle travel area."

Proximity to Households. A project with no single-building floor-plate greater than 50,000 square feet located within one-half mile of 1800 households is eligible.

C. Office Building

To be eligible for streamlining pursuant to Section 15183.3, a project must satisfy one of the following:

Regional Location. Office buildings, both commercial and public, are eligible if they. locate in a low vehicle travel area.

Proximity to a Major Transit Stop. Office buildings, both commercial and public, within1/2 mile of an existing major transit stop, or 1/2 mile of an existing stop along a high quality transit corridor, are eligible.

D. Transit

Transit stations, as defined in Section 15183.3(e)(1), are eligible.

E. Schools

Elementary schools within one mile of fifty percent of the projected student population are eligible. Middle schools and high schools within two miles of fifty percent of the projected student population are eligible. Alternatively, any school within 1/2 mile of an existing major transit stop or an existing stop along a high quality transit corridor is eligible.

Additionally, in order to be eligible, all schools shall provide parking and storage for bicycles and scooters and shall comply with the requirements in Sections 17213, 17213.1 and 17213.2 of the California Education Code.

F. Small Walkable Community Projects

Small walkable community projects, as defined in Section 15183.3, subdivision (e)(6), that implement the project features described in Section III above are eligible.

G. Mixed-Use Projects

Where a project includes some combination of residential, commercial and retail, office building, transit station, and/or schools, the performance standards in this Section that apply to the predominant use shall govern the entire project.

Authority: Public Resources Code 21083, 21094.5.5

Reference: Public Resources Code Sections 21094.5 and 21094.5.5
Revised December 28, 2018

CEQA APPENDIX N:
INFILL ENVIRONMENTAL CHECKLIST FORM

NOTE: This sample form is intended to assist lead agencies in assessing infill projects according to the procedures provided in Section 21094.5 of the Public Resources Code. Lead agencies may customize this form as appropriate, provided that the content satisfies the requirements in Section 15183.3 of the CEQA Guidelines.

1. Project title: _____

2. Lead agency name and address:

   _____
   _____

3. Contact person and phone number: _____

4. Project location: _____

5. Project sponsor's name and address:

   _____
   _____

6. General plan designation: _____ 7. Zoning: _____

8. Prior Environmental Document(s) Analyzing the Effects of the Infill Project (including State Clearinghouse Number if assigned): _____

9. Location of Prior Environmental Document(s) Analyzing the Effects of the Infill Project:

   _____
   _____

10. Description of project: (Describe the whole action involved, including but not limited to later phases of the project, and any secondary, support, or off-site features necessary for its implementation. Attach additional sheets if necessary.)

    _____
    _____
    _____

11. Surrounding land uses and setting: Briefly describe the project's surroundings, including any prior uses of the project site, or, if vacant, describe the urban uses that exist on at least 75% of the project's perimeter:

    _____
    _____
    _____

12. Other public agencies whose approval is required (e.g., permits, financing approval, or participation agreement.)

    _____
    _____
    _____

13. Have California Native American tribes traditionally and culturally affiliated with the project area requested consultation pursuant to Public Resources Code section 21080.3.1? If so, is there a plan for consultation that includes, for example, the determination of significance of impacts to tribal cultural resources, procedures regarding confidentiality, etc.?

    _____
    _____
    _____

Note: Conducting consultation early in the CEQA process allows tribal governments, lead agencies, and project proponents to discuss the level of environmental review, identify and address potential adverse impacts to tribal cultural resources, and reduce the potential for delay and conflict in the environmental review process. (See Public Resources Code section 21083.3.2.) Information may also be available from the California Native American Heritage Commission's Sacred Lands File per Public Resources Code section 5097.96 and the California Historical Resources Information System administered by the California Office of Historic Preservation. Please also note that Public Resources Code section 21082.3(c) contains provisions specific to confidentiality.

SATISFACTION OF APPENDIX M PERFORMANCE STANDARDS

Provide the information demonstrating that the infill project satisfies the performance standards in Appendix M below. For mixed-use projects, the predominant use will determine which performance standards apply to the entire project.

1. Does the non-residential infill project include a renewable energy feature? If so, describe below. If not, explain below why it is not feasible to do so. _____

_____

2. If the project site is included on any list compiled pursuant to Section 65962.3 of the Government Code, either provide documentation of remediation or describe the recommendations provided in a preliminary endangerment assessment or comparable document that will be implemented as part of the project.

_____

3. If the infill project includes residential units located within 500 feet, or such distance that the local agency or local air district has determined is appropriate based on local conditions, a high volume roadway or other significant source of air pollution, as defined in Appendix M, describe the measures that the project will implement to protect public health. Such measures may include policies and standards identified in the local general plan, specific plans, zoning code or community risk reduction plan, or measures recommended in a health risk assessment, to promote the protection of public health. Identify the policies or standards, or refer to the site specific analysis, below. (Attach additional sheets if necessary).

_____

4. For **residential** projects, the project satisfies which of the following?

☐ Located within a low vehicle travel area, as defined in Appendix M. (Attach VMT map.)

☐ Located within 1/2 mile of an existing major transit stop or an existing stop along a high quality transit corridor. (Attach map illustrating proximity to transit.)

☐ Consists of 300 or fewer units that are each affordable to low income households. (Attach evidence of legal commitment to ensure the continued availability and use of the housing units for lower income households, as defined in Section 50079.5 of the Health and Safety Code, for a period of as least 30 years, at monthly housing costs, as determined pursuant to Section 50053 of the Health and Safety Code.

5. For **commercial** projects with a single building floor-plate below 50,000 square feet, the project satisfies which of the following?

☐ Located within a low vehicle travel area, as defined in Appendix M. (Attach VMT map.)

☐ The project is within one-half mile of 1800 dwelling units. (Attach map illustrating proximity to households.)

6. For **office building** projects, the project satisfies which of the following?

☐ Located within a low vehicle travel area, as defined in Appendix M. (Attach VMT map.)

☐ Located within ½ mile of an existing major transit stop or within ¼ of a stop along a high quality transit corridor. (Attach map illustrating proximity to transit.)

7. For **school** projects, the project does all of the following:

☐ The project complies with the requirements in Sections 17213, 17213.1 and 17213.2 of the California Education Code.

☐ The project is an elementary school and is within one mile of 50% of the student population, or is a middle school or high school and is within two miles of 50% of the student population. Alternatively, the school is within ½ mile of an existing major transit stop or an existing stop along a high quality transit corridor. (Attach map and methodology.)

☐ The project provides parking and storage for bicycles and scooters.

8. For **small walkable community projects**, the project must be a residential project that has a density of at least eight units to the acre or a commercial project with a floor area ratio of at least 0.5, or both.

ENVIRONMENTAL FACTORS POTENTIALLY AFFECTED:

The infill project could potentially result in one or more of the following environmental effects.

☐ Aesthetics	☐ Agriculture and Forestry Resources	☐ Air Quality
☐ Biological Resources	☐ Cultural Resources	☐ Energy
☐ Geology / Soils	☐ Greenhouse Gas Emissions	☐ Hazards & Hazardous Materials
☐ Hydrology / Water Quality	☐ Land Use / Planning	☐ Mineral Resources
☐ Noise	☐ Population / Housing	☐ Public Services
☐ Recreation	☐ Transportation	☐ Tribal Cultural Resources
☐ Utilities / Service Systems	☐ Wildfire	☐ Mandatory Findings of Significance

DETERMINATION: (To be completed by the Lead Agency) On the basis of this initial evaluation:

☐ I find that the proposed infill project WOULD NOT have any significant effects on the environment that either have not already been analyzed in a prior EIR or that are more significant than previously analyzed, or that uniformly applicable development policies would not substantially mitigate. Pursuant to Public Resources Code Section 21094.5, CEQA does not apply to such effects. A Notice of Determination (Section 15094) will be filed.

☐ I find that the proposed infill project will have effects that either have not been analyzed in a prior EIR, or are more significant than described in the prior EIR, and that no uniformly applicable development policies would substantially mitigate such effects. With respect to those effects that are subject to CEQA, I find that such effects WOULD NOT be significant and a NEGATIVE DECLARATION, or if the project is a Transit Priority Project a SUSTAINABLE COMMUNITIES ENVIRONMENTAL ASSESSMENT, will be prepared.

☐ I find that the proposed infill project will have effects that either have not been analyzed in a prior EIR, or are more significant than described in the prior EIR, and that no uniformly applicable development policies would substantially mitigate such effects. I find that although those effects could be significant, there will not be a significant effect in this case because revisions in the infill project have been made by or agreed to by the project proponent. A MITIGATED NEGATIVE DECLARATION, or if the project is a Transit Priority Project a SUSTAINABLE COMMUNITIES ENVIRONMENTAL ASSESSMENT, will be prepared.

☐ I find that the proposed infill project would have effects that either have not been analyzed in a prior EIR, or are more significant than described in the prior EIR, and that no uniformly applicable development policies would substantially mitigate such effects. I find that those effects WOULD be significant, and an infill ENVIRONMENTAL IMPACT REPORT is required to analyze those effects that are subject to CEQA.

_____   _____

_____   _____

Signature   Date

EVALUATION OF THE ENVIRONMENTAL IMPACTS OF INFILL PROJECTS:

1) A brief explanation is required for all answers except "No Impact" answers that are adequately supported by the information sources a lead agency cites in the parentheses following each question. A "No Impact" answer is adequately supported if the referenced information sources show that the impact simply does not apply to projects like the one involved (e.g., the project falls outside a fault rupture zone). A "No Impact" answer should be explained where it is based on project-specific factors as well as general standards (e.g., the project will not expose sensitive receptors to pollutants, based on a project-specific screening analysis).

2) All answers must take account of the whole action involved, including off-site as well as on-site, cumulative as well as project-level, indirect as well as direct, and construction as well as operational impacts.

3) For the purposes of this checklist, "prior EIR" means the environmental impact report certified for a planning level decision, as supplemented by any subsequent or supplemental environmental impact reports, negative declarations, or addenda to those documents. "Planning level decision" means the enactment or amendment of a general plan, community plan, specific plan, or zoning code. (Section 15183.3(e).)

381

4) Once the lead agency has determined that a particular physical impact may occur as a result of an infill project, then the checklist answers must indicate whether that impact has already been analyzed in a prior EIR. If the effect of the infill project is not more significant than what has already been analyzed, that effect of the infill project is not subject to CEQA. The brief explanation accompanying this determination should include page and section references to the portions of the prior EIR containing the analysis of that effect. The brief explanation shall also indicate whether the prior EIR included any mitigation measures to substantially lessen that effect and whether those measures have been incorporated into the infill project.

5) If the infill project would cause a significant adverse effect that either is specific to the project or project site and was not analyzed in a prior EIR, or is more significant than what was analyzed in a prior EIR, the lead agency must determine whether uniformly applicable development policies or standards that have been adopted by the lead agency, or city or county, would substantially mitigate that effect. If so, the checklist shall explain how the infill project's implementation of the uniformly applicable development policies will substantially mitigate that effect. That effect of the infill project is not subject to CEQA if the lead agency makes a finding, based upon substantial evidence, that the development policies or standards will substantially mitigate that effect.

6) If all effects of an infill project were either analyzed in a prior EIR or are substantially mitigated by uniformly applicable development policies or standards, CEQA does not apply to the project, and the lead agency shall file a Notice of Determination.

7) Effects of an infill project that either have not been analyzed in a prior EIR, or that uniformly applicable development policies or standards do not substantially mitigate, are subject to CEQA. With respect to those effects of the infill project that are subject to CEQA, the checklist shall indicate whether those effects are significant, less than significant with mitigation, or less than significant. If there are one or more " Significant Impact" entries when the determination is made, an infill EIR is required. The infill EIR should be limited to analysis of those effects determined to be significant. (Sections 15128, 15183.3(d).)

8) "Less Than Significant With Mitigation Incorporated" applies where the incorporation of mitigation measures will reduce an effect of an infill project that is subject to CEQA from " Significant Impact" to a "Less Than Significant Impact." The lead agency must describe the mitigation measures, and briefly explain how those measures reduce the effect to a less than significant level. If the effects of an infill project that are subject to CEQA are less than significant with mitigation incorporated, the lead agency may prepare a Mitigated Negative Declaration. If all of the effects of the infill project that are subject to CEQA are less than significant, the lead agency may prepare a Negative Declaration.

9) This is only a suggested form, and lead agencies are free to use different formats; however, lead agencies should normally address the questions from this checklist that are relevant to an infill project's environmental effects in whatever format is selected.

10) The explanation of each issue should identify:

a) the significance criteria or threshold, if any, used to evaluate each question; and

b) the mitigation measure identified, if any, to reduce the impact to less than significance.

SAMPLE QUESTION

Issues:

	Significant Impact	Less Than Significant or Less than Significant with Mitigation Incorporated	No Impact	Analyzed in the Prior EIR	Substantially Mitigated by Uniformly Applicable Development Policies
I. AESTHETICS. Would the project:					
a) Have a substantial adverse effect on a scenic vista?	☐	☐	☐	☐	☐
b) Substantially damage scenic resources, including, but not limited to, trees, rock outcroppings, and historic buildings within a state scenic highway?	☐	☐	☐	☐	☐
c) In non-urbanized area, substantially degrade the existing visual character or quality of the site and its surroundings? (Public views are those that are experienced from publicly accessible vantage point.) If the project is in an urbanized area, would the project conflict with applicable zoning and other regulations governing scenic quality?	☐	☐	☐	☐	☐
d) Create a new source of substantial light or glare which would adversely affect day or nighttime views in the area?	☐	☐	☐	☐	☐

II. AGRICULTURE AND FORESTRY RESOURCES. In determining whether impacts to agricultural resources are significant environmental effects, lead agencies may refer to the California Agricultural Land Evaluation and Site Assessment Model (1997) prepared by the California Dept. of Conservation as an optional model to use in assessing impacts on agriculture and farmland. In determining whether impacts to forest resources, including timberland, are significant environmental effects, lead agencies may refer to information compiled by the California Department of Forestry and Fire Protection regarding the state's inventory of forest land, including the Forest and Range Assessment Project and the Forest Assessment project; and forest carbon measurement methodology provided in Forest Protocols adopted by the California Air Resources Board. Would the project:

	Significant Impact	Less Than Significant or Less than Significant with Mitigation Incorporated	No Impact	Analyzed in the Prior EIR	Substantially Mitigated by Uniformly Applicable Development Policies
a) Convert Prime Farmland, Unique Farmland, or Farmland of Statewide Importance (Farmland), as shown on the maps prepared pursuant to the Farmland Mapping and Monitoring Program of the California Resources Agency, to non-agricultural use?	☐	☐	☐	☐	☐
b) Conflict with existing zoning for agricultural use, or a Williamson Act contract?	☐	☐	☐	☐	☐
c) Conflict with existing zoning for, or cause rezoning of, forest land (as defined in Public Resources Code section 12220(g)), timberland (as defined by Public Resources Code section 4526), or timberland zoned Timberland Production (as defined by Government Code section 51104(g))?	☐	☐	☐	☐	☐
d) Result in the loss of forest land or conversion of forest land to non-forest use?	☐	☐	☐	☐	☐
e) Involve other changes in the existing environment which, due to their location or nature, could result in conversion of Farmland, to non-agricultural use or conversion of forest land to non-forest use?	☐	☐	☐	☐	☐

III. AIR QUALITY. Where available, the significance criteria established by the applicable air quality management district or air pollution control district may be relied upon to make the following determinations. Would the project:

	Significant Impact	Less Than Significant or Less than Significant with Mitigation Incorporated	No Impact	Analyzed in the Prior EIR	Substantially Mitigated by Uniformly Applicable Development Policies
a) Conflict with or obstruct implementation of the applicable air quality plan?	☐	☐	☐	☐	☐
b) Result in a cumulatively considerable net increase of any criteria pollutant for which the project region is non-attainment under an applicable federal or state ambient air quality standard?	☐	☐	☐	☐	☐
c) Expose sensitive receptors to substantial pollutant concentrations?	☐	☐	☐	☐	☐

	Significant Impact	Less Than Significant or Less than Significant with Mitigation Incorporated	No Impact	Analyzed in the Prior EIR	Substantially Mitigated by Uniformly Applicable Development Policies
e) Result in other emissions (such as those leading to odors) adversely affecting a substantial number of people?	☐	☐	☐	☐	☐

IV. BIOLOGICAL RESOURCES.

Would the project:

	Significant Impact	Less Than Significant or Less than Significant with Mitigation Incorporated	No Impact	Analyzed in the Prior EIR	Substantially Mitigated by Uniformly Applicable Development Policies
a) Have a substantial adverse effect, either directly or through habitat modifications, on any species identified as a candidate, sensitive, or special status species in local or regional plans, policies, or regulations, or by the California Department of Fish and Game or U.S. Fish and Wildlife Service?	☐	☐	☐	☐	☐
b) Have a substantial adverse effect on any riparian habitat or other sensitive natural community identified in local or regional plans, policies, regulations or by the California Department of Fish and Game or US Fish and Wildlife Service?	☐	☐	☐	☐	☐
c) Have a substantial adverse effect on state or federally protected wetlands (including, but not limited to, marsh, vernal pool, coastal, etc.) through direct removal, filling, hydrological interruption, or other means?	☐	☐	☐	☐	☐
d) Interfere substantially with the movement of any native resident or migratory fish or wildlife species or with established native resident or migratory wildlife corridors, or impede the use of native wildlife nursery sites?	☐	☐	☐	☐	☐
e) Conflict with any local policies or ordinances protecting biological resources, such as a tree preservation policy or ordinance?	☐	☐	☐	☐	☐
f) Conflict with the provisions of an adopted Habitat Conservation Plan, Natural Community Conservation Plan, or other approved local, regional, or state habitat conservation plan?	☐	☐	☐	☐	☐

385

	Significant Impact	Less Than Significant or Less than Significant with Mitigation Incorporated	No Impact	Analyzed in the Prior EIR	Substantially Mitigated by Uniformly Applicable Development Policies

V. CULTURAL RESOURCES. Would the project:

a) Cause a substantial adverse change in the significance of a historical resource pursuant to § 15064.5?	☐	☐	☐	☐	☐
b) Cause a substantial adverse change in the significance of an archaeological resource pursuant to § 15064.5?	☐	☐	☐	☐	☐
c) Disturb any human remains, including those interred outside of formal cemeteries?	☐	☐	☐	☐	☐

VI. ENERGY. Would the project:

a) Result in potentially significant environmental impact due to wasteful, inefficient, or unnecessary consuption of energy resources, during project construction or operation?	☐	☐	☐	☐	☐
b) Conflict with or obstruct a state or local plan for renewable energy or energy efficiency?	☐	☐	☐	☐	☐

VII. GEOLOGY AND SOILS. Would the project:

a) Directly or indirectly cause potential substantial adverse effects, including the risk of loss, injury, or death involving:	☐	☐	☐	☐	☐
i) Rupture of a known earthquake fault, as delineated on the most recent Alquist-Priolo Earthquake Fault Zoning Map issued by the State Geologist for the area or based on other substantial evidence of a known fault? Refer to Division of Mines and Geology Special Publication 42.	☐	☐	☐	☐	☐
ii) Strong seismic ground shaking?	☐	☐	☐	☐	☐
iii) Seismic-related ground failure, including liquefaction?	☐	☐	☐	☐	☐
iv) Landslides?	☐	☐	☐	☐	☐
b) Result in substantial soil erosion or the loss of topsoil?	☐	☐	☐	☐	☐
c) Be located on a geologic unit or soil that is unstable, or that would become unstable as a result of the project, and potentially result in on- or off-site landslide, lateral spreading, subsidence, liquefaction or collapse?	☐	☐	☐	☐	☐

	Significant Impact	Less Than Significant or Less than Significant with Mitigation Incorporated	No Impact	Analyzed in the Prior EIR	Substantially Mitigated by Uniformly Applicable Development Policies
d) Be located on expansive soil, as defined in Table 18-1-B of the Uniform Building Code (1994), creating substantial direct or indirect risks to life or property?	☐	☐	☐	☐	☐
e) Have soils incapable of adequately supporting the use of septic tanks or alternative waste water disposal systems where sewers are not available for the disposal of waste water?	☐	☐	☐	☐	☐
f) Directly or indirectly destroy a unique paleontological resource or site or unique geological feature?	☐	☐	☐	☐	☐

VIII. GREENHOUSE GAS EMISSIONS.
Would the project:

	Significant Impact	Less Than Significant or Less than Significant with Mitigation Incorporated	No Impact	Analyzed in the Prior EIR	Substantially Mitigated by Uniformly Applicable Development Policies
a) Generate greenhouse gas emissions, either directly or indirectly, that may have a significant impact on the environment?	☐	☐	☐	☐	☐
b) Conflict with an applicable plan, policy or regulation adopted for the purpose of reducing the emissions of greenhouse gases?	☐	☐	☐	☐	☐

IX. HAZARDS AND HAZARDOUS MATERIALS. Would the project:

	Significant Impact	Less Than Significant or Less than Significant with Mitigation Incorporated	No Impact	Analyzed in the Prior EIR	Substantially Mitigated by Uniformly Applicable Development Policies
a) Create a significant hazard to the public or the environment through the routine transport, use, or disposal of hazardous materials?	☐	☐	☐	☐	☐
b) Create a significant hazard to the public or the environment through reasonably foreseeable upset and accident conditions involving the release of hazardous materials into the environment?	☐	☐	☐	☐	☐
c) Emit hazardous emissions or handle hazardous or acutely hazardous materials, substances, or waste within one-quarter mile of an existing or proposed school?	☐	☐	☐	☐	☐
d) Be located on a site which is included on a list of hazardous materials sites compiled pursuant to Government Code Section 65962.5 and, as a result, would it create a significant hazard to the public or the environment?	☐	☐	☐	☐	☐

	Significant Impact	Less Than Significant or Less than Significant with Mitigation Incorporated	No Impact	Analyzed in the Prior EIR	Substantially Mitigated by Uniformly Applicable Development Policies
e) For a project located within an airport land use plan or, where such a plan has not been adopted, within two miles of a public airport or public use airport, would the project result in a safety hazard or excessive noise for people residing or working in the project area?	☐	☐	☐	☐	☐
f) Impair implementation of or physically interfere with an adopted emergency response plan or emergency evacuation plan?	☐	☐	☐	☐	☐
g) Expose people or structures, either directly or indirectly, to a significant risk of loss, injury or death involving wildland fires?	☐	☐	☐	☐	☐

X. HYDROLOGY AND WATER QUALITY.

Would the project:

	Significant Impact	Less Than Significant or Less than Significant with Mitigation Incorporated	No Impact	Analyzed in the Prior EIR	Substantially Mitigated by Uniformly Applicable Development Policies
a) Violate any water quality standards or waste discharge requirements or otherwise substantially degrade surface or ground water quality?	☐	☐	☐	☐	☐
b) Substantially decrease groundwater supplies or interfere substantially with groundwater recharge such that the project may impede sustainable groundwater management of the basin?	☐	☐	☐	☐	☐
c) Substantially alter the existing drainage pattern of the site or area, including through the alteration of the course of a stream or river or through the addition of impervious surfaces, in a manner which would:	☐	☐	☐	☐	☐
(i) result in substantial erosion or siltation on- or off-site;	☐	☐	☐	☐	☐
(ii) substantially increase the rate or amount of surface runoff in a manner which would result in flooding on- or offsite;	☐	☐	☐	☐	☐
(iii) create or contribute runoff water which would exceed the capacity of existing or planned stormwater drainage systems or provide substantial additional sources of polluted runoff; or	☐	☐	☐	☐	☐

	Significant Impact	Less Than Significant or Less than Significant with Mitigation Incorporated	No Impact	Analyzed in the Prior EIR	Substantially Mitigated by Uniformly Applicable Development Policies
(iv) impede or redirect flood flows?	☐	☐	☐	☐	☐
d) In flood hazard, tsunami, or seiche zones, risk release of pollutants due to project inundation?	☐	☐	☐	☐	☐
e) Conflict with or obstruct implementation of a water quality control plan or sustainable groundwater management plan?	☐	☐	☐	☐	☐

XI. LAND USE AND PLANNING. Would the project:

a) Physically divide an established community?	☐	☐	☐	☐	☐
b) Cause a significant environmental impact due to a conflict with land use plan, policy, or regulation adopted for the purpose of avoiding or mitigating an environmental effect?	☐	☐	☐	☐	☐

XII. MINERAL RESOURCES. Would the project:

a) Result in the loss of availability of a known mineral resource that would be of value to the region and the residents of the state?	☐	☐	☐	☐	☐
b) Result in the loss of availability of a locally-important mineral resource recovery site delineated on a local general plan, specific plan or other land use plan?	☐	☐	☐	☐	☐

XIII. NOISE. Would the project result in:

a) Generation of a substantial temporary or permanent increase in ambient noise levels in the vicinity of the project in excess of standards established in the local general plan or noise ordinance, or applicable standards of other agencies?	☐	☐	☐	☐	☐
b) Generation of excessive groundborne vibration or groundborne noise levels?	☐	☐	☐	☐	☐

389

	Significant Impact	Less Than Significant or Less than Significant with Mitigation Incorporated	No Impact	Analyzed in the Prior EIR	Substantially Mitigated by Uniformly Applicable Development Policies
c) For a project located within the vicinity of a private airstrip or an airport land use plan or where such a plan has not been adopted, within two miles of a public airport or public use airport, would the project expose people residing or working in the project area to excessive noise levels?	☐	☐	☐	☐	☐

XIV. POPULATION AND HOUSING. Would the project:

	Significant Impact	Less Than Significant or Less than Significant with Mitigation Incorporated	No Impact	Analyzed in the Prior EIR	Substantially Mitigated by Uniformly Applicable Development Policies
a) Induce substantial unplanned population growth in an area, either directly (for example, by proposing new homes and businesses) or indirectly (for example, through extension of roads or other infrastructure)?	☐	☐	☐	☐	☐
b) Displace substantial numbers of existing people or housing, necessitating the construction of replacement housing elsewhere?	☐	☐	☐	☐	☐

XV. PUBLIC SERVICES.

	Significant Impact	Less Than Significant or Less than Significant with Mitigation Incorporated	No Impact	Analyzed in the Prior EIR	Substantially Mitigated by Uniformly Applicable Development Policies
a) Would the project result in substantial adverse physical impacts associated with the provision of new or physically altered governmental facilities, need for new or physically altered governmental facilities, the construction of which could cause significant environmental impacts, in order to maintain acceptable service ratios, response times or other performance objectives for any of the public services:	☐	☐	☐	☐	☐
Fire protection?	☐	☐	☐	☐	☐
Police protection?	☐	☐	☐	☐	☐
Schools?	☐	☐	☐	☐	☐
Parks?	☐	☐	☐	☐	☐
Other public facilities?	☐	☐	☐	☐	☐

XVI. RECREATION.

	Significant Impact	Less Than Significant or Less than Significant with Mitigation Incorporated	No Impact	Analyzed in the Prior EIR	Substantially Mitigated by Uniformly Applicable Development Policies
a) Would the project increase the use of existing neighborhood and regional parks or other recreational facilities such that substantial physical deterioration of the facility would occur or be accelerated?	☐	☐	☐	☐	☐

	Significant Impact	Less Than Significant or Less than Significant with Mitigation Incorporated	No Impact	Analyzed in the Prior EIR	Substantially Mitigated by Uniformly Applicable Development Policies
b) Does the project include recreational facilities or require the construction or expansion of recreational facilities which might have an adverse physical effect on the environment?	☐	☐	☐	☐	☐

XVII. TRANSPORTATION. Would the project:

	Significant Impact	Less Than Significant or Less than Significant with Mitigation Incorporated	No Impact	Analyzed in the Prior EIR	Substantially Mitigated by Uniformly Applicable Development Policies
a) Conflict with a program, plan, ordinance or policy addressing the circulation system, including transit, roadway, bicycle and pedestrian facilities?	☐	☐	☐	☐	☐
b) Conflict or be inconsistent with CEQA Guidelines Section 15064.3, subdivision (b)?	☐	☐	☐	☐	☐
c) Substantially increase hazards due to a geometric design feature (e.g., sharp curves or dangerous intersections) or incompatible uses (e.g., farm equipment)?	☐	☐	☐	☐	☐
d) Result in inadequate emergency access?	☐	☐	☐	☐	☐

XVIII. TRIBAL CULTURAL RESOURCES.

	Significant Impact	Less Than Significant or Less than Significant with Mitigation Incorporated	No Impact	Analyzed in the Prior EIR	Substantially Mitigated by Uniformly Applicable Development Policies
a) Would the project cause a substantial adverse change in the significance of a tribal cultural resource, defined in Public Resources Code section 21074 as either a site, feature, place, cultural landscape that is geographically defined in terms of the size and scope of the landscape, sacred place, or object with cultural value to a California Native American tribe, and that is:	☐	☐	☐	☐	☐
i) Listed or eligible for listing in the California Register of Historical Resources, or in the local register of historical resources as defined in Public Resources Code Section 5020.1 (k), or	☐	☐	☐	☐	☐
ii) A resource determined by the lead agency, in its discretion and supported by substantial evidence, to be significant pursuant to criteria set forth in subdivision (c) of Public Resources Code Section 5024.1. In applying the criteria set forth in subdivision (c) of Public Resources Code Section 5024.1, the lead agency shall consider the significance of the resource to a California Native American tribe.	☐	☐	☐	☐	☐

XIX. UTILITIES AND SERVICE SYSTEMS.
Would the project:

	Significant Impact	Less Than Significant or Less than Significant with Mitigation Incorporated	No Impact	Analyzed in the Prior EIR	Substantially Mitigated by Uniformly Applicable Development Policies
a) Require or result in the relocation or construction of new or expanded water, wastewater treatment or storm water drainage, electric power, natural gas, or telecommunications facilities, the construction or relocation of which could cause significant environmental effects?	☐	☐	☐	☐	☐
b) Have sufficient water supplies available to serve the project and reasonably foreseeable future development during normal, dry and multiple dry years?	☐	☐	☐	☐	☐
c) Result in a determination by the wastewater treatment provider which serves or may serve the project that it has adequate capacity to serve the project's projected demand in addition to the provider's existing comments?	☐	☐	☐	☐	☐
d) Generate solid waste in excess of State or local standards, or in excess of the capacity of local infrastructure, or otherwise impare the attainment of solid waste reduction goals?	☐	☐	☐	☐	☐
e) Comply with federal, state, and local management and reduction statutes and regulations related to solid waste?	☐	☐	☐	☐	☐

XX. WILDFIRE
If located in or near state responsibility areas or lands classified as very high fire hazard severity zones, would the project:

	Significant Impact	Less Than Significant or Less than Significant with Mitigation Incorporated	No Impact	Analyzed in the Prior EIR	Substantially Mitigated by Uniformly Applicable Development Policies
a) Substantially impair an adopted emergency response plan or emergency evacuation plan?	☐	☐	☐	☐	☐
b) Due to slope, prevailing winds, and other factors, exacerbate wildfire risks, and thereby expose project occupants to, pollutant concentrations from a wildfire or the uncontrolled spread of a wildfire?	☐	☐	☐	☐	☐
c) Require the installation or maintenance of associated infrastructure (such as roads, fuel breaks, emergency water sources, power lines or other utilities) that may exacerbate fire risk or that may result in temporary or ongoing impacts to the environment?	☐	☐	☐	☐	☐
d) Expose people or structures to significant risks, including downslope or downstream flooding or landslides, as a result of runoff, post-fire slope instability, or drainage changes?	☐	☐	☐	☐	☐

	Significant Impact	Less Than Significant or Less than Significant with Mitigation Incorporated	No Impact	Analyzed in the Prior EIR	Substantially Mitigated by Uniformly Applicable Development Policies

XXI. MANDATORY FINDINGS OF SIGNIFICANCE.

a) Does the project have the potential to substantially degrade the quality of the environment, substantially reduce the habitat of a fish or wildlife species, cause a fish or wildlife population to drop below self-sustaining levels, threaten to eliminate a plant or animal community, substantially reduce the number or restrict the range of a rare or endangered plant or animal or eliminate important examples of the major periods of California history or prehistory?

☐ ☐ ☐ ☐ ☐

b) Does the project have impacts that are individually limited, but cumulatively considerable? ("Cumulatively considerable" means that the incremental effects of a project are considerable when viewed in connection with the effects of other current projects, and the effects of probable future projects)?

☐ ☐ ☐ ☐ ☐

c) Does the project have environmental effects which will cause substantial adverse effects on human beings, either directly or indirectly?

☐ ☐ ☐ ☐ ☐

Authority: Public Resources Code 21083, 21094.5.5
Reference: Public Resources Code Sections 21094.5 and 21094.5.5
Revised: December 28, 2018

393

Index
CEQA Guidelines

Topic .... Section

NOTES

NOTES